ISRAEL IN FUTURE PROPHECY

Is There a Larger Restoration of the Kingdom to Israel?

ISRAEL IN FUTURE PROPHECY

PROPHECY

Is There a Larger Restoration of the Kingdom to Israel?

J.K. McKee

TNN PRESS
www.tnnonline.net

Israel In Future Prophecy
Is There a Larger Restoration of the Kingdom to Israel?

Cover photos: Istockphoto

Published by TNN Press, a division of Outreach Israel Ministries
908 Audelia Rd. Suite 200-228
Richardson, Texas 75081
(407) 933-2002

www.tnnonline.net/tnnpress

Unless otherwise noted, Scripture quotations are from the *New American Standard, Updated Edition* (NASU), © 1995, The Lockman Foundation.

Unless otherwise noted, quotations from the Apocrypha are from the *Revised Standard Version* (RSV), © 1952, Division of Education of the National Council of the Churches of Christ in the United States of America.

Table of Contents

Abbreviation Chart and Special Terms

The following is a chart of abbreviations for reference works and special terms that are used in publications by TNN Press. Please familiarize yourself with them as the text may reference a Bible version, i.e., RSV for the Revised Standard Version, or a source such as *TWOT* for the *Theological Wordbook of the Old Testament*, solely by its abbreviation. Detailed listings of these sources are provided in the Bibliography.

Special terms that may be used have been provided in this chart:

ABD: *Anchor Bible Dictionary*

AMG: *Complete Word Study Dictionary: Old Testament, New Testament*

ANE: Ancient Near East(ern)

Apostolic Scriptures/Writings: the New Testament

Ara: Aramaic

ASV: American Standard Version (1901)

ATS: ArtScroll Tanach (1996)

b. Babylonian Talmud (*Talmud Bavli*)

B.C.E.: Before Common Era or B.C.

BDAG: *A Greek-English Lexicon of the New Testament and Other Early Christian Literature* (Bauer, Danker, Arndt, Gingrich)

BDB: *Brown-Driver-Briggs Hebrew and English Lexicon*

BECNT: *Baker Exegetical Commentary on the New Testament*

BKCNT: *Bible Knowledge Commentary: New Testament*

C.E.: Common Era or A.D.

CEV: Contemporary English Version (1995)

CGEDNT: *Concise Greek-English Dictionary of New Testament Words* (Barclay M. Newman)

CHALOT: *Concise Hebrew and Aramaic Lexicon of the Old Testament*

CJB: Complete Jewish Bible (1998)

DRA: Douay-Rheims American Edition

DSS: Dead Sea Scrolls

ECB: *Eerdmans Commentary on the Bible*

EDB: *Eerdmans Dictionary of the Bible*

eisegesis: "reading meaning into," or interjecting a preconceived or foreign meaning into a Biblical text

EJ: *Encylopaedia Judaica*

ESV: English Standard Version (2001)

exegesis: "drawing meaning out of," or the process of trying to understand what a Biblical text means on its own

EXP: *Expositor's Bible Commentary*

Ger: German

GNT: Greek New Testament

Grk: Greek

halachah: lit. "the way to walk," how the Torah is lived out in an individual's life or faith community

HALOT: *Hebrew & Aramaic Lexicon of the Old Testament* (Koehler and Baumgartner)

HCSB: Holman Christian Standard Bible (2004)

Heb: Hebrew

HNV: Hebrew Names Version of the World English Bible

ICC: *International Critical Commentary*

IDB: *Interpreter's Dictionary of the Bible*

IDBSup: *Interpreter's Dictionary of the Bible Supplement*

ISBE: *International Standard Bible Encyclopedia*

IVPBBC: *IVP Bible Background Commentary (Old & New Testament)*

Jastrow: *Dictionary of the Targumim, Talmud Bavli, Talmud Yerushalmi, and Midrashic Literature* (Marcus Jastrow)

JBK: New Jerusalem Bible-Koren (2000)

JETS: *Journal of the Evangelical Theological Society*

KJV: King James Version

Lattimore: The New Testament by Richmond Lattimore (1996)

LITV: *Literal Translation of the Holy Bible* by Jay P. Green (1986)

LS: *A Greek-English Lexicon* (Liddell & Scott)

LXE: *Septuagint with Apocrypha* by Sir L.C.L. Brenton (1851)

LXX: Septuagint

m. Mishnah

MT: Masoretic Text

NASB: New American Standard Bible (1977)

NASU: New American Standard Update (1995)

NBCR: *New Bible Commentary: Revised*

NEB: New English Bible (1970)

Nelson: *Nelson's Expository Dictionary of Old Testament Words*

NETS: New English Translation of the Septuagint (2007)

NIB: *New Interpreter's Bible*

NIGTC: *New International Greek Testament Commentary*

NICNT: *New International Commentary on the New Testament*

NIDB: *New International Dictionary of the Bible*

NIV: New International Version (1984)

NJB: New Jerusalem Bible-Catholic (1985)

NJPS: Tanakh, A New Translation of the Holy Scriptures (1999)

NKJV: New King James Version (1982)

NRSV: New Revised Standard Version (1989)

NLT: New Living Translation (1996)

NT: New Testament

orthopraxy: lit. "the right action," how the Bible or one's theology is lived out in the world

OT: Old Testament

PreachC: *The Preacher's Commentary*

REB: Revised English Bible (1989)

RSV: Revised Standard Version (1952)

t. Tosefta

Tanach (Tanakh): the Old Testament

Thayer: *Thayer's Greek-English Lexicon of the New Testament*

TDNT: *Theological Dictionary of the New Testament*

TEV: Today's English Version (1976)

TLV: Tree of Life Messianic Family Bible—New Covenant (2011)

TNIV: Today's New International Version (2005)

TNTC: *Tyndale New Testament Commentaries*

TWOT: *Theological Wordbook of the Old Testament*

UBSHNT: United Bible Societies' 1991 Hebrew New Testament revised edition

v(s). verse(s)

Vine: *Vine's Complete Expository Dictionary of Old and New Testament Words*

Vul: Latin Vulgate

WBC: *Word Biblical Commentary*

Yid: Yiddish

YLT: Young's Literal Translation (1862/1898)

Introduction

As a teacher, researcher, and apologist, it is my responsibility to address all manner of subjects and issues which are presented or inquired of me, from the Holy Scriptures, providing answers for the people of God. Many of these issues regard the essentials of faith, and how we, as a contemporary but yet still-emerging and developing Messianic movement, should approach them. My writings to date bear witness to the fact that I have had to address a whole host of topics, many of them relating to the challenges and controversies which our broad Messianic community is facing today. A variety of these issues are those upon which we all express a great deal of camaraderie and unity, as they concern the nature of Yeshua and His salvation. Some issues, however, are those which tend to get groups of people significantly divided and/or upset at one another, and which tend to make us rather uncomfortable. In far too many cases, issues which do get people divided or upset are not often approached with a great deal of objectivity, reason, innovation, or patience. *And the love of the Messiah, which we are to demonstrate one to another, can often just be thrown out the proverbial window...*[i]

There are three broad groups, which tend to make up the contemporary Messianic movement: Messianic Judaism, the One Law/One Torah sub-movement, and the Two-House sub-movement. **Messianic Judaism** as a modern movement, emerged in the late 1960s from the older Hebrew Christian movement, as a group of Jewish Believers wanting to acknowledge and worship Yeshua as the Messiah, in a widely Jewish cultural and religious context. As Messianic Judaism grew in the 1980s and 1990s, congregations and fellowships were established all throughout places such as North America, Europe, Israel, and the West in general. While many Jewish people rejoicingly came to a saving knowledge of Yeshua as the Messiah of Israel, a major unforeseen side-effect also took place: scores of non-Jewish Believers, evangelical Christians, entered into Messianic Judaism, and sincerely desired to not only learn more about the Jewish Jesus, but also live more like Him, embracing their Hebraic Roots in obedience to the Torah or Law of Moses.

As non-Jewish Believers have begun to utterly swell the Messianic community—indeed becoming the majority of it—many questions and answers to such questions have been proposed. For many of today's Messianic Jewish leaders, non-Jewish Believers entering into the Messianic movement is only the result of the Lord calling specific persons and families to assist in Jewish ministry and the redemption of their people, and for them to be in a unique, close communion with Jewish Believers. Others have thought that non-Jewish Believers entering into the Messianic community, embracing a life of submission and obedience to God's Torah, is a result of prophecies like Micah 4:1-3 or Isaiah 2:2-4 or Zechariah 8:23

---

[i] Deuteronomy 6:5; Leviticus 19:18; cf. Matthew 19:19; 22:39; Mark 12:31; Luke 10:27; Romans 13:9; Galatians 5:14; James 2:8.

taking place, and a more decisive understanding of the New Covenant being realized (Jeremiah 31:31-34; Ezekiel 36:25-27; Hebrews 8:8-12; 10:15-17). Such non-Jewish Believers are to be likened unto the *ger* (גֵּר) or sojourner in the Torah who entered into the community of Ancient Israel, who was widely anticipated to follow the same basic Instruction as the native Israelite. Those who have emphasized that non-Jewish Believers are part of an enlarged, Kingdom realm of Israel, are widely considered to be a part of the **One Law/One Torah** sub-movement, given the Torah's emphasis on "You shall have one law for him who does *anything* unintentionally, for him who is native among the sons of Israel and for the alien who sojourns among them" (Numbers 15:29).[ii]

Obviously in the realm of contemporary theological discussion, proposing that Jewish and non-Jewish Believers are to widely be in observance of the Torah or Law of Moses—including things like the seventh-day Sabbath/*Shabbat*, the appointed times of Leviticus 23, or eating kosher—is most controversial. And, such convictions certainly require a great deal of analysis and reflection from various passages in the Apostolic Scriptures or New Testament, which may seem to say otherwise—including the validity and relevance of the Torah for Messiah followers.[iii] Yet in the scope of Messianic discussion, no proposals can be more provocative than those often made by people composing the **Two-House** sub-movement.

In the scope of the history of Ancient Israel, following the death of King Solomon, no one can deny the fact that Israel's realm split into the Northern Kingdom of Israel, also called Ephraim, and the Southern Kingdom of Judah. In the course of Biblical history, as recorded within the Books of Kings and Chronicles, a mass from the Northern Kingdom of Israel was corporately taken into exile by the Assyrian Empire. Later in the course of Biblical history, the bulk of the Southern Kingdom of Judah was taken into exile by the Babylonian Empire, many of whom returned to the Holy Land following the conquering of the Babylonians by the much more tolerant and accepting Persian Empire. A huge mystery has ensued regarding the destiny of the descendants of the exiled Northern Kingdom of Israel—and their widescale non-return to the Holy Land—giving rise to all manner of interesting theories, speculations, and in far too many cases, outright myth and fantasy about the "Ten Lost Tribes."

A majority of people in today's Two-House sub-movement, while rightly raising the attention of Bible readers to the issue of the exiled Northern Kingdom in Scriptural history, have simply assumed that most of today's non-Jewish Believers

---

ii Other passages of importance include: : Exodus 12:48-49; Leviticus 7:7; 24:22; Numbers 9:14; 15:15-16, 29-30.

For a further discussion, consult the author's publication *One Law for All: From the Mosaic Texts to the Work of the Holy Spirit*. Some important related discussions are also found in the author's publication *Are Non-Jewish Believers Really a Part of Israel?*

iii Consult the author's books *The New Testament Validates Torah: Does the New Testament Really Do Away With the Law?*, *Torah In the Balance, Volume I* (and forthcoming *Volume II*), and the relevant volumes of the *Messianic Helper Series* by TNN Press.

are descendants of the exiled Northern Kingdom of Israel/Ephraim. This is no doubt due to the widespread—and most deplorable—complimentarianism of the broad Messianic movement, and concurrent with it the thought that those who are physical descendants of Abraham, Isaac, and Jacob somehow *must be* closer to God and His will than people of the nations generally. And not only this, but these non-Jewish individuals tend to call themselves "Ephraimites," although they lack any documentation or substantial proof for it, other than some sort of unobjective feeling or instinct. Suffice it to say, this is a huge debate—and one where reason, careful attention to detail, and a Thomas-level of skepticism (cf. John 20:25-27)—have not often been allowed to prevail. Yet, those Messianic people who identify themselves as being "Two-House," do make up a large and most noticeable sub-movement of the larger Messianic community, with which the ministry of Outreach Israel and TNN Online does interact with also. If any of us intend to be fair as God's people, the main Biblical passages which they consider to be of importance must be analyzed, and in such a way which does appropriate justice to the text, removed from any of the bad behavior, problems, or semi-racism which may be endemic of various Two-House adherents.

Outreach Israel and TNN Online *should not at all* be considered a "Two-House" ministry, given the wide and diverse array of Biblical and theological topics we address, germane to the broad Messianic community. Our ministry serves people in Messianic Judaism, as well as in the One Law/One Torah sub-movement and in the Two-House sub-movement—as we consider and analyze a wide series of issues and subjects which are thought to be of importance to people in all of those different sub-communities. If our ministry choice is to at all be honored by others in the Messianic world of ideas, we would consider ourselves **an egalitarian Messianic ministry**, sitting above these three different Messianic groupings. We are a ministry which regards both Jewish and non-Jewish Believers in Messiah Yeshua to be a part of the Commonwealth of Israel (Ephesians 2:11-13, 19; 3:6), and which advocates a mutual submission ideology (Ephesians 5:21; Philippians 2:3-4). We fully affirm that all Messianic Believers, Jewish and non-Jewish, male and female—are complete equals in the eyes of the Lord (Galatians 3:28; Colossians 2:11)—and should be encouraged to develop all of their gifts, talents, and skills as is proper in Him. We also believe that the Messianic movement's shared spiritual and theological heritage in the Jewish Synagogue and Christian Church, must be steadfastly honored.

As it concerns the specific issue of the Two-House teaching, Outreach Israel Ministries and TNN Online disavow the popular/populist variety of the Two-House teaching which has been promulgated since the 1990s, via a number of pseudo-denominations, sensationalistic groups, and dominant and/or presumed-prophetic personalities—which has not allowed itself to be often subject to constructive criticism and/or further theological refinement and engagement with conservative Biblical scholarship. Yet, in 2008, at least, one Messianic Jewish ministry actually allowed the following statement to be featured on its website: "The Two-House doctrine, in its most basic terms, simply maintains that the nation of Israel was divided following the reign of Solomon and will be reunited during the end times."[iv] This would be the basic or generic approach taken by our ministry to the issue of what happened to the exiled Northern Kingdom of Israel/Ephraim, in concert with the sentiments of pre-millennial eschaology.[v] We would affirm a larger restoration of Israel, involving those from the exiled Northern Kingdom as a participant, yet to occur in Biblical prophecy.

We would acknowledge a greater, end-time restoration of Israel to come that is prophesied, going beyond the rebirth of the State of Israel in 1948, as important as this has surely been. Such a larger restoration of Israel definitely involves the Jewish people, as well as descendants from the exiled Northern Kingdom, but also many welcome and valued scores of companions from the nations themselves. There are pockets of people in remote corners of places like Southeast Asia, Southern Asia, the Middle East, the Eastern Mediterranean basin, and the environs of Central Africa, who claim to be descendants of the exiled Northern Kingdom via some kind of oral tradition, and/or what can appear to be Jewish-style customs — *and most probably are.* (Sometimes this has been enjoined with some credible DNA analysis, confirming distant Semitic descent.) These are the areas which generally fall within the sphere of influence of the old Assyrian, Babylonian, and Persian Empires, and where the exiles of the Northern Kingdom could have been legitimately deported, scattered, and/or assimilated (cf. Jeremiah 31:10; Hosea 8:8-9; Amos 9:8-9).[vi]

We believe that the Lord will bring together, as one people in Him: the Jewish people, such aforementioned descendants of exiled Israel/Ephraim, and their many associated companions from all nations as one broad and inclusive community of people in Messiah Yeshua, before His return, in fulfillment of end-time prophecy (i.e., Isaiah 11:12-16; Jeremiah 31:6-10; Ezekiel 37:15-28; Zechariah 10:6-10). We **do not at all encourage** non-Jewish Believers (particularly those of Western European ancestry) who are a part of today's Messianic movement, and who recognize themselves as a part of the Commonwealth of Israel (Ephesians 2:11-13; 3:6) or the Israel of God (Galatians 6:16), grafted into Israel by faith in Israel's Messiah (Romans 11:17-18), to identify themselves as some sort of "Ephraimites." We especially do not encourage such non-Jewish people to make any kind of permanent pilgrimage or "*aliyah*" to the Holy Land, as there is no indication that all Messiah followers will, in total, ever live in the Land of Israel, even in the Messiah's Millennial Kingdom (cf. Isaiah 19:23-24; Zechariah 14:16-19).

[iv] (2008). *Two-House Doctrine Debate. The Messianic Center.* Retrieved 14 August, 2011 from <http://www.themessianiccenter.com>.

[v] Cf. Walter C. Kaiser, *Preaching and Teaching the Last Things: Old Testament Eschatology for the Life of the Church* (Grand Rapids: Baker Academic, 2011), pp 37-38, 47-49.

[vi] I.e., as would be particularly seen in a work like Quest for the Lost Tribes A&E, 1998, DVD 2006, hosted by Simcha Jacobovici, and the concurrent comments witnessed in Jonathan Bernis (2005), *The Scattering of the Tribes of Israel,* March/April 2005. *Jewish Voice Today.* Available via <http://www.jewishvoice.org> and Sid Roth, *The Incomplete Church: Bridging the Gap Between God's Children* (Shippensburg, PA: Destiny Image, 2007), pp 17-18.

An eschatology-based approach toward addressing this subject, with obviously various details needing to be left to an Eternal and Sovereign God, is frequently not the approach which one encounters in much of the well-known literature surrounding the subject matter. It can be said that there is a distinct difference between a populist Two-House teaching, which essentially advocates that the majority of non-Jewish Believers are distant descendants of the exiled Northern Kingdom (with various connections to be likely made with Nineteenth Century British-Israelism), versus a more Biblical approach to the issue that focuses on the specific prophecies of a larger restoration of Israel. While we would affirm a wide number of Tanach prophecies involving the exiled Northern Kingdom as a participant, as being unfulfilled at the present time, our ministry would not at all be considered a part of a Two-House sub-movement which practices a great deal of theological eisegesis, where many Biblical references to "two" are applied to Judah and Ephraim, and whose Hebrew and Greek examination is often limited to *Strong's Concordance* (among other things).

When this subject matter has been raised, we have definitely strived as a ministry—as best as we humanly can—to focus the attention of today's Messianic people on a larger scope of expectations regarding the restoration of Israel, with the exiled Northern Kingdom of Israel/Ephraim as a noticeable participant. *How does this affect our view of the end-times, and what is to transpire regarding the restoration of Israel before the Messiah's return?* Unlike the populist Two-House teaching that has garnered the most attention since the late 1990s, our ministry has made it clear that non-Jewish Messianic Believers thinking that they are mostly descendants of the exiled Northern Kingdom, is not at all a useful or profitable endeavor. Jeremiah 31:10 certainly directs Bible readers, "He who scattered Israel will gather him." **Many of the finer details of such a larger restoration of Israel to be anticipated are only known by our Eternal and Omnipresent Creator.** And, not at all to be ignored, is the steadfast Torah word of Deuteronomy 28:62, "Then you shall be left few in number, whereas you were as numerous as the stars of heaven, because you did not obey the LORD your God." Much of the popular/populist Two-House literature has actually posited that the physical numbers of descendants of Abraham, Isaac, and Jacob are in the hundreds of millions, if not billions, whereas the tenor of the Pentateuch itself does not at all convey this. Not only does this seem like a significant over-exaggeration, it makes the known Jewish population seem absolutely miniscule—especially in light of the 6 million Jews who were slaughtered in the Holocaust!

Perhaps most overlooked (and dismissed) in the whole discussion (and debate), is that there will be many associated companions/associates from the nations themselves involved in the restoration process (Ezekiel 37:16-19; Isaiah 49:6; cf. Luke 2:32; Acts 13:47), most definitely being the significant majority of those who participate, in what is mainly *not* the reunion of the Two Houses of Israel as has been popularly communicated—but in actuality, instead, what is **a larger restoration/expansion of Israel's Kingdom.** Such a restoration would involve a resolution to the issue of the exiled Northern Kingdom for sure, but would also incorporate the righteous from the nations, into an expanded realm of Israel's Kingdom (cf. Amos 9:11-12; Acts 15:15-18). Most of the non-Jewish Believers one is likely to encounter, forcibly identifying themselves as some sort of "Ephraimites," are not, and they have no Semitic genealogy of any kind. Yet, these people have been Divinely led by the Lord into the Messianic movement, certainly in fulfillment of prophecies like Micah 4:1-3 and Isaiah 2:2-3 and Zechariah 8:23, and should be considered welcome and valued members of the community of Israel. They are most certainly the equals of Jewish Believers in Messiah Yeshua (cf. Galatians 3:28).[vii] They are, without question, human beings made in God's image (Genesis 1:27), who are valued and loved by Him as the Eternal Creator!

Our ministry has a consistent track record of speaking out against many of the anti-Christian and anti-Jewish sentiments, which are often witnessed in the Two-House sub-movement and much of its popular literature.[viii] If there is genuinely a larger restoration of Israel to occur, which effectively involves all who acknowledge the God of Abraham, Isaac, and Jacob—*via the emergence of the modern Messianic movement*—then today's Messianic people must certainly show proper respect and honor to their Jewish and Christian forbearers, employing their great virtues to accomplish His mission and purpose for the final hour.

Today's Messianic community needs some preliminary resolution to the whole "Two-House" controversy, one which is not dismissive as it concerns unfulfilled prophetic words from the Tanach involving the descendants of the exiled Northern Kingdom of Israel (Isaiah 11:12-16; Jeremiah 31:6-10; Ezekiel 37:15-28; Zechariah 10:6-10), but one which is far more engaged with the Biblical text and contemporary scholarship than the populism which tends to utterly plague the Two-House sub-movement,[ix] and much of the religious posturing and/or total dismissal which can be seen against it.[x] *Israel in Future Prophecy: Is There a Larger*

---

vii Consult the author's exegesis paper on Galatians 3:28, "Biblical Equality and Today's Messianic Movement."

viii Consult the relevant sections of the author's book, *Confronting Critical Issues: An Analysis of Subjects that Affects the Growth and Stability of the Emerging Messianic Movement*.

ix The writings representing this perspective include, but are not limited to:

Batya Ruth Wootten, *Who Is Israel? And Why You Need to Know* (St. Cloud, FL: Key of David, 1998); *Who Is Israel?*, enlarged edition (St. Cloud, FL: Key of David, 2000); *Redeemed Israel—Restored and Reunited* (St. Cloud, FL: Key of David, 2006); *Israel's Feasts and their Fullness*, expanded edition (St. Cloud, FL: Key of David Publishing, 2008); *Who Is Israel? Redeemed Israel—A Primer* (St. Cloud, FL: Key of David, 2011); Angus Wootten, *Restoring Israel's Kingdom* (St. Cloud, FL: Key of David, 2000); Eddie Chumney, *Restoring the Two Houses of Israel* (Hagerstown, MD: Serenity Books, 1999); Moshe Koniuchowsky, *The Truth About All Israel: A Refutation of the I.M.J.A. Position Paper on the Two Houses of Israel* (Miami Beach: Your Arms to Israel, 2000); Sandy Bloomfield, *The Errors of "The Ephraimite Error": Disposing of the Lies and Hatred* (Lebanon, TN: Messianic Israel Alliance, 2008).

x The writings representing this perspective include, but are not limited to:

Kay Silberling (1999). *The Ephraimite Error: A Position Paper Submitted to the International Messianic Jewish Alliance*. Available online via <http://umjc.org>; (1999). *A Short Summary of "The Ephraimite Error."* Available online via <http://umjc.org>; Rich Robinson (2001). *The Two-House (Messianic Israel) Theory that Ephraim is the Church. Jews for Jesus*. Available online via <http://www.jfjonline.org>; Tim Hegg (2002). *The Two House Theory: Three Fatal Flaws. Torah Resource*. Available online via <http://torahresource.com>; Boaz Michael (2004). *Encounters with an Ephraimite: Identity through a Lost Heritage. First Fruits of Zion*. Available online via <http://ffoz.org>; Perry Trotter (2003). *A Brief Assessment of Two House Theology*, 07 January, 2003.

Restoration of the Kingdom to Israel? can hopefully provide some of the answers which are needed in the current season of Messianic development, and we would hope, Lord willing, also maturation. If any of you can understand what it means for a "third solution" to be offered to a theological controversy—then this is a publication which I believe is going to help you greatly!

J.K. McKee
Editor, TNN Online

Christian Witness Ministries. Available online via <http://www.christian-witness.org>; Boaz Michael, with Jacob Fronczak, *Twelve Gates: Where Do the Nations Enter?* (Marshfield, MO: First Fruits of Zion, 2012); Toby Janicki, *God-Fearers: Gentiles and the God of Israel* (Marshfield, MO: First Fruits of Zion, 2012).

Israel In Future Prophecy

-1-

Approaching Two-House Controversies

In our day, a wide number of non-Jewish Believers, in significant numbers, have chosen to address what many throughout religious history have called, "the Ten Lost Tribes" of Israel issue. This has often taken place because of a strong interest by many Christians in the Hebraic Roots of our faith, and a renewed interest in Israel and their faith heritage in Judaism. A loose sub-movement, commonly known by the descriptions "Judah and Ephraim" or "Two-House" or "Messianic Israel," has gained wide adherence in various sectors of the broad, modern Messianic movement. *There is no doubting the fact that it has caused controversy, consternation, and even division among many Believers...*

Appearing along with the article "Decoding the Priesthood" by Peter Hirschberg,[1] from the 10 May, 1999 edition of *The Jerusalem Report*, the adjunct "Report Card" by Tibor Krausz stated how, "An evolving doctrine in Christian Zionism and Messianic Judaism, based on a new interpretation of scripture, holds that most true Christians are descendants of the Lost Tribes of Israel."[2] This is certainly interesting, coming from a mainstream Jewish publication. What is going on, exactly? What might these sentiments mean? How do we properly approach the issues at hand, and what are at least, some thought-provoking statements issued? How can we know what is fact, and what is fiction?

What is the "Two-House teaching," which has gained a great deal of attention and controversy throughout the Messianic world since the late 1990s? What is it all about and what is its purpose? Does it actually advocate that all non-Jewish Believers are physical Israel? Or, could it be that there are elements of Israel's restoration which have been overlooked by Bible readers, requiring further analysis and contemplation? What questions are being asked today about "Israel" that we must take note of, and attempt to reasonably answer? What are some of the

---

[1] This article largely summarizes an ongoing project of trying to test various groups within the Jewish community, as well as those in some remote locations of South Asia, Southeastern Asia, and Central Africa, for particular DNA strands, trying to conclude who might be descended from the priestly class within Ancient Israel.

[2] Tibor Krausz (1999). *Report Card*, 10 May, 1999. *The Jerusalem Report*. Retrieved 11 April, 2011 from <http://jpost.com/JerusalemReport>.

over-statements and under-statements that we have to all sort through, from both the pro- and con- sides of this discussion? *How much data and noise have to actually be sifted through?*

Each of us needs to take to serious heart the words of Ezekiel 37:28. God says that "the nations will know that I am the LORD who sanctifies Israel, when My sanctuary is in their midst forever," *b'heyot miqdashi b'tokam l'olam* (בְּתוֹכָם לְעוֹלָם בִּהְיוֹת מִקְדָּשִׁי). Notice that our Heavenly Father does not say He sanctifies a separate group of elect called "the Church," and also notice that He does speak of a day coming when Israel is restored and His presence will be in the world forever. **We have obviously not reached this anticipated point in human history.**

We begin our discussions by examining some of the important questions concerning the subject matter commonly known by the label of "the Two-House teaching." We will consider the historical division and prophesied reunification of Israel from the Tanach or Old Testament. We will examine some of the objections that people commonly have associated with a larger restoration of Israel to come, involving those of the Northern and Southern Kingdoms. What are some things in the Bible concerning Israel and the Kingdom of God that readers may have overlooked or under-emphasized that can no longer be avoided? Is there a legitimate, larger restoration of Israel to take place before the return of the Messiah? If so, how many things have contemporary advocates of the "Two-House teaching" embellished and over-exaggerated, which need to be avoided?

The Commonwealth of Israel

In the Apostle Paul's letter to a largely non-Jewish audience in Asia Minor,[3] he makes a very intriguing statement. In Ephesians 2:11-13, he admonishes the non-Jewish Believers, "Therefore remember that formerly you, the Gentiles in the flesh, who are called 'Uncircumcision' by the so-called 'Circumcision,' *which is* performed in the flesh by human hands—*remember* that you were at that time separate from Messiah, excluded from the commonwealth of Israel, and strangers to the covenants of promise, having no hope and without God in the world. But now in Messiah Yeshua you who formerly were far off have been brought near by the blood of Messiah." The statement that Paul makes is that prior to their salvation in Yeshua the Messiah, these people were "alienated[4] from the commonwealth of

---

[3] Be aware of how "in Ephesus" (*en Ephesō*, ἐν Ἐφέσῳ) does not appear in the oldest manuscripts of Ephesians 1:1 (cf. Bruce M. Metzger, *A Textual Commentary on the Greek New Testament* [London and New York: United Bible Societies, 1975], 601), and that in all likelihood the Epistle of Ephesians was originally a circular letter written by the Apostle Paul to assemblies within Asia Minor, eventually making its way to Ephesus. The RSV notably rendered Ephesians 1:1 with: "Paul, an apostle of Christ Jesus by the will of God, to the saints who are also faithful in Christ Jesus."

For a further discussion, consult C.E. Arnold, "Ephesians, Letter to the: Destination," in Gerald F. Hawthorne, Ralph P. Martin, and Daniel G. Reid, eds., *Dictionary of Paul and His Letters* (Downers Grove, IL: InterVarsity, 1993), pp 243-245, and the author's entry for the Epistle of Ephesians in *A Survey of the Apostolic Scriptures for the Practical Messianic*.

[4] Grk. *apallotrioō* (ἀπαλλοτριόω), "to estrange, alienate" (H.G. Liddell and R. Scott, *An Intermediate Greek-English Lexicon* [Oxford: Clarendon Press, 1994], 87).

Israel" (RSV). Now, having come to faith, they have been "brought near by the blood of Messiah." In the view of Walter C. Kaiser, in his book *The Promise-Plan of God*,

"All Gentiles were Christless, stateless, promiseless, hopeless, and Godless (2:12)...But now in Christ's salvation, the Gentiles 'have been brought near' (2:13b), just as Israel had been described as being 'near' to God in Deuteronomy 4:7 and Psalm 148:14."[5]

When we review what Ephesians 2:11-12 communicates, what is Paul really saying? Is he saying that these non-Jewish Believers have become a part of "the Church," something separate from Israel? No. This is the last thing on his mind, especially if non-Jewish Believers are "joint heirs, [part of] a joint body and joint sharers with the Jews" (Ephesians 3:6, CJB). Paul communicates to those in Asia Minor that they have become part of the community of Israel by their salvation in Israel's Messiah—obviously a realm which has been expanded and enlarged, because of His work and the inclusive nature of the gospel. This is witnessed by the Greek word *politeia* (πολιτεία), often rendered as "commonwealth,"[6] which means **"the right to be a member of a sociopolitical entity, citizenship"** (BDAG).[7] Nowhere in Yeshua the Messiah's mission did He ever come to establish "the Church" as a second group of elect. On the contrary, He came to restore and rebuild Israel (Jeremiah 33:7; cf. Matthew 16:18).[8]

All of the negative conditions of once being unredeemed were reversed for Ephesians' non-Jewish audience. Being "brought near" to Israel is not just a kind of closeness; it is a statement of being integrated into the community of Israel, no different than how Ancient Israel in the wilderness was considered the people of God. The question of Deuteronomy 4:7 is, "For what great nation is there that has a god so near to it as is the LORD our God whenever we call on Him?" Psalm 148:14

---

[5] Walter C. Kaiser, *The Promise-Plan of God: A Biblical Theology of the Old and New Testaments* (Grand Rapids: Zondervan, 2008), 294.

[6] "citizenship" (NIV); "community" (REB/*Lattimore*); "citizens" (Common English Bible).

[7] Frederick William Danker, ed., et. al., *A Greek-English Lexicon of the New Testament and Other Early Christian Literature*, third edition (Chicago: University of Chicago Press, 2000), 845.

In some branches of today's Messianic Judaism, notably those that advocate what they call a "bilateral ecclesiology," non-Jewish Believers being a part of the Commonwealth of Israel is not quantitatively different from them being a part of a separate "Church" per dispensationalism. Such a Commonwealth of Israel is simply thought to compose two groups: the Jewish people and the Church. The Greek term *politeia* is approached from the perspective of it being "commonwealth" like the British Commonwealth of Nations, as Yeshua is King over the Jewish people and the Church much like Queen Elizabeth II is monarch of independent countries like the United Kingdom, Canada, Australia, New Zealand, etc.

The classical Greek meaning of *politeia* does not imply a kind of citizenship where a single monarch rules over a collection of separate states, but rather of either a single government or a way of conduct within a society (sometimes set within the context of a city). Cf. *LS*, 654; Plato *Republic* 10.619c; Aristotle *Politics* 3.6.1278b; 3.7.1279a; 2 Maccabees 8:17.

For a further discussion, consult the relevant sections of the author's commentary *Ephesians for the Practical Messianic.*

[8] Consult the author's article "When Did 'the Church' Begin?", for a further examination of how God has always had only *one* assembly of elect. Also consult the material in the author's publication, *Are Non-Jewish Believers Really a Part of Israel?*

further details, "And He has lifted up a horn for His people, praise for all His godly ones; *even* for the sons of Israel, a people near to Him. Praise the LORD!" Paul is certain to say, "So then you are no longer strangers and aliens, but you are fellow citizens with the saints, and are of God's household," the assessment being, "the Gentiles are fellow heirs and fellow members of the body, and fellow partakers of the promise in Messiah Yeshua through the gospel" (Ephesians 2:19; 3:6). While by no means replacing the Jewish people in God's salvation-historical plan, non-Jewish Believers do get to partake of the blessings and responsibilities of being a part of Israel's Kingdom along with them. A non-Jewish Believer is to be regarded as *sumpolitēs* (συμπολίτης), a *"fellow-citizen/compatriot"* (BDAG)[9] within the community of Israel. In fact, the reconciliation of Jewish people and those from the nations, together, is to be a testament to the greater reconciliation to come to the cosmos (Ephesians 3:10).

If we are to understand that non-Jewish Believers are a part of the community of Israel, an enlarged Kingdom realm, along with their fellow Jewish Believers, then questions will naturally be asked about what the Hebrew Scriptures or the Tanach tell us about Israel. Ultimately, it is safe to say that being a part of "the Israel of God" (Galatians 6:16), or being grafted into the olive tree (cf. Romans 11:17-18), is incumbent upon possessing faith in Israel's Messiah. Very sadly, there will be Jewish people who are physical descendants of the Patriarchs, who will in the end be considered "cut off" (Romans 11:17, 20). (Yet, this is something that *only* a Creator God and Final Judge is responsible for determining, and *not* any of us as limited and biased human beings.)[10] And, as Paul had to remind many of his non-Jewish readers in Rome, "Do not be conceited, but fear; for if God did not spare the natural branches, He will not spare you, either" (Romans 11:20b-21). Whenever the topic of who is, and who is not, a part of Israel comes up—each of us has to proceed very cautiously.

Focusing on Israel In Future Prophecy

The relatively young Two-House sub-movement today is broad, and as such it needs to be recognized how there are a wide array of proponents who teach about the subject matter. It is to be fairly observed, though, that after a decade or more of growth, expansion, and popular conference events from the late 1990s to early 2010s, that a significant number of Two-House proponents believe that the majority of non-Jewish Believers in today's Messianic movement are descendants of the exiled Northern Kingdom of Israel/Ephraim, and as such, they feel it is appropriate to refer to themselves as some sort of "Ephraimites." While it has been important that they have raised the awareness level of various Biblical passages, which may have otherwise gone unaddressed or ignored by many Messianic people—the things that they have done with those Biblical passages have not always been good.

---

[9] BDAG, 959; *"possessing the same citizenship with others, a fellow-citizen"* (Joseph H. Thayer, *Thayer's Greek-English Lexicon of the New Testament* [Peabody, MA: Hendrickson, 2003], 597).

[10] For some further thoughts, consult the author's exegesis paper on Romans 1:18-25, "Is Salvation Only Available for those who Profess Faith in Yeshua?"

Alternatively to much of the rhetoric and populism which can be witnessed from the Two-House/Ephraimite sub-movement, more thought-conscious Bible readers do need to recognize how there is a larger restoration of Israel prophesied in the Tanach, which has been a significantly overlooked component of what is to transpire prior to the return of Yeshua. *This is not something that should overly-comprise someone's personal identity in the Messiah.* A reasonable approach to the issue of the Northern and Southern Kingdoms of Israel being reunited, concerns eschatology, and should *not* manifest itself in promoting unwarranted speculations and/or Lost Tribes hunting. It should instead cause each of us to evaluate events that are foretold to transpire before the Messiah's return (i.e., Isaiah 11:12-16; Jeremiah 31:6-10; Ezekiel 37:15-28; Zechariah 10:6-10), and how soon, or not so soon, the Second Coming will actually take place.

It is factual to report that many Orthodox Jews believe in the reunification of those of the Northern and Southern Kingdoms of Israel before the coming of the Messiah. A relatively mainline resource like the *Encylopaedia Judaica* notes, "The belief in the continued existence of the ten tribes was regarded as an incontrovertible fact during the whole period of the Second Temple and of the Talmud."[11] While it is appropriate to consider the Jewish eschatological expectation, even more so we should force our evaluations to be placed within the world of the Biblical text, and a relatively conservative, evangelical theological framework, that places a high degree of integrity on the Biblical record and legitimate expectations of the Prophets of the Tanach (Old Testament). While it can be quite a chore, **focusing one's attention on what is foretold in the Scriptures is imperative,** especially given the many problems associated with the destiny of the Northern Kingdom of Israel, and those others who have widely addressed this subject matter in the past, and their false teachings—varying from British-Israel to Christian Identity heresies.[12] Ultimately, our attention as readers needs to be focused on the Biblical text and the verses and passages of relevance.

As we sort through various Bible passages, and reflect on what is occurring in the broad, contemporary Messianic movement—we should also recognize that both the Christian Church and the Jewish Synagogue have had a part to play in God's eternal plan, and at the same time *both* the Church *and* the Synagogue have had their shortcomings as human institutions. Is it merely a coincidence that in our day—unlike any other time in history—that many Jewish people are coming to faith in Messiah Yeshua, and non-Jewish Believers are turning toward their Hebraic Roots and are becoming Torah obedient? Is this happening just by circumstance? Or, is it happening because the final elements of the restoration of Israel's Kingdom are in the process of occurring, as the return of the Messiah draws near? What are some of the things which today's contemporary Messianic

---

[11] Louis Isaac Rabinowitz, "Ten Lost Tribes," in Enyclopaedia Judaica. MS Windows 9x. Brooklyn: Judaica Multimedia (Israel) Ltd, 1997.

[12] Consult Bruce Hoffman, *Inside Terrorism* (New York: Columbia University Press, 1998), 112; Walter R. Martin, *The Kingdom of the Cults* (Minneapolis: Bethany House, 1985), pp 303-337; Josh McDowell & Don Stewart, *Handbook of Today's Religions* (San Bernadino, CA: Here's Life Publishers, 1983), pp 114-122.

movement has properly evaluated, and what are some of the things which still require some fine-tuning and improvement?

Our Heavenly Father is seeking only *one* people for His own possession (Deuteronomy 4:20; Titus 2:14; 1 Peter 2:9). He wants all human beings to be a part of this people—a redeemed, collective, composite Kingdom of Israel, which King Yeshua will rule and reign over! It is the high, holy calling of God's people to take actions that will result in the fulfillment of the Disciples' question of Acts 1:6: "Lord, is it at this time You are restoring the kingdom to Israel?" (cf. Matthew 6:10). What we do today affects tomorrow, and as we seek to please the Lord in how we practice our faith, it should hopefully be in the light of seeing Israel's Kingdom restored—something that does involve *more* than just the Jewish people, *or even* those of the exiled Northern Kingdom (Isaiah 49:6). The larger restoration of Israel that we encounter in the Scriptures, is actually certainly something that will affect the entire world.[13]

These compelling ideas, as can and should be expected, create new questions that need to be examined. Even with previous abuses having been witnessed in past history regarding the subject matter of the Northern and Southern Kingdoms of Israel, it is a subject matter that will surely not go way—*if it indeed* involves future Biblical prophecies awaiting their completion.

The Northern and Southern Kingdoms of Israel

Surveying the Tanach, Bible readers should be able to fairly acknowledge how Ancient Israel reached its zenith during the time of King David and King Solomon. But after Solomon's death and with the reign of his son Rehoboam, the Kingdom of Israel split into two separate Kingdoms, also referred to as Houses.[14] These two Kingdoms are referred to as the Southern Kingdom of Judah and the Northern Kingdom of Israel throughout the Tanach (Old Testament), the latter also known as Joseph or Ephraim.

King Solomon sought after strange women and the worship of gods other than the Holy One of Israel. As a consequence of his idolatry, the Kingdom of Israel would be divided after his death (1 Kings 11:7-11).[15] The Lord told Solomon,

---

[13] If you have not already, do consult the author's publication *Are Non-Jewish Believers Really a Part of Israel?*, which addresses many of the different components and debates within contemporary Messianic ecclesiology.

[14] For a broad overview of the period, from the United Kingdom era to the Divided Kingdom era, and the exile and return, consult: C.F. Pfeieffer, "Israel, History of the People of," in *ISBE*, 2:913-922; A.E. Hill, "History of Israel 3: United Monarchy," in Bill T. Arnold and H.G.M. Williamson, eds., *Dictionary of the Old Testament Historical Books* (Downers Grove, IL: InterVarsity, 2005), pp 442-452; S.L. McKenzie, "History of Israel 4: Division of the Monarchy," in Ibid., pp 452-458; B.E. Kelle and B.A. Strawn, "History of Israel 5: Assyrian Period," in Ibid., pp 458-478; P.-A. Beaulieu, "History of Israel 6: Babylonian Period," in Ibid., pp 478-485.

[15] "Then Solomon built a high place for Chemosh the detestable idol of Moab, on the mountain which is east of Jerusalem, and for Molech the detestable idol of the sons of Ammon. Thus also he did for all his foreign wives, who burned incense and sacrificed to their gods. Now the LORD was angry with Solomon because his heart was turned away from the LORD, the God of Israel, who had appeared to him twice, and had commanded him concerning this thing, that he should not go after other gods; but he did not observe

"Nevertheless I will not do it in your days for the sake of your father David, *but* I will tear it out of the hand of your son. However, I will not tear away all the kingdom, *but* I will give one tribe to your son for the sake of My servant David and for the sake of Jerusalem which I have chosen" (1 Kings 11:12-13). We are further told that Jeroboam, at one time Solomon's high servant, was the one to whom the Lord would give ten tribes, affecting a split in the Kingdom of Israel:

"It came about at that time, when Jeroboam went out of Jerusalem, that the prophet Ahijah the Shilonite found him on the road. Now Ahijah had clothed himself with a new cloak; and both of them were alone in the field. Then Ahijah took hold of the new cloak which was on him and tore it into twelve pieces. He said to Jeroboam, 'Take for yourself ten pieces; for thus says the LORD, the God of Israel, "Behold, I will tear the kingdom out of the hand of Solomon and give you ten tribes (but he will have one tribe, for the sake of My servant David and for the sake of Jerusalem, the city which I have chosen from all the tribes of Israel)"''' (1 Kings 11:29-32).

For the sake of King David, whom the Lord loved, the Southern Kingdom of Judah would remain sovereign and keep Jerusalem. This time in Ancient Israel, which began in approximately 922 B.C.E., is commonly called the Divided Kingdom period. The Israelites were split into two Kingdoms of Israel: Israel/Ephraim in the north, and Judah in the south. This division was from God, and the Southern Kingdom Israelites were prevented by Him from attempting to reconquer the Northern Kingdom:

"It came about when all Israel [the Northern Kingdom] heard that Jeroboam had returned, that they sent and called him to the assembly and made him king over all Israel. None but the tribe of Judah followed the house of David. Now when Rehoboam had come to Jerusalem, he assembled all the house of Judah and the tribe of Benjamin, 180,000 chosen men[16] who were warriors, to fight against the house of Israel to restore the kingdom to Rehoboam the son of Solomon" (1 Kings 12:20-21).

These two separate Kingdoms had two separate monarchies,[17] they switched between worshipping the Holy One of Israel and false gods, and they frequently warred with one another (cf. 1 Kings 14:30; 15:16; 2 Kings 15:37; 16:5-6). The Northern Kingdom's first ruler, Jeroboam, saw to it that idolatry was immediately established as the approved method of worship, as he did not want the people to go to Jerusalem and demand reunification with the Southern Kingdom (1 Kings

---

what the LORD had commanded. So the LORD said to Solomon, 'Because you have done this, and you have not kept My covenant and My statutes, which I have commanded you, I will surely tear the kingdom from you, and will give it to your servant'" (1 Kings 11:7-11).

[16] Note how the Septuagint says that there were "a hundred and twenty thousand young men" (LXE). Given the issue present in Biblical Studies over what *elef* (אֶלֶף) can mean, either as "thousand" or "troop," it has been contested by some whether the army described here was really 180,000.

Cf. Simon J. DeVries, *Word Biblical Commentary: 1 Kings*, Vol 12 (Waco, TX: Word Books, 1985), 158.

[17] The fact that the Northern Kingdom of Israel/Ephraim actually had numerous dynasties rule, contrasted to the Southern Kingdom of Judah which consistently retained the House of David, is a testament to its instability.

12:26-33).[18] In modern terms, both the Northern Kingdom of Israel/Ephraim and the Southern Kingdom of Judah were two separate "states" of Israel. This continued until the Assyrian Empire finally encroached upon the region, conquering the Northern Kingdom in 722-721 B.C.E., and taking many of its people into captivity.[19] When this happened, a great number of these Northern Kingdom exiles, over a series of several generations, were absorbed into the mass of Assyria through transplantation and cultural assimilation. Those of the Northern Kingdom were never corporately heard from again, as the Assyrians displaced and intermingled peoples that they conquered to reduce the likelihood of rebellion against them.[20] The testimony of 2 Kings 17:22-23 says,

"The sons of Israel walked in all the sins of Jeroboam which he did; they did not depart from them until the LORD removed Israel from His sight, as He spoke through all His servants the prophets. So Israel was carried away into exile from their own land to Assyria until this day [or: and they are still there, NIV]."

At this same time, exiles from other parts of the Assyrian Empire were imported into the Land of Israel. They were forced to intermingle with many of the Northern Kingdom Israelites who had remained, resulting in the formation of the Samaritans (2 Kings 17:24-41). This group was greatly despised by the First Century Jewish community, as they practiced a hybrid religion based in God's Torah as well as various pagan rituals and superstitions.

Corporately, the Northern Kingdom was deported away how how "the king of Assyria captured Samaria and carried Israel away into exile to Assyria, and settled

---

[18] "Jeroboam said in his heart, 'Now the kingdom will return to the house of David. If this people go up to offer sacrifices in the house of the LORD at Jerusalem, then the heart of this people will return to their lord, *even* to Rehoboam king of Judah; and they will kill me and return to Rehoboam king of Judah.' So the king consulted, and made two golden calves, and he said to them, 'It is too much for you to go up to Jerusalem; behold your gods, O Israel, that brought you up from the land of Egypt.' He set one in Bethel, and the other he put in Dan. Now this thing became a sin, for the people went *to worship* before the one as far as Dan. And he made houses on high places, and made priests from among all the people who were not of the sons of Levi. Jeroboam instituted a feast in the eighth month on the fifteenth day of the month, like the feast which is in Judah, and he went up to the altar; thus he did in Bethel, sacrificing to the calves which he had made. And he stationed in Bethel the priests of the high places which he had made. Then he went up to the altar which he had made in Bethel on the fifteenth day in the eighth month, even in the month which he had devised in his own heart; and he instituted a feast for the sons of Israel and went up to the altar to burn incense'" (1 Kings 12:26-33).

[19] Cf. Hosea 8:8; 9:17; Amos 9:9.

"Assyria exiled many residents of the northern kingdom in 722 B.C.E." ("Israel, Land of," in Jacob Neusner and William Scott Green, eds., *Dictionary of Judaism in the Biblical Period* [Peabody, MA: Hendrickson, 2002], 322).

[20] As Biblical archaeologist Siegfried H. Horn attests,

"Conquered peoples from the western portions of the empire were resettled in Assyria and in the eastern provinces, while captives from the eastern and southern regions were resettled in the West. Thus we are told in 2 Kings 17:6 that Sargon transported the captive Israelites to Assyria and in 2 Kings 17:24 that he repopulated the cities of Samaria with the peoples from Babylonia and Elam (southwestern Iran). More specifically, the Israelites were resettled in Halah (northeast of Nineveh), on the Habor (the Khabor River, a tributary that flows south into Euphrates from the highlands of southern Turkey and northeastern Syria), and in the highlands of the Medes (northwestern Iran)" (Siegfried H. Horn, "The Divided Monarchy," rev. P. Kyle McCarter, Jr., in Hershel Shanks, ed., *Ancient Israel: From Abraham to the Destruction of the Temple* [Washington, D.C.: Biblical Archaeology Society, 1999], 174).

them in Halah and Habor, *on* the river of Gozan, and in the cities of the Medes" (2 Kings 17:6),[21] displacing them eastward. The observation of the author/editors of Kings is that such displaced persons remained eastward *ad ha'yom ha'zeh* (הַיּוֹם הַזֶּה עַד) or "until this day" (2 Kings 17:23). This would presumably be the time when the Books of Samuel-Kings reached their final form, either during or after the Southern Kingdom's exile to Babylon in the Sixth Century B.C.E. The later testimony of 2 Chronicles 10:19 says, "So Israel has been in rebellion against the house of David to this day," *ad ha'yom ha'zeh*. Given the fact that the Books of Chronicles are a post-exilic work, this could definitely be an observation that the people of the Northern Kingdom, exiled by Assyria, were to be corporately regarded as still in rebellion in the late Fifth to Fourth Centuries B.C.E., when Chronicles reached its final form.[22]

Enough people from the Northern Kingdom of Israel had to be dispersed by Assyria, being large enough for the Prophets to foresee a time in the future when they—whomever they would be *and* wherever they would be—would need to be reunited with those of the Southern Kingdom of Judah. One of the end-time expectations of the Prophets is undeniably the reunion of the scattered segments of the Northern Kingdom with those of the Southern Kingdom.

The Southern Kingdom of Judah also fell into gross idolatry and rebellion against God, being taken into exile by the Babylonian Empire in a series of dispersions from 597-587 B.C.E. (2 Kings chs. 24-25). But the exiles of Judah, unlike Ephraim, corporately returned to the Land of Israel in 539 B.C.E. after the Persian Empire conquered the Babylonians, as is recorded in the historical testimonies at the end of the Books of Chronicles and in Ezra-Nehemiah.

When we read in the Tanach Scriptures of "Judah and Israel" or "Judah and Ephraim" or some combination thereof, and sometimes we read just "Judah" or "Israel" by themselves (contingent on **context**), the two Kingdoms of Israel, from the Divided Kingdom era, are often being referred to. It is very interesting that we be aware that even prior to King Saul ascending to power a division between "Judah and Israel" existed (cf. Joshua 11:21; Judges 10:9; 1 Samuel 11:8), implying that there was probably some kind of division or preferential groupings sometime before the Divided Kingdom era.

---

[21] Cf. 1 Chronicles 5:26.

[22] Consult the entries for the Books of Samuel, Kings, and Chronicles, in the author's workbook *A Survey of the Tanach for the Practical Messianic*.

"All Israel" Escaped and Found, and Not Ignoring Future Prophecy

There are those who believe that the complete reunification of the Northern and Southern Kingdoms has already taken place in past history, and that treating this as a future event yet to occur is misplaced. Claims are often issued regarding post-exilic statements made in the Tanach that involve "all Israel." But a careful reading of these passages, does not conclusively prove that Judah and those of exiled Israel/Ephraim have been fully reunited. This is a convenient way for those who do not wish to examine the subject matter in any detail to dismiss it.

Perhaps the most significant reference to be considered is seen at an oath taking ceremony, where the returned Jewish exiles were forbidden from intermarrying local pagans. Ezra 10:5 tells us, "Then Ezra rose and made the leading priests, the Levites and all Israel, take oath that they would do according to this proposal; so they took the oath." According to some, because this event took place after the Babylonian exile, all Israel—both the Northern and Southern Kingdoms—were reunified because "all Israel" is mentioned. Yet a reading of significant end-time prophecies that speak of Israel's end-time restoration demonstrates that those of both the Northern and Southern Kingdoms have not at all been fully reunited. The kol-Yisrael (כָּל־יִשְׂרָאֵל) mentioned here in Ezra should be understood as all Israel, meaning the community present, available, or accessible for this event. This is confirmed by what we see earlier in Ezra 8:25, when gifts for the Second Temple had been collected:

"I weighed out to them the silver, the gold and the utensils, the offering for the house of our God which the king and his counselors and his princes and all Israel present there had offered."

The kol-Yisrael ha'nimtza'im (כָּל־יִשְׂרָאֵל הַנִּמְצָאִים), "all the Israelites who were present" (NEB), could have been "all the Israelites of that region" (New American Bible) who were able to attend. The verb matza (מָצָא), appearing in the Nifal stem (simple action, passive voice), means "be found," or possibly even "be found incidentally, by chance, happen to be found" (CHALOT).[23] The thought of the Keil & Delitzch Commentary on the Old Testament is that it was actually, "all Israelites who were found, met with, in Babylon, and were not going with them to Jerusalem."[24] The offerings presented were definitely presented on behalf of the known community of Israel, those who survived the challenges and difficulties of the exile, and who only by the sheer grace of God were able to be freed from Babylonian oppression. Even though the returnees to the Land of Israel were largely those of the Southern Kingdom, there is no reason why they should never have referred to themselves as kol Yisrael or as b'nei-Yisrael (בְּנֵי־יִשְׂרָאֵל), the "sons/children of Israel" (cf. Ezra 6:21).

---

[23] William L. Holladay, ed., A Concise Hebrew and Aramaic Lexicon of the Old Testament (Leiden, the Netherlands: E.J. Brill, 1988), 209.

[24] E-Sword 8.0.8: Keil & Delitzsch Commentary on the Old Testament. MS Windows 9x. Franklin, TN: Equipping Ministries Foundation, 2008.

There is also no compelling reason, that when the Second Temple was dedicated to God, that there should not have been various twelve sets of animal sacrifices made for all twelve tribes (Ezra 6:17; 8:35). In the view of a Jewish commentator like Judah J. Slotki, "The number included those tribes who had not returned or of whom only very few came back. The oneness of Israel was always emphasized at national assemblies....The remnant who had returned made solemn confession of sin in the name of the whole scattered and despised race."[25] There was certainly a hope, after all, that Israel would fully return to the Promised Land and be restored to right relationship with God. Those who issue a natural confession to the Lord, notably call themselves *pelei'tah* (פְּלֵיטָה),[26] an "escaped remnant" (Ezra 9:13-15) or "surviving remnant" (CJB).

Those of Israel who were found, who presented material offerings, and then presented various animal sacrifices, surely did so with the hope that there would never again be a terrible calamity befall the people. The "all Israel"[27] represented likely included survivors from the Northern Kingdom who had not been fully assimilated into the Assyrian Empire, and who joined with the Jewish exiles when the Persian Empire conquered the Babylonian Empire, and freed all of the conquered peoples of the region.[28] Also not to be overlooked is how various Northern Kingdom families and individuals had migrated into the Southern Kingdom centuries earlier, had been integrated into the Southern Kingdom, and whose descendants were taken to Babylon and had subsequently returned.[29] Yet, while language such as "all Israel that were found" (Ezra 8:25, LXE)[30] is witnessed in the post-exilic scene,[31] there is still **a significant, futuristic prophetic expectation** that cannot be disregarded. And, "all Israel found," after all, can be an admission that there was still some or a noticeable part of Israel still unaccounted for.

---

[25] Judah J. Slotki, *Soncino Books of the Bible: Daniel, Ezra, Nehemiah* (London: Soncino Press, 1973), 147.

[26] Meaning either "a survivor, survival, someone or something remaining," or "**escape, deliverance**" (Ludwig Koehler and Walter Baumgartner, eds., *The Hebrew & Aramaic Lexicon of the Old Testament*, 2 vols. [Leiden, the Netherlands: Brill, 2001], 2:932).

[27] ***Context*** should always determine who "all Israel" is, when being referred to. Consider how 1 Kings 12:20 speaks of "all Israel," and it is not "all Israel" in the sense of *both* the Northern and Southern Kingdoms: "It came about when all Israel heard that Jeroboam had returned, that they sent and called him to the assembly and made him king over all Israel. None but the tribe of Judah followed the house of David." In this verse "all Israel" referred to is the Northern Kingdom of Israel/Ephraim. In a similar manner, Ezra 10:5 refers largely to those of the Southern Kingdom.

[28] I.e., people possibly like Tobit of the tribe of Naphtali, exiled to Nineveh (Tobit 1:1-3).

[29] 2 Chronicles 11:16; 15:9; 30:11, 18; 34:9; cf. 35:16-19 and the *kol-Yehudah v'Yisrael ha'nimtza* (הַנִּמְצָא כָּל־יְהוּדָה וְיִשְׂרָאֵל), "all Judah and Israel who are found" (35:18, YLT), who were participants in King Josiah's Passover.

[30] The Greek Septuagint of Ezra 8:25 has *pas Israēl hoi euriskomenoi* (πᾶς Ισραηλ οἱ εὑρισκόμενοι); the verb *euriskō* (εὑρίσκω) actually meaning, "**to come upon someth. either through purposeful search or accidentally, find**" (*BDAG*, 411).

[31] Commenting on King Cyrus' decree made in Ezra 1:3, "Whoever there is among you of all His people...," *m'kol-amo* (מִכָּל־עַמּוֹ), H.G.M. Williamson, *Word Biblical Commentary: Ezra, Nehemiah*, Vol 16 (Waco, TX: Word Books, 1985), 13 notably says,

"[I]t is highly unlikely, either historically or on the basis of the ideological outlook of the writer, that any reference is intended to the lost tribes of the old Northern Kingdom."

If the Northern and Southern Kingdoms of Israel have been fully reunited, then what do Bible readers do with the prophetic oracle of Ezekiel 37:25-28, which is clearly futuristic?

"They will live on the land that I gave to Jacob My servant, in which your fathers lived; and they will live on it, they, and their sons and their sons' sons, forever; and David My servant will be their prince forever. I will make a covenant of peace with them; it will be an everlasting covenant with them. And I will place them and multiply them, and will set My sanctuary in their midst forever. My dwelling place also will be with them; and I will be their God, and they will be My people. And the nations will know that I am the LORD who sanctifies Israel, when My sanctuary is in their midst forever" (Ezekiel 37:25-28).

Has this prophecy been fulfilled? Is God's Sanctuary presently established in the Land of Israel for all the nations of the world to see? Also consider the fact that Ezekiel 37:24 plainly states, "My servant David will be king over them, and they will all have one shepherd; and they will walk in My ordinances and keep My statutes and observe them." "David," we should rightly conclude, is a reference to the Messiah. If indeed the Northern and Southern Kingdoms were fully reunited in past history, then Yeshua the Messiah should surely be present in Jerusalem *right now* ruling and reigning over the world. (At the very least, we would see Israel in a position of significant prominence and respect in the world.) But He has not yet returned, and we are still waiting for the complete reunion of Israel and all of the mighty acts that it involves.

Popular author Tim LaHaye tells us, in regard to Bible prophecy, "The Kingdom of David and Solomon split in 931 B.C., becoming Israel and Judah. In restored Israel, all tribes are represented and the nation will be united, as the sign of the fused stick reveals."[32] John F. Walvoord observes in his *Every Prophecy of the Bible*, "The situation where these two kingdoms were divided will end, and as this and other prophecies predict, the two kingdoms will become one nation (cf. Jer. 3:18; 23:5-6; 30:3; Hosea 1:11; Amos 9:11). No fulfillment has ever been recorded in history, and the future regathering of Israel will occur in the Millennium."[33] These two dispensationalists validly recognize some level of future fulfillment that cannot go unaddressed. If these two Christians—who think that much of Israel's end-time restoration will be actually preceded by a pre-tribulation rapture—can recognize that more is on the horizon, then today's Messianic Believers can certainly consider it as well.

Noting the contents of Haftarah *Va'yigash* (Genesis 44:18-47:27), Ezekiel 37:15-28, in the *JPS Bible Commentary: Haftorot*, Michael Fishbane rightly summarizes some of the main points of what the fulfillment of this oracle is to involve:

"The haftarah emphasizes the theme of national restoration, with specific focus on the promised reunification of the northern and southern tribes, the renewal of

[32] Tim LaHaye, ed., *Tim LaHaye Prophecy Study Bible* (Chattanooga: AMG Publishers, 2000), 873.

[33] John F. Walvoord, *Every Prophecy of the Bible* (Colorado Springs: Chariot Victor Publishing, 1999), pp 186-187.

the Davidic royal lineage, and the reestablishment of the covenant between God and Israel....Another theme of the haftarah is that of stability, expressed as a permanent change from the past and as a vision of a permanent future....[T]he haftarah achieves an intensity of focus and emphasis. Indeed, through [the terms used] the dispersed nation is given hope in a new future—unsullied by the defilements of sin and restored to their Land of God, one people forever. This is the new covenant of *shalom* prophesied to the people. It is a promise without condition....In the haftarah, God prophesies the unification of the northern and southern tribes, symbolized respectively by Judah and Joseph, along with their ingathering to the ancestral homeland."[34]

Have all of these things, notably called by Fishbane to be "a vision of a permanent future," **all come to pass?** Note how the descendants of the post-exilic community were eventually exiled again when the Romans destroyed Jerusalem in 70 C.E. Fulfillment of the Ezekiel 37:15-28 prophecy, subsequent to the Second Coming of Yeshua the Messiah, has to instead be on the horizon.[35] And not at all to be overlooked is Fishbane's assessment, "In the haftarah, the initiation of redemption belongs to God alone, as does its consummation."[36] This should draw our attention to the fact that even though there might be much abuse surrounding the issue, frequently found among those who address it and have popularized it, ultimately the sovereignty of our Creator as the One orchestrating events has to be supremely acknowledged.

In our day, given the significant growth and expansion of many diverse sectors of the Messianic movement, the Two-House sub-movement especially advocates that prophecies like Ezekiel 37:15-28 are in high gear. Many more people are just trying to honestly answer the question, **"Will you not show us what you mean by these?"** (Ezekiel 37:18, RSV). They do not know if they will be direct or indirect participants of what is to come, but they are certainly inquiring of the Heavenly Father to know what is going on and what He wants to do with all of His people. And perhaps most notably, regardless of how things actually play out, they do not want to be excluded from it.

There are many details regarding the exiled Northern Kingdom of Israel/Ephraim, that are only known to our Sovereign God. If, however, there are unfulfilled prophecies regarding the reunion of the Northern and Southern Kingdoms on the horizon, then He will be the One who Divinely brings all of His

---

[34] Michael Fishbane, *JPS Bible Commentary: Haftarot* (Philadelphia: Jewish Publication Society, 2002), pp 71, 72, 74.

[35] Even the largely liberal *Jewish Study Bible*, remarking on the genealogy of Ezra 8:1-4, leaves open the possibility for future prophetic fulfillment between the Northern and Southern Kingdoms, noting:

"While...these [ten] tribes had assimilated due to the Assyrian policy of forced population exchanges, the tradition of their continued existence is found in, for instance, Tobit...Emphasis is placed on genealogical connections to the priesthood and the Davidic line. These links are necessary if the preexilic and exilic Israelite prophecies of return are to be fulfilled (See, e.g., Ezek. 37.24-28)" (Hindy Najman, "Ezra," in Adele Berlin and Marc Zvi Brettler, eds., *The Jewish Study Bible*, NJPS [Oxford: Oxford University Press, 2004], 1682).

[36] Fishbane, 75.

people together. And, it cannot go overlooked that within the prophecies of Israel's restoration, companions of Judah and Ephraim are definitively included as well. As Ezekiel 37:16 says,

"And you, son of man, take for yourself one stick and write on it, 'For Judah and for the sons of Israel, **his companions** [*chavero*, וַחֲבֵרוֹ]'; then take another stick and write on it, 'For Joseph, the stick of Ephraim and all the house of Israel, **his companions** [*chavero*, חֲבֵרוֹ].'"

If you noticed carefully, in this prophecy of the two sticks, with each stick representing a separate Kingdom of Israel, is a reference to "his comrades" (ATS) or "his companions." There has definitely been a gross over-emphasis in the popular/populist Two-House literature given to Judah and Ephraim, when technically *three groups* are to be brought together according to prophecy: Judah, Israel/Ephraim, and companions from the nations. **There is no exclusion from those who are physically non-Israelites in what is to occur.**[37] On the contrary, the larger restoration of Israel that is to be anticipated, is to be a very *inclusive* process.[38] And, it is *most highly probable* that the significant majority of those involved in such a larger restoration of Israel are companions from the nations at large. It is important that we realize that the doors for membership in Israel have always been open to all, not those who are just physical Israelites. For, as the famed word of Isaiah 49:6 tells us,

"It is too small a thing that You should be My Servant to raise up the tribes of Jacob and to restore the preserved ones of Israel; I will also make You a light of the nations so that My salvation may reach to the end of the earth."

Key Prophecies of Israel's Restoration

Far too frequently, as has been encountered in the approach of many voices within the Two-House sub-movement, the issue of the reunion of Judah and Israel/Ephraim, is one of lost identity. Many non-Jewish Messianic Believers, reading various prophecies, and legitimately acknowledging them as futuristic and unfulfilled—have gone far beyond thinking that they might be *"to be determined..."* participants in them, but that they must absolutely be descendants, however distant, of the exiled Northern Kingdom of Israel/Ephraim. **This is an inappropriate way to approach the subject matter of a larger restoration of Israel.**

Aside from some of the controversies that have been spurred on, the issue is undeniably intertwined with end-time prophecy. As such, as the Second Coming approaches, Tanach prophecies regarding a larger restoration of Israel, should come clearer into focus—no differently than with Bible readers trying to understand the rise of the antimessiah/antichrist, a one world government, a World War III type event or events, massive Earth changes and catastrophes, the arrival of

---

[37] This is further examined in Chapter 2, "What About 'the Gentiles'?"

[38] The restoration of Israel is *no less* an inclusive process than the Sabbath was intended to be. As Exodus 20:10 indicates, "you shall not do any work, you or your son or your daughter, your male or your female servant or your cattle or your sojourner who stays with you," a command that is quite egalitarian. Israel's mission was to *always* include others in its community than just native Israelites.

a mark of the beast economic system, and a great apostasy of defectors away from Biblical faith and/or theism. Here is a selection of just four passages that need to be seriously considered by Bible readers:

"And He will lift up a standard for the nations and assemble the banished ones of Israel, and will gather the dispersed of Judah from the four corners of the earth. Then the jealousy of Ephraim will depart, and those who harass Judah will be cut off; Ephraim will not be jealous of Judah, and Judah will not harass Ephraim. They will swoop down on the slopes of the Philistines on the west; together they will plunder the sons of the east; they will possess Edom and Moab, and the sons of Ammon will be subject to them. And the LORD will utterly destroy the tongue of the Sea of Egypt; and He will wave His hand over the River with His scorching wind; and He will strike it into seven streams and make *men* walk over dry-shod. And there will be a highway from Assyria for the remnant of His people who will be left, just as there was for Israel in the day that they came up out of the land of Egypt" (Isaiah 11:12-16).

"For there will be a day when watchmen on the hills of Ephraim call out, 'Arise, and let us go up *to* Zion, to the LORD our God.' For thus says the LORD, 'Sing aloud with gladness for Jacob, and shout among the chief of the nations; proclaim, give praise and say, "O LORD, save Your people, the remnant of Israel." Behold, I am bringing them from the north country, and I will gather them from the remote parts of the earth, among them the blind and the lame, the woman with child and she who is in labor with child, together; a great company, they will return here. With weeping they will come, and by supplication I will lead them; I will make them walk by streams of waters, on a straight path in which they will not stumble; for I am a father to Israel, and Ephraim is My firstborn.' Hear the word of the LORD, O nations, and declare in the coastlands afar off, and say, 'He who scattered Israel will gather him and keep him as a shepherd keeps his flock'" (Jeremiah 31:6-10).

"Say to them, 'Thus says the Lord GOD, "Behold, I will take the sons of Israel from among the nations where they have gone, and I will gather them from every side and bring them into their own land; and I will make them one nation in the land, on the mountains of Israel; and one king will be king for all of them; and they will no longer be two nations and no longer be divided into two kingdoms. They will no longer defile themselves with their idols, or with their detestable things, or with any of their transgressions; but I will deliver them from all their dwelling places in which they have sinned, and will cleanse them. And they will be My people, and I will be their God. My servant David will be king over them, and they will all have one shepherd; and they will walk in My ordinances and keep My statutes and observe them. They will live on the land that I gave to Jacob My servant, in which your fathers lived; and they will live on it, they, and their sons and their sons' sons, forever; and David My servant will be their prince forever. I will make a covenant of peace with them; it will be an everlasting covenant with them. And I will place them and multiply them, and will set My sanctuary in their midst forever. My dwelling place also will be with them; and I will be their God, and they will be My people. And the nations will know that I am the LORD who sanctifies Israel, when My sanctuary is in their midst forever"'" (Ezekiel 37:21-28).

"I will strengthen the house of Judah, and I will save the house of Joseph, and I will bring them back, because I have had compassion on them; and they will be as though I had not rejected them, for I am the LORD their God and I will answer them. Ephraim will be like a mighty man, and their heart will be glad as if *from* wine; indeed, their children will see *it* and be glad, their heart will rejoice in the LORD. I will whistle for them to gather them together, for I have redeemed them; and they will be as numerous as they were before. When I scatter them among the peoples, they will remember Me in far countries, and they with their children will live and come back. I will bring them back from the land of Egypt and gather them from Assyria; and I will bring them into the land of Gilead and Lebanon until no *room* can be found for them" (Zechariah 10:6-10).

How some of these prophecies will transpire, are specifically unknown at this point in history. (Ezekiel 37:15-28 is examined in specific detail in **Chapter 6**.) Yet, we *really do* need to be carefully considering them as a part of our end-time scenarios. We must consider the fact that Yeshua **may have not presently returned**—as many have expected—because these prophecies have been overlooked, or at least under-emphasized. We must seek the Lord and through His Holy Spirit contemplate the prophecies before us and proceed carefully. Much will undoubtedly take place in a future time, when the global situation is much different than it is today. When one sees prophetic words that detail a great amount of people, presumably immigrating to the Land of Israel, for example—it may very well take place in a world environment and in circumstances that are much different than ours, presently in the early Twenty-First Century.

The Mission of Israel

By far, I would have to argue that the most important part of any person recognizing himself or herself as a part of the Commonwealth of Israel—especially if that person is a Jewish Believer or a non-Jewish Believer in Messiah Yeshua—is in trying to understand **the Divine mission that God gave Ancient Israel.**

In the scene of Genesis 32:28-29, as he was preparing himself for a confrontation with his estranged brother Esau, the Patriarch Jacob wrestles with the supernatural being all night, and is renamed "Israel." Part of his being renamed Israel has to do with the mission that the Lord had for both him and his descendants after him. We can also safely assume that such a mission regards those who are joined into Israel via their faith in its God, and now the Messiah:

"He said, **'Your name shall no longer be Jacob, but Israel; for you have striven with God and with men and have prevailed.'** Then Jacob asked him and said, 'Please tell me your name.' But he said, 'Why is it that you ask my name? And he blessed him there."

Prior to being renamed Israel, the Patriarch's name was *Ya'akov* (יַעֲקֹב), which has been traditionally interpreted as meaning "supplanter," although it more specifically means "heel holder," as he grabbed his brother's heel at the time of his birth (Genesis 25:26).[39] The Biblical story of Jacob reveals that he was very much a trickster and a swindler prior to this time. By being renamed *Yisrael* (יִשְׂרָאֵל), Jacob experienced a major status change. Jewish commentator J.H. Hertz observes in *Pentateuch & Haftorahs*, regarding the name Israel, that "The name is clearly a title of victory; probably 'a champion of God'. The children of the Patriarch are *Israelites*, Champions of God, Contenders for the Divine, conquering by strength from Above."[40] The thoughts of Joyce G. Baldwin, in her reflective commentary *The Message of Genesis 12-50*, are also rather useful to consider:

"In Jacob's case it took God twenty years to bring Jacob to this point of surrender on the border of the promised land; the Lord is not in any hurry, crucial as the transaction is. But when his time comes the transformation is complete: it is a transition from life to death, from self-help to faith in the God who cripples Jacob in order to bless him....In the same way as Jacob had needed the transforming power of God, so in every generation did his successors. The name *Jacob* stood for the raw material taken by the Lord to achieve his purposes, while *Israel* called to mind the transforming power which made a new man of Jacob, and which could have done the same for his descendants..."[41]

The Hebrew name *Yisrael* "Means 'he contends with God'" (*TWOT*), something which is surely intended to convey how "Jacob's struggle was spiritual...as well as physical. And in it the patriarch 'prevailed'" (*TWOT*).[42] Jacob or *Ya'akov* (יַעֲקֹב) was renamed Israel or *Yisrael* (יִשְׂרָאֵל) because **he had remained steadfast** in wrestling with the supernatural being during the night. Jacob's descendants, and/or those who consider themselves a part of the community that bears the name Israel, are likewise called to endure and strive through the power of God. It is sadly true that this has not always been the case, as evidenced by much of the Scriptural testimony of God's people falling into sin and needing to be *sternly and firmly* admonished to return to loyalty and obedience to Him. Yet as Believers in Yeshua, we should wholeheartedly embrace a spiritual ethos and dynamic deeply rooted within what it means to contend with God—the meaning of *Yisrael*. Such a call is witnessed in the Apostle Paul's word of Philippians 3:14:

"I keep pursuing the goal in order to win the prize offered by God's upward calling in the Messiah Yeshua" (Philippians 3:14, CJB).

As Believers in the Messiah of Israel, we are each called to press forward in our faith, the calling that the Lord has given us to achieve His mission, and never give up, no matter what the cost. We are called to endure for our God (cf. 2 Timothy 2:3-7). And as we need to perhaps remind ourselves, as it concerns the controversial subject matter of a larger restoration of Israel—indeed involving those of the

---

[39] L. Hicks, "Jacob (Israel)," in George Buttrick, ed. et. al., *Interpreter's Dictionary of the Bible*, 4 vols. (Nashville: Abingdon, 1962), 2:782-783.

[40] J.H. Hertz, ed., *Pentateuch & Haftorahs* (London: Soncino Press, 1960), *Pentateuch & Haftorahs*, 124.

[41] Joyce G. Baldwin, *The Message of Genesis 12-15* (Downers Grove, IL: InterVarsity, 1986), 139.

[42] J. Barton Payne, "יִשְׂרָאֵל; שָׂרָה," in R. Laird Harris, Gleason L. Archer, Jr., and Bruce K. Waltke, eds., *Theological Wordbook of the Old Testament*, 2 vols (Chicago: Moody Press, 1980), 2:883.

Northern and Southern Kingdoms, *and* many more companions from the nations themselves—only those who are *persistently reasonable* and who *strive to be fair* are those who are going to be rewarded by the Lord in the long run. This subject matter absolutely does concern the restoration of His Kingdom on Earth via the return of the Messiah, which is *no trivial matter* in the least. Those who are going to haphazardly dismiss and fail to read and consider a large(r) scope of unfulfilled, Biblical prophecies regarding Israel in the eschaton, *and/or* various popular/populist teachers who go out on the road for speaking trips and conference appearances, making a "quick buck"—are **surely not** those who are prevailing with Him. They possess no ability to see the long term future, and commit themselves to the daily and weekly tasks of His Kingdom, reaching for the age to come.

I think we should all choose to be a part of the holy and set-apart people which our Heavenly Father desires in Deuteronomy 28:9: "The LORD will establish you as a holy people to Himself, as He swore to you, if you keep the commandments of the LORD your God and walk in His ways." The Apostle Peter concurs, instructing how important it is that God's people obey Him and demonstrate proper conduct: "[B]ut like the Holy One who called you, be holy yourselves also in all *your* behavior; because it is written, 'YOU SHALL BE HOLY, FOR I AM HOLY' [Leviticus 11:44-45; 19:2; 20:7]" (1 Peter 1:15-16). Moses originally said in the Torah that obedience to God's commandments would naturally result in outsiders to Israel seeing the people blessed, and hence inquiring about Him as Creator:

"So keep and do *them,* for that is your wisdom and your understanding in the sight of the peoples who will hear all these statutes and say, 'Surely this great nation is a wise and understanding people.' For what great nation is there that has a god so near to it as is the LORD our God whenever we call on Him?" (Deuteronomy 4:6-7).

Considering oneself as a part of the community of Israel, in obedience to the Lord, should manifest itself in demonstrating His character and goodness to *all* we encounter—especially as it concerns the good news of salvation in Messiah Yeshua! How any person, ministry, or organization in today's broad Messianic world demonstrates such goodness, grace, and mercy to one another—has not typically been easy, and in a few cases, it has been quantitatively absent. Yet, it is those who are able to allow their hearts and minds to be transformed by the Messiah's love and character, who will be able to approach the different issues and sub-issues with the intention to let the Lord lead and have His Word be heard.

There is too much of a good thing going on in today's Messianic community, with Jewish and non-Jewish Believers being brought together as the "one new humanity" (Ephesians 2:15, NRSV), for unnecessary division and rivalry to manifest itself over issues associated with a larger restoration of Israel—which when properly diagnosed, concerns eschatology, and will manifest steadily as we edge closer to the Messiah's return. By its very nature, any interpretation regarding the end-times and future prophecy, **is not a salvation issue;** it is *adiaphora*.[43] But, if there really is a futuristic, larger restoration of Israel to come, it does need to be subject to further refinement, examination, and reflection.

---

[43] *Adiaphora* is Greek term for "things indifferent," largely meaning "Elements of faith regarded as neither commanded nor forbidden in Scripture and thus on which liberty of conscience may be exercised" (Donald S. McKim, *Westminster Dictionary of Theological Terms* [Louisville: Westminster John Knox, 1996], 4).

-2-

What About "the Gentiles"?
and the terms we use to speak of people

One of my all-time favorite films, going back to my experiences as a young child watching the Disney Channel, is the 1967 piece The Gnome Mobile, starring Walter Brennan as both the human D.J. Mulrooney and the gnome Knobby. Frequently throughout the story, as the much larger humans encounter the small gnomes, you hear the gnomes refer to the "big people" as **dudeens.** In the course of the story, it is entirely comedic, as the gnomes ride around in some old man's Rolls Royce, they are carried in a picnic basket, and they are stolen by a trickster named Quaxton of Quaxton's Academy of Fantastic Freaks. That the gnomes would have a term like dudeen to refer to big people makes the story rather humorous, but it cannot be denied that the gnomes—at least at first—have a strong distrust of humans. The 900-year old Knobby expresses to D.J. how the gnomes have almost gone extinct because of the chopping down of their redwood forest—with some "Mulrooney outfit" being the worst culprit. And to add to the irony of the story, at their first encounter, Knobby has no idea that D.J. is actually the owner of San Francisco-based Mulrooney Lumber. Suffice it to say, it is easily detected from watching The Gnome Mobile, that the term dudeen was probably not originally given out of some kind of respect to big people, in order to charm them.

Unfortunately due to some trends in Western society over the past two to three decades, it is no longer commonplace for a congregation leader, either in the Synagogue or Church, to be referred to by an appropriate title. Mr. and Mrs. Smith or Mr. and Mrs. Jones, are now often referred to by their first names by young people half their age. (To an extent, I can get upset at times when people I do not know do not refer to me as Mr. McKee, and instead call me John.) What happened to the doctors among us? Many are completely unaware if someone has ever served in the military, law enforcement, or some kind of other major service career. *Things are expected to now be more informal and less-stuffy.* Yet, from my early years of visiting my grandparents in Annapolis, MD, and going to the United States Naval Academy where my grandfather worked as museum director and chief archivist— it was always a thrill to see him referred to as Professor Jeffries. And, it was certainly rather impressive to see him call his colleagues titles like Commander,

Captain, and Admiral.[1] (I am sorry I was never there to see the President make a surprise visit.)

While the employment of proper titles is critical to establish some degree of formal respect for one's peers—especially those who have worked hard for some high achievement, like those in academia or those in uniform—terms used in the context of a community of faith, are something even more important.[2] How we refer to people in a local assembly or fellowship of Believers needs to convey not only a sense of respect, love, and a tenor of feeling welcome—but that we are, to some degree, to be sensitive to their various unique cultural and social needs.

A concept that is very popular not only in today's Messianic Jewish movement, but much of the broad Messianic community in general, is that of **"Jew and Gentile, one in Messiah."**[3] Technically speaking, what is intended by this sentiment is that *any person*, regardless of if he or she is Jewish or not, is to be viewed as equal not only in the eyes of God—but most especially with one's fellow Believers viewing one another as equal and valued because of saving faith in Yeshua (Jesus). For many of those in today's Messianic Jewish community, this is exactly what the message of the Apostles is all about: Jew and Gentile becoming one in Messiah. For many of those in evangelical Christianity, in slight contrast, it can be all about Jew and Gentile becoming one in Messiah as a part of "the Church," a group separated from Israel.

In the past two decades or so, given the significant growth of the Messianic movement via a large number of evangelical Christians embracing their Hebraic and Jewish Roots, in a very real and tangible way, various questions have been asked and trends can be noticed. A few of the claims of modern Christianity, and even Messianic Judaism, have been challenged on some noticeable levels. In a large part of today's broad Messianic movement, non-Jewish Believers consider themselves a part of the Commonwealth of Israel, and *equal partakers* in Israel's promises along with their fellow Jewish Believers (cf. Ephesians 2:11-13; 3:6). While these people are obviously not Jewish either ethnically or culturally, they do not consider their status as God's people to be something separate from Israel, in some

---

[1] My late grandfather, Prof. Jeffries, did retire as a Commander in the U.S. Naval Reserve. He arrived at Annapolis in 1942 subsequent to Pearl Harbor, as he received his doctorate at Vanderbilt University, written on the Battle of Mobile Bay. While originally a member of the commissioned faculty, he later served as a part of the civilian faculty. For more information, see William W. Jeffries Memorial Archives <usna.edu/LibExhibits/Archives/Academic.html>.

[2] I am innately aware of the debate surrounding the title "Rabbi" in the Messianic movement, which many oppose using on the basis of Yeshua's statements in Matthew 23:8. I think a better solution than a uniform moratorium on using the title "Rabbi" needs to be found, per the following word in Matthew 23:9 regarding the term "father," and a similar moratorium on calling human fathers "father" has never been proposed by any Messianic person I know.

Alas, though, many of the (male) Messianic Jewish congregational leaders who bear the term "Rabbi," whom I have encountered, have far less theological training than I do. Because of this, and the fact that I will never be ordained by any Messianic organization as a "rabbi," I have a personal tendency to only refer to such persons as Mr. ABC-XYZ or simply "sir."

Consult the FAQ on the TNN website, "Rabbi, Title."

[3] This exact sentence has been largely popularized, in no uncertain terms, due to the Joel Chernoff song "Jew and Gentile."

kind of a "Church" entity that sits off to the distance *or* even more closely alongside it.

This causes some problems, because in various parts of Messianic Judaism, non-Jewish Believers can find themselves in congregations relegated to an almost "second class" status to their Jewish constituents. The main purpose that any non-Jewish Believer, *a Gentile,* would need to recognize in such a place, is that he or she is probably there to have an appreciation for the Jewish Roots of Christianity. Yet in some settings it goes even further, as the non-Jewish person or family is only and exclusively there to supplement the congregation's outreach to the Jewish community (and perhaps with that only by financial offerings). Obviously, each individual Messianic congregation has to be evaluated on its own merits—and many places *can and do change* over the course of time—but in these sorts of environments, it is easy for many Messianic Jews' reference to non-Jewish Believers as just "Gentiles" or *"goyim"* to have some additional things attached to it.

A significant cause of the rise of various independent Messianic congregations from the late 1990s into the 2000s, and even now into the 2010s, has been when non-Jewish Believers find themselves unwelcome in a Messianic Jewish congregation—and they know that they do belong in the Messianic world. A feeling of being unwelcome, even in places where non-Jewish Believers want to clearly fellowship with their Jewish brothers and sisters in Messiah, and be very sensitive to their unique social and cultural needs—has helped give significant rise to the One Law/One Torah and Two-House sub-movements. While both of these sectors of the broader Messianic community have their issues, they do tend to more widely emphasize the word of Yeshua's prayer, "that they may be one, just as We are one" (John 17:22), more than some of today's Messianic Jews do. *The kind of unity that Messiah followers are to reach for is the kind of unity that the Father and Son—as God—have.* This presents us as limited mortals with an almost impossible goal to achieve, but a grand, magnanimous unity of this kind should not be left outside of our view.[4]

Within the Two-House sub-movement, it has become significantly commonplace for non-Jewish Believers to consider themselves "former Gentiles," based on one reading of Paul's statement "remember that formerly you, the Gentiles..." (Ephesians 2:11). Along with this, it is said that the word **Gentile** most always means **pagan**, and some verses can be quoted as support for this. 1 Corinthians 5:1, for example, where Paul is horrified upon hearing about "immorality of such a kind as does not exist even among the Gentiles," more specifically means "there is immorality among you, and of a kind that is not found even among pagans" (RSV). When various people speak about non-Jewish Believers with the term "Gentiles," there can be easily detected a wide amount of resentment and offense. Populist Two-House teachers have stirred their audiences to the point of not only resisting any kind of usage of the word "Gentile," but they

---

[4] For some useful thoughts, consult the article "Unity, Despite Diversity in the Body of Messiah" by Mark Huey, appearing in the December 2010 issue of Outreach Israel News.

frequently direct them to insist on being referred to as some sort of "Israelite(s)." Along with this, given their high emphasis on restoration of Israel prophecies that speak of the Southern Kingdom of Judah and Northern Kingdom of Israel/Ephraim, one can often fail to detect the inclusion of any Gentiles—those outside of the bloodlines of physical Israel—in such a restoration process. This presents some serious theological problems, including the warranted accusation that *their message* withholds God's salvation from the vast, vast majority of human beings, created by Him, who live on Planet Earth.

Among many of the advocates and adherents of the Two-House teaching, have certainly been found many overstatements made about the English word "Gentile" meaning "pagan." Some people have taken offense a little too readily. But at the same time, it would be disingenuous to think that terms such as "Gentile," the Hebrew noun "*goy*," or adjectives such as the Yiddish "*goyische*," as have been used in much of the Jewish community—have been in an entirely neutral sense, without any context of disparagement. Along these same lines, it should also be observed that there have been Messianic Jewish individuals, at least, who have used the term "Gentile" or "*goyim*" to refer to non-Jewish people as something *other than* not being Jewish. Some have used the English term Gentile as a means of disparagement, or even a derogative slur.

The issue regarding the term "Gentile" cannot be separated from a much bigger issue that has been present in a great deal of Christian theology, and to a lesser extent Jewish theology, over the past two decades: **the inclusive language debate.** Given the changing contours of modern English speech, be it in Great Britain, North America, Australia and New Zealand, or elsewhere—is it appropriate to *exclusively* use terms like man, men, mankind, and brothers where the community of God is concerned? Inclusive language advocates, even those of a more mild variety, would argue that terms such as human being(s), humanity, humankind, brothers and sisters (or perhaps the more generic, although older term brethren), and people—are far better and clearer to now use. Taking some cues from this, would it be advisable that today's Messianics employ some acceptable substitutes for the term Gentile(s), such as nation(s) or people(s)? Implementing some very easy alternatives, which are already known to Bible readers, might deflate an unnecessarily big balloon.

The "Gentiles" and the Two-House Controversy

Many in the Messianic community, including a great number of individual Messianic Jews I know, have no difficulty seeing Jewish and non-Jewish Believers work together as a part of the Commonwealth of Israel, an enlarged Kingdom realm of Israel, *as the people of God*. This is an inclusive body, where Jewish people are no doubt to be honored for sure (Romans 3:2; 9:4), but where others' place is not at all dishonored. It is not a single, homogeneous group of people—but rather a people made up of peoples (cf. Revelation 21:3, Grk.).

It is when the controversies of the Two-House issue of Judah and Ephraim comes up—that these open-minded people can often become close-minded, regarding the Biblical passages and prophecies. In my interactions over the years, the way they have often heard about the subject matter of a larger restoration of Israel, is that it is quite exclusive. They see it as such because what is popularly taught, emphasized, repeated, and even sung about at its popular conference events and gatherings, is that *Judah and Ephraim* are coming together as one in the Messiah. What they have been taught, guided by, repeated to others, and even sung about is that *Jew and Gentile* are to be one in Messiah. So naturally, the following can be issued:

> *What about the Gentiles? What do you do about Gentiles in this so-called coming together of the Two Houses of Israel? If there is no place for the Gentiles then you are preaching falsehoods.*

The Two-House teaching, which one will most probably encounter advocated from its literature and various pseudo-denominations, does focus on Judah and Ephraim being one. Biblically, this issue is a matter to be largely reserved to eschatology or future end-time prophecy (i.e., Isaiah 11:12-16; Jeremiah 31:6-10; Ezekiel 37:15-28; Zechariah 10:6-10), with many of the specific details only known by our Eternal God Himself. As such, there are various unknown details regarding the descendants of the exiled Northern Kingdom and their prophesied return to the Holy Land. But even so, is affirming that there is a futuristic, larger restoration of Israel to occur on the horizon, something that excludes true "Gentiles" from membership within the Kingdom of God—meaning those from the nations of Planet Earth at large, *without* any physical descent from the Patriarchs Abraham, Isaac, and Jacob?

The premise, that all Believers in Messiah Yeshua are somehow a part of the community of Israel, with non-Jewish Believers being grafted into the olive tree (Romans 11:17-18), is not really what is controversial for some.[5] Rather, for those who tend to hear about a larger restoration of Israel, involving Judah and Ephraim coming together (from populist Two-House literature), the issue concerns who a third group of people is: **the Gentiles.** Are they, too, involved in this reunification process? Or are they really to be excluded from it, meaning that God is only interested in saving physical Jews and (lost) physical descendants from the exiled Northern Kingdom? Because of what various outspoken voices have chosen to emphasize, many perceive the Two-House teaching as pushing a significant form of racially-based salvation. (And, based on some of the sentiments expressed by the recognized "leaders" of the Two-House sub-movement, it might very well be.) All I can tell you is that if I honestly believed that this was the only perspective to be offered regarding this subject matter, **I myself would be the first person to rally against the issue of Judah and Ephraim yet to be reunited in prophetic history.** Being an egalitarian, after all, I believe not only that "Jew or Greek" are equals in

---

[5] Be sure to consult the author's analysis of Romans 11:16-14, 25-29 in his publication *Are Non-Jewish Believers Really a Part of Israel?*

Messiah—but also "male and female" are complete equals (Galatians 3:28).[6] This is hardly a position that one can hold to if any group of people are to be *left out* of God's Kingdom and Yeshua's salvation, or be excluded from a place of service or leadership, because of biological factors![7]

Anyone who would affirm a larger restoration of Israel prophesied for the future, involving Judah and Israel/Ephraim, must properly answer the question: **"What about the Gentiles?"** Are those of the nations of Planet Earth, obviously human beings who God made in His image (Genesis 1:27) and who He loves dearly as His special creations, quantitatively *excluded* as participants from Israel's restoration?

In this examination, it is my intention to recognize a variety of ways that the Hebrew terms *goy/goyim* and the Greek term *ethnos* are witnessed in Scripture, and how they can refer to both Israel and the nations at large. I will be considering various opinions of what it means to be a "Gentile," specifically as it is sometimes seen in Jewish theology and commentary. Does it mean "pagan"? I will even show some specific examples of how in some English Bibles, the proper term "Greek" has been inappropriately rendered as "Gentile." We will also evaluate some of the main promises given to the Patriarchs Abraham, Isaac, and Jacob regarding their progeny, and how we can fairly sort through over-statements made regarding their multiplication by Two-House advocates. Most importantly, though, we will clarify how prophecies regarding a larger restoration of Israel *do not exclusively* concern physical descendants of Abraham, Isaac, and Jacob—but that many companions from the nations themselves are very much involved, welcome, and are the significant majority of participants in it.

Goy and Ethnos: "Gentile" or "Nation"?

In order to properly consider the issue surrounding the English term "Gentile," every Bible reader needs to know the underlying Hebrew and Greek terms appearing in the source text, which are commonly rendered as such. We need to have appropriate definitions of the Hebrew word *goy* (גּוֹי) and Greek word *ethnos* (ἔθνος), and have a good idea of how they were used in their original contexts.

The common Hebrew word that one will encounter, sometimes rendered as "Gentile" in older versions like the KJV, is the term **goy** (גּוֹי). Its plural form, and possibly more common usage that you will encounter is **goyim** (גּוֹיִם). The *HALOT* lexicon indicates that it relates to "**people**...whole population of a territory; עַם [*am*]

---

[6] For a further discussion, consult the author's exegetical paper on Galatians 3:28, "Biblical Equality and Today's Messianic Movement."

[7] The term "egalitarian" is simply derived from the French *égal*, meaning "equal." The position of being egalitarian is commonly associated with those who believe in the ordination of female clergy, as either pastors or rabbis, and with those who deny the concept of so-called "male headship," believing that husbands and wives *together* lead the home.

Consult the FAQs on the TNN website, "Women in Ministry" and "Male Headship," as well as the relevant sections of the author's commentaries *Ephesians for the Practical Messianic* and *The Pastoral Epistles for the Practical Messianic*.

rather stresses the blood relationship," "**nation**," "often the **pagan** peoples as opposed to Israel...the 'heathen,'" "people=**persons**."[8] The *BDB* lexicon states how *goy* means "nation, people," "spec. of descendants of Abraham," "definitely of Israel."[9]

Witnessed in the Hebrew Tanach, *goy/goyim* has a wide array of uses. In its most neutral sense, *goy/goyim* means nation/nations. This can relate to the masses of Planet Earth, those outside of the bloodlines of Israel, the enemies of Israel, sheer pagans and idolaters, and it can even relate to the people of Israel itself. Regarding the progeny of Abraham, the Patriarch was told by God, "I will make you a great nation [*goy gadol*, גּוֹי גָּדוֹל], and I will bless you, and make your name great" (Genesis 12:2). The assembly of the Ancient Israelites gathered at Mount Sinai was told by the Lord, "you shall be to Me a kingdom of priests and a holy nation [*goy qadosh*, גּוֹי קָדוֹשׁ]" (Exodus 19:6). The term *goyim* can even relate to the tribes of Israel, as Ezekiel 2:3 states, "I send you to the Children of Israel, to the rebellious nations [*el-goyim*, אֶל-גּוֹיִם] that have rebelled against Me; they and their fathers have defiantly sinned against Me; they and their fathers have defiantly sinned against Me to this very day" (ATS). Context in a Tanach passage where *goy/goyim* appears, ultimately determines the different contours of what is intended by its usage.

The Greek equivalent term for the Hebrew *goy* (גּוֹי) is *ethnos* (ἔθνος), and is used fairly consistently in the Septuagint translation of the Hebrew Tanach to render *goy/goyim*. The *BDAG* lexicon indicates how "(τὰ) ἔθνη [(ta) ethnē are] **people groups foreign to a specific people group**" which "corresp. to Heb. גּוֹיִם [*goyim*] in LXX; a nationalistic expression."[10] Being concerned with both Biblical and classical usages of *ethnos*, the *LS* lexicon offers us with a variety of definitions, including: "*a number of people accustomed to live together, a company, body of men*," "*a nation, people*," "*the nations, Gentiles, i.e. all but Jews and Christians*."[11] *TDNT* further observes that *ethnos* can mean "'mass,' 'multitude,' 'host,' and may be used for a 'herd' or 'swarm' as well as a human group."[12]

Unlike how the Hebrew *goy/goyim* is most always rendered in modern versions by the neutral nation/nations, usages of *ethnos* may considerably vary. Among modern versions *ethnos* will be translated as **both** "Gentile(s)" and "nation(s)." And it should not go unnoticed that in the LXX, when Ancient Israel was originally called in the Hebrew to be a *goy qadosh* (גּוֹי קָדוֹשׁ) in Exodus 19:6, in the Greek it reads with *ethnos hagion* (ἔθνος ἅγιον). Just like with *goy/goyim*, context in a New Testament passage will determine what is intended by *ethnos*. Yet unlike *goy/goyim*, which modern versions tend to leave as nation/nations, we have the added complexity of seeing *ethnos* rendered in at least two different ways. This can,

---

[8] *HALOT*, 1:183.

[9] Francis Brown, S.R. Driver, and Charles A. Briggs, *Hebrew and English Lexicon of the Old Testament* (Oxford: Clarendon Press, 1979), 156.

[10] *BDAG*, 276.

[11] *LS*, 226.

[12] K.L. Schmidt, "*éthnos*," in Geoffrey W. Bromiley, ed., *Theological Dictionary of the New Testament*, abrid. (Grand Rapids: Eerdmans, 1985), 201.

with some important passages, likely make reviewing their intended meaning(s) a bit more complicated.

Various general theological resources, in their entry for "Gentiles," have noted some of the translation issues for *goy/goyim* and *ethnos*, that each of us needs to be conscious of when reading a English translation, and considering the source vocabulary:

- *Baker's Dictionary of Theology:* "The Hebrew *gôyim* [גּוֹיִם] designates non-Jewish peoples, rendered by the AV as 'nations' or 'heathen,' by the RV frequently as 'Gentiles.' The 'people,' *'am* [עַם], is usually confined to Israel. The LXX makes a similar distinction between *ethnos* [ἔθνος] and *laos* [λαός]..."[13]

- *International Standard Bible Encyclopedia:* "The Heb. *gôy* [גּוֹי] is rendered 'Gentiles' in the AV in some thirty passages, but much more frequently 'heathen,' and still more often 'nation,' which is the usual rendering in later versions; but it is commonly used for a non-Israelite people, and thus corresponds to the meaning of 'Gentiles.'..In the NT Gk. *ethnos* [ἔθνος] is the word corresponding to *gôy* [גּוֹי] (usually rendered 'Gentiles' by the English versions)...The AV also renders Gk. *Hellēnes* ['Ελληνες] 'Gentiles' in six passages, but the RSV renders 'Greeks' throughout."[14]

A notable definition of the Greek *ethnos* (ἔθνος) that need not overlook us, in evaluating this term, is provided by BDAG: "those who do not belong to groups professing faith in the God of Israel, ***the nations, gentiles, unbelievers*** (in effect='polytheists')."[15] This is a lexical definition where substantiation for viewing the nations/Gentiles in the Greek Apostolic Scriptures as "pagans," would find some support. And indeed, in places like 1 Corinthians 5:1; 10:20, where a version like the NASU has "Gentiles," the RSV and NIV has "pagans":

> "It is actually reported that there is immorality among you, and immorality of such a kind as does not exist even **among the Gentiles** [*en tois ethnesin,* ἐν τοῖς ἔθνεσιν], that someone has his father's wife...No, but *I say* that the things **which the Gentiles sacrifice** [*hoti ha thuousin,* ὅτι ἃ θύουσιν; lit. 'that what they sacrifice,' HCSB][16], they sacrifice to demons and not to God; and I do not want you to become sharers in demons" (1 Corinthians 5:1; 10:20, NASU).

---

[13] Richard E. Higginson, "Gentiles," in Everett F. Harrison, ed., *Baker's Dictionary of Theology* (Grand Rapids: Baker Book House, 1960), 235.

[14] A. van Selms, "Gentile," in *ISBE,* 2:443.

[15] *BDAG,* 276.

[16] Most modern Bibles (RSV, NASU, NRSV, ESV, CJB) follow the textual variant *ha thousin ta ethnē* (ἃ θύουσιν τὰ ἔθνη), which as Metzger, *Textual Commentary,* 560 points out, is "considered to be an ancient gloss" in the event that anybody errantly thinks that the sacrifices of the Jerusalem Temple are somehow being referred to (1 Corinthians 10:18).

"It is actually reported that there is immorality among you, and of a kind that is not found even **among pagans**; for a man is living with his father's wife...No, I imply that **what pagans sacrifice** they offer to demons and not to God. I do not want you to be partners with demons" (1 Corinthians 5:1; 10:20, RSV).

"It is actually reported that there is sexual immorality among you, and of a kind that does not occur even **among pagans**: A man has his father's wife... No, but **the sacrifices of pagans** are offered to demons, not to God, and I do not want you to be participants with demons" (1 Corinthians 5:1; 10:20, NIV).[17]

One can easily see why versions like the RSV and NIV would choose to render *ethnos* as "pagan(s)" in the verses above (other verses that could be considered include 1 Thessalonians 4:5; 1 Peter 4:3). Yet at the same time, one can see a figure like the Apostle Paul say things in terms of "I am speaking to you who are Gentiles" (Romans 11:13), "the Gentiles in the flesh" (Ephesians 2:11), "I, Paul, [am] the prisoner of Messiah Yeshua for the sake of you Gentiles" (Ephesians 3:1)—all verses that employ the Greek *ethnos*. However, Paul would also instruct non-Jewish Believers, "So this I say, and affirm together with the Lord, that you walk no longer just as the Gentiles also walk [CJB: do not live any longer as the pagans live], in the futility of their mind" (Ephesians 4:17).

The issue regarding the Greek *ethnos* (ἔθνος), ultimately to be realized, is that while varied English translations can be found rendering it as "Gentile(s)," "nation(s)," or even "pagan(s)"—when the various Apostolic letters and documents were composed, they all used a single term. Readers and speakers in the First Century Mediterranean world could figure out, either because of how *ethnos* rendered *goy/goyim* in the Septuagint translation of the Tanach, or how it was used in the marketplace and on the street—what was really intended. In the English-speaking world, with our diverse vocabulary, we have to read the Apostolic Writings with some care. For some reason or another, many English Bibles have chosen to render *ethnos* as **both** "Gentile(s)" and "nation(s)," making somewhat of a value judgment for their readers. (Two notable exceptions to this, where *ethnos* is consistently rendered by the rather neutral nation/nations, are Young's Literal Translation and the Literal Translation of the Holy Bible by Jay P. Green.)

But where did we get the term "Gentile" from, if *ethnos* best means "nation"? The *Westminster Dictionary of Theological Terms* informs us:

Gentile (From Lat. *gentilis*, "member of a people") Term used by Jews for one who is not Jewish by racial origin. In the Old Testament, "the nations" (Heb. *goyim*) is used.[18]

---

[17] The Complete Jewish Bible, follows suit with the RSV and NIV quoted here, using "pagans."
1 Corinthians 12:2 in the NASU, interestingly enough, says "You know that when you were pagans [*ethnē*, ἔθνη], *you were* led astray to the mute idols, however you were led."
[18] McKim, 113.

The English term "Gentile" is actually derived from the Latin word *gentilis*, meaning "family, hereditary; national,"[19] being related to *gens* or "clan; tribe; family; race; nation."[20] One will find the term *gentilis* and its cognates employed in the Latin Vulgate translation of the Bible, and it is unavoidable for English at least, how this Latin term has influenced the history of English Bible translation. (And to perhaps make things even more complicated, one will also encounter the Latin term *nationis*, "tribe, race; breed class"[21] in the Vulgate, from which our English "nation" is derived as well.) What this means is that with two terms available for rendering the Hebrew *goy/goyim* and the Greek *ethnos*, there might not be as much consistency witnessed in an English Bible—that may actually be quite necessary where Tanach intertextuality is concerned. One example to be considered would be the quotation of Isaiah 9:1 in Matthew 4:15:

> "But there will be no gloom for her that was in anguish. In the former time he brought into contempt the land of Zebulun and the land of Naphtali, but in the latter time he will make glorious the way of the sea, the land beyond the Jordan, **Galilee of the nations** [*Galil ha'goyim*; גְּלִיל הַגּוֹיִם; Galilee of the Gentiles, NASU][22]" (Isaiah 9:1, RSV).

> "[T]HE LAND OF ZEBULUN AND THE LAND OF NAPHTALI, BY THE WAY OF THE SEA, BEYOND THE JORDAN, **GALILEE OF THE GENTILES** [*Galilaia tōn ethnōn*, Γαλιλαία τῶν ἐθνῶν]" (Matthew 4:15, NASU).

The best, most neutral rendering seen for both *Galil ha'goyim* and *Galilaia tōn ethnōn*, the latter clause witnessed in both the LXX of Isaiah 9:1 and Matthew 4:15, is **"Galilee of the nations"** (Isaiah 9:1, NETS). What is witnessed in the Vulgate for both Isaiah 9:1 and Matthew 4:15, however, is *Galileae gentium*. While this is not a problem if one were a Roman, Latin-speaking Christian in the early centuries of the faith, it does interject a dynamic for modern English speakers which we need to be aware of—a likely testament to English having mixed Latin and Germanic origins.

And perhaps interestingly enough, with this in mind, the closest, most wide-spoken relative to modern English, actually appears to lack the term "Gentile" in its vocabulary. If one turns to the rather massive *Langenscheidts New College German Dictionary*, the words offered for the English "Gentile" include the noun *Nichtjude* and the adjective *nichtjüdisch*,[23] which are pretty easily discernible to mean *non-Jew* and *non/not-Jewish*. How did a German Bible like the 1993 Elberfelder Bibel render *Galil ha'goyim* and *Galilaia tōn ethnōn?* In Isaiah 9:1 we encounter "den Kreis[24] der Nationen," and in Matthew 4:15, "Galiläa der Nationen." One can also

---

[19] *HarperCollins Latin Concise Dictionary* (Glasgow: HarperCollins, 1997), 94.

[20] *Pocket Oxford Latin Dictionary*, 60.

[21] *HarperCollins Latin Concise Dictionary*, 138.

[22] "the region of the nations" (ATS).

[23] *Langenscheidts New College German Dictionary, German-English* (Berlin and Munich: Langenscheidt KG, 1995), 275.

[24] The term *Kreis* should be understood here as *"adm.* district" (Ibid., 372), which is certainly allowable as the Hebrew *galil* (גְּלִיל) can mean "cylinder, rod, circuit, district" (*BDB*, 165).

do some quick surveying of this German Bible, and will find that where various English Bibles have "Gentile(s)," the term **Nation** [na'tsĭo:n][25] is used instead. So among many examples to be considered, when the Jerusalem Believers conclude, "God has granted **to the Gentiles** [*tois ethnesin*, τοῖς ἔθνεσιν] also the repentance *that leads* to life" (Acts 11:18), the Elberfelder Bibel has, "Dann hat Gott also **auch den Nationen** die Buße gegeben zum Leben."

It is at this point where we reach an impasse. What is the best approach to the Hebrew *goy/goyim* and Greek *ethnos*? Is it really Gentile/Gentiles—*or* is it nation/nations? Much of this is undeniably a perspective issue, and how in their most neutral context both of these words mean nation/nations. Seriously consider, what the Apostle Paul communicates to his dear friend Timothy in 2 Timothy 4:17, reflecting back on his life of ministry service to the Lord:

"But the Lord stood with me and strengthened me, so that through me the proclamation might be fully accomplished, and that **all the Gentiles** might hear; and I was rescued out of the lion's mouth."

That Paul had a unique calling to the world at large is easily understood (cf. Acts 9:15; Romans 11:13). But is "all the Gentiles" the best rendering for *panta ta ethnē* (πάντα τὰ ἔθνη)? In the view of some Pastoral Epistles commentators **"all the nations"** is what is to be missionally understood here, which does *not only* include the world at large. The view of William D. Mounce, who is most well known for authoring various collegiate level Greek textbooks, is that when *ethnē* is rendered as "nations" here, then "the phrase 'all the nations/Gentiles' can mean 'all groups of people,' Jew and Gentile alike."[26] From this viewpoint then, *panta ta ethnē* is akin "to those who had never heard" (The Message) the gospel message. We need to remember that even though Paul had a definite calling and skillset as a Jewish Believer that would help to bring the nations into the Commonwealth of Israel (cf. Ephesians 2:11-12), Paul never stopped believing that his own Jewish people needed salvation nor did he ever stop declaring Yeshua to them (cf. Romans 11:13-14). It would seem appropriate for us to view *panta ta ethnē* in 2 Timothy 4:17 as meaning *everyone* who needed to hear, **all nations** upon Planet Earth *including* Paul's own Jewish people. Philip H. Towner appropriately summarizes,

"[T]he phrase 'all the Gentiles/nations,' which certainly need not exclude the Jewish people, is a theologically loaded term in Pauline thought (Rom 15:11; 16:26; Gal 3:28). It sums up the universal scope of the salvation plan of God, from the Abrahamic promise and institution of the covenant to its full unveiling in the Psalms and prophets, from which Paul clearly took his cue (Romans 9-11; 15:9-13; Gal 1:15-16)."[27]

---

[25] *Langenscheidts New College German Dictionary*, 441.

[26] William D. Mounce, *Word Biblical Commentary: Pastoral Epistles*, Vol. 46 (Nashville: Thomas Nelson, 2000), 597.

In Ibid. his further conclusion is, "By proclaiming the gospel to all the authorities in Rome, Paul has now preached to all groups and all types of Gentiles and therefore has fulfilled his ministry."

[27] Philip H. Towner, *New International Commentary on the New Testament: The Letters to Timothy and Titus* (Grand Rapids: Eerdmans, 2006), 643.

The blessing of Abraham and the sacrifice of Yeshua, remitting the curse of the Law, are for "all nations" (Galatians 3:8, 14), which necessarily includes the Jewish people as well as the world at large.

Surely with what we witness in Yeshua's Great Commission of Matthew 28:18-20, the common rendering of "nations" is understood to convey a significant, worldwide effect:

"And Yeshua came up and spoke to them, saying, 'All authority has been given to Me in heaven and on earth. Go therefore and make disciples of **all the nations** [*panta ta ethnē*, πάντα τὰ ἔθνη], baptizing them in the name of the Father and the Son and the Holy Spirit, teaching them to observe all that I commanded you; and lo, I am with you always, even to the end of the age.'"

We may never be able to know why more English Bibles than not have chosen to render the Greek *ethnos* as both "Gentile(s)" and "nation(s)," and not just "nation(s)." But what we can know is that rendering this single Greek term, in two different ways, has created some confusion—if not some significant confusion in some quarters. **The most significant confusion caused by the term "Gentile" is that it can underplay the universal availability of God's salvation for all of humankind.** In Isaiah 49:6, Yeshua the Messiah has come not only to restore the tribes of Israel, but also to be the *or goyim* (אוֹר גּוֹיִם) or *phōs ethnōn* (φῶς ἐθνῶν), "a light of the nations." For consistency's sake, English Bible readers need to train their minds to recognize that "Gentile(s)" *really means* "nation(s)"—and today's Messianic teachers and leaders need to be a little more sensitive to this fact as well.

"Gentile" Can be an Offensive Term for Some

While among many Christians today, and in many theological works, the term "Gentile" is simply employed as a term to refer to a person who is not Jewish, meaning "one of the nations," it is obvious in Scripture that the Greek *ethnos* can be used in various pejorative contexts. Yeshua's direction regarding the reproof of someone who sins, includes the admonition, "If he refuses to listen to them, tell it to the [assembly]; and if he refuses to listen even to the [assembly], let him be to you **as a Gentile** and a tax collector" (Matthew 18:17). The clause *ho ethnikos kai ho telōnēs* (ὁ ἐθνικὸς καὶ ὁ τελώνης), is rendered into the 1991 UBSHNT as *k'goy v'k'mokeis* (וְכַמּוֹכֵס כַּגּוֹי). That both *ethnos* and *goy* can mean "a pagan" (CJB) here, does not go unnoticed.[28]

Of course, as we have tried to emphasize above, there are not only many neutral usages of the terms *goy/goyim* and *ethnos* witnessed in the Bible, but these same terms are used to describe Israel. Context and usage alone, in the various verses on a case-by-case basis, determines what is to be intended. But to act like the terms *goy/goyim* and *ethnos* can never be viewed from the perspective of "pagan," and that this does not in any way carry over into the English term "Gentile," would be dishonest. *ISBE*, for example, indicates how "The general tendency...was one of

---

[28] Matthew 6:32 could also be considered: "For the Gentiles [*ta ethnē*, τὰ ἔθνη] eagerly seek all these things..." This is also rendered with "pagans" (NIV/CJB) and "idolaters" (HCSB) elsewhere.

increasing hostility toward the Gentiles. They and their countries were considered unclean."[29] *EJ* further notes how from a Jewish perspective in much of the Bible, "the low moral, social, and ethical standards of the surrounding gentiles were continuously emphasized, and social contact with them was regarded as being a pernicious social and moral influence. As a result, during this period the world was regarded as divided, insofar as peoples were concerned, into the Jewish people and the 'nations of the world,' and insofar as individuals were concerned, into 'the Jew' and the idolater."[30]

Whether *goy/goyim* or *ethnos* carry with it the intention of "...of the nations" or "pagan" in the Bible, can only be determined in the places where it is used. And, we should think that "nations(s)" is a far better, uniform rendering for these terms, leaving its exact meaning up to the reader to decide. It is, however, to be noted that in Rabbinical literature, one will encounter the Hebrew term *goy* (גּוֹי) used to mean "gentile, idolator" (*Jastrow*).[31] An example provided by *Jastrow* to be considered is t.*Avodah Zarah* 3:4:

"A gentile woman should not be called upon to cut out the foetus in the womb of an Israelite girl. And she should not give her a cup of bitters to drink, for they are suspect as to the taking of life. And an Israelite should not be alone with a gentile either in a bathhouse or in a urinal. [When] an Israelite goes along with a gentile, he puts him at his right hand, and he does not put him at his left hand. R. Ishmael son of R. Yoḥanan b. Beroqah says, '[He goes along] with a sword in his right hand, with a staff in his left hand.' [If] there are two going up on an ascent or going down on a ramp, the Israelite goes up ahead, and the gentile behind."[32]

Some of the viewpoints here are obviously historically conditioned, and are the result of a longstanding distrust on the part of the Jewish community toward outsiders. But, the point is taken that the *goyim* (גּוֹיִם) are to be kept at a distance.

More present in Judaism today is the line of an ancient prayer, which is customarily recited as a part of the morning *Shacharit* blessings, when the observant declare, "Blessed are You, HASHEM, our God, King of the universe, for not having made me a gentile," *asani goy* (עָשַׂנִי גּוֹי).[33] When non-Jewish Believers in today's Messianic movement get wind of some Messianic Jews in the congregation they are attending, possibly saying this sort of thing before God every morning[34]—

---

[29] A. van Selms, "Gentile," in *ISBE*, 2:444.

[30] Editorial Staff, "Gentile," in *EJ*.

[31] Marcus Jastrow, *Dictionary of the Targumim, Talmud Bavli, Talmud Yerushalmi, and Midrashic Literature* (New York: Judaica Treasury, 2004), 220.

[32] Jacob Neusner, ed., *The Tosefta: Translated from the Hebrew With a New Introduction*, 2 vols. (Peabody, MA: Hendrickson, 2002), 2:1269.

[33] Nosson Scherman and Meir Zlotowitz, eds., *Complete ArtScroll Siddur, Nusach Ashkenaz* (Brooklyn: Mesorah Publications, 1984), pp 18-19.

[34] In complete fairness, it must be stressed that another edition of this same prayer, does not use the Hebrew term *goy*. This is seen in Joseph H. Hertz, ed., *The Authorised Daily Prayer Book*, revised (New York: Bloch Publishing Company, 1960), 18:

"Blessed art thou, O Lord our God, King of the universe, who hast not made me a **heathen** [*asani nakri*, עָשַׂנִי נָכְרִי]."

The Hebrew *nakri* (נָכְרִי) largely means, "foreign, alien" (*BDB*, 648).

and perhaps including some of their main leaders—they do get a little upset. *Some of them even get livid.* The Conservative Jewish *Siddur Sim Shalom* has thankfully changed much of this, only including the declaration "Praised are You Adonai our God, who rules the universe, making me a Jew" (although the Hebrew is actually *Yisrael*, יִשְׂרָאֵל) and "making me free."[35] For reciting traditional prayers from the Jewish community, I do think that many of us can certainly understand the value of what *Sim Shalom* offers, and that we can appreciate how it has removed the rather negative remarks about not being made a Gentile. Thanking God for being a Jew or an Israelite is one thing (that I personally do not have a problem with); thanking God for not being Nationality XYZ is something else.

So what does the non-Jewish person in a Messianic Jewish congregation, who finds out about the ancient prayer of "for not having made me a gentile"—and who is understandably a bit offended—then do about it? The first thing, that tends to happen, is that when the term "Gentile" tends to be spoken in various teachings or announcements or just common speech, the individual feels that he or she is likely being called some kind of a "pagan," "heathen," "idolater," or something worse. Secondly, if various Messianic Jews have not been careful with how they have employed the term "Gentile," at least also incorporating valid alternatives like "nations" or "peoples," then some significant resentment can build up (rather quickly). Thirdly, and what can frequently happen, is that the non-Jewish Messianic who has taken considerable offense at being called a "Gentile," will build a kind of personal credo around Ephesians 2:11, where the Apostle Paul says:

"Therefore remember **that formerly you, the Gentiles in the flesh,** who are called 'Uncircumcision' by the so-called 'Circumcision,' *which is* performed in the flesh by human hands—"

It is from a verse like this where many non-Jewish Messianic Believers will claim that they are *former Gentiles.* It is absolutely true that for any non-Believer to come to saving faith in Yeshua the Messiah (Jesus Christ), that he or she is no longer a kind of pagan, heathen, idolater, insolent rebel, or even atheist against the Creator. Yet Paul's words to those in Asia Minor are specific in that he speaks of those here as *ta ethnē en sarki* (τὰ ἔθνη ἐν σαρκί), "the nations in the flesh" (YLT) or "you who are Gentiles by birth" (NIV). When people come to faith in Yeshua, even though they may be saved and spiritually regenerated, their DNA does not change. He identifies these people as being of the nations, in the flesh. The former status that Paul is obviously more concerned about, **and so should any of us for that matter,** is detailed in Ephesians 2:11-12 together:

"Therefore remember that formerly...you were at that time separate from Messiah, excluded from the commonwealth of Israel, and strangers to the covenants of promise, having no hope and without God in the world."

A status of being removed from Israel's Messiah, Israel's polity, Israel's covenants, and being without the hope and knowledge of the Creator God—is

---

[35] Jules Harlow, ed., *Siddur Sim Shalom for Shabbat and Festivals* (New York: Rabbinical Assembly, 2007), 65.

what is really considered to be the former status for the non-Jewish Believers addressed in Ephesians. This is one which has been fully reversed. The non-Jewish Believers in Asia Minor now know Israel's Messiah, they are a part of Israel's polity, they now benefit from Israel's covenants, and they are truly known by the Creator God.[36]

The term "Gentile," *goy* (גּוֹי), need not always have a negative meaning, but in various places in Jewish theology and commentary it will. The *Dictionary of Judaism in the Biblical Period* observes how *goyim* is the "generic Israelite expression for all of humanity except Israel. Most often this common biblical expression has a pejorative connotation that parallels the Greek use of 'barbarians.' By virtue of its covenantal relationship to YHWH and its observance of the Torah, Israel is contrasted with the rest of humanity, which stands outside the scope of God's covenantal love."[37] This same entry is actually pretty even-handed, though, in further commenting, "While Gentiles are often pictured as sexually uninhibited and untrustworthy, they are also described as righteous and the progenitors of rabbis and even kings of Israel."[38]

But what meaning of *goyim* are we more likely to find for non-Jewish people, used in today's Judaism *and* even Messianic Judaism? Does it mean "pagan" *or* just a "non-Jew"?

When non-Jewish Believers in today's Messianic world know some of the theological background behind the term "Gentile," it often does not make them very happy when it is used to define them. Knowing that the term *goyim* can frequently mean "pagan," in many respects, can be offensive to more than a few. What is to be done about this?

When non-believing members of the Jewish community today, refer to those outside the Synagogue as "Gentiles" or "*goyim*," is it in the most positive of ways? When my mother grew up in Annapolis, Maryland with its sizeable Jewish population, she certainly witnessed the terms "*goy*" and "Gentile" used in some rather negative ways by her friends' parents. When she has been in some Messianic Jewish congregations, and heard the congregational leader or speaker refer to the non-Jews in the audience as "*goyim*," she has had difficulty separating it from her youth experience among her Jewish friends.

Non-Jewish Believers being referred to as "Gentiles" in the Messianic Jewish movement, or even some sectors of the independent Messianic world, can at times be suspect. I do know for certain that many Messianic Jews do not intend any offense when they use the term "Gentile," and I also know that they want all people to be welcome in their assemblies. The easiest way to deflate some of this potential unwelcomeness is to simply employ a number of valid alternatives like **"nations"** or **"peoples."** The neutral term **"non-Jew"** would also be appropriate to use.

---

[36] For a further discussion, consult the author's commentary *Ephesians for the Practical Messianic*.
[37] "Gentiles," in *Dictionary of Judaism in the Biblical Period*, pp 247-248.
[38] Ibid., 248.

The Promises That Were Made, Many Nations, and the Exile of the Northern Kingdom

Jewish Believers in Yeshua do not wonder about their personal pedigree or bloodline. Being born into a Jewish family, and being a part of the Jewish community (although many Messianic Jews are unfortunately ex-communicated and/or spurned from their families and communities for their faith in Yeshua), a Jewish Believer knows that his or her ancestors *definitely* stood at the base of Mount Sinai when Moses was given the Ten Commandments. Many Non-Jewish Believers who enter into the Messianic movement, and who are welcomed with open arms and acceptance by their fellow Jewish Believers into the Commonwealth of Israel, putting a complicated past of Christian anti-Semitism *in the past*, and integrated into various congregations and assemblies—do frequently have that nagging thought. Some days, they *wonder* if whether or not the reason God led them into a Messianic congregation and a Torah obedient lifestyle, was because they had lost Jewish ancestry from hundreds of years ago, and did not even know it. When discussions about the exiled and widely forgotten Northern Kingdom of Israel/Ephraim comes up, it naturally piques the interest of many. *Why am I here?*

It is necessary that we review some of the basic promises given to Abraham, Isaac, and Jacob regarding their physical seed, as the issue of who comprises their offspring has undoubtedly arisen, given the controversy of the Two-House teaching. All Bible readers should agree that their descendants were intended to be used by the Lord to bless all people and all nations in the world, so that **all human beings might hopefully come to a knowledge of Him as the One True God and be eternally redeemed.** When God originally told Abraham, "And I will make you a great nation, and I will bless you, and make your name great; and so you shall be a blessing" (Genesis 12:2), this is what the Apostle Paul would later testify as, "The Scripture, foreseeing that God would justify the Gentiles by faith, preached the gospel beforehand to Abraham, *saying*, 'ALL THE NATIONS WILL BE BLESSED IN YOU'" (Galatians 3:8), as the good news of salvation and redemption in Messiah Yeshua found its beginnings in this Abrahamic promise. To fail to recognize the seed of Abraham, Isaac, and Jacob as giving rise to *the Ultimate Seed*, Yeshua the Messiah (Jesus Christ),[39] will result in one not fully understanding how God had to choose the descendants of these people as His agents and representatives, so that *all peoples* might hopefully be reconciled to their Loving, yet All-Powerful and Magnificent Creator.

No one should ever be led into the simplistic thinking that every human being on Planet Earth is descended from the Patriarchs of Israel, or even just Abraham. Yet, all Bible readers can agree on the fact that it is very true that Abraham, Isaac, and Jacob were promised many descendants. And to this, it might also be said that there are a few unanswered questions and details to be reviewed concerning those descendants.

---

[39] Cf. Galatians 3:16.

Abraham

Regarding Abram, God "took him outside and said, 'Now look toward the heavens, and count the stars, if you are able to count them.' And He said to him, 'So shall your descendants be'" (Genesis 15:5). We are especially told how Abram "believed in the LORD; and He reckoned it to him as righteousness" (Genesis 15:6). Whatever this promise would mean for the future, Abram had the trust in his Creator that He would bring it to pass. Further on, when we see *Avram* (אַבְרָם) having his named changed to *Avraham* (אַבְרָהָם), meaning "father of a multitude,"[40] it is intended to be an affirmation of His promises to him:

"Abram fell on his face, and God talked with him, saying, 'As for Me, behold, My covenant is with you, and you will be the father of **a multitude of nations.** No longer shall your name be called Abram, but your name shall be Abraham; for I will make you the father of **a multitude of nations.** I will make you exceedingly fruitful, and I will make **nations of you,** and kings will come forth from you. I will establish My covenant between Me and you and your descendants after you throughout their generations for an everlasting covenant, to be God to you and to your descendants after you'" (Genesis 17:3-7).

A key part of the Abrahamic Covenant is that nations will come forth from the Patriarch: *hamon goyim* (הֲמוֹן גּוֹיִם; Genesis 17:4, 5), *u'nettati'kha l'goyim* (וּנְתַתִּיךָ לְגוֹיִם; Genesis 17:6)—"many nations" (NIV) and "turn you into nations" (Alter). As it regards the term *hamon* (הֲמוֹן), employed here, while the word can mean **"agitation," "turmoil,"** or **"noise, roar, din,"** it would be best that we simply take it to mean **"multitude, crowd"** (*HALOT*).[41] The Septuagint translated *hamon goyim* into Greek as *plēthous ethnōn* (πλήθους ἐθνῶν). The term *plēthos* (πλῆθος) similarly means *"a great number, a throng, crowd, multitude"* (*LS*).[42] The point to be taken from Genesis 17:3-7 is that a large group of people will come from Abraham, and come to be associated with him. A Jewish commentator like J.H. Hertz states in his *Pentateuch & Haftorahs* that such *"a multitude of nations"* would be mainly "The Israelites; the Arabs, descended from Ishmael; and the tribes enumerated in [25:1ff]."[43]

In Genesis 22:17-18, the Lord promises Abraham that He will multiply his descendants greatly:

"[I]ndeed I will greatly bless you, and I will greatly multiply your seed as the stars of the heavens and as the sand which is on the seashore; and your seed shall possess the gate of their enemies. In your seed all the nations of the earth shall be blessed, because you have obeyed My voice."

---

[40] Cf. J. Barton Payne, "'āb," in *TWOT*, 1:5-6.

[41] *HALOT*, 1:250.

As Baker and Carpenter, 267 further indicate of *hamon*, "In general usage, it also indicates wealth (Ps. 37:16) and a great supply or mass of things (1 Chr. 29:16; 2 Chr. 31:10; Jer. 49:32)," buttressing the concept of multitude in Genesis 17:4, 5.

[42] *LS*, 646.

[43] Hertz, *Pentateuch & Haftorahs*, 58.

The Hebrew term zera (זֶרַע) has a variety of meanings, including "sowing, seed, descendants, offspring, children, and posterity" (*AMG*).[44] Its equivalent in the Greek Septuagint and in the Greek Messianic Scriptures is *sperma* (σπέρμα).[45] It is is natural to take the main words of Genesis 22:17-18 as speaking of physical people. But, while it is said b'zar'akha (בְּזַרְעֲךָ) or "by your offspring" (NRSV), *kol goyei ha'eretz* (כֹּל גּוֹיֵי הָאָרֶץ), "all the nations of the earth" will be blessed; it does not at all say that all the nations, people groups, or ethnicities on Planet Earth will be physically descended from or genetically related to Abraham. (Throughout history, the Jewish people and the Arabs, to be sure, have claimed actual physical lineage from Abraham.) It may, however, be certainly taken to mean that the physical progeny of Abraham—obviously climaxing with the arrival of Yeshua the Messiah onto the scene of human history—will impact the nations of the world at large in a very significant way.

Many readers and interpreters have associated the reference to "many nations" (Genesis 17:3-7) coming from Abraham, as meaning that the goodness of Abraham's God, and the life example of Abraham, have touched them (Genesis 22:17-18)—even with them likely not being physical descendants of Abraham. In Galatians 3:29, for example, we read, "If you belong to Christ, then you are Abraham's seed, and heirs according to the promise" (NIV), meaning that there is an attachment to Abraham for many people who are not his physical progeny. Many are to be regarded as Abraham's *sperma*, even if they do not bear his DNA. Still, it cannot be avoided that there are many dimensions to what the seed of Abraham is in Galatians 3:29, because there were surely beneficiaries of the Abrahamic promise in the First Century C.E., Jewish Believers, who partook of the gospel message largely because of what was originally declared to their ancient ancestor, and they responded favorably to it.[46]

Jacob

Moving forward in the Book of Genesis, in the second scene (cf. Genesis 32:24-32) where the Patriarch Jacob is renamed from *Ya'akov* (יַעֲקֹב) to Israel or *Yisrael* (יִשְׂרָאֵל), God gives him a confirmation of the Abrahamic promise that he would have multitudes of descendants:

"Then God appeared to Jacob again when he came from Paddan-aram, and He blessed him. God said to him, 'Your name is Jacob; you shall no longer be called Jacob, but Israel shall be your name.' Thus He called him Israel.' God also said to him, 'I am God Almighty; **be fruitful and multiply; a nation and a company of nations shall come from you,** and kings shall come forth from you. The land which I gave to Abraham and Isaac, I will give it to you, and I will give the land to your descendants after you'" (Genesis 35:9-12).

---

[44] Warren Baker and Eugene Carpenter, eds., *Complete Word Study Dictionary: New Testament* (Chattanooga: AMG Publishers, 2003), 304.

[45] *"seed, offspring, issue"* (*LS*, 740).

[46] An appropriate summary of what the seed of Abraham involves is offered by David H. Stern, *Jewish New Testament Commentary* (Clarksville, MD: Jewish New Testament Publications, 1995), 549.

The word issued by the Lord here to Jacob is *p'rei u'reveih goy u'qahal goyim yih'yeh m'mekha* (פְּרֵה וּרְבֵה גּוֹי וּקְהַל גּוֹיִם יִהְיֶה מִמֶּךָּ). The word *goy u'qahal goyim*, is rendered by ATS with "a nation and a congregation of nations," the NIV has "a nation and a community of nations," and YLT has "a nation and assembly of nations." The LXX Greek rendering of this is actually *ethnē kai sunagōgai ethnōn* (ἔθνη καὶ συναγωγαὶ ἐθνῶν), to be viewed as "nations and gatherings of nations" (Genesis 35:11, LXE/NETS). While the promise given to Abraham, who is widely regarded in the Judeo-Christian world as the progenitor of both the Arabs and the Jews, can be taken as a rather general word—here the promise that Jacob himself would give rise to *goyim* (גּוֹיִם) or "nations," obviously has to be considered.

What is the word that from Jacob/Israel would arise an assembly of nations? A safe way to definitely take this would be that the *goyim* referred to are the Twelve Tribes of Israel that would arise, as *goyim* can be used (cf. Ezekiel 2:3). We can also, safely, take the word of Genesis 25:9-12 as an extension of the Abrahamic promise, and that it is the specific line of Jacob/Israel which will be responsible for blessing all in the world, as those from the nations find themselves associated in the same Kingdom community with His descendants. The most provocative suggestion, that could be made, would be that beyond the twelve sons of Jacob/Israel, who would give rise to the Twelve Tribes, and beyond the nations of Planet Earth being blessed by and associated with the community of Israel via Israel's God—would be that nations in addition to the Twelve Tribes of Israel would arise from Jacob's physical progeny.

Much needs to be tempered with how, "A nation and a company of nations shall come from you," is paralleled with the word, "And kings shall come forth from you" (Genesis 35:11), which would obviously relate to the monarchs of Ancient Israel. Recognizing the original vantage point of Jacob, following the incident with his sons in Shechem (Genesis 34), and having relocated to Bethel (35:1-8)—it would have been most significant for the Creator God not only to reaffirm promises of descendants, but that kings would actually come from him. The Lord's declarations of the promises of multiplicity, be they by physical bloodline or others being associated with those who could come from him, would have been most crucial—especially as his beloved Rachel was soon to die (Genesis 35:16-19), and Jacob/Israel was surely shaken by a series of tragic events. He could have been thinking that his family was about to fall apart.

The English of Genesis 35:11 can confuse some readers, as there are some who conclude that both "A nation and a company of nations ," as well as "kings shall come forth from you," all mean that these are the products of Jacob's physical seed. In the statement *u'melakim m'chaltzey'kha yeitzei'u* (וּמְלָכִים מֵחֲלָצֶיךָ יֵצֵאוּ), "kings shall come forth from you," the verb *yatza* (יָצָא), appearing in the Qal stem (simple action, active voice), means "go or come out" (BDB).[47] "Sometimes yāṣa' is used with a special emphasis on source or origin" (TWOT),[48] which in the case of Israel's

---

[47] BDB, 442.
[48] Paul R. Gilchrist, "יָצָא," in TWOT, 1:393.

kings, would necessarily mean that they are Jacob/Israel's physical descendants, as opposed to some outsiders.

Contrary to this, in the preceding clause in Genesis 35:11, *p'rei u'reveih goy u'qahal goyim yih'yeh m'mekha*, one only sees the verb *hayah* (הָיָה), a standard Hebrew verb meaning "to be." A nation and a company of nations coming from Jacob, meaning being associated with him, does not require that all those who would be associated with Israel must be born of Jacob/Israel's physical line. *Yih'yeh m'mekha* (יִהְיֶה מִמֶּךָ) was actually rendered by the Septuagint as *esontai ek sou* (ἔσονται ἐκ σοῦ), "shall be of thee" (LXE), which can relate to both physical descendants **and** those who would come to be associated with those physical descendants.

In Genesis 35:11, we see a combination of promises given to the Patriarch Jacob/Israel: "I am God Almighty: be fruitful and multiply. A nation and a company of nations shall come from you, and kings shall come from your own body" (ESV).[49] Jacob/Israel would obviously multiply physically, but the nations of Planet Earth themselves are not quantitatively excluded from being incorporated into Israel's Kingdom realm. At the same time, the kings of Israel would come directly from Jacob/Israel, with King Yeshua (Jesus) being such a chief descendant.

Ephraim and Manasseh

Promises of multiplicity are witnessed in some of the final words of Jacob, as he prepared to bless his family before dying. The expectation that some of their descendants would become prolific, is witnessed when Jacob blessed his two grandsons from Joseph, who was viceroy of Egypt, Manasseh and Ephraim, who he would adopt as his own:

"He blessed Joseph, and said, 'The God before whom my fathers Abraham and Isaac walked, the God who has been my shepherd all my life to this day, the angel who has redeemed me from all evil, bless the lads; and may my name live on in them, and the names of my fathers Abraham and Isaac; and **may they grow into a multitude in the midst of the earth.'** When Joseph saw that his father laid his right hand on Ephraim's head, it displeased him; and he grasped his father's hand to remove it from Ephraim's head to Manasseh's head. Joseph said to his father, 'Not so, my father, for this one is the firstborn. Place your right hand on his head.' But his father refused and said, 'I know, my son, I know; he also will become a people and he also will be great. However, his younger brother shall be greater than he, and his descendants shall become **a multitude of nations**'" (Genesis 48:15-19).

The first major word issued by Jacob, regards Manasseh and Ephraim's multiplicity: *v'yidgu l'rov b'qerev ha'eretz* (וְיִדְגּוּ לָרֹב בְּקֶרֶב הָאָרֶץ; Genesis 48:16). This is a very unique phrase, which various Two-House advocates have tended to draw readers' attention toward. Here, regardless of what conclusions or opinions we

---

[49] "a nation and a company of nations shall be of thee, and kings shall come out of thy loins" (Jerusalem Bible-Koren); "a nation and an assembly of nations will come from you and kings will emerge from your loins" (Keter Crown Bible).

have, we do have to remember that Ephraim would legitimately be a designation for the Northern Kingdom of Israel, as borne out in the Historical Books of the Tanach. It is unavoidable that the Hebrew can be rendered with, "may they like the fishes increase into a multitude in the midst of the earth" (LITV), or "may they proliferate abundantly like fish within the land" (ATS).

The Hebrew verb often rendered as "grow" is dagah (דָּגָה), meaning *multiply, increase*" (TWOT),[50] and is related to the noun dag (דָּג) or "fish." The perspective of the *ArtScroll Chumash* on Genesis 48:16 of these descendants is, "May be like fish, which are fruitful and multiply and which are not affected by the evil eye."[51] This itself is based on some commentary from the Talmud:

"He said to them, 'I come from the seed of Joseph, over which the evil eye does not rule. For it is written, "Joseph is a fruitful vine, a fruitful vine above the eye" (Gen. 49:22).' And R. Abbahu said, 'Do not read what is written, but rather, "superior to the evil eye."' R. Yosé b. R. Hanina said, 'Proof comes from here: "And let them multiply like fishes in the midst of the earth" (Gen. 48:16). Just as the fish of the sea are covered by water so that the evil eye cannot get at them, so the evil eye cannot get at the seed of Joseph'" (b.Berachot 20a).*[52]

In ancient Jewish thought, the presence of the evil eye was a real, negative spiritual force, of which one needed to beware.[53] Of course, while this Talmudic perspective might imply that the seed of Joseph could hide from the evil eye, as fish hide underneath the water, fish underneath the water—whether they be just underwater a few feet or deep underwater hundreds of feet—are definitely known by a Sovereign Creator to be there.

The perspective of the descendants of Manasseh and Ephraim, or Joseph, multiplying as though they were fish underwater, is a bit strange and odd to many English Bible readers—especially if connections between the Hebrew verb *dagah* and the noun *dag* are not able to be made. A wide variety of Genesis commentators, more Christian than Jewish actually, in working from the Hebrew text, have had to recognize some sort of issue regarding multiplicity at work in Genesis 48:16.[54]

What, if anything, might this obscure promise by the Patriarch Jacob, to his grandsons Ephraim and Manasseh in Genesis 48:16—*v'yidgu l'rov b'qerev ha'eretz*—teach us about their descendants? The Targum Onkelos on Genesis 48:16 actually offers the paraphrase, "The Angel who redeemed me from all evil, bless the youths;

[50] Earl S. Kalland, "דגה," in *TWOT*, 1:182; cf. *HALOT*, 1:213.

[51] Nosson Scherman, ed., *ArtScroll Chumash, Stone Edition* (Brooklyn: Mesorah Publications, Ltd., 2000), 273.

[52] *The Babylonian Talmud: A Translation and Commentary.* MS Windows XP. Peabody, MA: Hendrickson, 2005. CD-ROM.

[53] Cf. "evil eye, in rabbinic Judaism," in *Dictionary of Judaism in the Biblical Period*, 212.

[54] Nahum M. Sarna, *JPS Torah Commentary: Genesis* (Philadelphia: Jewish Publication Society, 1989), 328; Gordon J. Wenham, *Word Biblical Commentary: Genesis 16-50*, Vol 1b (Dallas: Word Books, 1994), 465; Victor P. Hamilton, *New International Commentary on the Old Testament: The Book of Genesis, Chapters 18-50* (Grand Rapids: Eerdmans, 1995), 633 fn#22; Bruce K. Waltke, *Genesis: A Commentary* (Grand Rapids: Zondervan, 2001), 599; Kenneth A. Mathews, *New American Commentary: Genesis 11:27-50:26* (Nashville: Broadman & Holman, 2005), 880.

and let my name be called upon them, and the name of my fathers Abraham and Izhak; and as the fish of the sea may they multiply among the children of men upon the earth!"[55]

Many Two-House advocates have claimed that with the future deportation and exile of the Northern Kingdom, with the Ephraim reference to be applied to the scattered exiles, that there would be a future multiplication of their descendants in exile—a multiplication largely known to a Sovereign God, but not necessarily to mortals at large, or even to many of the descendants themselves. This is certainly one way to take Jacob's prophecy made to his grandsons. The challenge is, of course, if there are such descendants of the exiled Northern Kingdom "out there" in the world—then why do a majority of the non-Jewish Believers in the Two-House sub-movement *just assume*, without any hard evidence, that they absolutely must be such descendants? **Would it not be better, and much safer, for our Sovereign God to know all of the finer details of Israel's restoration?**

Concurrent with this, it is specifically communicated by Jacob/Israel to Ephraim, and possibly by extension to the Northern Kingdom of Israel as a whole, that "his descendants shall become **a multitude of nations**," *melo-ha'goyim* (הַגּוֹיִם־מְלֹא), which would suggest some level of abundance. This most probably relates to how Ephraim would be one of the main names for the Northern Kingdom, and would incorporate a wide number of Israel's tribes into itself, certainly in name.

Many Two-House advocates think that this implies a multiplication of the descendants of the Northern Kingdom of Israel, in their exile, to the point of somehow being reckoned as a very numerous body, or bodies, of people. This tends to be connected to the Apostle Paul's word of Romans 11:25, speaking of the salvation-historical redemption of Israel: "For I do not want you, brethren, to be uninformed of this mystery—so that you will not be wise in your own estimation—that a partial hardening has happened to Israel until **the fullness of the Gentiles has come in.**" Many Two-House advocates take this as meaning that "all Israel will be saved" (Romans 11:26) will only take place, at the point when various scores of descendants of the exiled Northern Kingdom have entered back into the fold.

No one should deny the fact that Romans chs. 9-11 in total, include some significantly "loaded" words as they involved the Jewish and non-Jewish Believers in Rome, the widescale First Century Jewish rejection of Yeshua, the Apostle Paul's lamentation over the great dismissal of the Messiah by his countrymen, and warnings issued to Believers from the nations to take significant care in how they approach this. Generally speaking, many interpreters will recognize that Romans chs. 9-11 speaks, at the very least, of a condition regarding the First Century Jewish people, to be contrasted with a future, fully restored eschatological Kingdom of Israel. When Israel is fully restored in the eschaton, this would necessarily have to involve the complete reunion of the descendants of the Northern and Southern Kingdoms.

---

[55] BibleWorks 7.0: Targum Onkelos on the Pentateuch. MS Windows XP. Norfolk: BibleWorks, LLC, 2006. CD-ROM.; cf. Hamilton, 633 fn#22.

However, the Septuagint translated *melo-ha'goyim* in Genesis 48:19 as *plēthos ethnōn* (πλῆθος ἐθνῶν), "a multitude of nations" (LXE), when *to plērōma tōn ethnōn* (τὸ πλήρωμα τῶν ἐθνῶν) is what actually appears in Romans 11:25. It would be inappropriate to absolutely equate *to plērōma tōn ethnōn* in Romans 11:25 with the *melo-ha'goyim* of Genesis 48:19. What can go significantly overlooked is how *plērōma* (πλήρωμα) or "fullness," when applied to human beings, generally regards ethical, moral, or spiritual maturity in the Pauline letters[56]—which is certainly the case when he previously speaks of his Jewish brethren: "Now if their transgression is riches for the world and their failure is riches for the Gentiles, how much more will their fulfillment [*plērōma*; fullness, NIV] be!" (Romans 11:12).

Given the prior usage of *plērōma* in Romans 11:12, the primary purpose of Paul stating that the "fullness of the nations" must enter in, in Romans 11:25, should be taken so that non-Jewish Believers (particularly those he writes to in Ancient Rome) can overcome any arrogant attitudes, and instead strive to be an spiritual/ethical/moral fullness, as grand vessels of mercy and grace to the Jewish people who are widely hardened to the Messiah: "so these also now have been disobedient, that because of the mercy shown to you they also may now be shown mercy" (Romans 11:31). Only when this takes place at an ultra-high level, can the hardening be gone! Paul has already said that the non-Jewish Believers are grafted into the community of Israel via Messiah faith (Romans 11:17-18). When non-Jewish Believers, operating at their grand spiritual fullness *as vessels of grace and mercy* to the Jewish people, arrive on the scene, then the complete restoration of Israel—obviously involving a massive salvation of Jews recognizing Yeshua as Redeemer—can manifest.

Notably at some point in future history, as a component of "all Israel" being saved, (Romans 11:25-27), there will be a return and restoration of the exiled Northern Kingdom with those of the Southern Kingdom, as witnessed within the Tanach intertexuality (cf. Isaiah 59:20-21; 27:9 [12-13]; Jeremiah 31:31-34).[57] Given that Romans 11:25 labels the entering of the "the fullness of the nations" as a mystery, no fair reader should suffice for a simplistic explanation. Non-Jewish Believers reaching for a high spiritual, ethical, moral, and intellectual "fullness of the nations" status as grand vessels of mercy and grace—perhaps even overcoming some of their own hardness toward the Jewish people—is something which **is far more difficult to see achieved,** even in much of today's Messianic movement, than a return of descendants from the exiled Northern Kingdom of Israel/Ephraim.[58]

---

[56] Cf. D.S. Lim, "Fullness," in *Dictionary of Paul and His Letters* (Downers Grove, IL: InterVarsity, 1993), 319.

[57] Kurt Aland, et. al., *The Greek New Testament, Fourth Revised Edition* (Stuttgart: Deutche Bibelgesellschaft/United Bible Societies, 1998), 551.

[58] For a further discussion, consult Chapter 5 of the author's book *When Will the Messiah Return?*, "The Restoration of All Things and the Emergence of the Messianic Movement," as well as the relevant sections of his publication *Are Non-Jewish Believers Really a Part of Israel?*

The Exile of the Northern Kingdom,
and Evaluating the Numbers of Physical Israel

It can be observed that there have been some over-statements made, or at least not enough careful attention given to, various multiplication promises of the descendants of Abraham, Isaac, and Jacob, as can commonly be seen by many within today's Two-House sub-movement.

When one evaluates Israel in future prophecy, and sees a significant expectation about the reunion of Judah and Israel/Ephraim, one legitimately wonders about who composes this latter group of people. Obviously there are small groups of people in parts of Southeast Asia, South Asia, the Middle East, Central Africa, and the Mediterranean basin who claim to be descendants of the exiled Northern Kingdom. These people are normally monotheistic, they practice what appear to be some sort of Jewish religious customs, and they will usually have an oral tradition associated with themselves going back to the ancient Kingdom of Israel, as seen in the Books of Kings and Chronicles, in some way.

Are there people descended from the exiled Northern Kingdom of Israel really "out there" in the nations? In Hosea 8:8-9, for example, we see how "Israel is swallowed up; they are now among the nations [*b'goyim*, בַּגּוֹיִם] like a vessel in which no one delights. For they have gone up to Assyria, *like* a wild donkey all alone; Ephraim has hired lovers." The Hebrew verb *bala* (בָּלַע), appearing here in the Nifal stem (simple action, passive voice), does mean **"be swallowed up"** (CHALOT),[59] obviously in the form of judgment.[60] The view of a Jewish commentator like S.M. Lehrman, is that "The prophecy has been literally fulfilled. The Ten Tribes have disappeared from the scene of Jewish history, and their identity is now only a subject for far-fetched conjecture."[61] And indeed, none of us wants to wander off into the realm of off-the-wall conjecture regarding those of the exiled Northern Kingdom; what we want to do is to stay true to the Word of God, doing justice to the text and affirming that its descendants will be gathered back at the right time in fulfillment of prophecy.

Concurrent with this, Amos 9:8-9 informs us, in a word primarily issued to the Northern Kingdom, "'Behold, the eyes of the Lord GOD are on the sinful kingdom, and I will destroy it from the face of the earth; nevertheless, I will not totally destroy the house of Jacob,' declares the LORD. 'For behold, I am commanding, and I will shake the house of Israel among all nations [Heb. MT: *b'kol-ha'goyim*, הַגּוֹיִם־בְּכָל; Grk. LXX: *en pasi tois ethnesin*, ἐν πᾶσι τοῖς ἔθνεσιν] as *grain* is shaken in a sieve, but not a kernel will fall to the ground." The Divine punishment to be issued against a rebellious and idolatrous Northern Kingdom is a significant calamity, doubtlessly in the form of besiegement and massive deaths at the hands of Assyria, as well as various survivors being shaken among the nations. The leaders of the

---

[59] *CHALOT*, 41.
[60] Cf. Walter C. Kaiser, "בָּלַע," in *TWOT*, 1:110-111.
[61] S.M. Lehrman, "Hosea: Introduction and Commentary," in *Soncino Books of the Bible: The Twelve Prophets*, 30.

Northern Kingdom would no doubt fall, but survivors would be shaken like grain into the nations—and regardless of what would happen, they would surely be known by the One shaking them.

Can we know the real numbers of descendants of Abraham, Isaac, and Jacob? I want all reading this to know that **this is an area that makes me feel extremely uncomfortable.** The reason is that many people, be they Jewish *or* they have a feeling that they think they are of the exiled Northern Kingdom, get the idea that their ethnicity and background will merit them special favors before God. The Scriptures stand clearly against this: "sin entered the world through one man, and death through sin, and in this way death came to all people" (Romans 5:12, TNIV). In Adam and Eve, every person on Planet Earth is a sinner in a condition of separation from his or her Creator, and this can only be rectified by us receiving salvation in Yeshua (Jesus). The baseline for all of us is that **we are fallen human beings in need of redemption.** The presence of some group called "Ephraim," however large or small, coming back, whether they are hidden away out in the nations, or have been assimilated into the nations here or there, is *only* necessary for the fulfillment of future prophecies.

But what about the numbers? This is an area where there has been some significant abuse, embellishment, and over-exaggeration witnessed within a significant majority of the Two-House sub-movement. But, it also probably needs to be considered, that the total numbers of descendants of Abraham, Isaac, and Jacob, do probably go beyond the known 14-15 million Jews of today:

- Today's Two-House populists tend to claim that there are somewhere in the range of 2-3 billion descendants of Israel on Planet Earth, multiplying 2-3 million Ancient Israelites in the wilderness (Deuteronomy 1:10) by a factor of 1,000 (Deuteronomy 1:11).[62] But, given the controversy over the Semitic term *elef* (אֶלֶף), and whether or not it means "thousand" *or* something along the lines of "company" or "troop," the population statistics seen of Ancient Israel in the Books of Exodus and Numbers are probably considerably less than 2-3 million, and perhaps even less than 600,000.[63] If there are 2-3 billion descendants of the exiled Northern

---

[62] Moses said, "The LORD your God has multiplied you, and behold, you are this day like the stars of heaven in number. May the LORD, the God of your fathers, increase you a thousand-fold more than you are and bless you, just as He has promised you!" (Deuteronomy 1:10-11, NASU).

[63] K.A. Kitchen, *On the Reliability of the Old Testament* (Grand Rapids: Eerdmans, 2003), 264 astutely informs us,

"In the Biblical texts, the actual words for 'ten(s)' and 'hundred(s)' are not ambiguous, and present no problem on that score; the only question (usually) is whether they have been correctly recopied down the centuries. With 'eleph, 'thousand,' the matter is very different, as is universally accepted. In Hebrew, as in English (and elsewhere), words that look alike can be confused when found without a clear context. On its own, 'bark' in English can mean the skin of a tree, the sound of a dog, and an early ship or an ancient ceremonial boat. Only the content tells us which meaning is intended. The same applies to the word(s) 'lp in Hebrew. (1) We have 'eleph, 'thousand,' which has clear contexts like Gen. 20:16 (price) or Num. 3:50 (amount). But (2) there is 'eleph for a group—be it a clan/family, a (military) squad, a rota of Levites or

Kingdom on Planet Earth, then it makes the 14-15 million Jews of today seem absolutely miniscule, or even practically like nothing, especially in light of the 6 million who perished in the Holocaust.

• A Messianic Jewish evangelist like Jonathan Bernis actually thinks, "Today we find that there are around 6 million Jews living in Israel but there are physical descendants of Abraham, Isaac and Jacob dwelling in almost every nation on the planet. In fact, there are estimates that the total dispersed Jewish population is anywhere from 20 to 30 million."[64] It is uncertain if he is using the label of "Jewish population" to include those small groups in places like India or Africa which claim to be descended from the exiled Northern Kingdom. Yet, 20 to 30 million is almost twice the known Jewish population.

The total numbers of descendants of the exiled Northern Kingdom, prophesied to have been widely swallowed up, are in all likelihood between two or three or four times the known Jewish population or so—and are not at all in the hundreds of millions, and especially not in the billions, as is widely touted throughout the Two-House sub-movement. The word of Deuteronomy 28:62 is especially poignant to keep in mind, and has been almost totally overlooked, ignored, and perhaps even derided by Two-House proponents: **"Then you shall be left few in number** [Heb MT: *b'mtei m'at,* בִּמְתֵי מְעָט; Grk. LXX: *arithmō brachei,* ἀριθμῷ βραχεῖ], **whereas you were as numerous as the stars of heaven, because you did not obey the LORD your God."** While there are promises that God will multiply the physical descendants of Abraham, Isaac, and Jacob—there is also a surety that if they disobey Him, that they will be reduced in number to a fraction of what they could have been.

Unfortunately, though, given the reality of human sin, a great majority of any descendants of Abraham, Isaac, and Jacob—however tabulated or guess-timated, and whether they know they are such descendants or not—**is likely to die in trespasses and sins** (Ephesians 2:1) *the same* as any human being who fails to acknowledge Yeshua as Savior. Just as Paul said, "the Scripture has shut up everyone under sin" (Galatians 3:22), meaning "both Jews and Greeks are all under sin" (Romans 3:9) without Divine intervention.

When the Northern Kingdom of Israel/Ephraim was corporately deported into exile, they were taken away into the nations as a punishment for rebellion against God, who knows where they fully are. As *IDB* summarizes,

---

priests, etc....It is plain that in other passages of the Hebrew Bible there are clear examples where *'eleph* makes no sense if translated 'thousand' but good sense if rendered otherwise, e.g., as 'leader' or the like."

Consult the FAQ on the TNN website "Exodus, numbers of."

[64] Jonathan Bernis (2005). *The Scattering of the Tribes of Israel,* March/April 2005. *Jewish Voice Today.* Retrieved 17 April, 2011 from <http://www.jewishvoice.org>.

"Samaria, capital of Israel, held out until early in 721, the siege having been laid by Shalmaneser V (727-722) and the fall of the city effected by Sargon II (722-705). This marked the end of the ten tribes: 'None was left but the tribe of Judah only' (II Kings 17:18). According to the biblical account the Assyrians exiled the Israelites to Assyria in Halah (cf. Obad. 20), on the Habor, the river of Gozan, and in the cities of the Medes (II Kings 17:6; 18:11); on the other hand, they brought people from Babylon, Cuthah, Hamath, and Sephar-vaim to the cities of Samaria (II Kings 17:24; cf. Ezra 4: 10).

"The displacement of populations was, it seems, so complete so far as the identity of the N ten tribes is concerned; for they eventually assimilated beyond the point of return to any historical continuum with their Israelite origins..."[65]

As a Biblical examiner, I can go as far as to say that there are likely groups of people—some of them who know, and others of them who do not readily know—with a line of ancestry from the deportees of the Northern Kingdom of Israel/Ephraim "out there" in the nations.[66] Objectively speaking from Biblical history, we should be considering the descendants of the exiled Northern Kingdom to be placed among people groups located within the sphere of influence of the ancient Assyrian, Babylonian, and Persian Empires—*not* Northwestern Europe and the British Isles or the South Seas and Polynesia. (There are groups of people who similarly, whether they have kept it relatively hidden, or they only need some genealogical research conducted, who have Jewish ancestry.) I trust that our Sovereign Eternal God will bring these people back in fulfillment of His Word in His timing, as the return of Yeshua draws closer:

"For there will be a day when watchmen on the hills of Ephraim call out, 'Arise, and let us go up *to* Zion, to the LORD our God.' For thus says the LORD, 'Sing aloud with gladness for Jacob, and shout among the chief of the nations; proclaim, give praise and say, "O LORD, save Your people, the remnant of Israel." Behold, I am bringing them from the north country, and I will gather them from the remote parts of the earth, among them the blind and the lame, the woman with child and she who is in labor with child, together; a great company, they will return here. With weeping they will come, and by supplication I will lead them; I will make them walk by streams of waters, on a straight path in which they will not stumble; for I am a father to Israel, and Ephraim is My firstborn.' Hear the word of the LORD, O nations, and declare in the coastlands afar off, and say, **'He who scattered Israel will gather him and keep him as a shepherd keeps his flock'**" (Jeremiah 31:6-10).[67]

---

[65] J.A. Sanders, "Exile," in *IDB*, 2:186-187.

[66] As is discussed in Chapter 3, "Cross-Examining the Two-House Teaching," there were certainly some Northern Kingdom Israelites who escaped to the Southern Kingdom.

[67] While this prophecy is sometimes often applied to support the return of Jewish people in the former Soviet Union to Israel, and by all means **we should support** this, the specific context of "Israel" in Jeremiah 31:1, "I will be the God of all the families of Israel, and they shall be My people," is to those of the Northern Kingdom. Jeremiah 31:5-6 has previously specified,

Our thrust as Bible readers is to simply affirm key, eschatological words like this, and allow prophecy to naturally take shape as time moves forward. For ultimately, only the One who exiled the Northern Kingdom of Israel/Ephraim in the nations, the Lord Himself, is He who can gather them back. And most significantly, it is only the Lord Himself *by the power of His Holy Spirit* who can unite Judah, Israel/Ephraim, *and* their many companions from all the nations as one in Him!

Never, EVER, exclude or forget the companions!

Because of the emphasis that one commonly sees in the Two-House sub-movement upon Judah and Ephraim, outsiders often conclude that not only does their anticipated reunion *only involve* the physical descendants of Abraham, Isaac, and Jacob—but that the Two-House teaching actually **withholds salvation** to non-Israelites. Notwithstanding the fact that many of those non-Jewish Messianics, who have self-adopted the label of "Ephraim" for themselves, are in all probability not descendants of the exiled Northern Kingdom at all—it is **frequently under-emphasized** within the Two-House sub-movement that the restoration of the God's Kingdom actually involves the nations at large. Yet as it is clearly emphasized within the mission of the Servant Messiah,

"It is too small a thing that You should be My Servant to raise up the tribes of Jacob and to restore the preserved ones of Israel; I will also make You a light of the nations so that My salvation may reach to the end of the earth" (Isaiah 49:6).

Here, we are specifically told that "It is too light a thing" (RSV) for only the tribes of Israel to be restored; Yeshua must also be an *or goyim* (אוֹר גּוֹיִם) or "a light of the nations," in order for salvation to be declared *ad-qetzeih ha'eretz* (קְצֵה הָאָרֶץ־עַד). As Duane L. Christensen astutely reminds us in the *ABD* entry for "Nations": "it is clear that 'Israel as a light to the nations' is no peripheral theme within the canonical process. The nations are the matrix of Israel's life, the raison d'être of her very existence."[68] Israel is to be a beacon of the Creator's goodness and love to all! Sojourners or *gerim* (גֵּרִים) have always been welcome within the community of Israel,[69] especially per the Divine mandate given to Abraham and later Ancient Israel for the people to be a blessing to the whole world (Genesis 12:2; Deuteronomy 4:6). The key declaration of Psalm 24:1 is, "The earth is the LORD'S, and all it contains, the world, and those who dwell in it." Our Sovereign God loves all people who He has created, regardless of if they are of the physical line of Israel

---

"Again you will plant vineyards on the hills of Samaria; the planters will plant and will enjoy *them*. For there will be a day when watchmen on the hills of Ephraim call out, 'Arise, and let us go up *to* Zion, to the LORD our God.'"

Remarking on this, a Jewish commentator like H. Freedman, *Soncino Books of the Bible: Jeremiah* (London: Soncino, 1968), 204 states that this is "An indication that the breach between Samaria and Judea will have been healed, and Jerusalem resume its rightful place as the religious centre of a reunited Israelite nation."

[68] Duane L. Christensen, "Nations," in David Noel Freedman, ed., *Anchor Bible Dictionary*, 6 vols. (New York: Doubleday, 1992), 4:1037.

[69] Cf. Exodus 22:21; 23:9; Leviticus 19:33-34; 24:22.

or not! *He desires all to be reconciled and redeemed unto Himself* (cf. 1 Timothy 2:3-4).

While any teaching on the Southern and Northern Kingdoms of Israel being reunited in fulfillment of prophecy, will necessarily focus upon "Judah and Ephraim," in too many circles there has been such an over-emphasis upon this—that the nations at large themselves have been greatly overlooked. So, what about those who have no physical claim to being descended from Abraham, Isaac, and Jacob/Israel? Are they excluded from the Kingdom realm of Israel? Are they not a part of the prophesied restoration of Israel? Do they have no hope of salvation? If we see what is spoken of in Ezekiel 37:15-28, which details the two sticks coming together, it clearly includes "companions":

"The word of the LORD came again to me saying, 'And you, son of man, take for yourself one stick and write on it, "For Judah and for the sons of Israel, **his companions** [*chavero*, חֲבֵרוֹ]"; then take another stick and write on it, "For Joseph, the stick of Ephraim and all the house of Israel, **his companions** [*chavero*, חֲבֵרוֹ]"'" (Ezekiel 37:15-16).

Who are these "companions" or "comrades" (ATS)? It should be quite obvious that connected to either Judah or Ephraim are various associates—those from the nations who are to be involved in the restoration process! The Hebrew word here in its singular form is *chaver* (חָבֵר), "**comrade, companion**" (CHALOT),[70] "*an associate, a companion, fellow*" (Gesenius' Hebrew-Chaldee Lexicon),[71] which is "A masculine noun indicating friendship, association with, being friends with, companion" (AMG).[72] In modern Hebrew, the term *chaverim* (חברים) actually means "friends." In other words, we see that when those of the Southern and Northern Kingdoms of Israel are together in the end-times there will be *far more* than just physical Israelites as part of the unification; their "friends," if you will, are going to very much be involved in the process as well.

The companions which are involved in the reunification process of Israel are physical non-Israelites, but they are surely a part of the Commonwealth of Israel through Messiah Yeshua (Ephesians 2:11-13) or the Israel of God (Galatians 6:16), grafted-in as wild olive branches (Romans 11:17-18), similarly likened unto the ancient sojourner or *ger* (גֵּר) in the Torah. They will be most certainly *included* as participants within Israel's restoration. With this in mind, it should never be thought that there is an exclusion of true "Gentiles" from God's salvation in Yeshua. One way or another, these *chaverim* from the nations—**most probably being *the significant majority* of those involved in the restoration process**—will be a part of a larger restoration of Israel, and are considered full-fledged citizens of the Commonwealth of Israel.

While I have never had difficulty comprehending that scores of companions from the nations themselves, are to be involved as participants in a greater

---

[70] *CHALOT*, 94.

[71] H.F.W. Gesenius: *Gesenius' Hebrew-Chaldee Lexicon to the Old Testament*, trans. Samuel Prideaux Tregelles (Grand Rapids: Baker, 1979), 259.

[72] Baker and Carpenter, 311.

restoration of Israel—the fact does remain that today a significant amount of what you will hear in the Two-House sub-movement has decisively *left out* such companions. And a considerable challenge, for those who have popularized much of this, is what happens if in the reunification they so desperately seek, there actually ends up involving a significant majority, i.e., eighty to ninety percent or more, of companions. Most of the non-Jewish Believers one is likely to encounter, identifying themselves as some sort of "Ephraimites," are not. **This is why a focus on the equality of all people in the Lord** (cf. Galatians 3:28; Colossians 3:11), **and all people feeling welcome and a sense of belonging and usefulness within the Messianic movement, is so imperative!** Most sadly, such a Messianic community that is welcoming of Jewish *and* non-Jewish Messianic Believers—is not something that enough people often encounter.

Going to the Source Text:
When did "Jew and Greek" become "Jew and Gentile"?

When we hear many people within today's Messianic movement talk about "Jew and Gentile" being one in the Messiah, the intention is to surely encourage unity and camaraderie—which is good. At the same time, though, some of the verses commonly quoted to support "Jew and Gentile" being one in Messiah, if examined much more carefully, **do not actually have this terminology employed.** In the New International Version, and to a greater extent, the Complete Jewish Bible (which is widely used in the Messianic community), one can find some specific places where the proper noun *Hellēn* ('Ελλην) has been rendered as "Gentile." Is this something that is appropriate? Surely, rendering *Ioudaios* ('Ιουδαῖος) as anything other than "Jew," "Jewish," or perhaps in some places "Judean," would not be proper.

In various places within the Apostolic Scriptures, where versions like the NIV or CJB might speak of "Jew and Gentile," the actual source text instead reads as "Jew and Greek." To take a specific nationality like "Greek," and instead replace it with "Gentile," is an inappropriate liberty. Once again, this cues us into the fact that as Believers in Yeshua—who make up a multi-national Commonwealth of Israel—that we need to be sensitive to the terms that we use. For in the case of the Greeks, even though there were many injustices done to the Jewish people by the Syrian-Greeks during the Maccabean crisis of the Second Century B.C.E., the fact does remain that both "Jews and Greeks" were some of the first *major* recipients of the good news.[73] Obviously the good news would reach far beyond Greek areas as time would advance, but by translating a specific term with a generic term, at the very least some significant historical settings of various Bible verses can be skewed.

I would ask you to consider a listing of passages where the NIV and CJB have noticeably taken a few liberties. You may have read some of these verses before, and have not thought anything of it. The chart below compares the NIV and CJB against the Greek New Testament (UBS Fourth Revised Edition), Young's Literal

---

[73] Acts 14:1; 18:4; 19:10, 17; 20:21; 1 Corinthians 1:22, 24; 12:13.

Translation (YLT), and the New American Standard Bible (NASU). Do note that some verses in the NIV have properly rendered "Greek" as "Greek":

"JEW AND GENTILE" IN THE GREEK APOSTOLIC SCRIPTURES

ROMANS 1:16

NIV: I am not ashamed of the gospel, because it is the power of God for the salvation of everyone who believes: first for the Jew, then for the Gentile.

CJB: For I am not ashamed of the Good News, since it is God's powerful means of bringing salvation to everyone who keeps on trusting, to the Jew especially, but equally to the Gentile.

GNT: Οὐ γὰρ ἐπαισχύνομαι τὸ εὐαγγέλιον, δύναμις γὰρ θεοῦ ἐστιν εἰς σωτηρίαν παντὶ τῷ πιστεύοντι, Ἰουδαίῳ τε πρῶτον καὶ Ἕλληνι.

Ou gar epaischunomai to euangelion, dunamis gar Theou estin eis sōtērian panti tō pisteuonti, **Ioudaiō** [Jew] te prōton kai **Hellēni** [Greek].

YLT: [F]or I am not ashamed of the good news of the Christ, for it is the power of God to salvation to every one who is believing, both to Jew first, and to Greek.

NASU: For I am not ashamed of the gospel, for it is the power of God for salvation to everyone who believes, to the Jew first and also to the Greek.

ROMANS 2:9-10

NIV: There will be trouble and distress for every human being who does evil: first for the Jew, then for the Gentile; but glory, honor and peace for everyone who does good: first for the Jew, then for the Gentile.

CJB: Yes, he will pay back misery and anguish to every human being who does evil, to the Jew first, then to the Gentile; but glory and honor and shalom to everyone who keeps doing what is good, to the Jew first, then to the Gentile.

GNT: θλῖψις καὶ στενοχωρία ἐπὶ πᾶσαν ψυχὴν ἀνθρώπου τοῦ κατεργαζομένου τὸ κακόν, Ἰουδαίου τε πρῶτον καὶ Ἕλληνος· δόξα δὲ καὶ τιμὴ καὶ εἰρήνη παντὶ τῷ ἐργαζομένῳ τὸ ἀγαθόν, Ἰουδαίῳ τε πρῶτον καὶ Ἕλληνι

Thlipsis kai stenochōria epi pasan psuchēn anthrōpou tou katergazomenou to kakon, **Ioudaiou** [Jew] te prōton kai **Hellēnos** [Greek] doxa de kai timē kai eirēnē panti tō ergazomenō to agathon, **Ioudaiō** [Jew] te prōton kai **Hellēni** [Greek].

Israel In Future Prophecy

YLT: [T]ribulation and distress, upon every soul of man that is working the evil, both of Jew first, and of Greek; and glory, and honour, and peace, to every one who is working the good, both to Jew first, and to Greek.

NASU: *There will be* tribulation and distress for every soul of man who does evil, of the Jew first and also of the Greek, but glory and honor and peace to everyone who does good, to the Jew first and also to the Greek.

ROMANS 10:12

NIV: For there is no difference between Jew and Gentile—the same Lord is Lord of all and richly blesses all who call on him.

CJB: That means that there is no difference between Jew and Gentile—*Adonai* is the same for everyone, rich toward everyone who calls on him.

GNT: οὐ γάρ ἐστιν διαστολὴ Ἰουδαίου τε καὶ Ἕλληνος, ὁ γὰρ αὐτὸς κύριος πάντων, πλουτῶν εἰς πάντας τοὺς ἐπικαλουμένους αὐτόν

Ou gar estin diastolē **Ioudaiou** [Jew] te kai **Hellēnos** [Greek], ho gar autos Kurios pantōn, ploutōn eis pantas tous epikaloumenous auton.

YLT: [F]or there is no difference between Jew and Greek, for the same Lord of all {is} rich to all those calling upon Him.

NASU: For there is no distinction between Jew and Greek; for the same *Lord* is Lord of all, abounding in riches for all who call on Him.

1 CORINTHIANS 10:32

NIV: Do not cause anyone to stumble, whether Jews, Greeks or the church of God.

CJB: Do not be an obstacle to anyone—not to Jews, not to Gentiles, and not to God's Messianic Community.

GNT: ἀπρόσκοποι καὶ Ἰουδαίοις γίνεσθε καὶ Ἕλλησιν καὶ τῇ ἐκκλησίᾳ τοῦ θεου

Aproskopoi kai **Ioudaiois** [Jews] ginesthe kai **Hellēsin** [Greeks] kai tē ekklēsia tou Theou

YLT: [B]ecome offenceless, both to Jews and Greeks, and to the assembly of God.

NASU: Give no offense either to Jews or to Greeks or to the church of God.

1 CORINTHIANS 12:13

NIV: For we were all baptized by one Spirit into one body—whether Jews or Greeks, slave or free—and we were all given the one Spirit to drink.

CJB: For it was by one Spirit that we were all immersed into one body, whether Jews or Gentiles, slaves or free; and we were all given the one Spirit to drink.

GNT: καὶ γὰρ ἐν ἑνὶ πνεύματι ἡμεῖς πάντες εἰς ἓν σῶμα ἐβαπτίσθημεν, εἴτε Ἰουδαῖοι εἴτε Ἕλληνες εἴτε δοῦλοι εἴτε ἐλεύθεροι, καὶ πάντες ἓν πνεῦμα ἐποτίσθημεν

Kai gar en eni pneumati hēmeis pantes eis hen sōma ebaptisthēmen, eite **Ioudaioi** [Jews] eite **Hellēnes** [Greeks] eite douloi eite elutheroi, kai pantes hen pneuma epotisthēmen

YLT: [F]or also in one Spirit we all to one body were baptized, whether Jews or Greeks, whether servants or freemen, and all into one Spirit were made to drink.

NASU: For by one Spirit we were all baptized into one body, whether Jews or Greeks, whether slaves or free, and we were all made to drink of one Spirit.

GALATIANS 3:28

NIV: There is neither Jew nor Greek, slave nor free, male nor female, for you are all one in Christ Jesus.

CJB: [T]here is neither Jew nor Gentile, neither slave nor freeman, neither male nor female; for in union with the Messiah Yeshua, you are all one.

GNT: οὐκ ἔνι Ἰουδαῖος οὐδὲ Ἕλλην, οὐκ ἔνι δοῦλος οὐδὲ ἐλεύθερος, οὐκ ἔνι ἄρσεν καὶ θῆλυ· πάντες γὰρ ὑμεῖς εἷς ἐστε ἐν Χριστῷ Ἰησοῦ.

ouk eni **Ioudaios** [Jew] oude **Hellēn** [Greek], ouk eni doulos oude eleutheros, ouk eni arsen kai thēlu pantes gar humeis heis este en Christō Iēsou.

YLT: [T]here is not here Jew or Greek, there is not here servant nor freeman, there is not here male and female, for all ye are one in Christ Jesus.

NASU: There is neither Jew nor Greek, there is neither slave nor free man, there is neither male nor female; for you are all one in Christ Jesus.

COLOSSIANS 3:11

NIV:
Here there is no Greek or Jew, circumcised or uncircumcised, barbarian, Scythian, slave or free, but Christ is all, and is in all.

CJB:
The new self allows no room for discriminating between Gentile and Jew, circumcised and uncircumcised, foreigner, savage, slave, free man; on the contrary, in all, the Messiah is everything.

GNT:
ὅπου οὐκ ἔνι Ἕλλην καὶ Ἰουδαῖος, περιτομὴ καὶ ἀκροβυστία, βάρβαρος, Σκύθης, δοῦλος, ἐλεύθερος, ἀλλὰ [τὰ] πάντα καὶ ἐν πᾶσιν Χριστός

Hopou ouk eni Hellēn [Greek] kai Ioudaios [Jew], peritomē kai akrobustia, barbaros, Skuthēs, doulos, eleutheros, alla [ta] panta kai en pasin Christos

YLT:
[W]here there is not Greek and Jew, circumcision and uncircumcision, foreigner, Scythian, servant, freeman—but the all and in all—Christ.

NASU:
a renewal in which there is no *distinction between* Greek and Jew, circumcised and uncircumcised, barbarian, Scythian, slave and freeman, but Christ is all, and in all.

A comparison of these different passages shows that there is some inaccuracy on the part of a few Bible translators in regard to "Jew and Greek," and its improper translation as "Jew and Gentile."[74]

Some may say that pointing out some discrepancies among versions like NIV and CJB, where "Jew and Gentile" has been used instead of "Jew and Greek," is going a little far—or at the very least is "nit picking." Yet, how many things can be missed from the Bible, if we get into the habit of skewing some specific details? By missing some specific details, how might this affect our interpretation of a Biblical passage? It should be clear, in a verse like Colossians 3:11 at least, that some significant historical and cultural issues can be overlooked when *Hellēn* (Ἕλλην) is improperly rendered as "Gentile" and not "Greek"—especially as it sits alongside "circumcised and uncircumcised, barbarian, Scythian, slave and freeman."

In the case of the Ancient Greeks, this is a specific nationality that undeniably has made some significant contributions to human civilization[75]—and neither they,

---

[74] The 2011 Messianic version, *Tree of Life—The New Covenant*, has properly rendered the proper noun *Hellēn* (Ἕλλην) as "Greek" in Romans 1:16; 2:9-10; 10:12; 1 Corinthians 10:32; 12:13; Galatians 3:28; Colossians 3:11.

[75] Do be quite aware of the fact that it is quite commonplace in some quarters of the Messianic movement to hear claims made against a so-called "Greek mindset" or "Greek perspective" on various spiritual issues. How much of this quantitatively lacks engagement with the relevant Hellenistic philosophers or ancient voices/historians? Should we ever allow statements made about "the Rabbis," positive or negative, when no specific Rabbinical voices or references are really made? If Greek philosophy

nor any other ethnic group, should be allowed in Bible translation to be recognized by the generic term "Gentile" or "nation" when their proper name is used. For some reason or another, though, much of today's contemporary Messianic movement does not often make the effort to pay attention to these kinds of specific issues.

Should we really use the term "Gentile"?
What are other terms we need to be careful of?

No one in today's Messianic community should ever "freak out" when they hear the term "Gentile" used, because it is going to be heard at the very least from various English Bible translations and various theological resources. There can probably be, however, some better ways to communicate that are more sensitive to a group's needs. If a Messianic congregational leader knows that there is a group of non-Jewish Believers in the assembly who might be offended if the term "Gentile" is used, then it might be incumbent to employ some worthwhile and valid alternatives like "nation(s)" or "people(s)" to offset a potential problem.

Many non-Jewish Messianics are asked to be sensitive to Jewish concerns with their usage of terms like "cross," given the reality of many heinous acts of anti-Semitism committed in history involving the cross. While we may never totally stop using terms like "cross" or "crucified," it is fair and advisable to employ valid alternatives like "tree" and "executed."[76] Is it too much, given some of the post-Second Temple usage of terms like *"goy"* and *"goyim"* and possible negative aspects surrounding the term "Gentile" in current Jewish culture, that some alternatives likewise be used? I have a feeling that in the case of many people in the Messianic movement, especially in much of Messianic Judaism, that for the considerable time being we may be dealing **with a one-way street** on this issue. Consider some of the thoughts offered by Toby Janicki in his article "What is a Gentile?":

"The word 'Gentile' is not a negative term, nor does it refer to idolaters in any essential way. Although it has had various implications in different contexts, its primary meaning is that of 'one from the nations.' This is the designation that the apostles used to distinguish non-Jewish believers from Jewish believers. If it was good enough for them, it should be good enough for us."[77]

The Biblical terms that are actually used to describe that nations are *goy/goyim* and *ethnos* — **nation(s).** While context determines whether people in general, or some kind of pagan idolaters are intended, it is disingenuous of anyone in either Messianic Judaism or the broader Messianic world to fail to recognize that in the Twenty-First Century, the English term "Gentile" can offend some non-Jewish Believers. It is also disingenuous to think that in some modern Jewish cultural

---

is targeted as being in error, or Rabbinic/Talmudic perspectives are touted as valued, then appropriate references should be provided.

For a specific example of how this works, consult the FAQ on the TNN website, "Dualism."

[76] Consult the FAQ on the TNN website, "Crucifixion."

[77] Toby Janicki. "What is a Gentile?" <u>Messiah Journal</u> Issue 101, Summer 2009/5770:44.

contexts, when the *goyim* or Gentiles are referred to, it is speaking of non-Jews in a totally neutral way.

But let us consider for a moment some more of the shortcomings found in the broad Messianic world as it concerns the terms used to describe people in general. A fair majority of today's Messianic community balks at using any degree of inclusive language, dismissing it as being the product of so-called "political correctness"—even though it is adhered to in part by many conservative evangelical Christians, and is actually reflected in much of David Stern's Complete Jewish Bible (1998), as well as in the new Tree of Life Bible—The New Covenant (2011).[78] *What is the inclusive language debate?* A big part of it is recognizing that there are some specific terms in the Hebrew and Greek Scriptures where a masculine-centric rendering is less-than-accurate, especially given some of the changing dynamics of modern English speech. The major terms to be aware of include:

- The generic *adam* (אָדָם) and *anthrōpos* (ἄνθρωπος), can be better rendered with **"humanity"** or **"humankind,"** rather than "man" or "mankind"; or in the case of individuals, **"human being(s),"** **"mortal(s),"** or **"person(s)."**
- The specific *ish* (אִישׁ) and *anēr* (ἀνήρ), relates to a person who is a **man** or of the **male** gender, and can sometimes refer to a **husband.**
- The specific *ishah* (אִשָּׁה) and *gunē* (γυνή), relates to a person who is a **woman** or of the **female** gender, and can sometimes refer to a **wife.**

Obviously, some renderings of these Hebrew and Greek terms are largely dependent on their usage in a passage. But in general when people at large are described, it is probably safe to say that calling them "men" has become more than a bit out of place in normal, everyday English language across the world. So even if a Bible version might use "men" when "people" is intended, such as where Yeshua calls His disciples to be "fishers of men[79]" (Mark 1:17; cf. Matthew 4:19), we need to be geared toward speaking on these sorts of passages relating to "fish for people" (NRSV/NLT/TNIV). A key passage where an inclusive language rendering will convey a far better and clearer understanding for Messianics, is where Ephesians 2:15 speaks of *kainon anthrōpon* (καινὸν ἄνθρωπον), the **"one new humanity"** (NRSV/CJB), as opposed to "one new man." Obviously, what the Father has brought about via the magnanimous work of His Son is to influence far more than just those of the male gender.

Once again, reality being what it is, not enough of today's Messianic teachers and leaders may be sensitive to employing a little bit of inclusive language in their speech. *In fact, more than a few Messianic leaders are probably some of the greatest offenders when it comes to not using any degree of inclusive language.* I want you to know that I myself do not get upset when I see terms like "man" or "mankind"

---

[78] Other Bible versions that employ a principle of inclusive language, to one degree or another, include: the New Revised Standard Version (1989), the Revised English Bible (1989), and the Today's New International Version (2005).

[79] Grk. *alieis anthrōpōn* (ἁλιεῖς ἀνθρώπων).

used to refer to the human race, because I do use them from time to time. Yet we do need to recognize the various limitations present in modern English speech, by only using terms like "man," "men," or "mankind."

In the Twenty-First Century, we have more than a few Messianic voices who are still quite prone to using "men," when in normal speech "people" is far more natural and preferable. Does it at all offend you when a Messianic speaker says—regardless of which slice of the broad Messianic movement in which the statement is made—says something like, "God is raising up men in this hour" and the audience is clearly mixed? Why would we not hear something more like, "God is raising up men *and women* in this hour" **or** "God is raising up *people* in this hour"? How would you feel if you were a woman and you heard terms like men, mankind, and brothers ***exclusively*** used? Speaking for myself, I know that I am offended when I only hear male-specific terms used, and I am a male!

Obviously, if some of today's Messianic Believers cannot compute the fact that using male-centric terms exclusively might cause some discord—would they even be able to see that using a term like "Gentile" exclusively, might also create some angst?

The issue of the terms we use affects our historical readings of the Scriptures. How many of today's Messianic Jews, even among those who are well-educated Bible teachers (with significant degrees), will say things along the lines of, "when God brought the Jewish people out of Egypt..."? Now it is certainly true that God brought the ancestors of today's Jewish people out of Egypt, but it is largely and historically incorrect to use the term "Jew" or *Yehudi* (יְהוּדִי) to describe anyone prior to the dispersion of the Southern Kingdom of Judah. As the entry for "Jew" in *IDB* directs us,

"In the OT, יהוד ('Jew') is not used for members of the old tribe of Judah or even to distinguish persons of the Southern Kingdom from those of the Northern Kingdom...It is scarcely used until the kingdom of Judah had survived N Israel (II Kings 25:25; Jer. 38:19; 52:28-30). In postexilic times 'Jew' refers to a subject of the Babylonian or Persian province of Judah or of the Maccabean state (Esth. 9:15-19; Neh. 4:1-H 3:33; Zech. 8:23; I Macc. 8:20; Jos. Antiq. XI.v.7)."[80]

There is, of course, nothing wrong with using terms such as "Jew" or "Jewish," provided that we are able to recognize when in Biblical history that *Yehudi* started being legitimately used, in association with the Southern Kingdom. The point to be taken is ***not*** that "Jew" is a bad term to use; rather, "strictly speaking, it is anachronistic to use the term with reference to the Hebrews or Israelites of an earlier period" (*ISBE*).[81] Yet many of today's Messianic Jews were raised in an environment where the Ancient Israelites at the foot of Mount Sinai, to those who made up the populations of both the Northern and Southern Kingdoms, to those

---

[80] J.A. Sanders, "Jew," in *IDB*, 2:897.
[81] W.W. Gasque, "Jew," in *ISBE*, 2:1056.

who returned from Babylon—were *all* "*Jews.*"[82] Specificity in terms of Biblical history, for such people, is not only something that is overlooked, but it is actually reinforced in some Jewish teaching materials. The Orthodox Jewish *ArtScroll Tanach*, for example, renders Exodus 21:2 with, "If you buy a Jewish bondsman...," when the source text clearly has *Ivri* (עִבְרִי) or "Hebrew." Its chart detailing the rulers, of both the Northern and Southern Kingdoms, is actually labeled to be "The Jewish Monarchy."[83] Even Stern's Jewish New Testament/Complete Jewish Bible may be said to have made a faux paux when labeling the Epistle to the Hebrews as "Messianic Jews," when modern Hebrew New Testaments tend to have *Ivrim* (עְבְרִים), Hebrew for "Hebrews," instead (for the Greek title ΠΡΟΣ ΕΒΡΑΙΟΥΣ, *Pros Hebraious*).[84]

Not paying attention to specific details in Biblical history has enabled many throughout the Messianic world to say things along the lines of, "When Paul writes to the Gentiles in Letter XYZ..." While it may be true that there was a large, non-Jewish readership for many of Paul's epistles, almost all of the Pauline letters are titled by a geographic-specific audience—in addition to having Jewish readers as well. Why would any of us ever speak in terms of Paul writing *the Gentiles*, when what we should be more tuned into is Paul writing the Romans, the Corinthians, the Galatians, the Philippians, the Colossians, the Thessalonicans, etc.?[85] Cultural and historical circumstances in places such as Rome, Corinth, Galatia, Philippi, and Colossae in the ancient Mediterranean world might factor into us understanding some difficult verses, and some of the location-specific issues ancient groups of Messiah followers faced.

---

[82] In the annotation for John 4:22-24, appearing in Daniel Gruber, trans., *The Messianic Writings* (Hanover, NH: Elijah Publishing, 2011), 148, it is actually stated, "After the Babylonians exiled the Jewish inhabitants of Shomron [Samaria], they brought other captive people to live there. (2K 17:22-41)."

This statement is not at all true to history, and even the text of 2 Kings 17:22-41 itself, as it details the exile of the Northern Kingdom of Israel by the Assyrians, not the Babylonians. Yet, these kinds of remarks litter the Messianic Jewish spectrum, and often go unnoticed by even those leaders who have weighty post-graduate degrees.

[83] Nosson Scherman and Meir Zlotowitz, eds., *ArtScroll Tanach* (Brooklyn: Mesorah Publications, 1996), 2026.

In contrast, *JPS Guide: The Jewish Bible* (Philadelphia: Jewish Publication Society, 2008), 188 correctly refers to "The Kingdoms of Israel and Judah."

[84] The Phillips New Testament has also incorrectly labeled the Epistle to the Hebrews as "The Letter to Jewish Christians."

[85] You do probably need to be aware of the textual issues in Ephesians 1:1, and how "in Ephesus" (*en Ephesō*, ἐν Ἐφέσῳ) does not appear in the oldest manuscripts (cf. Metzger, *Textual Commentary*, 601). In all likelihood the Epistle of Ephesians was originally a circular letter written by the Apostle Paul to assemblies within Asia Minor, eventually making its way to Ephesus. The RSV notably rendered Ephesians 1:1 with: "Paul, an apostle of Christ Jesus by the will of God, to the saints who are also faithful in Christ Jesus."

Specific Pauline letters that actually concern the Believers in Ephesus, are actually the Epistles of 1&2 Timothy, as Timothy served as Paul's duly-appointed superintendent to Ephesus and the surrounding region. For more information, consult the entries for the Epistles of 1&2 Timothy in the author's workbook *A Survey of the Apostolic Scriptures for the Practical Messianic*.

The Terms We Use, and Your Messianic Speech

Sensitivity toward non-Jewish Believers who may be a little upset when they are called "Gentiles," does need to be recognized by many within the broad Messianic community. Sensitivity toward people of both genders, when terms like "man" or "mankind" or "brothers" are exclusively used, needs to *also* be recognized. And above all, when contemplating the prophecies of a larger restoration of Israel, the place of the nations as *welcomed companions* within what is going on, need not at all be overlooked. **Does our Creator God have a program for the wide world that He has made, or does He not?**

It will be a challenge for all parties concerned to begin employing terms like "nations" or "peoples" to refer to non-Jewish Believers. Some will strongly resist speaking in terms of "humanity" and "brothers *and* sisters." And in terms of much of what is commonly encountered surrounding the Two-House issue, we may not see any significant shift toward an emphasis on the companions of either Judah and Ephraim, being a valued part of the restoration process too, anytime soon in the populist literature. Yet if we can be committed to seeing a Messianic movement, and indeed an "Israel of God" (Galatians 6:16), where are all welcomed and can be involved in the unique work He has begun in our day—**then we will go far.** For, it is only our Sovereign Creator who can bring diverse groups of people together: Jews, Christians, men, women, and everyone on Planet Earth who He loves, in a unique Messianic community that can see His Kingdom fully restored.

-3-

Cross-Examining
the Two-House Teaching
sifting through the claims of the Two-House sub-movement,
what is Biblical, and what is not

Since the early 2000s, various parts of the broad Messianic community have been bombarded with an array of issues and teachings that have been anything but good. These things have challenged our collective understanding of who Messiah Yeshua is, the recorded history of the First Century, hermeneutics and how we are to understand the Bible, and indeed the very authority of the Scriptures themselves. Since such a wave of "teachings" has hit, and the consequent damage that they have caused, many of us have had to reevaluate and reconsider some things that we have picked up in our days in the Messianic movement. With some issues, we have had to return to previous beliefs and practices, discarding things that were passing themselves off as "true," but we discovered were not. With other things, we have had to fine-tune our theology and make sure that it is in fuller alignment with Scripture, eliminate any unsound elements that may have been allowed to creep in, and pull the reigns back a considerable bit.

While this has been especially true of some fringe teachings and beliefs that we may have all gotten wind of, one issue that needs to be truly cross-examined by many people is **the Two-House teaching.** I have always believed that we must approach the subject matter of the reunification of the Northern and Southern Kingdoms of Israel from the Biblical text and from what should be read as unfulfilled prophecies. One must not make unsubstantiated claims about the descendants of the exiled Northern Kingdom, nor can one ignore the Jewish expectations of Israel's restoration. We have to understand that the message of Israel's restoration is ultimately the message of God's Kingdom coming to Earth — and Israel just happens to be the vehicle that God is going to use to accomplish it. *It is something that truly welcomes all human beings who look to Him for deliverance and salvation!*

It is necessary to cross-examine and revisit various elements of the Two-House teaching. There are some important Bible passages that advocates of the Two-House teaching have brought to the attention of today's Messianic Believers. Yet, as with many theological issues which have to be frequently fine-tuned, we will be examining some aspects of the Two-House teaching that are assumed to be true by many proponents and adherents of it, but Biblically and historically are overstated, or even unsustainable.

In what way may we all be considered "Israel"?

A major issue in theology today is determining what the purpose of the Messiah coming to Earth was, aside from being sacrificed for the sins of fallen humanity at Golgotha (Calvary) and providing permanent atonement and forgiveness to those who look to Him. Many are of the mistaken impression that Yeshua came to inaugurate a new program via the establishment of "the Church," when in actuality this is not attested to in any of His teachings or in the testimony of the Apostles. Yeshua the Messiah came to bring about the restoration of Israel (Matthew 16:18; cf. Jeremiah 33:6-8).[1] This restoration was to involve both the tribes of Jacob and the nations at large (Isaiah 49:6). **The God of Israel has always had a global vision of saving all members of the human race who would recognize Him.** While Israel is His chosen nation, it is nevertheless to function as the vehicle for Him to communicate His truth to the entire world. When one recognizes the God of Israel as the One True God, that person then becomes a part of the community, or Kingdom realm, of Israel. The salvation of every person is innately connected to Israel, and its prophesied restoration.

The Apostle Paul recognized this global vision as he was specially commissioned to be the "apostle of the nations[2]" (Romans 11:13, LITV). For his time in the First Century, Paul had the training of a Jewish rabbi and was a Roman citizen, so he could go out into the Mediterranean basin and ably testify to others about the God of Israel and His Son, Yeshua, to both Diaspora Jews and diverse groups of people. Paul plainly wrote non-Jewish Believers in Asia Minor that prior to their salvation experience they were separate from the Commonwealth of Israel, yet as a result of their faith they had been "brought near":

"Therefore remember that formerly you, the Gentiles in the flesh, who are called 'Uncircumcision' by the so-called 'Circumcision,' *which is* performed in the flesh by human hands—*remember* that you were at that time separate from Messiah, excluded from the commonwealth of Israel, and strangers to the covenants of promise, having no hope and without God in the world. But now in Messiah Yeshua you who formerly were far off have been brought near by the blood of Messiah."

What does it mean to be "brought near"? The Torah testifies of Ancient Israel, "For what great nation is there that has a god so near to it as is the LORD our God whenever we call on Him?" (Deuteronomy 4:7). Psalm 148:14 exclaims, "And He has lifted up a horn for His people, praise for all His godly ones; *even* for the sons of Israel, a people near to Him. Praise the LORD!" When those from the nations have recognized Israel's Messiah, it is clear that they have been made one with

---

[1] For a further discussion of this issue, consult the author's article "When Did 'the Church' Begin?" as well the examination of Matthew 16:18-19 in his publication, *Are Non-Jewish Believers Really a Part of Israel?*

[2] Grk. *ethnōn apostolos* (ἐθνῶν ἀπόστολος).

their Jewish brethren within the Commonwealth of Israel, *tēs politeias tou Israēl* (τῆς πολιτείας τοῦ Ἰσραὴλ). The Greek word *politeia* (πολιτεία), rendered as "commonwealth" or "citizenship" (NIV),[3] means **"the right to be a member of a sociopolitical entity, citizenship"** (BDAG).[4] Paul's further writing specifies how non-Jewish Believers are to be regarded as a part of the community of Israel:

"So then you are no longer strangers and aliens, but you are fellow citizens with the saints, and are of God's household, having been built on the foundation of the apostles and prophets, Messiah Yeshua Himself being the corner *stone*, in whom the whole building, being fitted together, is growing into a holy temple in the Lord, in whom you also are being built together into a dwelling of God in the Spirit...the Gentiles are fellow heirs and fellow members of the body, and fellow partakers of the promise in Messiah Yeshua through the gospel" (Ephesians 2:19-22; 3:6).

The term *sumpolitēs* (συμπολίτης) means *"fellow-citizen/compatriot"* (BDAG).[5] Paul definitely believed that non-Jews who recognize Israel's Messiah have been given citizenship in Israel, even though they are not ethnically or culturally Jewish. Such persons certainly benefit from the rich root of Israel (cf. Romans 11:18), **but** they also have a definite responsibility to live appropriately as a part of Israel, in holiness, as well (cf. 1 Peter 2:9-10).

Many non-Jewish Believers who have entered into the Messianic community are of the strong conviction that they are a part of the polity of Israel, along with their fellow Jewish Believers, and that God's Torah is relevant instruction for them. There are many open-minded Messianic Jewish congregational leaders who have no problem with considering such people a part of Israel along with them, *provided* that there is an extreme level of respect and sensitivity realized for Jewish concerns (cf. Romans 11:21, 29). Paul himself, in telling the non-Jewish Believers in Rome that they had been grafted into Israel's olive tree, also warned how they could be broken off from it because of arrogance issued against the natural Jewish branches (Romans 11:17-18).

While aspects of the Messianic lifestyle and Torah observance tend to garner a great deal of attention (especially considering that they involve one's day-to-day activities), all of those who compose the Messianic movement and consider themselves as being a part of an enlarged Kingdom realm of Israel—need to recognize that the prophecies detailing Israel's restoration somehow involve "them." But how they *specifically involve* "them" has been a question generating a variety of answers. Much confusion has been caused by errant teachings such as the pre-tribulation rapture, built upon a dispensational foundation of God having two groups of elect, Israel and "the Church." Obviously, when such a presupposition is removed—and Bible readers can be more honest with what "after the tribulation of those days" means (cf. Matthew 24:29-31)[6]—then end-time

---

[3] "community" (REB/*Lattimore*); "citizens" (Common English Bible).

[4] *BDAG*, 845.

[5] Ibid., 959.

[6] For a detailed study, consult the author's report *The Dangers of Pre-Tribulationism*.

prophecies which regard Israel's restoration can be viewed as being far more applicable *and relevant* to all of those within today's Messianic movement. Such prophecies, while including participation within Tribulation-period events, also involve a larger anticipated restoration of Israel *beyond* the rebirth of the State of Israel and a return of many Jewish people to the Holy Land—as important as these have undeniably been.

When we review the prophecies of Israel's end-time restoration, a major, and frequently overlooked component of it, is the reunion the House of Judah and the exiled House of Israel, or Ephraim[7]—those of the Southern and Northern Kingdoms of Israel which divided following the death of King Solomon. Judah, of course, may be rightly considered to largely compose today's Jewish people, who have been the principal torchbearers of Israel for over two-and-a-half millennia. Ephraim composes the descendants of the exiled Northern Kingdom of Israel that was taken corporately away into Assyrian exile and deported. Various pockets of people found in remote corners of Southeast Asia, South Asia, the Middle East, Central Africa, and the Eastern Mediterranean basin, have claimed, at one point or another, to be their descendants—and today can even be recognized as their descendants by various Jewish historians and/or religious authorities in modern Israel.

According to Biblical prophecy, the Lord is going to restore those of the Northern and Southern Kingdoms of Israel in the Last Days. God's plan has always been that by restoring Israel the message of salvation may finally reach to the ends of the Earth (cf. Matthew 24:14). The challenge is with understanding who is to be reunited in the Last Days. **Do we leave much of this to our Sovereign Creator to determine when all is completed—or should we appropriate this role for ourselves?** In what way are we "Israel"? How far do we take this? What are some of the issues that have arisen?

The controversy which has arisen in the Messianic community, known as "the Two Houses of Israel," has grown steadily since the mid-to-late 1990s. Many non-Jewish Believers, who have been led to embrace their Hebraic Roots, consider themselves to be a part of the Commonwealth of Israel (Ephesians 2:11-13) or the Israel of God (Galatians 6:16), grafted-in to the olive tree (Romans 11:17-18), along with their fellow Jewish Believers. But this is not just on a spiritual or citizenship/membership level, but also on a physical level. They (strongly) assert themselves to be "of Ephraim," meaning that they are convinced that they must be descendants of the exiled Northern Kingdom of Israel deported as captives by Assyria in 722-721 B.C.E. Suffice it to say, in many sectors this viewpoint is seen by Messianic Jews with some extreme skepticism, if not hostility.

While there are doubtlessly problems which have been caused by many proponents and popular voices promoting the Two-House teaching, it is also true

---

[7] Isaiah 11:12; Jeremiah 3:18; 30:3; 31:31; 33:7, 14; 50:4, 20; Ezekiel 37:15-28; Hosea 1:11; Zechariah 8:13; 9:13; Hebrews 8:8, et. al.

that there are claims being made from Biblical history and future prophecy which must be evaluated.

The Exile of the Northern Kingdom of Israel

The period of Ancient Israel's history that directly affects the subject matter commonly called or referenced as "the Two Houses of Israel," concerns the Divided Kingdom era which occurred following the reigns of Kings David and Solomon.[8] Because of the intense idolatry and apostasy of King Solomon, God decreed that following his death, ten of the tribes would break away from the Kingdom of Israel, being given to his servant Jeroboam:

"So the LORD said to Solomon, 'Because you have done this, and you have not kept My covenant and My statutes, which I have commanded you, I will surely tear the kingdom from you, and will give it to your servant. Nevertheless I will not do it in your days for the sake of your father David, *but* I will tear it out of the hand of your son. However, I will not tear away all the kingdom, *but* I will give one tribe to your son for the sake of My servant David and for the sake of Jerusalem which I have chosen" (1 Kings 11:11-13).

Ancient Israel quantitatively experienced a split into two different Kingdoms or Houses: the Northern House or Kingdom of Israel, also known as Ephraim, and the Southern House or Kingdom of Judah. Judah primarily consisted of the tribes of Judah, Benjamin, and some Levites. Ephraim summarily entailed the remaining ten tribes: Reuben, Simeon, Levi, Zebulun, Issachar, Dan, Gad, Asher, Naphtali, Manasseh, and Ephraim (the last two represent "Joseph"). The Divided Kingdom era (Tenth-Eighth Centuries B.C.E.) is a rather complicated period of Ancient Israelite history, largely having to do with how the Southern Kingdom of Judah continued to be ruled by the House of David, and the Northern Kingdom of Israel/Ephraim was ruled by a series of successive royal dynasties. The impression that one gets, from surveying the Books of Kings and Chronicles,[9] is that corruption and idolatry were rampant all over Israel, although the Southern Kingdom was a bit more godly.

While problems with sin and infidelity to the LORD God were present in both the Southern and Northern Kingdoms, the Northern Kingdom of Israel/Ephraim had a particular problem with idolatry from the very beginning. This is best evidenced by its first king, Jeroboam, setting up temples for golden calf worship and proclaiming, "behold your gods, O Israel, that brought you up from the land of Egypt" (1 Kings 12:28). Jeroboam's justification for setting up high places in Bethel and Dan (1 Kings 12:29) was his concern that if the people of the newly established Northern Kingdom went to Jerusalem to offer sacrifices, that they would insist on reunification with the Southern Kingdom (1 Kings 12:27).

---

[8] For a summary of this time, consult C.F. Pfeiffer, "Israel, History of the People of: Divided Kingdom," in *ISBE*, 2:916-918; B.E. Kelle and B.A. Strawn, "History of Israel 5: Assyrian Period," in *Dictionary of the Old Testament Historical Books*, pp 458-478.

[9] Consult the summaries provided for the Books of Kings and Books of Chronicles in the author's workbook *A Survey of the Tanach for the Practical Messianic.*

The Divided Kingdom era existed for about two centuries, and during this time the Northern and Southern Kingdoms of Israel had good relations, bad relations, they fought with one another—and they all committed sins together. Various groups of people from the tribes of the largely idolatrous Northern Kingdom, loyal to the God of Israel, did migrate to, and were integrated into, the Southern Kingdom. Eventually, the Northern Kingdom of Israel/Ephraim saw itself caught in the politics of the wider Ancient Near East. The Northern Kingdom found itself steadily encroached upon by the forces of the expanding Assyrian Empire, which was not only a brutal, militaristic state, but also was a widescale practitioner of transplanting conquered peoples to other parts of their realm. The *ISBE* entry by C.F. Pfeiffer offers us the following useful summary of what occurred to the Northern Kingdom:

> "Israel's prosperity under Jeroboam II [cf. 2 Kings 14:28] was short-lived. Assyrian power was on the increase, and the entire Syria-Palestine area was considered suitable prey. In the reign of Menahem [cf. 2 Kings 15:14-22], Israel became tributary to Assyria. Northern Israel, including Naphtali, was carried into captivity by Tiglath-pileser (733 B.C.). His son Shalmaneser V besieged Samaria, which fell to Shalmaneser's successor, Sargon II (722 B.C.). Israel had placed confidence in Egypt for assistance against Samaria, but the days of Egyptian might were past.
>
> "The Assyrian policy of transportation had an important effect upon subsequent history. Captive peoples were transported to new areas in an attempt to break up any possible national resistance. Israelites were taken to Halah and Gozan on the banks of the river Habor in northern Mesopotamia. Similarly, peoples from Babylonia, Syria, Elam, and elsewhere were settled in Samaria (2 K. 17:24). The subsequent intermarriage of these peoples with the Israelites who were left in the land produced the people known as the Samaritans (v. 29). It was precisely this policy of transportation that made impossible the return of the people of the northern kingdom in a way comparable to the return of the Judeans after the decree of Cyrus."[10]

The *Jewish Study Bible* adds to this how "The Assyrian empire conquered the Northern Kingdom of Israel in 722 and exiled its people. The Assyrians were well-known for their massive building projects and for their cruelty in war."[11]

Two prophecies regarding the punishment to be meted by God upon the Northern Kingdom of Israel, for their sins and widescale rejection of Him, need not be overlooked. Amos 9:9 first decreed, "For behold, I am commanding, and I will shake the house of Israel among all nations as *grain* is shaken in a sieve, but not a kernel will fall to the ground." Israel would be shaken b'kol-ha'goyim (בְּכָל־הַגּוֹיִם). Hosea 8:8-9 follows this up with, "Israel is swallowed up; they are now among the nations like a vessel in which no one delights. For they have gone up to Assyria, *like* a wild donkey all alone; Ephraim has hired lovers." The verb *bala* (בָּלַע),

---

[10] Pfeiffer, "Israel, History of the People of," in *ISBE*, 2:917.

[11] *Jewish Study Bible*, 2124.

appearing in the Nifal stem (simple action, passive voice), means "**be swallowed up**" (CHALOT).[12] The observation of a Jewish commentator like S.M. Lehrman, should be well taken here: "The prophecy has been literally fulfilled. The Ten Tribes have disappeared from the scene of Jewish history, and their identity is now only a subject for far-fetched conjecture."[13]

Our job as Bible readers is to obviously stay, as best as we can, true to what the text communicates to us about what happened to the Northern Kingdom of Israel/Ephraim. The testimony of 2 Kings 17:22-23, which serves as a kind of epithet for the Northern Kingdom, is, "The sons of Israel walked in all the sins of Jeroboam which he did; they did not depart from them until the LORD removed Israel from His sight, as He spoke through all His servants the prophets. So Israel was carried away into exile from their own land to Assyria **until this day**." The key clause of interest is obviously *ad ha'yom ha'zeh* (עַד הַיּוֹם הַזֶּה), extrapolated by the NIV as, "and they are still there." The volume of Samuel-Kings is widely agreed by conservatives to have reached its final form after the Babylonian exile of the Southern Kingdom, which likely makes "until this day" in 2 Kings 17:23 an editorial remark from the Sixth-Fifth Centuries B.C.E. An additional testimony of what occurred to is seen in 1 Chronicles 5:25-26:

"But they acted treacherously against the God of their fathers and played the harlot after the gods of the peoples of the land, whom God had destroyed before them. So the God of Israel stirred up the spirit of Pul, king of Assyria, even the spirit of Tilgath-pilneser king of Assyria, and he carried them away into exile, namely the Reubenites, the Gadites and the half-tribe of Manasseh, and brought them to Halah, Habor, Hara and to the river of Gozan, **to this day**."

Some readers of 1 Chronicles 5:25-26,[14] take its statements to mean that only those from the tribes of Reuben, Gad, and half-tribe of Manasseh, were those really taken away into Assyrian exile. This does not, though, stand up well to scrutiny.

The main issue, in 1 Chronicles 5:25-26, is how the Hebrew preposition *l* (ל) functions in the clause: *l'Reuveini v'l'Gadi v'l'chatzi sheivet Menashe* (וְלַחֲצִי שֵׁבֶט מְנַשֶּׁה לְרֹאוּבֵנִי וְלַגָּדִי). The purpose of 1 Chronicles ch. 5 is to summarize a listing of the descendants of Reuben, Gad, and Manasseh, and how a great many of them were taken away into Assyrian captivity. The presence of these specific tribal names is not to detract from the many others in the Northern Kingdom of Israel who likewise went into exile; it is to instead draw the attention of the reader of these genealogies how these tribes were met with exile. The translation of the preposition *l* (ל) as "namely" fits well, following what Bill T. Arnold and John H. Choi consider "*Specification*," which "calls to attention the object of the preposition."[15]

---

[12] CHALOT, 41.

[13] Lehrman, "Hosea: Introduction and Commentary," in *Soncino Books of the Bible: The Twelve Prophets*, 30.

[14] Cf. David Rothstein, "First Chronicles," in *Jewish Study Bible*, 1724.

[15] Bill T. Arnold and John H. Choi., *A Guide to Biblical Hebrew Syntax* (New York: Cambridge University Press, 2003), 113.

Secondly, the statement of 1 Chronicles 5:25-26, as J.A. Thompson properly notes for us, "concerns the deportation of Transjordanian tribes in 734 B.C. (2 Kgs 15:29) in the days of Tiglath-Pileser III (745-727 B.C.)."[16] The chronicler intended to attach the exile of those widely from Reuben, Gad, and the half-tribe of Manasseh, to the main reason of why the Northern Kingdom was corporately dispersed with the fall of Samaria, a little more than a decade later, in 722-721 B.C.E., which took place during the reign of Shalmaneser V (727-722 B.C.E.; cf. 2 Kings 18:9). H.G.M. Williamson confirms, "Its effect is to transfer to the earlier deportation of the two and a half tribes the description and explanation of the later exile of the main part of the northern kingdom."[17] While 2 Kings 17:22-23 and 1 Chronicles 5:25-26 *together* speak of people being exiled "until this day"—a post-exilic scene—the group of 1 Chronicles 5:26-27 composing those from Reuben, Gad, and the half-tribe of Manasseh was actually exiled *earlier* (2 Kings 15:29) than the main part of the Northern Kingdom that tends to garner most attention. 2 Chronicles 10:18-19 further clarifies, regarding the split of the Northern and Southern Kingdoms:

"Then King Rehoboam sent Hadoram, who was over the forced labor, and the sons of Israel stoned him to death. And King Rehoboam made haste to mount his chariot to flee to Jerusalem. So Israel has been in rebellion against the house of David **to this day** [*ad ha'yom ha'zeh*]."

The Books of Chronicles or *Divrei HaYamim* (דברי הימים), actually called *Paraleipomenōn* (ΠΑΡΑΛΕΙΠΟΜΕΝΩΝ), meaning "things omitted" in the Greek Septuagint, often include various miscellaneous accounts from sources that were not included in the Books of Samuel-Kings. All expositors, conservative and liberal, agree that the Books of Chronicles reflect a post-exilic composition, at the earliest in the 400s B.C.E. The statement about the Northern Kingdom of Israel being in rebellion against the House of David, "to this day," is a good indication that the chronicler continued to believe that there was a rift yet to be fixed. Jewish commentator I.W. Slotki views this to mean, "The split in the kingdom was never healed."[18]

The fact that the Northern Kingdom was corporately deported, with many of the exiles scattered and assimilated into other nations, is evidenced by the fact that the Assyrian Empire would take conquered peoples and transplant them in the lands of other conquered peoples, forcing them to relocate among foreigners to decrease the possibility of rebellion. Biblical archaeologist Siegfried H. Horn summarizes,

"Conquered peoples from the western portions of the empire were resettled in Assyria and in the eastern provinces, while captives from the eastern and southern regions were resettled in the West. Thus we are told in 2 Kings 17:24 that Sargon transported the captive Israelites to Assyria and in 2 Kings 17:24 that he

---

[16] J.A. Thompson, *New American Commentary: 1,2 Chronicles* (Nashville: Broadman & Holman, 1994), 82.

[17] H.G.M. Williamson, *New Century Bible Commentary: 1 and 2 Chronicles* (Grand Rapids: Eerdmans, 1982), 67.

[18] I.W. Slotki, *Soncino Books of the Bible: Chronicles* (London: Soncino Press, 1965), 209.

repopulated the cities of Samaria with the peoples from Babylonia and Elam (southwestern Iran). More specifically, the Israelites were resettled in Halah (northeast of Nineveh), on the Habor (the Khabor River, a tributary that flows south into Euphrates from the highlands of southern Turkey and northeastern Syria), and in the highlands of the Medes (northwestern Iran)."[19]

Approximately 135 years later, between 597-587 B.C.E., the Southern Kingdom of Judah was widely deported to Babylon for also transgressing God's commands and succumbing to idolatry. Those exiles from the Southern Kingdom of Judah, however, returned to the Land of Israel 70 years later (cf. 2 Chronicles 36:21), and in spite of terrible hardships since, they continue to exist until today as the Jewish people. But those from the Northern Kingdom of Israel, aside from various family lines and groups, were never corporately heard from again.

It is from this widescale silence in Biblical history that has come forth much speculation regarding the "Ten Lost Tribes" of Israel. While much of this speculation has not at all been healthy or good, when we consider the scholastic evidence of Assyria's displacement of the Israelites, we can logically assume that many from the Northern Kingdom did become "lost" among foreign nations. Many either forgot their Israelite heritage via intermarriage and/or assimilation, or hid it from wide view, keeping it quiet as some kind of oral tradition passed down in a particular family line. The challenge for many, however, is in recognizing that our Eternal God is the One who ultimately scattered the Northern Kingdom (cf. Jeremiah 31:10). And, the exiles of the Northern Kingdom being deported and/or assimilated, is something that should be kept largely within the ancient sphere of influence of the ancient Assyrian, Babylonian, and Persian Empires—*not* Northwestern Europe and the British Isles or the South Seas and Polynesia.

Not all hope is lost for the descendants of the exiled Northern Kingdom, though. Hosea 1:10 tells us that "in the place where it is said to them, 'You are not My people,' it will be said to them, '*You are* the sons of the living God'" (cf. Romans 9:25-26; 1 Peter 2:10). **There will be a future restoration of the Southern and Northern Kingdoms.** There are *specific end-time prophecies* that detail their reunion that have yet to be accomplished. These prophecies have not been fulfilled, because if they truly were then Messiah Yeshua would be physically present in Jerusalem right now reigning over the Earth.

Key Prophecies of Israel's Restoration—Repeated

The subject matter of a larger restoration of Israel is closely intertwined with end-time prophecy. My own approach, especially given some of the controversies associated with this issue, has always been based in what I read to be unfulfilled prophecies regarding Judah, Ephraim, and their many associated companions from the nations being gathered together as one, albeit, diverse people of God. Here is a selection of just four passages that need to be seriously considered by Bible readers:

---

[19] Horn, "The Divided Monarchy," in *Ancient Israel: From Abraham to the Destruction of the Temple*, 174.

"And He will lift up a standard for the nations and assemble the banished ones of Israel, and will gather the dispersed of Judah from the four corners of the earth. Then the jealousy of Ephraim will depart, and those who harass Judah will be cut off; Ephraim will not be jealous of Judah, and Judah will not harass Ephraim. They will swoop down on the slopes of the Philistines on the west; together they will plunder the sons of the east; they will possess Edom and Moab, and the sons of Ammon will be subject to them. And the LORD will utterly destroy the tongue of the Sea of Egypt; and He will wave His hand over the River with His scorching wind; and He will strike it into seven streams and make *men* walk over dry-shod. And there will be a highway from Assyria for the remnant of His people who will be left, just as there was for Israel in the day that they came up out of the land of Egypt" (Isaiah 11:12-16).

"For there will be a day when watchmen on the hills of Ephraim call out, 'Arise, and let us go up *to* Zion, to the LORD our God.' For thus says the LORD, 'Sing aloud with gladness for Jacob, and shout among the chief of the nations; proclaim, give praise and say, "O LORD, save Your people, the remnant of Israel." Behold, I am bringing them from the north country, and I will gather them from the remote parts of the earth, among them the blind and the lame, the woman with child and she who is in labor with child, together; a great company, they will return here. With weeping they will come, and by supplication I will lead them; I will make them walk by streams of waters, on a straight path in which they will not stumble; for I am a father to Israel, and Ephraim is My firstborn.' Hear the word of the LORD, O nations, and declare in the coastlands afar off, and say, 'He who scattered Israel will gather him and keep him as a shepherd keeps his flock'" (Jeremiah 31:6-10).

"Say to them, 'Thus says the Lord GOD, "Behold, I will take the sons of Israel from among the nations where they have gone, and I will gather them from every side and bring them into their own land; and I will make them one nation in the land, on the mountains of Israel; and one king will be king for all of them; and they will no longer be two nations and no longer be divided into two kingdoms. They will no longer defile themselves with their idols, or with their detestable things, or with any of their transgressions; but I will deliver them from all their dwelling places in which they have sinned, and will cleanse them. And they will be My people, and I will be their God. My servant David will be king over them, and they will all have one shepherd; and they will walk in My ordinances and keep My statutes and observe them. They will live on the land that I gave to Jacob My servant, in which your fathers lived; and they will live on it, they, and their sons and their sons' sons, forever; and David My servant will be their prince forever. I will make a covenant of peace with them; it will be an everlasting covenant with them. And I will place them and multiply them, and will set My sanctuary in their midst forever. My dwelling place also will be with them; and I will be their God, and they will be My people. And the nations will know that I am the LORD who sanctifies Israel, when My sanctuary is in their midst forever"'" (Ezekiel 37:21-28).

"I will strengthen the house of Judah, and I will save the house of Joseph, and I will bring them back, because I have had compassion on them; and they will be as though I had not rejected them, for I am the LORD their God and I will answer them. Ephraim will be like a mighty man, and their heart will be glad as if *from* wine; indeed, their children will see *it* and be glad, their heart will rejoice in the LORD. I will whistle for them to gather them together, for I have redeemed them; and they will be as numerous as they were before. When I scatter them among the peoples, they will remember Me in far countries, and they with their children will live and come back. I will bring them back from the land of Egypt and gather them from Assyria; and I will bring them into the land of Gilead and Lebanon until no *room* can be found for them" (Zechariah 10:6-10).

How some of the prophecies regarding the manner in which both Judah and Ephraim will be reunited and return to the Land of Israel, are specifically unknown at this point in history. Affirming that these prophecies are unfulfilled, many of the circumstances surrounding their completion will undoubtedly become clearer as time moves forward and we get closer and closer to the return of Yeshua. There is much witnessed within these various prophetic words, that needs to be seriously factored into one's end-time scenario(s). As things stand today, though, too many have not seriously considered the reunification of Judah and Ephraim as an end-time "event," no different than the rise of the antimessiah/antichrist or the arrival of a mark of the beast economic system.

Ezekiel 37:15-28 is probably the most frequently referenced word concerning a greater restoration of Israel. Ezekiel 37:15-19 speaks of Judah, Ephraim, and associated companions from the nations coming together, as one in the hand of the Son of Man:

"The word of the LORD came again to me saying, 'And you, son of man, take for yourself one stick and write on it, "For Judah and for the sons of Israel, his companions"; then take another stick and write on it, "For Joseph, the stick of Ephraim and all the house of Israel, his companions." Then join them for yourself one to another into one stick, that they may become one in your hand. When the sons of your people speak to you saying, "Will you not declare to us what you mean by these?" say to them, "Thus says the Lord GOD, 'Behold, I will take the stick of Joseph, which is in the hand of Ephraim, and the tribes of Israel, his companions; and I will put them with it, with the stick of Judah, and make them one stick, and they will be one in My hand.'"

We further see in the two-stick oracle how there will be an everlasting covenant of peace established (Ezekiel 37:26a), that God's Sanctuary will be established (Ezekiel 37:26b), that His dwelling place will be in the midst of Israel (Ezekiel 37:27), and perhaps most importantly: "Then the nations shall know that I the LORD sanctify Israel, when my sanctuary is among them forevermore[20]" (Ezekiel 37:28, NRSV). **It is obvious that we have yet to reach such a point in human history.**

A big problem that has been caused, by many popular voices and leaders within the Two-House sub-movement, is not drawing the attention of Messianic Believers to the fact that according to prophecy, more is on the horizon in terms of

---

[20] Heb. *b'heyot miqdashi b'tokam l'olam* (בִּהְיוֹת מִקְדָּשִׁי בְּתוֹכָם לְעוֹלָם).

Israel's restoration. Their challenge is in communicating that there are **three**, not two groups of people, who are to be brought together. The very fact that many of them would label themselves "Two-House," can give the distinct impression that all God is concerned with in His plan for the ages is *just* Judah and Ephraim. This is not true, as a third group—*the companions* (Ezekiel 37:16, 19)—the nations or the Gentiles of Planet Earth, are also included in the restoration process.[21] The Lord has a global vision for all of humanity that extends well beyond the people of Israel themselves. *Israel is His tool by which the whole world may be saved.*

Much of the discussion and debate surrounding the Two-House teaching, within today's broad Messianic movement, has not been focused around prophecies like those listed above. Because of many abuses regarding the subject matter of the "Ten Lost Tribes" seen in history, many of today's Messianic leaders refuse to touch the subject matter—if for any other reason because they think it is just too controversial. Is this really a responsible approach, especially when Bible readers ask legitimate questions about an oracle witnessed in Scripture like Ezekiel 37:15-28? While there are specific details regarding the restoration of Israel, which can only be fully understood subsequent to the Second Coming of Yeshua, the observations of Peter C. Craigie on Ezekiel 37:15-28 have to be noted:

> "It is difficult to know how to apply or interpret the oracle. The northern kingdom no longer existed, and many of its peoples had been scattered and long absorbed by other cultures. How could it be restored to the land? Recognising this mystery, several cults and sects in recent centuries have sought to identify themselves with the lost tribes of Israel, and thus find a place in prophecy. But it is safer to recognise the necessary element of mystery involved in any language addressing the future. **The main thrust of the prophecy is that *all* of God's people would somehow participate in the future restoration; how this could be is not known, yet it is the essence of the prophet's affirmation**....It is clear, with the benefit of hindsight, that the prophecy concerns a distant future. The preceding passage, concerning the dry bones [Ezekiel 15:1-14], could be interpreted simply in terms of exiles returning to their homeland. But this oracle moves out of the realm of history, as we commonly understand it, and anticipates a future time in which God will bring a new kind of reality into being. While the precise significance of each part of the prophecy may elude us, the broad thrust in clear: God had not forgotten his people and had determined their restoration" (emphasis mine).[22]

Craigie's approach should be the perspective of all of us, as God's sovereign plan for His people simply manifests as salvation history moves forward in time. Who one specifically is, as a person in the flesh, *ultimately does not matter*. The participants of the prophecy are stated to be Judah, Israel/Ephraim, and their many companions or associates. Much of what is to transpire is unknown to us at present, but as many interpreters of Ezekiel 37:15-28 have concluded, the two-stick

---

[21] This has just been discussed in Chapter 2, "What About 'the Gentiles'?"

[22] Peter C. Craigie, *Daily Study Bible Series: Ezekiel* (Philadelphia: Westminster Press, 1983), pp 263-264.

oracle has a unique place within the Tanach, to convey a grand message of unity and camaraderie for all who look to the God of Israel for deliverance.[23]

There Were Northern Kingdom Israelites Who Became "Jews"

There is often a great omission on the part of many people within today's Two-House sub-movement, recognizing the historical fact that a sizeable enough sector of people from the Northern Kingdom of Israel/Ephraim became integrated into the Southern Kingdom of Judah, and thus would be considered to be "Jews" until this day. A commentator like H.L. Ellison indicates for us how, "2 Ch[ronicles] 11:16;[24] 15:9;[25] 30:11,[26] 18;[27] 34:9[28] stress that a considerable number of northerners had joined Judah at various times."[29] A proper approach is needed regarding the fact that people from the Northern Kingdom, those loyal to the God of Israel and who rejected the idolatry established by Jeroboam (2 Chronicles 11:16; 15:9), did migrate to the Southern Kingdom, and were integrated into it.

A common claim made against a future reunion of people from the Northern and Southern Kingdoms of Israel, is that people from all Twelve Tribes of Israel are represented among today's Jews, and there is apparently no need to anticipate any future restoration of Judah and Ephraim. But, does some level of representation, of persons from all Twelve Tribes of Israel within the Jewish community, constitute a complete, corporate reunion of Israel as anticipated by the Prophets? Let us engage with the relevant Biblical data that demonstrates how various Northern Kingdom Israelites became integrated into the Southern Kingdom of Judah.

1 Chronicles 9:3, for example, states how "Some of the sons of Judah, of the sons of Benjamin and of the sons of Ephraim and Manasseh lived in Jerusalem." This needs to be kept in view of how after the end of the Southern Kingdom's Babylonian exile, the people started returning to where they had previously lived (1 Chronicles 9:2). Why would those from the tribes of Ephraim and Manasseh, which were clearly a part of the Northern Kingdom, return and live in Jerusalem? Would it not make sense for them to reclaim their holdings in the northern regions of the Land of Israel? One of the factors that can elude Bible readers, is precisely how these people from Ephraim and Manasseh, were not those who had been

---

[23] For a further, and much more detailed investigation, consult Chapter 6, "Ezekiel 37:15-28: Have the Two Sticks Been Reunited?"

[24] "Those from all the tribes of Israel who set their hearts on seeking the LORD God of Israel followed them to Jerusalem, to sacrifice to the LORD God of their fathers" (2 Chronicles 11:16).

[25] "He gathered all Judah and Benjamin and those from Ephraim, Manasseh and Simeon who resided with them, for many defected to him from Israel when they saw that the LORD his God was with him" (2 Chronicles 15:9).

[26] "Nevertheless some men of Asher, Manasseh and Zebulun humbled themselves and came to Jerusalem" (2 Chronicles 30:11).

[27] "For a multitude of the people, even many from Ephraim and Manasseh, Issachar and Zebulun, had not purified themselves, yet they ate the Passover otherwise than prescribed" (2 Chronicles 30:18).

[28] "They came to Hilkiah the high priest and delivered the money that was brought into the house of God, which the Levites, the doorkeepers, had collected from Manasseh and Ephraim, and from all the remnant of Israel, and from all Judah and Benjamin and the inhabitants of Jerusalem" (2 Chronicles 34:9).

[29] H.L. Ellison, "1 and 2 Chronicles," in NBCR, pp 375-376.

taken into Assyrian exile, and then somehow joined the Jewish community in its Babylonian exile. Rather, these people—whose ancestors had clearly been a part of the Northern Kingdom at one point—*never went* into Assyrian exile. They were integrated into the Southern Kingdom before the Northern Kingdom's downfall, they settled in the capital of Jerusalem, they went into Babylonian captivity, and then they returned. Noting the genealogical list of 1 Chronicles ch. 9, the *ArtScroll Tanach* indicates how "This chapter explains why only some of the tribal genealogies were given at length in the preceding chapters. They were the ones who lived among the people of Judah, and returned with them from the Babylonian exile."[30]

In the Tanach, the Northern Kingdom of Israel/Ephraim is regarded as being corporately exiled by Assyria (2 Kings 17:23), but it is clear from any objective reading of the Historical Books that not all of the people from the Northern Kingdom were taken away. The Passover commemoration of King Hezekiah of Judah (715-690 B.C.E.; 2 Chronicles 30:6-15), definitely did include people from the Northern Kingdom of Israel, specified to be "those of you who escaped *and* are left from the hand of the kings of Assyria[31]" (2 Chronicles 30:6), as they had avoided capture and exile.[32] While many of those left from the fallen Northern Kingdom mocked the idea of remembering Passover (2 Chronicles 30:10), some of them did accept Hezekiah's invitation (2 Chronicles 30:11), including "many from Ephraim and Manasseh, Issachar and Zebulun" (2 Chronicles 30:18).

Later, during the reign of King Josiah of Judah (649–609 B.C.E.), the Temple in Jerusalem was repaired, and it is recorded how "the doorkeepers, had collected [money] from Manasseh and Ephraim, and from all the remnant of Israel, and from all Judah and Benjamin and the inhabitants of Jerusalem" (2 Chronicles 34:9). These people are labeled as *sh'eirit Yisrael* (שְׁאֵרִית יִשְׂרָאֵל). It is obvious that they are not all of the Northern Kingdom corporate, but instead those who escaped captivity and exile, constituting a remnant.

---

[30] Scherman and Zlotowitz, *ArtScroll Tanach*, pp 1894-1895.

[31] Heb. *v'yashov el-ha'peleitah ha'nisheret l'khem m'kaf malkei' Ashur* (הַנִּשְׁאֶרֶת לָכֶם מִכַּף מַלְכֵי אַשּׁוּר וְיָשֹׁב אֶל־הַפְּלֵיטָה); "and he will return again the remnant of you, who have escaped out of the hand of the kings of Assur" (Jerusalem Bible-Koren); "and He will return to the remnant of you still left from the hands of the kings of Assyria" (Keter Crown Bible).

Not to be overlooked here is the clause *ha'peleitah ha'nisheret*, "those of you who escaped *and* are left" (NASU), meaning those of the Northern Kingdom of Israel/Ephraim who avoided exile by the Assyrians. Appearing in the Nifal stem (simple action, passive voice), the verb *sha'ar* (שָׁאַר) means, "**be left, over, remain**" (*CHALOT*, 357). This is "the remnant of you that still remains from the hands of the kings of Assyria" (ATS).

A less than literal rendering would appear in a version like the RSV, which says, "that he may turn again to the remnant of you who have escaped from the hand of the kings of Assyria." Interestingly enough, though, a less-than-literal CJB has the much more preferred, "Then he will return to those of you who remain, who escaped capture by the kings of Ashur."

[32] "[2 Chronicles] 30:6, like the rest of the section, implies that the Northern Kingdom had fallen to the Assyrians, who are pictured as leaving behind only a 'remnant'" (Richard J. Coggins, "1 and 2 Chronicles," in James D.G. Dunn and John W. Rogerson, eds., *Eerdmans Commentary on the Bible* [Grand Rapids: Eerdmans, 2003], 308).

The resettlement of outsiders from the east, by the Assyrians, to the former holdings of the Northern Kingdom, and their intermarriage with those who remained, needs to also be kept in mind. This produced the people which became known as the Samaritans, who had a hybrid religion of worshiping the God of Israel *along with* various pagan customs (2 Kings 17:24-41). The Samaritans continued to exist at the time of Yeshua, being treated with a great deal of disgust and contempt by much of the First Century Jewish community. The Samaritans did constitute, however, one of the well-known segments of people who were descended from the tribes of the fallen Northern Kingdom.

In terms of the Assyrian exile of those from the Northern Kingdom, there are indications that not all of those taken away were culturally and religiously assimilated, forgetting who they were as Israelites. In the Apocrypha, we see the account of the family a Northern Kingdom exile, Tobit, who remained faithful to the God of Israel while in Nineveh. Tobit specifies that he was of the tribe of Naphtali:

"I, Tobit, walked in the ways of truth and righteousness all the days of my life, and I performed many acts of charity to my brethren and countrymen who went with me into the land of the Assyrians, to Nineveh. Now when I was in my own country, in the land of Israel, while I was still a young man, the whole tribe of Naphtali my forefather deserted the house of Jerusalem. This was the place which had been chosen from among all the tribes of Israel, where all the tribes should sacrifice and where the temple of the dwelling of the Most High was consecrated and established for all generations for ever" (Tobit 1:3-4).[33]

Obviously, the account of Tobit details the early period of the Northern Kingdom exiles' displacement to Assyria. The example of such a person like Tobit, though, may be the exception. Assuming that (enough of) his family remained faithful to the God of Israel while in Assyrian exile, they may have integrated themselves into the larger Jewish world exiled to Babylon, especially as all exiles were emancipated by the Persian Empire when it finally became dominant. A standard view present, among some readers and interpreters, is that when Babylon was engulfed by Persia, a major part of the exiles made their way back to the Land of Israel—including the so-called "Lost Tribes." To an extent this is true. Many of the Northern Kingdom exiles did not forget their Israelite heritage and integrated themselves into the Jewish groups returning to the Land of Israel from Babylon.

In the First Century, at the dedication of Yeshua the Messiah at the Temple, we see a reference to "Anna the daughter of Phanuel, of the tribe of Asher" (Luke 2:36). No detailed backstory is given regarding Anna's family, meaning that all we

---

[33] For readers of the Book of Tobit, it needs to be noted that there is a significant textual variant in Tobit 11:17, which reads either *pasi tois en Nineuē adelphois autou* (πᾶσι τοῖς ἐν Νινευη ἀδελφοῖς αὐτοῦ), "all his brethren in Nineveh" (RSV; cf. LXE, ESV), or *pasin tois Ioudaiois tois ousin en Nineuē* (πᾶσιν τοῖς Ἰουδαίοις τοῖς οὖσιν ἐν Νινευη), "all the Jews who were in Nineveh" (NRSV; cf. NEB, REB). The former is what would be historically correct.

Cf. Alfred Rahlfs, ed., *Septuaginta* (Stuttgart: Deutsche Bibelgesellschaft, 1979), 1030; Alexander A. Di Lella, "Tobit," in Albert Pietersma and Benjamin G. Wright, eds., *A New English Translation of the Septuagint* (Oxford and New York: Oxford University Press, 2007), pp 472-473.

can safely conclude is that her original ancestors were a part of the Northern Kingdom. Anna's ancestors could have been like Tobit, and remained somewhat faithful to the Lord when in Assyrian exile. Or, Anna's ancestors could have migrated to the Southern Kingdom during the Divided Kingdom era, only to be taken into Babylonian captivity, and then returned when Persia became the dominant Ancient Near Eastern power. The thought of David H. Stern, in his *Jewish New Testament Commentary*, regarding Anna of the tribe of Asher, is that "individual families could preserve their identities and transmit their genealogies."[34]

There were enough Northern Kingdom Israelites, who had integrated themselves into the Southern Kingdom of Judah—either by migrating south during the Divided Kingdom period, or with some returning with those exiled to Babylon—that by the First Century there were indeed "Northern Kingdom Jews." But does the presence of people descended from all Twelve Tribes, present within the Jewish community up until today, qualify as "fulfillment" of the prophecies detailing a grand restoration of Judah and Ephraim? Some—especially in much of Messianic Judaism—say yes, but they do not tend to substantiate why they think so. We should be much more cautious, and not think that a representation here or there of various Jews in history, having a descent from one of the ten tribes of the old Northern Kingdom, justifies a complete restoration of Israel.

Remarking on 2 Kings 17:23—"So the Israelites were deported from their land to Assyria, as is still the case" (NJPS)—Terrence E. Fretheim gives us some important direction:

"The Israelites remain exiled to the time of the narrator (v. 23). We know that they became so thoroughly integrated into these foreign populations that they ceased to exist as a people (hence 'the ten lost tribes'); yet many fled to the south and were preserved within that grouping of the people of God (see also 2 Chron. 30:6-11)."[35]

To this, we can add the observations of Hebrew Christian scholar Alfred Edersheim, who in his classic work *The Life and Times of Jesus the Messiah*, said, "there is reason to believe that part of them [the Northern Kingdom], at least, had coalesced with their brethren of the later exile."[36] He references a Talmudic statement for this, **"Ten castes came up from Babylonia"** (b.*Kiddushin* 69b).[37] Yet, Edersheim goes on to notably conclude, "Still the great mass of the ten tribes was in the days of Christ, as in our own, lost to the Hebrew nation."[38]

Are there members of the Northern Kingdom of Israel/Ephraim found among today's Jewish people? Yes. Are there descendants of the Northern Kingdom of Israel/Ephraim "out there" in the nations today as well? Yes, even though their

---

[34] Stern, *Jewish New Testament Commentary*, 110.
[35] Terrence E. Fretheim, *Westminster Bible Companion: First and Second Kings* (Louisville: Westminster John Knox, 1999), 193.
[36] Alfred Edersheim, *The Life and Times of Jesus the Messiah* (Peabody, MA: Hendrickson, 1993), 11.
[37] *The Babylonian Talmud: A Translation and Commentary.*
[38] Edersheim, 11.

descendants have been customarily sought for within the spheres of influence of both Ancient Israel and the ancient Assyrian, Babylonian, and Persian Empires (namely Southeast Asia, South Asia, the Middle East, Central Africa, and the Eastern Mediterranean basin). **There can admittedly be a tension** between the fact that there were Northern Kingdom Israelites who somehow became a part of the Southern Kingdom of Judah, and are to be reckoned as "Jews" today—versus the eschatological reality that there is a larger restoration of Israel prophesied in the Tanach, which surely did not occur after the conclusion of the Babylonian exile.

Were the Lost Tribes really lost?
How many were really deported to Assyria?

A Bible teacher, or a Bible reader, has to have a great deal of courage and fortitude when approaching the subject matter of the exiled Northern Kingdom of Israel, because of the great number of abuses which have stigmatized the issue of the Ten Lost Tribes over the centuries. In a relatively conservative resource like the *Archaeological Study Bible*, for example, one finds the following remark issued on 2 Kings 17:3-6:

"Much mythology has been developed around the theme of the so-called ten lost tribes of Israel. A close examination of Assyrian records reveals that the deportations approximated only a limited percentage of the population..."[39]

No one can deny the fact that throughout history since the downfall of the Northern Kingdom, various sectarian associations have arisen—which to some degree or another have claimed that *they are* the Lost Ten Tribes of Israel. **Their views need to be significantly avoided.** The liberal *JPS Guide: The Jewish Bible* is a bit fairer, though, in how it states "After the Assyrian conquest, the scattered northern tribes become known as the Ten Lost Tribes. They never return to Canaan, giving birth to numerous tales and legends about their history and whereabouts."[40]

But what do we actually classify as "mythology" as it pertains to the Northern Kingdom of Israel? Claiming that this tribe "went here," and that tribe "went there," with no documentation or proof of substance? Or, affirming from the prophecies of Holy Scripture, that a larger restoration of Israel is to be anticipated *and* actually occur immediately prior to the return of the Messiah?

About as "mythological" as any of us should be allowed to get, is perhaps seen in John Milton's 1671 work *Paradise Regained*, where it is asserted that the exiles of the Northern Kingdom will come back when the Messiah reigns over the world:

---

[39] Duane A. Garrett, ed., et. al., *NIV Archaeological Study Bible* (Grand Rapids: Zondervan, 2005), 555.
[40] *JPS Guide: The Jewish Bible*, 182.

In David's royal seat, his true successor,
Deliverance of thy brethren, those ten tribes
Whose offspring in his territory yet serve
In Habor, and among the Medes dispersed,
Ten sons of Jacob, two of Joseph lost
Thus long from Israel; serving as of old
Their fathers in the land of Egypt served,
This offer sets before thee to deliver.
These if from servitude thou shalt restore
To their inheritance, then, nor till then,
Thou on the throne of David in full glory,
From Egypt to Euphrates and beyond
Shalt reign, and Rome or Caesar need not fear.
To whom our savior answered thus unmoved.[41]

All Milton did was to paraphrase a selection of Tanach verses and prophecies on the matter.

A wide number of the contemporary evangelical Christian materials, which in some form or another mention what happened to the Northern Kingdom of Israel, tend to be concerned with refuting the abuses of Nineteenth and Twentieth Century British-Israelism, and figures like Herbert W. Armstrong, more than anything else.[42] This material, while brief, tends to completely sidestep or ignore Bible prophecies which indicate that a larger restoration of Israel—*including* the return of the descendants of the exiled Northern Kingdom—is yet to occur. Author William Varner of the book *Jacob's Dozen*, which is frequently encountered in many sectors of today's Messianic community, is one of these people. He makes some statements about the numbers of people taken away by the Assyrians, concluding that there were actually no ten tribes of Israel ever taken into exile:

"Excavations have revealed that the population of Judah rapidly increased after the fall of the northern kingdom as a result of the many refugees mentioned in 2 Chronicles 11:14-16. Furthermore, archaeologists have uncovered the annals of the Assyrian Sargon, in which he tells that he carried away only 27,290 people and 50 chariots (*Biblical Archaeologist*, VI, 1943, p. 58). Since estimates of the population of the northern kingdom at that time range from 400,000 to 500,000, clearly less than one-twentieth of the population was deported, primarily the leaders from the area around Samaria. The ten tribes, therefore, were never *lost* because they were never deported! Their kingdom was destroyed and ceased to exist, but most of them stayed..."[43]

Is Varner at all correct with what he says here, especially given how God Himself said in Jeremiah 7:15, "I will cast you out of My sight, as I have cast out all

[41] John Milton, *The Major Works* (New York: Oxford University Press, 2003), 652.

[42] Cf. William Varner, *Jacob's Dozen: A Prophetic Look at the Tribes of Israel* (Bellmawr, NJ: Friends of Israel Gospel Ministry, 1987), pp 94-95.

[43] Varner, pp 96-97.

your brothers, all the offspring of Ephraim[44]"? In the previous section, we have already noted how people from the Northern Kingdom became integrated into the Southern Kingdom. Varner's claim is that there were really no people from the Northern Kingdom quantitatively taken into Assyrian captivity—"The ten tribes...were never *lost* because they were never deported,"[45] as he says—other than just 27,290 people. These statements from a fundamentalist Christian are notably contrary to my relatively liberal Hebrew civilization professor at the University of Oklahoma (2001), Dr. Daniel C. Snell, who believed in JEDP Pentateuchal source criticism and held to a rather low view of the reliability of the Tanach's Historical Books. In his book *Life in the Ancient Near East*, he just asserts "...the northern kingdom succumbed earlier to Assyrian exile..."[46]

Most of the attention, regarding the exile of the Northern Kingdom of Israel, is understandably given to the final fall of its capital, Samaria, as summarized by 2 Kings 17:3-6:

"Shalmaneser king of Assyria came up against him, and Hoshea became his servant and paid him tribute. But the king of Assyria found conspiracy in Hoshea, who had sent messengers to So king of Egypt and had offered no tribute to the king of Assyria, as *he had done* year by year; so the king of Assyria shut him up and bound him in prison. Then the king of Assyria invaded the whole land and went up to Samaria and besieged it three years. In the ninth year of Hoshea, the king of Assyria captured Samaria and carried Israel away into exile to Assyria, and settled them in Halah and Habor, *on* the river of Gozan, and in the cities of the Medes."

Following this, it is asserted in the narrative of the history, that by the time of the final composition of Samuel-Kings, these people taken into exile were still there (2 Kings 17:23). As Bible readers, this is where our ultimate loyalty must be found, as according to Scripture, those Northern Kingdom Israelites taken captive by Assyria from Samaria, did not return back home to the Land of Israel. But does this mean that only a small number of people were exiled by Assyria, thus implying that there were no Ten Lost Tribes of Israel? The number of 27,290 taken away, is frequently referenced in a wide array of study Bibles accessible to the normal layperson.[47] This number itself is a part of ancient, extant archaeological finds, which have been collected and translated into English by Ancient Near Eastern specialists. "The Fall of Samaria" from the reign of Sargon II (721-705), paralleling 2 Kings 17:4ff, details,

---

[44] Heb. *et-kol-achei'khem et kol-zera Efraim* (אֶת־כָּל־אֲחֵיכֶם אֵת כָּל־זֶרַע אֶפְרָיִם).

[45] Ibid., 97.

[46] Daniel C. Snell, *Life in the Ancient Near East* (New Haven and London: Yale University Press, 1997), 133.

[47] These include, but are not limited to: Herbert G. May and Bruce M. Metzger, eds., *The New Oxford Annotated Bible With the Apocrypha*, RSV (New York: Oxford University Press, 1977), 478; Kenneth L. Barker, ed., et. al., *NIV Study Bible* (Grand Rapids: Zondervan, 2002), pp 555-556; Claude F. Mariottini, "2 Kings," in Walter J. Harrelson, ed., et. al., *New Interpreter's Study Bible*, NRSV (Nashville: Abingdon, 2003), 553; *Archaeological Study Bible*, 554.

"I besieged and conquered Samaria (*Sa-me-ri-na*), led away as booty 27,290 inhabitants of it. I formed from among them a contingent of 50 chariots and made remaining (inhabitants) assume their (social) positions. I installed over them an officer of mine and imposed upon them the tribute of the former king."[48]

Many people just stop examining the issue of how many people were taken away from the Northern Kingdom by Assyria, but there is actually more Biblical data to be reckoned with. There was a previous assault recorded of how during the reign of King Pekah (737-732 B.C.E.) of the Northern Kingdom, Tiglath-Pileser of Assyria (745–727 B.C.E) carried a significant number away from the northern territories of Israel/Ephraim. In *A Biblical History of Israel* by Ian Provan, V. Philips Long, and Tremper Longman III, it is summarized how "During the reign of Pekahiah's successor Pekah…we read in both Kings and Chronicles of the Assyrian annexation of much of Israel's northern and eastern territory, and the deportation to Assyria of a significant percentage of her population (2 Kgs. 15:29-31; 1 Chr 5:26)."[49] Also to be considered is how during the reign of King Hezekiah of Judah (715-690 B.C.E.), Sennacherib of of Assyria (704-681 B.C.E) launched an attack on the Southern Kingdom and on Jerusalem:

Tiglath-Pileser of Assyria: "In the days of Pekah king of Israel, Tiglath-pileser king of Assyria came and captured Ijon and Abel-beth-maacah and Janoah and Kedesh and Hazor and Gilead and Galilee, all the land of Naphtali; and he carried them captive to Assyria. And Hoshea the son of Elah made a conspiracy against Pekah the son of Remaliah, and struck him and put him to death and became king in his place, in the twentieth year of Jotham the son of Uzziah. Now the rest of the acts of Pekah and all that he did, behold, they are written in the Book of the Chronicles of the Kings of Israel" (2 Kings 15:29-31).

Sennacherib of Assyria: "Now in the fourteenth year of King Hezekiah, Sennacherib king of Assyria came up against all the fortified cities of Judah and seized them. Then Hezekiah king of Judah sent to the king of Assyria at Lachish, saying, 'I have done wrong. Withdraw from me; whatever you impose on me I will bear.' So the king of Assyria required of Hezekiah king of Judah three hundred talents of silver and thirty talents of gold" (2 Kings 18:13-14; cf. Isaiah 36:1ff).

When these Biblical accounts are taken into consideration, as well as the extant Assyrian historical records that confirm them—one finds that there were far more than just 27,290 people taken into Assyrian exile. K.A. Kitchen is compiler of the massive work *On the Reliability of the Old Testament* (Grand Rapids: Eerdmans, 2003), a definite powerhouse in conservative Biblical scholarship. This resource has

---

[48] A. Leo Oppenheim, trans., "Assyrian and Babylonian Historical Texts," in James B. Pritchard, ed., *The Ancient Near East Volume I: An Anthology of Texts and Pictures* (Princeton, NJ: Princeton University Press, 1958), 195.

[49] Iain Provan, V. Philips Long, and Tremper Longman III, *A Biblical History of Israel* (Louisville: Westminster John Knox, 2003), 270.

put together a great deal of external data from Ancient Near Eastern civilizations contemporary to Ancient Israel, confirming the veracity of the Hebrew Tanach. This is what Kitchen has to say about those who were taken captive by the Assyrian Empire, factoring in the Biblical information seen in 2 Kings 15:29-31; 17:1-23; and 18:13-14:

> "Tiglath-pileser III removed people from Galilee and environs in the 730s; Shalmaneser V and Sargon II between them sent away many Israelites to eastern lands in 722-720; and Sennacherib did this to Judah in 701. Tiglath-pileser III took 13,520 people (totaled from lesser amounts—226, 400 + x, 656, and [lost]). Then Sargon II boasts of having removed 27,290 (var. 27,280) people from Samaria. And in 701 Sennacherib claimed to have reduced forty-six of Hezekiah's walled towns and to have taken 200,150 people from them. Such measures did not necessarily depopulate a region entirely, and some Assyrian kings brought in new populations from elsewhere (Sargon II and 2 Kings 17; contrast Tiglath-pileser III). But 'the Assyrian exile' of both Israelites and Judeans was considerable—and in the former case, permanent."[50]

According to Kitchen and his sources, some 13,520 people were taken away by the Assyrians in the exile of 2 Kings 15:29-31 (cf. 1 Chronicles 5:26). Following this were the 27,290 people taken away after the fall of Samaria in 2 Kings 17:1-23. Unlike what William Varner has done in his book *Jacob's Dozen*, K.A. Kitchen has referenced not only 13,520 more from the Northern Kingdom of Israel taken away into Assyrian exile—but he has perhaps most shockingly referenced that in the siege upon the Southern Kingdom of Judah seen in 2 Kings 18:13-14, some 200,150 people were taken away! "The Siege of Jerusalem" from the reign of Sennacherib (704-681 B.C.E.), details,

> "As to Hezekiah, the Jew, he did not submit to my yoke, I laid siege to 46 of his strong cities, walled forts and to the countless small villages in their vicinity, and conquered (them) by means of well-stamped (earth-)ramps, and battering-rams brought (thus) near (to the walls) (combined with) the attack by foot soldiers, (using) mines, breeches as well as sapper work. I drove out (of them) 200,150 people, young and old, male and female, horses, mules, donkeys, camels, big and small cattle beyond counting, and considered (them) booty."[51]

If we were to only go by the numbers from extant Assyrian records—more people were presumably taken into exile from the Southern Kingdom of Judah than the Northern Kingdom of Israel/Ephraim—in the course of Assyria's expansion into the region. Recognizing how there were people from the Northern Kingdom who had migrated into the Southern Kingdom, since the time of the division, it would seem likely that among the 200,150 taken by Sennacherib were a large number not only of Southern Kingdom Israelites, but Northern Kingdom

---

[50] Kitchen, *On the Reliability of the Old Testament*, 65.
[51] *The Ancient Near East Volume I*, 200.
This is actually noted in the *Archaeological Study Bible*, 558 in its notes on 2 Kings 18:13-14.

Israelites who had relocated south. Could there have been more taken away, than those just seen in the Assyrian records? Yes. But the ANE data currently available confirms that there was a substantial number taken away into Assyrian captivity, a wide number of whom then probably assimilated away and forgot its Israelite heritage after a few generations.

That a significant judgment would be issued by God upon the Northern Kingdom of Israel, especially for the opulence and oppression caused by the wealthy, is certain. Amos 4:1-3 decreed, "Hear this word, you cows of Bashan who are on the mountain of Samaria, who oppress the poor, who crush the needy, who say to your husbands, 'Bring now, that we may drink!' The Lord GOD has sworn by His holiness, 'Behold, the days are coming upon you when they will take you away with meat hooks, and the last of you with fish hooks. You will go out *through* breaches *in the walls*, each one straight before her, and you will be cast to Harmon,' declares the LORD." Amos 5:3 follows this up with a very sobering word: "For thus says the Lord GOD, 'The city which goes forth a thousand *strong* will have a hundred left, and the one which goes forth a hundred *strong* will have ten left to the house of Israel.'" What does this declaration imply regarding the Assyrian siege upon the Northern Kingdom? Amos 9:10 further states, "All the sinners of My people will die by the sword, those who say, 'The calamity will not overtake or confront us.'"

During the Assyrian encroachment upon the Northern Kingdom of Israel, and the subsequent battles that ensued, it is likely probable that a wide number of the civilian population became collateral damage, meeting the destiny of the sword.[52] The impression that we get from Amos 5:3, for example, is that as high as ninety-percent of some of its towns' populations, or at least its fighting force, would be decimated by war. Of course in warfare, many civilians are able to escape as refugees—and surely many from the Northern Kingdom of Israel made it to the Southern Kingdom of Judah. It is also possible that other groups of civilians from the Northern Kingdom escaped elsewhere within the immediate Eastern Mediterranean. The word of Hosea 9:17, regarding those of Ephraim, is that "My God will cast them away because they have not listened to Him; and they will be wanderers among the nations [*b'goyim*, בַּגּוֹיִם]." Thankfully, a major theme of the Prophets is that on a future day the Kingdoms of Israel and Judah will be formally reunited.

When someone in today's Messianic community, who asks questions about what happened to the Northern Kingdom of Israel/Ephraim—and is then handed a copy of a publication like Varner's *Jacob's Dozen*—one should wonder why no attention is expelled at all to various prophetic words that speak of a reunion of Judah and Ephraim subsequent to the eschaton. It is inappropriate, both Biblically

---

[52] K.A. Kitchen, *The Bible In Its World: The Bible & Archaeology Today* (Exeter: Paternoster, 1977), pp 112-113 details how brutal some of this was:

"Tiglath-pileser III devastated northern Israel, including Hazor (2 Kings 15:29) where have been found eloquent traces of the ferocity of that destruction in a layer of ashes a metre thick over the ruined buildings."

and historically, to act as though there was only a small number of people taken into exile by Assyria. It might be "easier" to ignore or disregard sections of Scripture that speak of the future destiny of the descendants of the exiled Northern Kingdom of Israel—given abuses that have transpired, per British-Israelism or Armstrongism. *But ignoring the implications of Tanach prophecies like Isaiah 11:12-16; Jeremiah 31:6-10; Ezekiel 37:15-28; Zechariah 10:6-10, would be irresponsible for any Bible teacher to do.* In fact, Christians ignoring Tanach prophecies that speak of a larger restoration of Israel, perhaps because others have abused them—is not too dissimilar from how many Jews in history have ignored the Messianic claims of Jesus of Nazareth, because of the unfortunate fact of Christian anti-Semitism.

Where some of today's conservative Christians do not want to consider the implications of what is to happen in the future, regarding the reunion of Judah and Ephraim—some liberal Bible scholars will stridently step in and correctly acknowledge that the Prophets indeed spoke of future activities of the exiled Northern Kingdom of Israel. Those who would disregard Tanach prophecies that speak of a larger restoration of Israel to come, **need to take serious notice** of how liberals have often approached them.

A liberal Jewish scholar like Zvi Ben-Dor Benite, in his book *The Ten Lost Tribes*, is one who is marked by his commitment to be an historical minimalist, meaning that he has a very low estimation for the Tanach's reliability. He is one who specifically believes that "the first book of Kings...is considered by biblical scholars to be almost entirely fictional,"[53] meaning that there really was no Kingdom of Israel ruled by a King David.[54] Ben-Dor Benite's view of 2 Kings is that there is much pseudo-history interspersed within the text, and that its "biblical depiction exaggerates the totality of the deportations as part of a specifically Israelite narrative of loss and promised redemption."[55] In terms of the future, though, Ben-Dor Benite honestly recognizes that the Prophets anticipate a regathering of the exiled Northern Kingdom back to the fold of Israel.[56] But, unlike a conservative who would treat such oracles as being Divinely inspired by God Himself, Ben-Dor Benite's conclusion is that the Prophets were actually master manipulators. He summarizes his view as follows:

---

[53] Zvi Ben-Dor Benite, *The Ten Lost Tribes: A World History* (New York: Oxford University Press, 2009), 8.

The two books previously referenced in this chapter, *A Biblical History of Israel* and *On the Reliability of the Old Testament*, both directly refute the presuppositions of minimalism.

[54] And of course, if this is true of King David, what of the other Biblical accounts preceding 1 Kings? Such minimalists deny that figures such as Abraham, Isaac, Jacob, and Moses ever existed, and that there was no Exodus or Conquest.

[55] Ben-Dor Benite, 35.

[56] Ibid., 53 references Amos 5:5, 27; Hosea 8:8; Isaiah 11:11-12.

"Isaiah, Hosea, and Amos illustrate how the lens of divine punishment transformed the deportations of the Israelites into the exile of an entire people. They were the first to put their oracles into writing; as such, they were hugely influential in turning the exile of Israel into a historical paradigm. They elaborated the notion of exile as it appears in 2 Kings and transformed the kernel of actual history, the patchy narrative of deportations, into an invented Israelite history of sin and all-encompassing divine punishment. The mundane history of several small-scale Assyrian deportations was transformed into a large-scale forced migration enacted by Isaiah's 'Rod of God.' So it is that, while Assyrian kings deported some Israelites for military and political purposes, the Judahite authors of the biblical narrative 'exiled' the entire Israelite kingdom for their own theological and ideological reasons."[57]

Were the Prophets of the Tanach, at all promoting fantasy, in their depiction of a future restoration of Israel, involving the exiles of the Northern Kingdom? **A conservative Bible reader would be aghast at the suggestion that what the Prophets communicated was anything less than Divine inspiration from the Holy One.** Most of today's Messianic Believers—especially those who affirm that the creation of the modern-day State of Israel was prophesied in Scripture (Isaiah 66:8)—would absolutely be horrified over the mere suggestion that the Tanach Scriptures are full of pseudo-histories and that the Prophets of Ancient Israel are *essentially liars and deceivers*. I, for one, certainly do not believe that the Prophets were just some sort of master manipulators.

Why have various conservative interpreters of the Bible ignored various prophecies about the reunion of Judah and Ephraim to come? Why are there various conservative interpreters, who actually cast their lot in with liberals, who claim that the idea of the Northern Kingdom being exiled is fallacious?

Is it really true that there are no Ten Lost Tribes of any kind "out there" in the world? Holding to a rigid "No!" is a position that some are realizing that they cannot take.

In his 1915 book *The History of the Ten "Lost" Tribes: Anglo-Israelism Examined*, Hebrew Christian David Baron—who while largely disregarding the idea that there were descendants from the exiled Northern Kingdom of Israel "out there," mostly in an effort to refute British-Israelism—had to at least be honest and admit that there could be people in remote regions of South Asia, descended from the Northern Kingdom exiles. Baron said, "It *may* be true that the Nestorians, and the Afghans, and some other Eastern tribes are descendants of the original Israelitish exiles in Assyria, but [have] more or less mixed themselves up by inter-marriage

---

[57] Ibid., 50.

Tudor Parfitt, *The Lost Tribes of Israel: The History of a Myth* (London: Phoenix, 2002), pp 4-5 referencing Ezekiel 37:16; Isaiah 11:11-12; and Jeremiah 31:7 is even more direct, as he states, "The fate of the ten tribes as an imagined mythical community started to assume great importance in the prophecies...where the final redemption of Israel was linked to the reunion of the Lost Tribes..."

with the surrounding nations…"[58] Holding to a position of "no Lost Tribes in any form, anywhere," is steadily proving to be unsustainable. Even with all of Varner's protestations, he still had to reluctantly refer to Ethiopian Jews possibly composing the tribe of Dan, and the Pashtu of Afghanistan as composing members of the exiled Northern Kingdom.[59]

The argument that there are no descendants of people, anywhere on Earth, from the exiled Northern Kingdom of Israel *and* being separated from the Jewish community at large, is often found in teachings intended to refute British-Israelism, and its commonly associated anti-Semitism. In wanting to rightly affirm the legitimate place of the Jewish people, how God has blessed and preserved them in history, and how they are indeed true descendants of the Patriarchs—some Christians go too far, and they end up disregarding or nullifying Bible prophecies that speak of the return of scattered Israel/Ephraim. The same attitude, of wanting to associate *any discussion* on the exiled Northern Kingdom, with something like British-Israelism, is present in much of today's Messianic Judaism.

Not dealing with the issue of the exiled Northern Kingdom of Israel/Ephraim, is something which has, thankfully, started to slowly change. A liberal resource like *JPS Guide: The Jewish Bible* (2008), at least offers the general summary:

"The 10 tribes of **Israel**…disappeared from Biblical accounts after the Northern Kingdom of Israel was conquered by the Assyrians in 722/1 B.C.E. The tribes lost their separate identity during their exile and captivity and are thought by some to have intermarried with the Assyrians. Throughout history, various groups around the world have claimed that they are descendants of the lost tribes, pointing to their ancient Hebraic customs and beliefs as proof. Perhaps the best known of these are the Falashas of Ethiopia and the **Samaritans** of Nablus."[60]

For our own Messianic faith community, evangelist Jonathan Bernis of Jewish Voice Ministries, wrote a short article in 2005 called "The Scattering of the Tribes of Israel." He referenced 2 Kings 17:22-23 about the Northern Kingdom being taken into Assyria "until this day," and appealed to Jeremiah 31:35-37[61] as evidence of future fulfillment regarding the return of the descendants of the Northern Kingdom. He was quite keen to assert how "Sadly exactly what happened to the 10 Northern Tribes is not known. There are many theories enough to fill a library. Some are bizarre and clearly false (like the British-Israel theory taught by one prominent American television Bible teacher until his death), while others are more feasible. In fact, where these descendants of Abraham, Isaac and Jacob eventually

---

[58] David Baron, *The History of the Ten "Lost" Tribes: Anglo-Israelism Examined* reprint (London: Morgan & Scott Ld., 1915), pp 47-48.

[59] Varner, pp 91-92.

[60] *JPS Guide: The Jewish Bible*, 231.

[61] "Thus says the LORD, who gives the sun for light by day and the fixed order of the moon and the stars for light by night, who stirs up the sea so that its waves roar; the LORD of hosts is His name: 'If this fixed order departs From before Me,' declares the LORD, 'Then the offspring of Israel also will cease from being a nation before Me forever.' Thus says the LORD, 'If the heavens above can be measured and the foundations of the earth searched out below, then I will also cast off all the offspring of Israel for all that they have done,' declares the LORD" (Jeremiah 31:35-37).

ended up is so shrouded in mystery and intrigue that these ten Tribes have come to be known as the 'Ten Lost Tribes of Israel!'"[62] Bernis actually concludes, "While the rest of the world might have lost these scattered 'outcasts of Israel'—God certainly has not! In fact, I am convinced that in these Last Days He is now uncovering the descendants of these Tribes and gathering them back to Himself in order to fulfill His Word."[63]

Similar sentiments are expressed by Sid Roth in his 2007 book *The Incomplete Church*, as he commented on the miracles that God has wrought in preserving the Jewish people throughout history. He observes, "The ancient rabbis believed that three things had to take place before the Messiah would appear. First, Israel had to be restored as a Jewish nation, which occurred in 1948. Second, the temple had to be rebuilt in Jerusalem. This could happen very quickly. And third, the ten lost tribes had to be restored to Israel (see Jer. 31:7-11). This seemed impossible—until now."[64] Roth goes on to summarize,

> "Filmmaker Simcha Jacobovici, a traditional Jew, read about the locations where the lost tribes were scattered in Isaiah 11:11. He set up an exploratory expedition to find and document the existence of these tribes. Not only did he find them exactly where God had scattered them, but he also discovered that they had not assimilated into their surrounding environments. {as seen in <u>Quest for the Lost Tribes</u> A&E, 1998, DVD 2006}
>
> "For example, he found descendants from the tribe of Manasseh living in northeast India. They observe the Sabbath, the festivals, and the biblical Jewish laws. In 2000, the Israeli Ministry of the Interior granted citizenship to the first one hundred members of that tribe.
>
> "All ten 'lost' tribes have been located. They say, 'We are not lost!' Many of the tribes practice an aberrant form of Judaism, but all have relics and customs proving their heritage. I agree with them and the Word of God—they are not lost."[65]

It is most unfortunate, given the current controversies which have ensued from various leaders and teachers in the Two-House sub-movement, that the sentiments of those such as Bernis or Roth have not been given a bit more publicity to facilitate more reasonable and constructive discussion (as opposed to the over-statements and religious politics and posturing of the 1999 white paper, "The Ephraimite Error," produced by the International Messianic Jewish Alliance or IMJA). Roth was quite fair to acknowledge,

---

[62] Jonathan Bernis (2005). *The Scattering of the Tribes of Israel*, March/April 2005. *Jewish Voice Today*. Retrieved 17 April, 2011 from <http://www.jewishvoice.org>.

[63] Ibid.
There are also some concurrent thoughts offered about this in Bernis' book, *A Rabbi Looks at the Last Days: Surprising Insights on Israel, the End Times and Popular Misconceptions* (Bloomington, MN: Chosen Books, 2013).

[64] Sid Roth, *The Incomplete Church: Bridging the Gap Between God's Children* (Shippensburg, PA: Destiny Image, 2007), 17.

[65] Ibid., pp 17-18.

"Followers of the Two-House Theology love the Jewish people, but they take the spiritual truth of Jew and Gentile becoming One New Man [cf. Ephesians 2:15] too far. They are trying to *physically* become Israel, as though this would give them a special place in God's Kingdom. They are wrong. The special place in the Kingdom is being a child of God."[66]

Isaiah 11:11 communicates, "Then it will happen on that day that the Lord will again recover the second time with His hand the remnant of His people, who will remain, from Assyria, Egypt, Pathros, Cush, Elam, Shinar, Hamath, and from the islands of the sea." Obviously, the first places which people must look for the descendants of the exiled Northern Kingdom should be within the sphere of influence of the old Assyrian, Babylonian, and Persian Empires: **the places where the original exiles were deported and/or immediately migrated.**

The customary places where the descendants, of the exiled Northern Kingdom of Israel, have been searched for, are often limited to remote and rural parts of the third world: in Southeast Asia, South Asia, the Middle East, Central Africa, and the Eastern Mediterranean basin. This would include various isolated groups, which to various degrees are monotheistic, who practice what appear to be some form of Jewish customs, and/or appear to have some odd oral traditions or customs which likely originate from Ancient Israel. *The New Encyclopedia of Judaism* has a fair summation:

> "Today, legends of descent from the 'lost' ten tribes abound. Jewish communities of Kurdish, Bokharan, and Indian (the BENÉ ISRAEL) origin claim their forefathers were exiled from the Kingdom of Israel, while the Israel Chief Rabbinate has taken the position that the Jews of Ethiopia come from the tribe of Dan. In addition, a wide range of non-Jewish tribes and groups claim descent from the Israelites, ranging from sections of the Nigerian Yoruba tribe to the 'Manipur Jews' from northeast India, who claim to belong to the tribe of Manasseh. Fifteen million Pathans spread over Afghanistan and Pakistan (now Kashmir) are divided into sub-tribal groupings with names like Reubeni (Reuben), Efridar (Ephraim), and Ashuri (Asher), leading to the suggestion that they come from the lost tribes."[67]

Tibor Krausz wrote an article in 1999 *for The Jerusalem Report,* in which he summarized some of the groups which claimed to have descent from the exiled Northern Kingdom of Israel. The more legitimate groups to be considered, included:

- **Shinlung:** A group of tribes in northeastern India, Burma, Thailand and Bangladesh boast 1.5 million members and trace their ancestry to the biblical tribe of Menashe. They call their deity Y'wa, have their own Exodus story and feast days corresponding

---

[66] Ibid., pp 41-42.
[67] "Tribes, Ten Lost," in Geoffrey Wigoder, ed. et. al., *The New Encyclopedia of Judaism* (Jerusalem: Jerusalem Publishing House, 2002), 784.

to the Jewish holidays, and many say they want to immigrate to Israel, in the footsteps of the few dozen who already have.

- **Telugu:** Some 30 families of the Indian village of Kottareddipalem, who have converted to Judaism, believe that their ancestors belonged to the lost tribe of Ephraim.
- **Iddao Ishaak:** This small tribe, which claims to be of Jewish origin, lives in Nigeria's Asakrei Valley.
- **Kaifeng:** Distant descendants of the Chinese Jews of Kaifeng, they still mark "Jew" as their ethnic identity in the government census. Some believe their ancestors were descendants of a lost tribe of Israel that settled between Tibet and Szechuan.
- **Pathans:** The 15 million Pathans, Sunni Muslims, comprise about 40 percent of Afghans and also live in Pakistan. Some call themselves "Bani Israel" and consider themselves descendants of the Israelites who found a home in ancient Hindustan.[68]

Another group to be added to Krausz' list can be the Lemba people, a small group of people living in Zimbabwe and South Africa. A BBC article from 2010 details,

> "The Lemba people of Zimbabwe and South Africa may look like their compatriots, but they follow a very different set of customs and traditions.
> "They do not eat pork, they practise male circumcision, they ritually slaughter their animals, some of their men wear skull caps and they put the Star of David on their gravestones.
> "Their oral traditions claim that their ancestors were Jews who fled the Holy Land about 2,500 years ago.
> "It may sound like another myth of a lost tribe of Israel, but British scientists have carried out DNA tests which have confirmed their Semitic origin."[69]

These are the sorts of small groups of people, who practice what appear to be some kind of Jewish customs, and who have an oral tradition tracing their origins back to Ancient Israel, who are likely to be true descendants of the Lost Tribes. In some cases, they might even have some DNA evidence to back up their claims.

When I took Ancient Hebrew Civilization at the University of Oklahoma in 2001, Dr. Daniel Snell told our class that he believed that the Lost Tribes of the Northern Kingdom were basically constrained to a belt of people in what is today Southern Turkey, Northern Iraq, Northern Iran, and into Afghanistan—and now they were all likely Muslim. Kitchen would confirm how Bible readers can at least

---

[68] Tibor Krausz (1999). *Report Card*, 10 May, 1999. *The Jerusalem Report*. Retrieved 11 April, 2011 from <http://jpost.com/JerusalemReport>.

[69] Steve Vickers (2010). *Lost Jewish tribe 'found in Zimbabwe,'* 08 March, 2010. *BBC News*. Retrived 08 April, 2012 from <http://news.bbc.co.uk/>.

be assured, "the exiled Hebrews were progressively assimilated into the Assyrian-Aramean amalgam of peoples inhabiting northern Mesopotamia."[70]

Another small group to consider could be how in 1 Maccabees 12:21, as the Jews were trying to elicit the support of allies against the Seleucid-Greeks, a letter was sent to the Spartans with the statement, "It has been found in writing concerning the Spartans and the Jews that they are brethren and are of the family of Abraham [ek genous Abraam, ἐκ γένους Αβρααμ]." Lee I. Levine, a professor of Jewish history and archaeology at Hebrew University, states, "According to 1 Maccabees (12:5-23)...a bond was forged between the citizens of Jerusalem and the people of Sparta, who saw themselves as descendants of Abraham and who sought to forge an alliance with Jerusalem."[71] Alas, though, Ancient Sparta, a part of the Greek Peloponnesus, sat within the sphere of influence of the old Assyrian, Babylonian, and Persian Empires—as opposed to tall tales like escapees from the Northern Kingdom migrating to the British Isles (or even the Americas!).

It is highly problematic, though, that when most people in today's Two-House sub-movement have considered where the exiles of the Northern Kingdom of Israel were deported—that they tend to look entirely outside of the Ancient Near East, and the places actually listed by the Holy Scriptures themselves. This is a serious issue which has been rightly noted by Boaz Michael & Jacob Fronczak in their publication, *Twelve Gates*:

> "Many of those who were deported from the Northern Kingdom did not return; those who lost their identity as Israelites would have assimilated into Assyrian society and culture. Their descendants would be found today among the Syrian people, many of whom are Christian and belong to various Oriental churches (the Assyrian Church of the East and the Syriac Orthodox Church among others) which split off from Catholicism after the Council of Chalcedon in 451 CE. This is one case in which a non-Jewish people group might have some claim to significant Israelite ancestry. Yet one rarely (if ever) hears Two-House proponents single the Syrian people out as potential 'Ephraimites.'"[72]

The great irony of the whole issue, of the exiled Northern Kingdom of Israel/Ephraim, is that most of the controversy has been caused by searching for groups of descendants well outside of people groups native to the Ancient Near East and immediately surrounding areas. If one were to propose that a wide number of Assyrian, Lebanese, Iraqi, Iranian, or Armenian Christians, among others, for example, were descended from the exiled Northern Kingdom of Israel, there were hardly be any problems, as these people groups largely sit within the confines of the Ancient Near East. It is when groups well outside what was legitimately feasible in ancient times, are posited, that problems ensue.

---

[70] Kitchen, *The Bible In Its World*, 113.

[71] Lee I. Levine, "The Age of Hellenism," in *Ancient Israel: From Abraham to the Destruction of the Temple*, 233.

[72] Boaz Michael, with Jacob Fronczak, *Twelve Gates: Where Do the Nations Enter?* (Marshfield, MO: First Fruits of Zion, 2012), 26.

Many of today's popular/populist Two-House proponents have essentially advocated that there are descendants of the exiled Northern Kingdom represented in every ethnicity, country, and corner of Planet Earth, from far Northwestern Europe to the South Seas, and possibly also to the ancient Americas. The traditional areas where the Lost Tribes have been searched for—are actually *the last places* where Two-House people tend to look. While it is true that in the course of two-and-a-half millennia, people from the Ancient Near East have migrated across the Earth, a substantial amount of that migration has actually only taken place in the past two centuries with European colonialism and de-colonization following the end of World War II.

A non-Jewish Believer of Northwestern European ancestry, who has been led by the Lord into today's Messianic movement, is actually going to have a far better chance at finding a Jewish ancestor or two who assimilated into Christianity during the Middle Ages—than being a descendant of the deported Northern Kingdom, which was largely spread *eastward*.

The need for Bible readers to stay away from unwarranted speculation—and widely let God's Word and prophecy take care of themselves—**is quite imperative.** This is something that far too many people who make up the Two-House sub-movement have utterly failed to do. As the *Encyclopaedia Judaica* entry on the "Ten Lost Tribes" rightly directs, "Various theories, one more farfetched than the other, have been adduced, on the flimsiest of evidence, to identify different peoples with the ten lost tribes. There is hardly a people, from the Japanese to the British, and from the Red Indians to the Afghans, who have not been suggested, and hardly a place, among them Africa, India, China, Persia, Kurdistan, Caucasia, the U.S., and Great Britain."[73] More often than not, theories about where Tribe XYZ have gone have not proven useful.

Some Ancient Views on the Lost Tribes from Extra-Biblical Jewish Sources

Various interpreters one may encounter today—Jewish, Christian, or even Messianic Jewish—may tend to favor the position that the Northern and Southern Kingdoms were corporately reunited following the end of the Babylonian exile in the Sixth Century B.C.E. While the evidence from unfulfilled prophecy does not favor such a conclusion, it also has to be recognized that the widespread Jewish position from the broad First Century B.C.E.-C.E., attested in an array of extra-Biblical sources, favors the view that the ten tribes of the Northern Kingdom of Israel were still largely "out there," waiting to be restored in the future. The *Encyclopaedia Judaica* entry on the "Ten Lost Tribes" notes that "The belief in the continued existence of the ten tribes was regarded as an incontrovertible fact during the whole period of the Second Temple and of the Talmud."[74] **It may be safely argued that the ancient Jewish expectation for Israel's complete**

---

[73] Louis Isaac Rabinowitz, "Ten Lost Tribes," in *EJ*.
[74] Ibid.

restoration, is widely yet to be realized. What is some of the relevant data that needs to be reckoned with? The *EJ* further informs us,

> "The Kingdom of Israel, consisting of the ten tribes (the twelve tribes excluding Judah and Benjamin who constituted the southern Kingdom of Judah), which fell in 722 B.C.E. and its inhabitants were exiled to 'Halah and Habor by the river Gozan, and in the cities of the Medes' (II Kings 17:6 and 18:11; for details and conjectures as to their ultimate fate, see Assyrian Exile), but in general it can be said that they disappeared from the stage of history. However, the parallel passage in I Chronicles 5:26 to the effect that the ten tribes were there 'unto this day' and the prophecies of Isaiah (11:11), Jeremiah (31:8), and above all of Ezekiel (37:19–24) kept alive the belief that they had maintained a separate existence and that the time would come when they would be rejoined with their brethren, the descendants of the Exile of Judah to Babylon...
>
> "The belief in the continued existence of the ten tribes was regarded as an incontrovertible fact during the whole period of the Second Temple and of the Talmud. Tobit, the hero of the apocryphal book of his name, was depicted as a member of the tribe of Naphtali; the Testament of the 12 Patriarchs takes their existence as a fact; and in his fifth vision, IV Ezra (13:34–45) saw a 'peaceable multitude...these are the ten tribes which were carried away prisoners out of their own land.' Josephus (Ant., 11:133) states as a fact 'the ten tribes are beyond the Euphrates till now, and are an immense multitude and not to be estimated in numbers.' Paul (Acts 26:6) protests to Agrippa that he is accused 'for the hope of the promise made unto our fathers, unto which promise our twelve tribes, instantly serving God, hope to come,' while James addresses his epistle to 'the twelve tribes which are scattered about' (l:l). The only opposing voice to this otherwise universal view is found in the Mishnah. R. Eliezer expresses his view that they will eventually return and 'after darkness is fallen upon the ten tribes light shall thereafter dwell upon them,' but R. Akiva expresses his emphatic view that 'the ten tribes shall not return again' (Sanh. 10:3). In consonance with this view, though it is agreed that Leviticus 26:38 applies to the ten tribes, where R. Meir maintains that it merely refers to their exile, Akiva states that it refers to their complete disappearance (Sifra, Be-Hukkotai, 8:1)."[75]

Having already summarized some of the Biblical evidence in favor of a larger restoration of Israel to come in the future, involving those of the Southern *and* Northern Kingdoms—it is appropriate that we see a summary of extra-Biblical opinions, which confirm that exiles from the Northern Kingdom of Israel, were indeed "out there" in the world. These opinions are surely varied in their approach and perspective, and some of the ancient Jews believed that those from the Northern Kingdom of Israel were permanently cut off from the rest of Israel, and even though deported and exiled, would never be restored. Yet when one surveys the Apocrypha, Pseudepigrapha, the historian Josephus, the Mishnah, Tosefta, and the Talmud—the belief that there were exiles from the Northern Kingdom of Israel somewhere on Earth, separated from the known Jewish community—is detectable. This may be considered to be a relatively "safe" array of extra-Biblical literature to

---

[75] Ibid.

engage with, as these same resources are consulted by mainstream scholars today to evaluate an entire selection of theological topics as they concern the teachings and perspective of Yeshua and the Apostles.

So what were some ancient views on the Lost Tribes from extra-Biblical Jewish sources?

Apocrypha: "He will afflict us for our iniquities; and again he will show mercy, and will gather us from all the nations among whom you have been scattered. If you turn to him with all your heart and with all your soul, to do what is true before him, then he will turn to you and will not hide his face from you. But see what he will do with you; give thanks to him with your full voice. Praise the Lord of righteousness, and exalt the King of the ages. I give him thanks in the land of my captivity, and I show his power and majesty to a nation of sinners. Turn back, you sinners, and do right before him; who knows if he will accept you and have mercy on you?" (Tobit 13:5-6, RSV).

Apocrypha: "For we have hope in God that he will soon have mercy upon us and will gather us from everywhere under heaven into his holy place, for he has rescued us from great evils and has purified the place" (2 Maccabees 2:18, RSV).

Apocrypha: "[A]nd an innumerable multitude shall be gathered together, as you saw, desiring to come and conquer him. But he shall stand on the top of Mount Zion. And Zion will come and be made manifest to all people, prepared and built, as you saw the mountain carved out without hands. And he, my Son, will reprove the assembled nations for their ungodliness (this was symbolized by the storm), and will reproach them to their face with their evil thoughts and the torments with which they are to be tortured (which were symbolized by the flames), and will destroy them without effort by the law (which was symbolized by the fire). And as for your seeing him gather to himself another multitude that was peaceable, these are the ten tribes which were led away from their own land into captivity in the days of King Hoshea, whom Shalmaneser the king of the Assyrians led captive; he took them across the river, and they were taken into another land. But they formed this plan for themselves, that they would leave the multitude of the nations and go to a more distant region, where mankind had never lived, that there at least they might keep their statutes which they had not kept in their own land. And they went in by the narrow passages of the Euphrates river. For at that time the Most High performed signs for them, and stopped the channels of the river until they had passed over. Through that region there was a long way to go, a journey of a year and a half; and that country is called Arzareth" (4 Esdras 13:34-45, RSV).

Pseudepigrapha: "Nevertheless, I shall also write to your brothers in Babylon, as you have said to me, and I shall send it by means of men. Also I shall write to the nine and a half tribes, and send it by means of a bird. And it happened on the twenty-first day of the ninth month that I, Baruch, came and sat down under the oak in the shadow of the branches, and nobody was with me; I was alone. And I wrote two letters. One I sent by means of an eagle to the nine and a half tribes, and the other I sent by means of three men to those who were in Babylon. And I called an eagle and said to him these words: You have been created by the

Most High that you should be higher than any other bird. But now go and do not stay in any place, do not go into a nest, do not sit on any tree until you have flown over the breadth of the many waters of the river Euphrates and have come to the people that live there and cast down to them this letter. Remember that Noah at the time of the flood received the fruit of the olive tree from a dove when he sent it away from the ark. And also the ravens served Elijah when they brought food to him as they were commanded. Also Solomon, in the time of his kingship, commanded a bird whither he wanted to send a letter and in whatever he was in need of and it obeyed him as he commanded it. And do not be reluctant and do not deviate to the right nor to the left, but fly and go straight away that you may preserve the command of the Mighty One as I said to you" (*2 Baruch* 77:17-26).[76]

Pseudepigrapha: "But in your allotted place will be the temple of God, and the latter temple will exceed the former in glory. The twelve tribes shall be gathered here and there and all the nations, until such time as the Most High shall send forth his salvation through the ministration of the unique prophet" (*Testament of Benjamin* 9:2).[77]

Pseudepigrapha: "Then, considering themselves like a lioness in a dusty plain, hungry and parched, the two tribes will call upon the ten tribes, and shall declare loudly, 'Just and holy is the Lord. For just as you sinned, likewise we, with our little ones, have now been led out with you.' Then, hearing the reproachful words of the two tribes, the ten tribes will lament and will say, 'What shall we, with you, do, brothers? Has not this tribulation come upon the whole house of Israel?' Then all the tribes will lament, crying out to heaven and saying, 'God of Abraham, God of Isaac, and God of Jacob, remember your covenant which you made with them, and the oath which you swore to them by yourself, that their seed would never fail from the land which you have given them. Then, in that day, they will remember me, saying from tribe to tribe, even each man to his neighbor, 'Is this not that which was made known to us in prophecies by Moses, who suffered many things in Egypt and at the Red Sea and in the wilderness for forty years (when) he solemnly called heaven and earth as witnesses against us that we should not transgress God's commandments of which he had become the mediator for us? These things which have come upon us since that time are according to his admonition declared to us at that time. And (those words) have been confirmed even to our being led as captives in the land of the East.' And they will be as slaves for about seventy-seven years.

"Then one who is over them will come upon the scene, and he will stretch forth his hands, and bow his knees and pray for them, saying 'Lord of all, king on the lofty throne, you who rules the world, who has willed that this people be for you a chosen people, yea, who has willed to be called their God according to the covenant which you made with their fathers, yet they, with their wives and children, have gone as captives into a foreign land, surrounded by the gates of strangers where there is great majesty. Have regard for them, and have

---

[76] A.F.J. Klijn, trans., "2 (Syriac Apocalypse of) Baruch," in James H. Charlesworth, ed., *The Old Testament Pseudepigrapha*, Vol 1 (New York: Doubleday, 1983), 647.

[77] H.C. Kee, trans., "Testaments of the Twelve Patriarchs," in Ibid., 827.

compassion for them, O heavenly Lord.' Then God will remember them because of the covenant which he made with their fathers and he will openly show his compassion. And in those times he will inspire a king to have pity on them and send them home to their own land. Then some parts of the tribes will arise and come to their appointed place, and they will strongly build its walls. Now, the two tribes will remain steadfast in their former faith, sorrowful and sighing because they will not be able to offer sacrifices to the Lord of their fathers. But the ten tribes will grow and spread out among the nations during the time of their captivity" (*Testament of Moses* 3:4-4:9).[78]

Pseudepigrapha: "Bring together the dispersed of Israel with mercy and goodness, for your faithfulness is with us" (*Psalms of Solomon* 8:28).[79]

Josephus: "[T]herefore there are but two tribes in Asia and Europe subject to the Romans, while the ten tribes are beyond Euphrates till now, and are an immense multitude, and not to be estimated by numbers" (*Antiquities of the Jews* 11.133).[80]

Mishnah: "The ten tribes are not destined to return, since it is said *And he cast them into another land, as on this day* (Dt. 29:28). Just as the day passes and does not return, so they have gone their way and will not return,' the words of R. Aqiba" (m.*Sanhedrin* 10:3).[81]

Tosefta: "The ten tribes have no portion in the world to come and will not live in the world to come, as it is said, *And the Lord drove them out of their land with anger and heat and great wrath* (Deut. 29:28)—in this world; *and cast them forth into another land* (Deut. 29:28)—in the world to come. R. Simeon b. Judah of Kefar Akkum says, 'Scripture said, *As at this day*—If their deeds remain as they are this day, they will [not] reach it, and if not, they will (not) reach it.' Rabbi says, 'Both these and those have a portion in the world to come, as it is said, *And it shall come to pass in that day that those who are perishing in the land of Assyria and those who are driven away into the Land of Egypt shall come and worship the Lord in the holy mountain, in Jerusalem* (Is. 27:13)" (t.*Sanhedrin* 13:12).[82]

Talmud: "'The ten tribes are not destined to return, since it is said, "And he cast them into another land, as on this day" (Deu. 29:28). Just as the day passes and does not return, so they have gone their way and will not return,' the words of R. Aqiba. R. Eliezer says, 'Just as this day is dark and then grows light, so the ten tribes for whom it now is dark — thus in the future it is destined to grow light for them.'

"*Our rabbis have taught on Tannaite authority:* 'The ten tribes have no portion in the world to come [T.: and will not live in the world to come], as it is said, "And the Lord drove them out of their land with anger and heat and great wrath" (Deu. 29: 8) — in this world; and cast them forth into another

[78] J. Priest, trans., "Testament of Moses," in Ibid., pp 928-929.
[79] R.B. Wright, trans., "Psalms of Solomon," in James H. Charlesworth, ed., *The Old Testament Pseudepigrapha*, Vol 2 (New York: Doubleday, 1985), 660.
[80] *The Works of Josephus: Complete and Unabridged*, 294.
[81] Neusner, *Mishnah*, 605.
[82] Neusner, *Tosefta*, 2:1191-1192.

land' (Deu. 29:28) — in the world to come,' the words of R. Aqiba. R. Simeon b. Judah of Kefar Akkum says in the name of R. Simeon, 'Scripture said, "As at this day" — if their deeds remains as they are this day, they will [not] reach it, and if not, they will (not) reach it.' Rabbi says, '[Both these and those] have a portion in the world to come, as it is said, "And it shall come to pass in that day that the trumpet shall be blown [and those who are perishing in the land of Assyria and those who are driven away in to the Land of Egypt shall come and worship the Lord in the holy mountain, in Jerusalem]" (Isa. 27:13).' [T. San. 13:12]." (b.Sanhedrin 110b).[83]

Talmud: "Said R. Judah said R. Assi, 'A gentile who betrothed an Israelite woman at this time — they take account of the possibility of the validity of the betrothal, since he might derive from the Ten Tribes.' *But lo, whatever falls from a mixed lot is assumed to have fallen from the majority thereof! The statement speaks of places in which the ten tribes took up residence, for* said R. Abba bar Kahana, "'And he put them in Halah and in Habor, on the river of Gozan, and the cities of the Medes' (2Ki. 18:11) — 'Halah' — this is Halwan; 'Habor' — this is Adiabene; 'the river of Gozan' — this is in Ginzaq; 'the cities of the Medes' — these are Hamdan and the neighboring towns.' Others say, 'Nihar and its neighboring towns'" (b.Yevamot 16b).[84]

There is certainly a variance of perspectives witnessed in an array of selections from mainline, extra-Biblical Jewish literature, on what was or is to happen, regarding the exiled Northern Kingdom of Israel, and even whether or not ancient Jews would encounter them. Some of the details seen in this wide array of quotes obviously seem more plausible than others. At least when 4 Esdras 13:45 says that the ten tribes went to Arzareth, this basically just means that they went to "Another Land,"[85] and that the while the author reflects on the anticipation of their descendants returning, the material does contain speculation. *Testament of Moses* 4:9 actually remains fairly true to the Biblical and prophetic picture, not adding speculative statements, other than the descendants of the exiled Northern Kingdom multiplying in their captivity. And perhaps quite intriguing is the statement seen in b.Yevamot 16b about a non-Jew marrying a Jewish woman being permitted, because he just might be a descendant of the exiled Northern Kingdom, and as such would ultimately be an Israelite too—although this was notably limited to a few specific towns to the East in Media-Persia, where the deportees of the Northern Kingdom were legitimately transported and/or migrated.

To the list seen above can probably be added the thoughts of a Fourth-Fifth Century Christian leader from Gaul, Sulpitus Severus, who said,

---

[83] *The Babylonian Talmud: A Translation and Commentary.*
[84] Ibid.
[85] *New Oxford Annotated Bible*, Apocrypha p 55.

"…[T]he ten which had previously been carried away being scattered among the Parthians, Medes, Indians, and Ethiopians never returned to their native country, and are to this day held under the sway of barbarous nations" (*Sacred History* 11).[86]

A variety of academic resources, knowing that the discussion about the exiled Northern Kingdom of Israel, was a subject of interest and speculation within the Jewish world prior to and immediately after, the time of Yeshua and the Apostles, has offered some useful summaries that today's Messianic Believers need to be familiar with:

Dictionary of Judaism in the Biblical Period: "In 1 Kings 11-12, the prophet Ahijah gives the new king, Jeroboam, ten of the twelve piece into which he had torn a new garment; these symbolized the tribes (other than Judah and apparently Benjamin) over which he was to rule. This realm existed until 722-721 B.C.E., when the Assyrians killed or deported thousands (see 2 Kings 15-17). The fact that these tribes are not mentioned again in the Hebrew Bible has given rise to the idea of the ten lost tribes. They do, however, play a part in some extrabiblical texts. The Testament of Moses 3-4 predicts that the other two tribes, when exiled, will summon the ten to repent. They do so, but eventually they grow and spread out among the nations. In 2 Baruch (c. 100 C.E.), the remaining two tribes are said to have done more evil than the ten who were deported; 4 Ezra 13:39-50 looks to a return of the ten tribes in the last days."[87]

Anchor Bible Dictionary: "The 3rd century Christian Latin poet Commodian (in the *Carmen* and *Instructiones*) and author of the *Acts of St. Matthew* may preserve an otherwise lost Jewish apocalyptic and apocryphal work that apparently described the living conditions of the lost ten (or nine and a half) tribes which were taken into exile by the king of Assyria. According to early rabbinics Rabbi Akiba claimed these tribes would not return, but Rabbi Eliezer disagreed, arguing that they shall move from darkness to light (*m. Sanh.* 10.3). We cannot yet be certain that an early Jewish apocryphon existed; but it is clear that the legend was widely known and influential. Did a Jew, perhaps in the late 1st century compose an exegetical expansion based on OT passages, especially 2 Kgs 17:23 (cf. 1 Chr 5:26, Isa 11:1, Jer 31:8, and Eze 37:19-28)? Around 100 C.E. three Jewish works—namely 4 *Ezra* (13:34-51), 2 *Baruch* (77:17-26), and Josephus' *Antiquities* (11.5)—referred to this legend or document.

"If Commodian excerpts this apocryphon in his *Instructiones*, and if the passage that refers to the destruction of Jerusalem in 70 C.E. is from this Jewish work, then the document must postdate 70, and was probably contemporaneous with 4 *Ezra*, 2 *Baruch*, and the *Antiquities*. The parallels with the *History of the Rechabites* are numerous and significant. M.R. James suggested that 'there evidently was a writing (presumably Jewish) which described the conditions under which the lost tribes lived.'"[88]

[86] BibleWorks 8.0: Schaff, Early Church Fathers. MS Windows Vista/7 Release. Norfolk: BibleWorks, LLC, 2009-2010. DVD-ROM.
[87] "tribes, ten," in *Dictionary of Judaism in the Biblical Period*, pp 648-649.
[88] James H. Charlesworth, "Lost Tribes, The," in *ABD*, 4:372.

While there was undoubtedly talk and speculation within the Jewish world of Yeshua and the Apostles, about what actually happened to *and* what will happen concerning the exiled Northern Kingdom of Israel, New Testament scholars have tended to stay away from the issue. What is usually witnessed, is that two specific references made to "the twelve tribes" (Acts 26:7; James 1:1) are taken to exclusively apply to the First Century Jewish community, and thus there is to be no future expectation of an ingathering to occur, with people "out there" in the nations, either in some isolated area, or assimilated descendants of, the exiled Northern Kingdom.

In Paul's defense of believing in Yeshua the Messiah, before Agrippa, the Apostle stated, "And now I am standing trial for the hope {the resurrection} of the promise made by God to our fathers; *the promise* to which our twelve tribes hope to attain, as they earnestly serve *God* night and day" (Acts 26:6-7).[89] In the Acts commentaries of two very highly regarded theologians, F.F. Bruce and I. Howard Marshall, we find an immediate dismissal of anything having to do with an exiled Northern Kingdom of Israel—in spite of these two often being well-acquainted with Second Temple Judaism and its associated literature. Bruce asserts, "Neither Paul nor any other NT writer knows anything of the fiction of the ten 'lost' tribes,"[90] followed by Marshall who says, "The idea that only returned exiles from Judah and Benjamin (the southern part of the kingdom) composed the Jewish people in New Testament times is a myth that dies hard."[91]

One would have expected better from these two, with more even-handed statements. However, we cannot totally blame either Bruce or Marshall from employing words like "fiction" or "myth" regarding Acts 26:6. In his commentary on Acts, Stanley D. Toussaint gives us a clue as to why various New Testament examiners are so insistent there is no one from the Northern Kingdom of Israel/Ephraim "out there" in the world: "Paul's reference to the **12 tribes** of Israel shows the error of British-Israelism with its '10 lost tribes of Israel.'"[92]

These three interpreters (Bruce, Marshall, Toussaint), unfortunately, have probably allowed a rightful rejection of British-Israelism (even though Bruce and Marshall do not mention it by name), to cause them to go too far so as to suggest that there is really no group of people from the exiled Northern Kingdom of Israel "out there" in the world, separate from the known and recognizable Jewish community. We have to be able to see over-reactionary statements when we encounter them, and think critically.

---

[89] With the verb *latreuō* (λατρεύω) employed for "serve," this is likely a reference to the offerings presented for the community of Israel in the Temple. Included within the First Century Temple worship would have been hymns and psalms issued for the redemption of Israel.

[90] F.F. Bruce, *New International Commentary on the New Testament: The Book of the Acts* (Grand Rapids: Eerdmans, 1983), 489 fn#13.

[91] I. Howard Marshall, *Tyndale New Testament Commentaries: Acts* (Grand Rapids: Eerdmans, 1980), 392.

[92] Stanley D. Toussaint, "Acts," in John F. Walvoord and Roy B. Zuck, eds., *The Bible Knowledge Commentary: New Testament* (Wheaton, IL: Victor Books, 1983), 424.

So, when Paul said to Agrippa, "...to which our twelve tribes hope to attain, as they earnestly serve *God* night and day..." (Acts 26:7), did he deny that there was a future, larger restoration of Israel to come, involving various people descended from the Northern Kingdom of Israel? It is very true that there were individuals like Anna of the tribe of Asher (Luke 2:36) who were a part of the First Century Jewish community, and that there were others in the ancient Jewish community who could trace their lineage to one of the twelve tribes (discussed previously). Still, reading a larger scope of Tanach prophecies, it is clear that the grand restoration of Israel—of both Judah and Ephraim—has not even occurred in our own day. So why would Paul testify to a leader like Agrippa, that "our twelve tribes hope"? Craig S. Keener offers us a useful perspective in *IVPBBC* that we need not overlook:

"Two of the most basic future hopes of most Jews were the resurrection of the bodies of the righteous and the restoration of the twelve tribes at the same time."[93]

David G. Peterson also interjects a useful thought to keep in mind:

"Perhaps the reference to *our twelve tribes* (*to dōdekaphylon hēmōn* [τὸ δωδεκάφυλον ἡμῶν], 'out twelve-tribe unit') implies an ideal Israel, comprising all true Israelites across time and scattered among the nations. Ezekiel 37:15-28 certainly envisages a reunification of the tribes of Israel when the Lord resurrects his people and brings them under the eternal rule of his servant David."[94]

It is difficult to refute the idea that the Apostles all recognized that they were living in a time when the restoration of Israel's Kingdom was something *in process* (cf. Acts 1:6). In some way or another, the gathering together of all of Israel—known and unknown—and the salvation of the nations at large who would acknowledge Israel's Messiah, King Yeshua, was taking place (cf. Isaiah 49:6; Acts 13:47). The Apostles ministered and served in an era when the final stages of Israel's restoration had begun.

James the Just's greeting in his epistle is, "To the twelve tribes who are dispersed abroad" (James 1:1). Many of those who want to completely disregard the subject matter of the exiled Northern Kingdom of Israel/Ephraim, offer James 1:1 as a proof. While no intelligent reader of James doubts the fact that this letter was written to ancient Jewish Believers in the First Century C.E., a non-Jewish readership of James as well cannot at all be excluded. The Epistle of James has parallels to not only ancient Rabbinic literature, but *also* to classical literature as well (see esp. James 3:4-6).[95] But where various Two-House populists would likely step in, and claim that James wrote to the Lost Tribes, we should be much, much more tempered. First of all, if James intended any members of dispersed Northern Kingdom being among his audience, assimilated or not, it would have been within the immediate sphere of influence of the old Assyrian Empire, in the Eastern

---

[93] Craig S. Keener, *The IVP Bible Background Commentary: New Testament* (Downers Grove, IL: InterVarsity, 1993), 399.

[94] David G. Peterson, *Pillar New Testament Commentary: The Acts of the Apostles* (Grand Rapids: Eerdmans, 2009), 662.

[95] Cf. Pheme Perkins, "The Letter of James," in *New Interpreter's Study Bible*, 2176.

Mediterranean, in the vicinity of "Phoenicia and Cyprus and Antioch" (Acts 11:19).[96]

Also to keep in mind, is how in his commentary on James, Dan G. McCartney directs our attention to how "twelve tribes" should be viewed not as the Jewish people exclusively, but rather a Kingdom of Israel in the process of restoration:

"The 'twelve tribes in the Diaspora' is, of course, a reference to Israel. Although many Jews had some knowledge of their tribal connections (e.g., Paul the Benjamite, Symeon the Levite), the twelve tribes as distinct and discernible units or clans within Judaism were a thing of the past, especially the 'northern' tribes (though the Samaritans probably were largely derived from northern Israelites). But the OT and later Jewish writings sometimes speak of the twelve tribes as an aspect of the restored Israel (Ezek. 47:13; T. Benj. 9.2)…"[97]

(James the Just's statements in James 1:1, regarding "the twelve tribes," can by no means be separated from his expectations at the Jerusalem Council in Acts 15:15-18, regarding the salvation of the nations, where he quotes Amos 9:11-12.)

The attestations regarding the twelve tribes of Israel elsewhere in the Apostolic Scriptures (Matthew 19:28; Luke 22:30; Revelation 7:4-8; 21:12), depict them in an eschatological setting, often regarding the restored Kingdom of God. When seeing "twelve tribes" referred to in either Acts 26:7 or James 1:1, it is far better for readers to associate these verses not with the First Century Jewish people exclusively—but instead with a Kingdom of Israel in the process of being restored in the Messiah Yeshua. This would have surely included the Jewish people *and* those of the exiled Northern Kingdom, but would **not at all exclude** the nations at large, either. This is an audience of the people of God, which are to be especially noted by the twelve tribes of Israel brought together. Bible readers are on safe ground to recognize that places in the Apostolic Scriptures which refer to Israel's "twelve tribes," refer to the in-process restoration of Israel's Kingdom brought about via the arrival of the Messiah. Such a restoration would, of course, also welcome in those of the nations who have recognized Israel's God and Israel's Messiah.[98]

While today's New Testament theologians, given various abuses about the Ten Lost Tribes witnessed via phenomenon like Nineteenth/Twentieth Century British-Israelism, tend to dismiss the entire subject matter, Christian Old Testament theologians tend to be far more honest about the issue. Referencing 2 Kings 15:29; 17:6; and 18:11 in his discussion, as well as the exile of the Southern Kingdom to Babylon, Kitchen reminds us how, "once the crash *had* come and the people were carried off into seeming despair, then both Jeremiah (30-31, etc.) and Ezekiel (36-37, etc.) had to proclaim that all was *not* finished, that in God's plan for the ages there

---

[96] Cf. Donald W. Burdick, "James," in Frank E. Gaebelein, ed. et. al., *Expositor's Bible Commentary*, 12 vols (Grand Rapids: Zondervan, 1981), 12:162-163.

[97] Dan G. McCartney, *Baker Exegetical Commentary on the New Testament: James* (Grand Rapids: Baker Academic, 2009), 79; cf. Douglas J. Moo, *Pillar New Testament Commentary: The Letter of James* (Grand Rapids: Eerdmans, 2000), pp 49-50.

[98] Consult the author's commentary *James for the Practical Messianic*, for an evaluation of this, and related issues.

was a future for his erring people."[99] This would notably include the promise of the New Covenant, the promise of return, and the promise of a Greater David to reign over a restored Israel *and* Planet Earth itself.

While people—Jews, Christians, Messianic Jews, theologians, and laypersons alike—may want to find little reasons here or there, to dismiss the issue of a larger restoration of Israel, **God Himself has not dismissed the issue.** As Craigie observes on Ezekiel 37:15-28,

"Long since, [the Jews in Babylonian exile] had ceased to wonder whether or not there was a future for their relatives in the northern kingdom, which had been defeated in war in 722 B.C. But where human memory ceases, often through selfish lack of concern for others, the divine memory is still at work. All God's people were important to him, whether from Joseph or Judah; all would eventually share in this salvation."[100]

It has only been in the era of critical Bible scholarship, which challenges the integrity and believability of Holy Writ, that much of the ancient Jewish hope of the exiled Northern Kingdom returning home, has been denied and derided. This has been coupled with the many abuses of phenomena like British-Israelism, and the less-than-reliable theological perspectives of Armstrongism, giving many evangelical Christians and Messianic Jews a convenient "excuse" to disregard the whole subject matter. Far too many in the Two-House sub-movement have also fallen prey to many tall tales and unwarranted speculation. However, if we are true to the Biblical text *and* to valuing the Bible in its world, as many ancient Jews did believe in people from the exiled Northern Kingdom "out there" among the nations—then we can have confidence that one day the dilemma that the Prophet Daniel prayed about will be over:

"Righteousness belongs to You, O Lord, but to us open shame, as it is this day—to the men of Judah, the inhabitants of Jerusalem and all Israel, those who are nearby and those who are far away in all the countries [*b'kol-ha'eratzot,* בְּכָל־הָאֲרָצוֹת] to which You have driven them, because of their unfaithful deeds which they have committed against You" (Daniel 9:7).

How much did the Apostles emphasize the exiled Northern Kingdom?

It is commonly thought that the Apostolic Scriptures or New Testament are largely silent about what happened to the exiled Northern Kingdom of Israel. Are they? No objective Bible reader would conclude that the complete restoration of Israel's Kingdom in the eschaton is a theme missing from the Apostolic Scriptures. From the Tanach, such a restoration would necessarily include the return of the descendants of the exiled Northern Kingdom to not only the community of Israel, but also that many are to return to the Promised Land itself. Many of today's popular/populist Two-House teachers have claimed that there are scores of

---

[99] Kitchen, *The Bible In Its World*, 121.
[100] Craigie, 264.

references to this in the Apostolic Scriptures, but such teachers can certainly be found to employ too much eisegesis, i.e., reading messages into the text that might not really be there.

In what is commonly called the Great Commission, Yeshua the Messiah bid His Disciples, "Go therefore and make disciples of all the nations[101]..." (Matthew 28:19a). Not only is there no distinction here between descendants of the exiled Northern Kingdom of Israel/Ephraim, and the nations/Gentiles in general—"all the nations" also necessarily includes the Jewish people themselves, who need the Messiah every bit as much as well. A wide number of the Two-House advocates, which one will encounter today, claim that the good news going forth the world is largely about finding "lost Israelites," and not really about people at large simply receiving the message—so that _all_ unsaved human beings might be redeemed by Israel's Messiah. ***This goes unacceptably too far.***

What should not be disputed is that the non-Jewish Believers were considered a part of the Commonwealth of Israel (cf. Ephesians 2:11-13). We also need to each consider how the Apostle Paul noted how, "For not all Israelites truly belong to Israel" (Romans 9:6, NRSV),[102] meaning that in the end, those who are considered or reckoned to be a part of "the Israel of God" (Galatians 6:16) by God, must have faith in Israel's Messiah, Yeshua (and in the case of Romans 9:6 that there will be Jewish people removed from Israel's polity).[103] If people do not have salvation in Yeshua—even if they are of physical Israel (physical descendants of either the known Jewish people or descendants of exiled Israel/Ephraim)—**they cannot ultimately be considered "Israel."**

In the teachings of the Apostles in the Messianic Scriptures, we see references to the exiled Northern Kingdom, but they may not be as direct as various popular/populist Two-House advocates, who you are likely to encounter, would at all like them to be. It can certainly be recognized, though, that themes regarding the end-time restoration of Israel are applied to the salvation of the nations at large. It cannot be denied, with some rudimentary investigation into the text, that Tanach passages regarding the exiled Northern Kingdom of Israel as a participant—are applied to the salvation of the nations by the Apostles. This does beg a few questions of how far certain elements of such a restoration can be pushed.

It would have been most odd and irregular—and perhaps even a bit sloppy on their part—if the Apostles associated restoration of Israel prophecies and terms, to the salvation of the nations, if they did not at least consider the nations to be some sort of participants in them. They surely recognized, that as the good news went forth, the God of Israel was in the process of restoring His Kingdom. Their job was to declare the good news and see that new Believers—whether they be Jewish or those of the nations—were properly discipled and set on the right path of maturity

---

[101] Grk. _panta ta ethnē_ (πάντα τὰ ἔθνη).

[102] Grk. _hoi ex Israēl houtoi Israēl_ (οἱ ἐξ Ἰσραὴλ οὗτοι Ἰσραήλ); "for not all who _are_ of Israel are these Israel" (YLT); "For not everyone from Isra'el is truly part of Isra'el" (CJB).

[103] Consult the discussion on Romans 9:3-6 in the author's publication _Are Non-Jewish Believers Really a Part of Israel?_

in the Messiah. Much of what would relate to the issue of exiled Northern Kingdom (cf. Hosea 8:8; Amos 9:9), obviously had to be left to the natural course of prophecy and the sovereign will and knowledge of God alone. The Apostles' primary mission was the same as any of us: seeing human individuals restored to their Creator via Yeshua's salvation, and seeing them develop in faith and holiness (cf. 1 Corinthians 1:9, 23-24).[104]

It is useful that we review a series of important examples of where the Apostles allude to Israel's restoration, and where the redeemed from the nations are decisively included within it.

James the Just

At the Jerusalem Council in Acts 15, James the Just, the half-brother of Yeshua, got up and explained how the Lord planned all along to receive from the nations a people for Himself. He says, "With this the words of the Prophets agree, just as it is written" (Acts 15:15). James then proceeded to quote from Amos 9:11-12, which says in its entirety, "In that day I will raise up the fallen booth of David, and wall up its breaches; I will also raise up its ruins and rebuild it as in the days of old; that they may possess the remnant of Edom and all the nations who are called by My name,' declares the LORD who does this." What is important to recognize is that in James' quotation of Amos, he actually said, "AFTER THESE THINGS I will return, AND I WILL REBUILD THE TABERNACLE OF DAVID WHICH HAS FALLEN, AND I WILL REBUILD ITS RUINS, AND I WILL RESTORE IT, SO THAT THE REST OF MANKIND MAY SEEK THE LORD, AND ALL THE GENTILES WHO ARE CALLED BY MY NAME" (Acts 15:16-17).

The difference between what actually James said in Acts 15:13-18 and the Hebrew text in Amos, is that James followed the Septuagint rendering which reads with *hoi kataloipoi tōn anthrōpōn* (οἱ κατάλοιποι τῶν ἀνθρώπων) for the Hebrew *sh'eirit Edom* (שְׁאֵרִית אֱדוֹם). The LXX translators understood *Edom* (אֱדוֹם) to be connected to *adam* (אָדָם), also the Hebrew word for "**mankind, people**" (*HALOT*),[105] and rendered it in Greek as "the remnant of men" (Apostle's Bible) or "those remaining of humans" (NETS), referring to God's faithful remnant that would come forth from humanity's masses.

James associated the nations coming to faith with the restoration of the Tabernacle of David, or Israel's Kingdom, by quoting Amos 9:11-12. Previously in Amos 9:9 is a declaration from the Lord of judgment on the Northern Kingdom of Israel/Ephraim: "I will shake the house of Israel among all nations [*b'kol-ha'goyim*, בְּכָל־הַגּוֹיִם] as *grain* is shaken in a sieve, but not a kernel will fall to the ground." The restoration of David's Tabernacle is to obviously bring resolution to this problem. Amos 9:14 further decrees, though, "I will restore [Heb. verb *shuv*, שׁוּב; Grk. LXX verb *epistrephō*] the captivity of My people Israel." It cannot be avoided that in Acts

---

[104] "God is faithful, through whom you were called into fellowship with His Son, Yeshua the Messiah our Lord...[B]ut we preach Messiah crucified, to Jews a stumbling block and to Gentiles foolishness, but to those who are the called, both Jews and Greeks, Messiah the power of God and the wisdom of God" (1 Corinthians 1:9, 23-24).

[105] *HALOT*, 1:14.

15:19, when James says, "wherefore I judge: not to trouble those who from the nations do turn back to God" (YLT), that the verb *epistrephō* has been employed to label the salvation of the non-Jewish Believers. The verb *epistrephō* was used in the Septuagint rendering of Amos 9:14, to essentially describe the restoration and return of the Northern Kingdom.

Whether a few of the early non-Jewish Believers coming to faith, from the Mediterranean basin, were assimilated descendants of exiled Israel/Ephraim in their ranks or not, was completely unknowable to the Jewish Apostles. *The main emphasis seen is on the nations' salvation and redemption from sin, after all!* But what is knowable to Bible readers is how such new, non-Jewish Believers were attested to be participants in the restoration of Israel. Concurrent with the restoration of David's Tabernacle, whether one follows the Hebrew MT or Greek LXX of Amos 9:11-12, is that Israel's Kingdom realm is expanded beyond the Twelve Tribes. This does mean that although there will be people descended from the exiled Northern Kingdom return to the Promised Land one day, that when the Messiah finally returns, situated around the restored Twelve Tribes will be the righteous from the nations incorporated into Israel's expanded polity. These people will not be ethnically or culturally Jewish, and they will maintain a high level of their own ethnic and cultural distinctiveness (obviously purged of sin)—but they will be observing God's Torah (Micah 4:1-3; Isaiah 2:2-4).[106]

The Apostle Peter

In his first epistle, the Apostle Peter directed his message to a broad geographical area in Asia Minor: "To those who reside as aliens, scattered throughout Pontus, Galatia, Cappadocia, Asia, and Bithynia, who are chosen" (1 Peter 1:1). Writing to a mixed group of ancient Believers, both Jewish and non-Jewish,[107] he applies Hosea's word of exiled Israel to their salvation experience: "I will sow her for Myself in the land. I will also have compassion on her who had not obtained compassion, and I will say to those who were not My people, 'You are My people!' And they will say, '*You are* my God!'" (Hosea 2:23). This was a prophecy that was given to the Northern Kingdom of Israel regarding their dispersion. Peter tells his audience, "for you once were NOT A PEOPLE, but now you are THE PEOPLE OF

---

[106] For a further evaluation, consult the author's examination of Acts 15:15-18, in his publication *Are Non-Jewish Believers Really a Part of Israel?*

[107] That there was a non-Jewish audience of 1 Peter as well is easily seen by statements such as, "the former lusts *which were yours* in your ignorance" (1 Peter 1:14), which included "sensuality, lusts, drunkenness, carousing, drinking parties and abominable idolatries" (1 Peter 4:3). The presence of pagan idolatry does not apply too well if the audience of 1 Peter is exclusively Jewish.

For a further review, consult the entry for the Epistle of 1 Peter in the author's workbook *A Survey of the Apostolic Scriptures for the Practical Messianic.*

Also useful to consider should be the sentiments issued in the *Tree of Life—The New Covenant*, 413.

GOD; you had NOT RECEIVED MERCY, but now you have RECEIVED MERCY" (1 Peter 2:10).[108]

The Apostle Peter recognized that a larger restoration of Israel was at hand, as many of his own Jewish people—as well as many from the nations—were receiving the good news. But Peter's quotation from Hosea 2:23, applied to non-Jewish readers of 1 Peter, is the furthest extent that Peter goes in addressing the subject. He does not at all identify any non-Jewish Believer with a particular tribe of the Northern Kingdom, but instead focuses on individuals' spiritual well-being, their discipleship in the faith, and their proper conduct in holiness. This would fit well with his words proclaimed at *Shavuot*/Pentecost: "For the promise is for you and your children and for all who are far off, **as many as the Lord our God will call to Himself**" (Acts 2:39). Peter's vision was a global vision, as he wanted "all whom the Lord our God will call" (NIV) to know Yeshua.[109]

The Apostle Paul

The Apostle Paul, just like James and Peter, recognized that the restoration of God's Kingdom was steadily at work in his assignments among the nations. He had no difficulty placing the salvation of the nations within the expectations of a larger restoration of Israel. As the message of the good news went forth to the world, God's Kingdom was in the process of being restored. Paul did not at all attempt to prove the ancestry of anyone who was saved by the Lord and freed from the power of sin. He could not have humanly discerned if, per chance, a few of the ancient, non-Jewish people coming to faith in Yeshua, included assimilated descendants of the exiled Northern Kingdom. Yet, prophecies and concepts regarding the exiled Northern Kingdom were applied to the salvation of the nations.

In his letter to the Romans, Paul applies prophecies from Hosea 2:23 and 1:10 to the salvation of the nations:

"And *He did so* to make known the riches of His glory upon vessels of mercy, which He prepared beforehand for glory, *even* us, whom He also called, not from among Jews only, but also from among Gentiles [*ex ethnōn*, ἐξ ἐθνῶν]. As He says also in Hosea, 'I WILL CALL THOSE WHO WERE NOT MY PEOPLE, 'MY PEOPLE,' AND HER WHO WAS NOT BELOVED, 'BELOVED'" [Hosea 2:23]. AND IT SHALL BE THAT IN THE PLACE WHERE IT WAS SAID TO THEM, 'YOU ARE NOT MY PEOPLE,' THERE THEY SHALL BE CALLED SONS OF THE LIVING GOD" [Hosea 1:10]" (Romans 9:23-26).

Paul has said that God has called people to Himself "not only out of Jews, but also out of nations" (Romans 9:24, YLT). In Paul's application of Hosea 2:23 and 1:10, why would he quote a passage with the Northern Kingdom of Israel intended

---

[108] A wider array of Tanach passages describing Israel, to this mixed audience of ancient Believers, is witnessed in 1 Peter 2:9-10, including: Deuteronomy 7:6; 10:15; Exodus 19:6; Isaiah 61:6; 43:21; Deuteronomy 4:20; 14:2; and Hosea 2:23.

Cf. Aland, *GNT*, pp 788-789.

[109] For a further evaluation, consult the author's examination of 1 Peter 2:9-11, in his publication *Are Non-Jewish Believers Really a Part of Israel?*

as the main subject, and apply it to the nations' reception of the good news? If Paul were trying to speak of just the salvation of the nations, generically in general, there were other Tanach prophecies which he could have referred to—that the Jewish Believers in Rome would have taken notice of and understood. You will notice that in Romans 9:23-26 Paul **does not at all** call the non-Jewish Believers "Ephraim," here, as many Two-House people automatically would. Yet, in applying a prophetic word regarding the restoration of Israel to the nations, Paul surely believed the non-Jews he ministered to were participants in Israel's restoration. Such a restoration of Israel's Kingdom, having started in the First Century C.E., necessarily had a few details that only God Himself could know.

In his comments to the Corinthians, Paul summarizes quite well what we need to all be emphasizing today in the Messianic community. He writes, "For I do not want you to be unaware, brethren, that our fathers were all under the cloud and all passed through the sea; and all were baptized into Moses in the cloud and in the sea; and all ate the same spiritual food; and all drank the same spiritual drink, for they were drinking from a spiritual rock which followed them; and the rock was Messiah" (1 Corinthians 10:1-4). Paul did recognize both the Jewish and non-Jewish Corinthian Believers as partaking of the same spiritual heritage in Ancient Israel. Paul emphasizes, "brothers and sisters...our ancestors were all[110] under the cloud, and all passed through the sea" (NRSV). Paul wanted all of the Corinthians to understand that all Believers are part of the same community of faith, and that they all partake of the same spiritual heritage. This is true if one is a physical descendant of the Patriarchs or not. **In the Messiah Yeshua, all are a part of the community of Israel**—and all need to learn from the mistakes of the Ancient Israelites in the wilderness! I do not think any of us would argue, by extension, that there are serious mistakes that we all have to take instruction and warnings from, as they concern the Divided Kingdom era in the Books of Kings and Chronicles, as well.

In Paul's letter to the Galatians, he communicates to his readers that "if you belong to Christ, you are the 'issue' of Abraham and heirs by virtue of the promise" (Galatians 3:29, REB). Various Two-House advocates have overstated Paul's words "you are Abraham's seed" (NIV; Grk. *sperma*, σπέρμα) to the point that only physical descendants or "sperm" of Abraham can really be those who are saved,[111] which is of course *doctrinal heresy*.[112] Paul's statement immediately preceding is most frequently hailed as the quintessential egalitarian credo: "There is neither Jew nor Greek, there is neither slave nor free man, there is neither male nor female; for you are all one in Messiah Yeshua" (Galatians 3:28; contra. t.*Berachot* 6:18). **All human beings are welcome into the people of God,** and are to be regarded as "one" in the Messiah. The Apostle Paul wanted the good news of salvation **to go to all people.** And, much to the chagrin of quite a few Messianics today (*including* many Two-

---

[110] Grk. *hoi pateres hēmōn pantes* (οἱ πατέρες ἡμῶν πάντες); the TNIV follows with, "our ancestors were all."

[111] This is at least partially implied by Wootten, *Restoring Israel's Kingdom*, 79.

[112] It can be, of course, legitimate to render the Greek *sperma* as "sperm," but the best, most neutral rendering is probably "seed" (American Standard Version, LITV, NIV).

House advocates), not only did Paul advocate the equality of Jewish and Greek Believers in the Body of Messiah, but most imperatively male and female Believers as well![113]

Born again Believers are to be regarded as the seed of Abraham certainly through their union with the Messiah; they are the seed of Abraham if they live like Abraham; they are the seed of Abraham if they partake of Abraham's covenant promises. And, many people who are the seed of Abraham are his physical descendants. *Paul's intention in Galatians 3:29 was to surely draw his readers' attention to the multi-faceted theological aspects of* sperma.[114]

Keep in mind how Paul appeals to how even Abraham had the good news proclaimed to him: "The Scripture, foreseeing that God would justify the Gentiles by faith, preached the gospel beforehand to Abraham, *saying*, 'ALL THE NATIONS[115] WILL BE BLESSED IN YOU'" (Galatians 3:8; cf. Genesis 12:2-3). This good news has obviously come to its fullest manifestation in the work of the Messiah Yeshua (Christ Jesus), in being sacrificed for all sinners. If we forget that by restoring Israel, God will bring salvation to the whole world, then we forget the mission that God has for Israel to make Israel a light to all of humankind (cf. Isaiah 49:6). While Paul considered the redeemed from the nations to be a part of "the Israel of God" (Galatians 6:16), along with the redeemed from the Jewish people—*nowhere* does he consider membership in such an Israel to be limited to only the physical descendants of Abraham, Isaac, and Jacob.[116]

The Author of Hebrews

Interestingly enough, one of the most direct statements in the Apostolic Scriptures regarding the reunion of the Northern and Southern Kingdoms of Israel is in the anonymous Epistle to the Hebrews. Its author quotes directly from Jeremiah 31:31-34 (in its Septuagint translation), concluding that the New Covenant has now been brought to fruition via the priestly work of Yeshua the Messiah. While Hebrews' audience was primarily First Century Jews in the Mediterranean Diaspora, likely in Rome, we cannot disclude or discount non-Jewish Believers from also reading or encountering it. The author of Hebrews writes about the Levitical priesthood, about to fall via the impending destruction of the Second Temple in 70 C.E., which was to naturally give way to the priesthood of Melchizedek served by Yeshua in Heaven. This priesthood has been inaugurated

---

[113] For a further examination, consult the author's exegesis paper on Galatians 3:28, "Biblical Equality and Today's Messianic Movement." Also consult the FAQ on the TNN website, "Women in Ministry."

See also the useful resource, Philip B. Payne, *Man and Woman, One in Christ: An Exegetical and Theological Study of Paul's Letters* (Grand Rapids: Zondervan, 2009).

[114] Heb. equiv. *zera* (זֶרַע).

Cf. Stern, *Jewish New Testament Commentary*, 549.

[115] Grk. *panta ta ethnē* (πάντα τὰ ἔθνη), which also appears in Matthew 28:19.

[116] For a further evaluation of some significant Pauline passages regarding non-Jewish inclusion in the community/Commonwealth of Israel (Romans 2:28-29; 9:3-6, 23-29; 11:16-24, 25-29; 16:4; 1 Corinthians 10:1-11, 18; Galatians 2:7-10; 6:15-16; Ephesians 2:11-13; 3:6; Titus 2:13-14), consult the author's publication *Are Non-Jewish Believers Really a Part of Israel?*

by the work of the Messiah, and with it has come the reality of the New Covenant with its promises of permanent atonement, forgiveness from sin, and a supernatural transcription of the Torah onto the hearts and minds of the redeemed. What the author of Hebrews writes is very important for us as Messianic Believers to understand:

"But now He has obtained a more excellent ministry, by as much as He is also the mediator of a better covenant, which has been enacted on better promises. For if that first [tabernacle/priesthood/service][117] had been faultless, there would have been no occasion sought for a second. For finding fault with them, He says, 'BEHOLD, DAYS ARE COMING, SAYS THE LORD, WHEN I WILL EFFECT A NEW COVENANT WITH THE HOUSE OF ISRAEL AND WITH THE HOUSE OF JUDAH; NOT LIKE THE COVENANT WHICH I MADE WITH THEIR FATHERS ON THE DAY WHEN I TOOK THEM BY THE HAND TO LEAD THEM OUT OF THE LAND OF EGYPT; FOR THEY DID NOT CONTINUE IN MY COVENANT, AND I DID NOT CARE FOR THEM, SAYS THE LORD. FOR THIS IS THE COVENANT THAT I WILL MAKE WITH THE HOUSE OF ISRAEL AFTER THOSE DAYS, SAYS THE LORD: I WILL PUT MY LAWS INTO THEIR MINDS, AND I WILL WRITE THEM ON THEIR HEARTS. AND I WILL BE THEIR GOD, AND THEY SHALL BE MY PEOPLE. AND THEY SHALL NOT TEACH EVERYONE HIS FELLOW CITIZEN, AND EVERYONE HIS BROTHER, SAYING, 'KNOW THE LORD,' FOR ALL WILL KNOW ME, FROM THE LEAST TO THE GREATEST OF THEM. FOR I WILL BE MERCIFUL TO THEIR INIQUITIES, AND I WILL REMEMBER THEIR SINS NO MORE'" (Hebrews 8:6-12).

The New Covenant was promised to a people of Israel, Judah and Israel, in the process of restoration (cf. Ezekiel 36:25-27). However, it is also true that the Holy Spirit was to be poured out upon *kol-basar* (כָּל־בָּשָׂר) or "all flesh" (Joel 2:28, RSV; cf. Acts 2:17). All men and women who place their trust in Israel's Messiah, are to receive the benefits of the New Covenant inaugurated by Yeshua (Luke 22:20)— whether they be of Judah or Israel *or* the nations—and are to have Moses' Teaching supernaturally inscribed upon their psyche (cf. Romans 8:1-4). Only those who are members of Israel's Kingdom realm, which would by necessity include those of the nations redeemed by grace as well, can benefit from the New Covenant's promise of a permanent sacrifice and atonement, and permanent forgiveness, available for transgressions and sins.[118]

---

[117] The NASU is unique, in that it has "For if that first *covenant* had been faultless," with "*covenant*" appearing in *italics*, which is not often present in other versions like the RSV/NRSV/ESV or NIV. All the Greek has is *Ei gar hē prōtē ekeinē* (Εἰ γὰρ ἡ πρώτη ἐκείνη), with no specific noun attached to *prōtē* or "first."

While the feminine term *diathēkē* (διαθήκη) or "covenant" could be referred to, given what is witnessed in the surrounding cotext (Hebrews 7:22; 8:6, 9, 10; 9:4, 16, 17, 20), so also could *skēnē* (σκηνή) or "tabernacle" (Hebrews 8:2, 5; 9:2, 3, 6, 8, 11, 21), *hierōsunē* (ἱερωσύνη) or "priesthood" (Hebrews 7:11, 12, 24), or even *leitourgia* (λειτουργία) or "ministry/service" (Hebrews 8:6; 9:21). The latter three would be used as referents to the Levitical sacrificial system, which the author of Hebrews affirms is surpassed in effectiveness by the Melchizedekian priesthood of Yeshua.

[118] This subject is examined in more detail in the author's article "What Is the New Covenant?" appearing in his book *The New Testament Validates Torah*.

Also be sure to consult the entry for the Epistle to the Hebrews in the author's workbook *A Survey of the Apostolic Scriptures for the Practical Messianic* and the commentary *Hebrews for the Practical Messianic*.

The Apostle John

In the Book of Revelation, we see twelve tribes of Israel mentioned. When the 144,000 sealed witnesses are commissioned by the Lord to perform their work, John records that 12,000 are sealed from each tribe:

"And I heard the number of those who were sealed, one hundred and forty-four thousand sealed from every tribe of the sons of Israel: from the tribe of Judah, twelve thousand *were* sealed, from the tribe of Reuben twelve thousand, from the tribe of Gad twelve thousand, from the tribe of Asher twelve thousand, from the tribe of Naphtali twelve thousand, from the tribe of Manasseh twelve thousand, from the tribe of Simeon twelve thousand, from the tribe of Levi twelve thousand, from the tribe of Issachar twelve thousand, from the tribe of Zebulun twelve thousand, from the tribe of Joseph twelve thousand, from the tribe of Benjamin, twelve thousand *were* sealed" (Revelation 7:4-8).

These individuals are going to be physical descendants of Abraham, Isaac, and Jacob. While tribal delineation has widely been lost due to the Assyrian and Babylonian exiles, those who are sealed know what tribe of Israel they are from, because God Himself is the One who performs the sealing—and it is likely that many of them are not all from the Holy Land, with various persons in the Diaspora. John records that 12,000 from every tribe are sealed. Notably missing is the Tribe of Dan, because for whatever reason, Dan is incapable of performing the functions that God would assign to it. Instead, it is replaced with "Joseph," and Levi or the priestly tribe is also included on the list. Undoubtedly included among these people will be various descendants of the exiled Northern Kingdom of Israel, which was corporately taken captive by Assyria in a series of dispersions in the Eighth Century B.C.E., and whose return to the Holy Land will be a sign of the end-times.[119]

It is witnessed that there are references to a larger restoration of Israel detectable in the Apostolic Scriptures or New Testament, involving the descendants of the exiled Northern Kingdom, but they are given in the context of the spread of the good news among the nations. Some of today's well-known Messianic teachers have taken note of how Tanach verses like Hosea 1:10 and 2:23 are quoted in Romans 9:6 and 1 Peter 2:10, and applied to the early non-Jewish Believers. They conclude that some kind of typological or allegorical application, regarding the exiled Northern Kingdom of Israel/Ephraim, is present.[120] Yet, they widely leave the question of *why* a figure like Peter or Paul would apply words regarding the those of the exiled Northern Kingdom to the nations unanswered or

---

[119] For a further evaluation consult Chapter 8 of the author's book *When Will the Messiah Return?*, "The Gospel of the Kingdom: Who Are the 144,000?"

Also consult the examination of Revelation 1:6; 5:10; 20:6 in the author's publication *Are Non-Jewish Believers Really a Part of Israel?*

[120] D. Thomas Lancaster, *The Mystery of the Gospel* (Littleton, CO: First Fruits of Zion, 2003), pp 82-83, 140 en#30; Tim Hegg, *Paul's Epistle to the Romans Volume 2: Chapters 9-16* (Tacoma, WA: TorahResource, 2007), pp 298-300.

unaddressed, if indeed those from the nations brought to Messiah faith in the First Century C.E. did not include some small level of descendants of the exiled Northern Kingdom among them in the Mediterranean basin.

On the flip side of this, though, there are Two-House populists who will without hesitation claim that the non-Jewish Believers referred to in Romans 9:6 and 1 Peter 2:10 were all pretty much "Ephraimites,"[121] and that they were all some sort of lost Israelites in dispersion. This goes much too far in the other direction, and may be tantamount to putting words in the Apostles' mouths. (And, it is something that has been further embellished, often rather dangerously, by many of such teachers' ardent followers.)

Any kind of spiritualized or typological application of restoration of Israel passages to the nations does not do enough. Isaiah 49:6 is clear to explain, "It is too small a thing that You should be My Servant to raise up the tribes of Jacob and to restore the preserved ones of Israel; I will also make You a light of the nations so that My salvation may reach to the end of the earth." The salvation of the nations, generally, is a part of the grand restoration of Israel. Isaiah 49:6 is appealed to, for certain, concerning the nations' redemption (Luke 2:32; Acts 13:47; 26:23). But why also apply words and terms regarding the Northern Kingdom of Israel/Ephraim to the nations' redemption?

Any assumption that all, or even most, of the non-Jewish Believers in Yeshua from the First Century were "Ephraimites," draws a conclusion that not only the Apostles themselves did not make—it is something that the Apostles could not have humanly known, if there were a few descendants of the Northern Kingdom "swallowed up" (Hosea 8:8) and assimilated within small parts of their First Century world in the Mediterranean basin. The term "Ephraimite" does not appear anywhere in the Apostolic Scriptures or New Testament.

The safe approach—that the nations are participants in a larger restoration of Israel—does the Biblical text its proper justice, focuses on what is most important, and is by far the most inclusive regarding the people of God. Those in passages like Romans 9:26 and 1 Peter 2:10 should be regarded as people genuinely of the nations at large, and at best only included a few assimilated descendants of the exiled Northern Kingdom of Israel here or there (cf. Deuteronomy 28:62). Yet, if the Lord can demonstrate mercy and grace to the descendants of the exiled Northern Kingdom—whose ancestors once lived in the Promised Land, saw the Temple of Solomon and God's presence within it, and then fell into gross idolatry—would He not also be compelled to save those of the nations, who were just turned over to sin and their lusts (cf. Romans 1), welcoming them as participants in Israel's restoration?

None of the Apostles labeled the non-Jews coming to faith in the First Century as "Ephraimites," a common term used throughout the Two-House sub-movement today that has become anachronistic and has been significantly abused.[122] The

---

[121] Cf. Wootten, *Who Is Israel?*, enlarged edition, pp 43-44.
[122] Cf. Wootten, *Redeemed Israel—Restored and Reunited*, 153.

Apostles never identify a particular nationality with Tribe XYZ, nor do they ever identify non-Jewish Believers as "Ephraim."

The Apostles *do apply* prophetic passages regarding the exiled Northern Kingdom of Israel/Ephraim to the nations (notably, in the First Century Mediterranean basin). The Apostles *do affirm* that by receiving the gospel message and salvation in Messiah Yeshua, a non-Jewish person partakes of the spiritual heritage of Israel, and that figures like Abraham, Isaac, and Jacob are to be regarded as their "ancestors" too (1 Corinthians 10:1, NRSV). The Apostles *do recognize* that a non-Jewish Believer is every bit a contributing member of the community/Commonwealth of Israel as a Jewish person. If a very small few of the non-Jewish Believers in the First Century world of the Apostles were indeed descendants of the exiled Northern Kingdom of Israel/Ephraim—then not unlike the true identity of the Unknown Soldier, such knowledge would have only been known to God. **The Apostles were more concerned about the salvation of a human being from sin and eternal punishment, something which heredity of any kind does not guarantee.**

A considerable challenge in the Two-House sub-movement is that too many of its teachers and leaders have been caught overemphasizing the return of descendants of the Northern Kingdom of Israel/Ephraim *at the expense of the universal availability of the gospel for all of humanity!* Just like many evangelical Christians understand the fact that God's Kingdom is to be restored on Earth via the return of Jesus, and that as Believers we are to work toward this goal via the proclamation of the good news—many of the same forget that God's Kingdom happens to be the Kingdom of Israel. Many Messianics have made the reverse mistake of forgetting that the Kingdom of Israel being restored is the Kingdom of God being brought to Earth, which is to welcome in all people from the masses of humankind who acknowledge Him as the Eternal One.

The only way God's Kingdom can be restored is by the restoration of individuals to their Creator, by knowing Yeshua the Messiah as their Personal Savior, and then having them properly discipled in their relationship with Him. If this does not happen, it does not matter if one is of Judah, Ephraim, or the nations.

Yeshua the Messiah
and "the Lost Sheep of the House of Israel"

One of the most difficult sayings of Yeshua the Messiah to reckon with, for many people within today's broad Messianic movement, is where He declares, **"I was sent only to the lost sheep of the house of Israel"** (Matthew 15:24; cf. 10:6). Many of today's Messianic Jews and Two-House proponents have been found to use "lost sheep of the house of Israel," as a convenient and significant sound byte, to promote various activities or positions. Many of those involved in Jewish evangelism have used "lost sheep of the house of Israel," as a way to promote their ministries. Many teachers and leaders within the Two-House sub-movement have been caught using, "I was sent only to the lost sheep of the house of Israel," as implying that salvation is only intended for the Jewish people and/or those of the exiled Northern Kingdom of Israel/Ephraim, with the nations at large a distant afterthought in the intention of God (that is, if God is even interested in the nations at all). *What do we do with Yeshua's words about the "lost sheep"?* A much better handle on what "lost sheep of the house of Israel" actually means, in the verses where it appears, is surely needed by **all Messianic people.**

There are some legitimate questions to be asked when one sees Yeshua's instruction to His Disciples, "Do not go in *the* way of *the* Gentiles, and do not enter *any* city of the Samaritans; but rather go to the lost sheep of the house of Israel" (Matthew 10:5-6).[123] It should be quite apparent from this, that these directions from the Messiah are bound by some kind of a timestamp or set time period. The idea that Yeshua *completely prohibited* His Disciples from ever going to the nations, or to the Samaritans, runs into a significant continuity problem when we see later instructions from the Lord—to actually go to all the nations and into Samaria (Matthew 28:19; Acts 1:8). The Book of Acts easily attests to how the gospel spread among the Samaritans and the nations at large. The word that the Disciples were to only go "to the lost sheep of the house of Israel" had to regard various ministry assignments and tasks which were to take place during Yeshua's specific, personal time with His Disciples. Once the Messiah ascended into Heaven, any limitation on working with those who were outside of the classification of "lost sheep of the house of Israel" was lifted by His own instruction to them.

For many Two-House advocates, there is some confusion regarding the terms witnessed, because many automatically assume that the Ten Lost Tribes of the Northern Kingdom are referred to when "the lost sheep of the house of Israel"[124] are spoken of. This is an easy conclusion to pass along, because the Northern Kingdom of Israel/Ephraim is frequently called the House of Israel in the Tanach, and they may be regarded as generally lost among the nations. Yet, when we read the various passages in the Gospels that mention "the lost sheep of the house of Israel" (Matthew 15:21-28; Mark 7:24-30), the idea that this is in reference to the Ten Lost Tribes runs into a few problems.

Most interpreters have rightly associated Yeshua's references to "lost sheep," with His Messianic role as the Good Shepherd. D.H. Johnson points out how "The OT language behind the saying about sheep without a shepherd is clear (Num 27:17; 1 Kings 22:17 par. 2 Chron 18:16; Eze 34:5)."[125] The tenor of Jeremiah 50:6 is, "My people have become lost sheep; their shepherds have led them astray. They have made them turn aside *on* the mountains; they have gone along from mountain

---

[123] It is interesting to suggest that the Greek term *hodos* (ὁδός), "way" (NASU) or "road" (HCSB), could be viewed in the sense of *"a way* or *manner"* (LS, 543), as does Wootten, *Restoring Israel's Kingdom*, pp 99-101. So, it might be said that the Disciples were prohibited from acting in the "ways of the nations," or their behavior. This is a tenuously difficult view to hold here, though, as *hodos* has to be kept in view of *polis* (πόλις), which is a town or a city. A locational orientation for both *hodos* and *polis* is required for Matthew 10:5.

[124] Grk. *ta probata ta apolōlota oikou Israēl* (τὰ πρόβατα τὰ ἀπολωλότα οἴκου Ἰσραήλ); Delitzch Heb. NT *ha'tzon ha'ovdot asher l'Beit-Yisrael* (הַצֹּאן הָאֲבֻדוֹת אֲשֶׁר לְבֵית־יִשְׂרָאֵל).

[125] D.H. Johnson, "Shepherd, Sheep," in Joel B. Green, Scot McKnight, and I. Howard Marshall, eds., *Dictionary of Jesus and the Gospels* (Downers Grove, IL: InterVarsity, 1992), 751.

to hill and have forgotten their resting place." The main issue is Yeshua's ministry to those of Israel who have gone astray and are perishing in their trespasses and sins, in need of a return to a proper path that pleases the Holy One.

So, who are the specific "the lost sheep of the house of Israel" referred to, and in focus, in the Gospels? Are they the descendants of the exiled Northern Kingdom of Israel/Ephraim? A careful view of Yeshua's encounter with the Syrophoenician, or Canaanite woman, is in order:

> "Yeshua got up and went away from there to the region of Tyre. And when He had entered a house, He wanted no one to know *of it*; yet He could not escape notice. But after hearing of Him, a woman whose little daughter had an unclean spirit immediately came and fell at His feet. Now the woman was a Gentile, of the Syrophoenician race. And she kept asking Him to cast the demon out of her daughter. And He was saying to her, 'Let the children be satisfied first, for it is not good to take the children's bread and throw it to the dogs.' But she answered and said to Him, 'Yes, Lord, *but* even the dogs under the table feed on the children's crumbs.' And He said to her, 'Because of this answer go; the demon has gone out of your daughter.' And going back to her home, she found the child lying on the bed, the demon having left" (Mark 7:24-30).

> "Yeshua went away from there, and withdrew into the district of Tyre and Sidon. And a Canaanite woman from that region came out and *began* to cry out, saying, 'Have mercy on me, Lord, Son of David; my daughter is cruelly demon-possessed.' But He did not answer her a word. And His disciples came and implored Him, saying, 'Send her away, because she keeps shouting at us.' But He answered and said, 'I was sent only to the lost sheep of the house of Israel.' But she came and *began* to bow down before Him, saying, 'Lord, help me!' And He answered and said, 'It is not good to take the children's bread and throw it to the dogs.' But she said, 'Yes, Lord; but even the dogs feed on the crumbs which fall from their masters' table.' Then Yeshua said to her, 'O woman, your faith is great; it shall be done for you as you wish.' And her daughter was healed at once" (Matthew 15:21-28).

Any idea that "I was sent only to the lost sheep of the house of Israel," means that the good news of salvation is to be constrained only to a particular group of people on Planet Earth—is easily refuted when one witnesses how the Syrophoencian or Canaanite woman's request is answered by Yeshua. *Her daughter is released from the demon, and Yeshua lauds her great faith.* To use Yeshua's statement, "I was sent only to the lost sheep of the house of Israel," to promote some kind of racially-based salvation plan or preference—as it can be seen among a wide number of Two-House people—has no basis from either Mark 7:24-30 or Matthew 15:21-28. If some Messianic Jews claim that "I was sent only to the lost sheep of the house of Israel," means that Yeshua was sent exclusively to see the Jewish people redeemed, this conclusion, as well, has no basis in either Mark 7:24-30 or Matthew 15:21-28—and even more so given Yeshua's emphasis on the good news to be declared to all nations (Matthew 24:14; 28:19-20). The statement, "I was sent only to the lost sheep of the house of Israel" is instead to highlight who the first recipients of the gospel were.[126]

So who are, specifically, "the lost sheep of the house of Israel"? Apparently, such persons do not include the Syrophoenician or Canaanite woman. Likewise, such "lost sheep of the house of Israel" would have excluded the Samaritans (Matthew 10:5-6). If by "lost sheep of the house of Israel" are intended, as many Two-House proponents think, a reference to the good news going out to the descendants of the Ten Lost Tribes—why would the Samaritans then be excluded? The Samaritans, if "the lost sheep of the house of Israel" spoken of by Yeshua were intended to be the Ten Lost Tribes, should have been some of the *first candidates* to receive the good news, after all. 2 Kings 17:24-41 records how the Assyrians relocated foreigners to what was left of the Northern Kingdom of Israel, and they intermarried with many of the remaining Northern Kingdom Israelites, producing the Samaritan people.

Viewing "the lost sheep of the house of Israel" as a reference to the gospel message, only going to those people descended from the exiled Northern Kingdom, runs into some observable challenges. What about the gospel going to those descended from the Southern Kingdom? For that same matter, Yeshua's prohibition of Matthew 10:5, "Don't take the road leading to other nations, and don't enter any Samaritan town" (HCSB), could be taken as meaning that the Disciples were not to go into the Mediterranean basin, where a large number of the Diaspora Jewish population itself resided!

A static reading of passages like Matthew 10:5-6; 15:21-28; Mark 7:24-30, with its prohibitions of the Disciples only going "to the lost sheep of the house of Israel," is problematic. These instructions had to have been temporal, to the scope of time during the ministry of Yeshua, as they are constrained to a limited geographical area. At a later point in time, the Disciples certainly went to the nations at large, and even to the Samaritans.

So who are **"the lost sheep of the house of Israel"** in Matthew 10:5-6; 15:21-28; Mark 7:24-30? These lost sheep are not only Yeshua's own fellow Jews, but they are specifically the Jewish people who Yeshua reached out to in Jerusalem, Judea, and Galilee. The "house of Israel" Yeshua has been sent to, as specified in these verses, excludes not only those people descended from the exiled Northern Kingdom of Israel/Ephraim, but could be taken to exclude those of the Diaspora Jewish community. Yet on the day of *Shavuot*/Pentecost, as witnessed in Acts ch. 2, many scores of Diaspora Jews would come to faith in Him.

Because of how the terminology "lost sheep of the house of Israel" has been used in the vast majority of the Two-House sub-movement, as applied to the exiled Northern Kingdom, it is difficult for some to see the fact that such "lost sheep of the house of Israel" are classified as Yeshua's own Jewish people. As Bible readers who have to be honest with the text and Biblical history, the Northern Kingdom

---

[126] Craig S. Keener, *IVP New Testament Commentary Series: Matthew* (Downers Grove, IL: InterVarsity, 1997), 202.

would quantitatively become "not My people" (Hosea 1:9-10) and be removed from Israel. With the downfall of the Northern Kingdom to Assyria, the Southern Kingdom inherited all of the titles and rights and honors of being "Israel" as the legitimate successor state (cf. Ezra 6:17). The Samaritans in Matthew 10:5-6, while perhaps having physical descent from the tribes of the Northern Kingdom, are notably excluded from being classified as the House of Israel.

The House of Israel that Yeshua refers to in Matthew 10:5-6; 15:21-28; Mark 7:24-30, is actually intended to be those who recognize the God of Israel as Supreme Deity, the ones who He came to first minister to. This would not be the Samaritans with their hybrid religion, nor would it be the nations at large. For the purposes of these passages, the Jewish people within Jerusalem, Judea, and Galilee are the House of Israel. D. Thomas Lancaster's observations, in his book *The Mystery of the Gospel* (2003), are somewhat useful:

"Who are the lost sheep of Israel that Yeshua sought? They are clearly not Gentiles or even to be found among the Gentiles. They are not the Ten Lost Tribes. They are the sinners and the tax collectors, the backsliders and the irreligious of the Master's countrymen. They are the Jewish people."[127]

Of course, no Bible reader can rightly argue that the good news was intended exclusively and only for First Century Jewish people in the Holy Land who had spiritually gone astray. The instructions of Matthew 10:5-6; 15:21-28; Mark 7:24-30 were temporal for the period of Yeshua's ministry, and draw the attention of how the good news was first declared to those Jews in Jerusalem, Judea, and Galilee.

One can see how "the lost sheep of the house of Israel" within the Gospels, does refer to Yeshua's own Jewish people who are spiritually perishing. But does the subject matter of the exiled Northern Kingdom "out there" among the nations, get totally nullified from the House of Israel being the Jews? It might come as a surprise to some Bible readers, but in the Book of Ezekiel itself—where the two-stick oracle of Ezekiel 37:15-28, detailing a futuristic reunification of Judah and Ephraim, appears—the House of Israel can often be used as terminology to refer to the Southern Kingdom of Judah! Steven Tuell informs us of how,

"Typically in Ezekiel, 'Israel' is used for *all* Israel, or even for Judah alone since, with the loss of the northern tribes, Judah is all of Israel that remains…[W]hen Ezekiel is certainly referring to the northern kingdom, he does not usually use the term Israel (see 23:4, where the wicked sister Oholah is Samaria, capital of the northern kingdom, and 37:16, where the northern kingdom is designated Ephraim)."[128]

The House of Judah actually being referred to as the House of Israel ***does not mean*** that there are not people from the exiled Northern Kingdom "out there" among the nations; it does mean that by all rights and privileges the Jewish people are the inheritors of the title "Israel." When Yeshua the Messiah refers to His fellow Jews as "the lost sheep of the house of Israel," it was certainly with this in mind.

---

[127] Lancaster, *The Mystery of the Gospel*, 111.

[128] Steven Tuell, *New International Biblical Commentary: Ezekiel* (Peabody, MA: Hendrickson, 2009), 26.

However, prophecy is clear that there will be a regathering together of a larger and fuller flock of Israel. As it concerns the community of Ancient Israel, of both the Northern and Southern Kingdoms as the flock of the Lord, it is useful for us to take serious note of Jeremiah 50:17:

"**Israel is a scattered flock, the lions have driven** *them* **away. The first one** *who* **devoured him was the king of Assyria, and this last one** *who* **has broken his bones is Nebuchadnezzar king of Babylon."**

Israel here is obviously a reference to both the Northern and Southern Kingdoms, how they have been scattered,[129] and how they have been hurt by both the Assyrians and Babylonians. The Northern Kingdom, though, may be regarded as having been devoured or eaten[130]—whereabouts largely unknown. The Southern Kingdom, though, may be regarded as having its bones broken.[131] The Northern Kingdom was not only scattered, but devoured; the Southern Kingdom was scattered, but only broken. The expectation from God is, "'And I will bring Israel back to his pasture and he will graze on Carmel and Bashan, and his desire will be satisfied in the hill country of Ephraim and Gilead. In those days and at that time,' declares the LORD, 'search will be made for the iniquity of Israel, but there will be none; and for the sins of Judah, but they will not be found; for I will pardon those whom I leave as a remnant'" (Jeremiah 50:19-20). There will be a reunification of the greater flock of Israel, obviously including those from the exiled Northern Kingdom.

Keener astutely indicates, on Matthew 10:1-4, how "Most Jewish people expected an eschatological restoration of the lost tribes (e.g., Tob 13:6; 2 Macc 2:18; Ps. Sol. 8:28; Test. Benj. 9:2; Pesiq. Rab Kah. Sup. 5:3; Gen. Rab. 98:9...)...though some dissent seems to have arisen (m. Sanh. 10:5; t. Sanh. 13:12)."[132] We have previously discussed how speculation on what happened to the Northern Kingdom of Israel, was present within the Jewish world of Yeshua and the Apostles. An end-time restoration of the descendants of these people is talked about in ancient Jewish literature. Simply because the Jewish people of the First Century were the House of Israel (cf. Acts 2:36)—especially because the widely exiled and scattered Northern Kingdom of Israel was no longer to be regarded as God's people (Hosea 1:9-10)—does not mean that there were not people from the Northern Kingdom "out there" among the nations. The Samaritans themselves, who were descended from some of the Northern Kingdom survivors, were not even regarded as the House of Israel.

Yeshua's word of "I was sent only to the lost sheep of the house of Israel," is akin to how Paul would later say, "I am not ashamed of the gospel, for it is the power of God for salvation to everyone who believes, to the Jew first and also to the Greek" (Romans 1:16). The Jewish people of the First Century were to surely be

---

[129] Heb. verb *pazar* (פָּזַר).

[130] Heb. verb *akal* (אָכַל).

[131] Heb. verb *atzam* (עָצַם); "gnawed" (RSV).

[132] Craig S. Keener, *The Gospel of Matthew: A Socio-Rhetorical Commentary* (Grand Rapids: Eerdmans, 2009), 310 fn#2.

recognized as the House of Israel, those who were loyal to the God of Israel, but who were perishing without the Good Shepherd. The Jewish people being such a House of Israel, does not at all, though, rule out various pockets of people in the nations being descended from the exiled Northern Kingdom of Israel/Ephraim.

The condition of anyone from the nations, without knowledge of Israel's God, is a removal from Israel—meaning that they are not a part of the House of Israel. Paul told those in Asia Minor, after all, "you were at that time separate from Messiah, excluded from the commonwealth of Israel, and strangers to the covenants of promise, having no hope and without God in the world" (Ephesians 2:12). Whether a small few non-Jewish Believers among them had a lineage from the exiled Northern Kingdom, or not, **before faith in Yeshua they were not a part of the community of Israel.** They were outside of the realm where the promises and blessings of God—especially the Messianic promise—could be legitimately realized.

Yeshua the Messiah Himself spoke of how, "I have other sheep, which are not of this fold; I must bring them also, and they will hear My voice; and they will become one flock *with* one shepherd" (John 10:16). Commentators on the Gospel of John are in general agreement that the "other sheep"[133] is an anticipatory remark made by the Lord, about the missions the Apostles would go on among the nations declaring of His salvation.[134] Yeshua the Messiah did envision His followers composing a larger flock of sheep, than just those whom He classified as "the lost sheep of the house of Israel" in Jerusalem, Judea, and Galilee. There were also "the children of God who are scattered abroad" (John 11:52) which were to hear of Him as well. Sheep from the Jewish Diaspora outside of the Land of Israel, and from the nations generally, would need to come to a knowledge of Him as Savior. The "Israel of God" (Galatians 6:16) as rightly manifested via the Messiah's work, is to be regarded as something rather large and inclusive—composed of all who recognize Him as Redeemer. When Yeshua says, "there will be one flock, one shepherd" (John 10:16, CJB), any idea of this being a flock of people with sub-divisions rigidly emphasized, should be disregarded when kept in view of how the unity His followers are to have is like the unity He has with the Father (John 17:21-23).

Today's Messianic Believers need to be quite cautious when using the terminology "the lost sheep of the house of Israel." It was used by Yeshua to describe His fellow Jews in the vicinity of Jerusalem, Judea, and Galilee. The good news of His salvation, in fact, was to go out to the Diaspora Jewish community, the Samaritans, *and* the whole world, and as a result would have certainly expanded the spiritual borders of Israel's commonwealth (cf. Ephesians 2:11-13). It would be

---

[133] Grk. *alla probata* (ἄλλα πρόβατα).

[134] Cf. Leon Morris, *New International Commentary on the New Testament: The Gospel According to John* (Grand Rapids: Eerdmans, 1971), 512; F.F. Bruce, *The Gospel of John* (Grand Rapids: Eerdmans, 1983), pp 227-228; George R. Beasley-Murray, *Word Biblical Commentary: John*, Vol 36 (Waco, TX: Word Books, 1987), 171; D.A. Carson, *Pillar New Testament Commentary: The Gospel According to John* (Grand Rapids: Eerdmans, 1991), 388; Colin G. Kruse, *Tyndale New Testament Commentaries: John* (Grand Rapids: Eerdmans, 2003), 237.

advised for today that one *really not use* "the lost sheep of the house of Israel" to describe the current Jewish people who need Yeshua, and especially not those of the exiled Northern Kingdom. For Jewish evangelism, quoting Romans 1:16, "to the Jew first," is a far better option. And, simply referring to "the exiled/scattered Northern Kingdom" would be what is historically accurate and the least controversial.[135]

Recognizing the Variant Uses of "Israel"

Far too frequently, not only among your average Christians—but also among many Messianic Jews—when they encounter usages of "Israel," in the Bible, it is automatically assumed that only the Jewish people are being referred to. Does this at all properly align with what we see in Biblical history? Is there not some variance of how the term "Israel" is used? Those who are more historically conscious in their Bible reading, do recognize that it is inappropriate to simply equate all uses of "Israel" as being synonymous with "the Jewish people." This is especially true the further and further back you go in Biblical history.

In the *International Standard Bible Encyclopedia* or *ISBE*, which is often considered to be a general conservative resource, the entry "Israel, History of the People of" by C.F. Pfeieffer (2:908-924), includes references to ten different periods of time in Biblical history which "Israel," in some form or another, is featured as a player. These include:

1. Pre-Mosaic Israel
2. Moses and the Exodus
3. Conquest of Canaan
4. Period of the Judges
5. United Kingdom
6. Divided Kingdom
7. Babylonian Exile
8. Return from Exile and Restoration
9. The Jews under Alexander and His Successors
10. The Jews under the Romans[136]

The main periods where there is confusion, regarding how the term "Israel" appears in Biblical history, occur from the Divided Kingdom period to Second Temple Judaism. The Northern Kingdom that broke off from the Southern Kingdom was known as "Israel," and this is borne out in prophetic texts like Hosea and Amos, where the "Israel" being referred to is principally a Northern Kingdom audience.[137] This can be confusing for many Bible readers, who may not make

---

[135] For a further evaluation, consult the author's examination of John 10:14-18, in his publication *Are Non-Jewish Believers Really a Part of Israel?*

[136] The outline in C.F. Pfeieffer, "Israel, History of the People of," in *ISBE*, 2:908-909.

[137] Cf. R.K. Harrison, *Introduction to the Old Testament* (Grand Rapids: Eerdmans, 1969), pp 860, 869 (Hosea); pp 884-885, 887 (Amos); Raymond B. Dillard and Tremper Longman III, *An Introduction to the Old Testament* (Grand Rapids: Zondervan, 1994), pp 354-356 (Hosea); pp 375-376 (Amos).

enough of an effort to place such prophetic books within their original setting. Further confusion ensues later in a text like Ezekiel, where following the fall of the Northern Kingdom, when "Israel" is used it can be as a reference to the Southern Kingdom, as the legitimate successor state to the title and the whole of the rights of "Israel." In the Apostolic Scriptures, "Israel" does largely represent the Jewish community, but that does not mean that non-Jews were excluded from being a part of Israel's Kingdom realm, as their Messiah faith certainly gave them citizenship within Israel (Ephesians 2:11-13; 3:6; cf. Galatians 6:16), being grafted-in to the olive tree (Romans 11:16-18).

There is a significant amount of debate among Romans interpreters, as to how many different variances regarding "Israel" are present in the Apostle Paul's discussion of Romans chs. 9-11. Generally speaking, at least two different views of "Israel" are believed to be present: the First Century Jewish community that had largely rejected the Messiah, and the restored eschatological Kingdom of Israel. Within Paul's salvation-historical perspective of "Israel" in Romans chs. 9-11—which is intended to direct the reader to the point of "all Israel will be saved" (Romans 11:25-26)—it may even be that there are as high as five different detectable variances in which "Israel" is used:

- the historical ancient community (Romans 9:4-5[138]; 10:19-21[139]; 11:7-10[140])
- God's corporate elect, and/or an eschatological, restored Kingdom of Israel composed of righteous people (Romans 9:6[141]; 11:25-27[142])
- Paul's First Century Jewish countrymen (Romans 9:4[143]; 11:1[144], 11-15[145], 28[146])

---

[138] "[W]ho are Israelites, to whom belongs the adoption as sons, and the glory and the covenants and the giving of the Law and the *temple* service and the promises, whose are the fathers, and from whom is the Messiah according to the flesh, who is over all, God blessed forever. Amen" (Romans 9:4-5).

[139] "But I say, surely Israel did not know, did they? First Moses says, 'I WILL MAKE YOU JEALOUS BY THAT WHICH IS NOT A NATION, BY A NATION WITHOUT UNDERSTANDING WILL I ANGER YOU' [Deuteronomy 32:21]. And Isaiah is very bold and says, 'I WAS FOUND BY THOSE WHO DID NOT SEEK ME, I BECAME MANIFEST TO THOSE WHO DID NOT ASK FOR ME' [Isaiah 65:1]. But as for Israel He says, 'ALL THE DAY LONG I HAVE STRETCHED OUT MY HANDS TO A DISOBEDIENT AND OBSTINATE PEOPLE' [Isaiah 65:2]" (Romans 10:19-21).

[140] "What then? What Israel is seeking, it has not obtained, but those who were chosen obtained it, and the rest were hardened; just as it is written, 'GOD GAVE THEM A SPIRIT OF STUPOR, EYES TO SEE NOT AND EARS TO HEAR NOT, DOWN TO THIS VERY DAY' [Deuteronomy 29:4; Isaiah 29:10]. And David says, 'LET THEIR TABLE BECOME A SNARE AND A TRAP, AND A STUMBLING BLOCK AND A RETRIBUTION TO THEM. LET THEIR EYES BE DARKENED TO SEE NOT, AND BEND THEIR BACKS FOREVER' [Psalm 69:22-23; 35:8]" (Romans 11:7-10).

[141] "But *it is* not as though the word of God has failed. For they are not all Israel who are *descended* from Israel" (Romans 9:6).

[142] "For I do not want you, brethren, to be uninformed of this mystery—so that you will not be wise in your own estimation—that a partial hardening has happened to Israel until the fullness of the Gentiles has come in; and so all Israel will be saved; just as it is written, 'THE DELIVERER WILL COME FROM ZION, HE WILL REMOVE UNGODLINESS FROM JACOB. THIS IS MY COVENANT WITH THEM, WHEN I TAKE AWAY THEIR SINS' [Isaiah 59:20-21; 27:9; Jeremiah 31:33-34]" (Romans 11:25-27).

[143] "[W]ho are Israelites, to whom belongs the adoption as sons, and the glory and the covenants and the giving of the Law and the *temple* service and the promises" (Romans 9:4).

- the Jewish people of largely the Second Temple era (Romans 9:31[147])
- the Northern Kingdom of Israel (Romans 11:2-4[148]; cf. 1 Kings 19:10, 14)

One of the key points in this section of Paul's letter to the Romans is not to exclude the nations from being grafted-in to the community of Israel (Romans 11:17-21), but to instead speak more against widescale Greek and Roman arrogance, toward the Jewish people who have largely rejected the Messiah. Such people are to still certainly be regarded and treated as "Israel," as God alone is the final arbiter of any person, as He is the One who has broken off natural branches (Romans 11:17). The non-Jewish Believers in Rome were carefully instructed, "because of the mercy shown to you they also may now be shown mercy" (Romans 11:31). If some Jewish branches have been broken off of Israel's olive tree, non-Jewish Believers who have received Israel's Messiah have the profound responsibility to be vessels of mercy and grace to such people—**and not be arrogant or disrespectful**—so that such Jewish people might be shown Messiah Yeshua.

It might be easier or more convenient for some people in today's Messianic Judaism to simply assume that when "Israel" is spoken of in the Bible, it is *just* the ancestors of today's Jewish people. A more careful survey of the Bible, across multiple centuries, reveals that more specificity is indeed involved. Ultimately, we are reminded that in the post-resurrection era, knowing Israel's Messiah Yeshua is required for one to ultimately be considered a part of the Kingdom (cf. Romans 9:6). There are sadly going to be some Jewish people, who because of their rejection of Yeshua, will be excluded from being considered as "Israel" in the end. Because of arrogance and disrespect of the Jewish people, there will probably also be many non-Jews who thought they were a part of the Commonwealth of Israel via their faith in Yeshua, but in the end are excluded precisely because they did not have a true heart change and were never moved to be vessels of mercy and grace toward Yeshua's own physical Jewish brethren.

---

[144] "I say then, God has not rejected His people, has He? May it never be! For I too am an Israelite, a descendant of Abraham, of the tribe of Benjamin" (Romans 11:1).

[145] "I say then, they did not stumble so as to fall, did they? May it never be! But by their transgression salvation *has come* to the Gentiles, to make them jealous. Now if their transgression is riches for the world and their failure is riches for the Gentiles, how much more will their fulfillment be! But I am speaking to you who are Gentiles. Inasmuch then as I am an apostle of Gentiles, I magnify my ministry, if somehow I might move to jealousy my fellow countrymen and save some of them. For if their rejection is the reconciliation of the world, what will *their* acceptance be but life from the dead?" (Romans 11:11-15).

[146] "From the standpoint of the gospel they are enemies for your sake, but from the standpoint of God's choice they are beloved for the sake of the fathers" (Romans 11:28).

[147] "[B]ut Israel, pursuing a law of righteousness, did not arrive at *that* law" (Romans 9:31).

[148] "God has not rejected His people whom He foreknew. Or do you not know what the Scripture says in *the passage about* Elijah, how he pleads with God against Israel? Lord, 'THEY HAVE KILLED YOUR PROPHETS, THEY HAVE TORN DOWN YOUR ALTARS, AND I ALONE AM LEFT, AND THEY ARE SEEKING MY LIFE' [1 Kings 19:10]. But what is the divine response to him? 'I HAVE KEPT for Myself SEVEN THOUSAND MEN WHO HAVE NOT BOWED THE KNEE TO BAAL' [1 Kings 19:14]" (Romans 11:2-4).

What Is "the Synagogue of Satan"?

It is not uncommon for various people in the Two-House sub-movement, to actually be told by some Messianic Jews, that they are actually a part of the "synagogue of Satan" mentioned in the Book of Revelation. While it is true that there are many people, teachers, and leaders within the Two-House sub-movement who have some significant and most serious, spiritual and theological problems, to work through—is there any basis to this? What is the synagogue of Satan, really?

Any interpretation over what "the synagogue of Satan" is, as it appears in Revelation 2:9 and 3:9, is going to be controversial. In order to fairly evaluate what "the synagogue of Satan" actually is, one needs to carefully recognize some of the ancient historical issues, which did involve some conflicts the ancient Believers had with some parts of the local Jewish community. At the same time, any conclusion about what "the synagogue of Satan" is, also needs to steadfastly recognize that there is nothing that requires the Greek term *sunagōgē* (συναγωγή) or "synagogue" to always represent an assembly of Jews.

There is nothing particularly special about the Greek word *sunagōgē* (συναγωγή), often translated "synagogue." The term *sunagōgē* is derived from the verb *sunageirō* (συναγείρω), meaning *"to gather together, come together, assemble"* (LS).[149] Although *sunagōgē* is the root word for our modern term "synagogue," usually associated with a Jewish place of worship, it could just as well mean an assemblage or a gathering of something. There is a pre-Jewish usage of the term *sunagōgē*, attested by the *Liddell-Scott* lexicon, which is primarily interested in classical Greek meanings. For its entry on the term *sunagōgē*, it lists the possible meanings:

- *a gathering in of* harvest, Polyb.
- *a drawing together, contracting,* ς. στρατιᾶς [s. *stratias*] *a forming* an army *in column,* Plat.; ς. τοῦ προσώπου [s. *tou prosōpou*] *a pursing up* or *wrinkling* of the face, Isocr.
- *a collection* of writings, Arist.
- *a conclusion, inference,* Id.[150]

A general meaning of the Greek term *sunagōgē* (συναγωγή) is simply **"gathering,"** as BDAG notes, "Orig. in act. sense 'a bringing together, assembling.'"[151] With this in mind, if we can refer to "the synagogue of Satan" via the more neutral **"the gathering of Satan,"** then it should be clear to anyone that such a gathering or group of people is composed of *all of those* who are accomplishing Satan's tasks and assignments—the foremost of which is keeping people away from the truth of the gospel and the saving power of Yeshua (Jesus). **"The gathering of Satan"** engulfs all of Satan's forces. Such people are a part of what we might call a **"macro-synagogue of Satan,"** involving members of false religions who actively blaspheme the Lord, and atheists who want people to deny

---

[149] LS, 766.
[150] Ibid.
[151] BDAG, 963.

the existence of God and His intelligent design. At the same time, there is also what we might call a **"micro-**synagogue of Satan," composing some Jewish people, who are actually out there accomplishing the enemy's tasks. It should not be hard for any good Messianic Believer to classify Jewish anti-missionaries, for example—those who are actively out there trying to get people, particularly Jewish people, to deny Yeshua as the Messiah—as being among the Adversary's forces.

The terminology *sunagōgē tou Satana* (συναγωγὴ τοῦ σατανᾶ) appears twice in the Book of Revelation:

> "I know your tribulation and your poverty (but you are rich), and the blasphemy by those who say they are Jews and are not, but are a synagogue of Satan [*sunagōgē tou Satana*, συναγωγὴ τοῦ σατανᾶ]" (Revelation 2:9).

> "Behold, I will cause *those* of the synagogue of Satan [*tēs sunagōgēs tou Satana*, τῆς συναγωγῆς τοῦ σατανᾶ], who say that they are Jews and are not, but lie—I will make them come and bow down at your feet, and *make them* know that I have loved you" (Revelation 3:9).

Approaching the term *sunagōgē* (συναγωγή) more as **"gathering"** is appropriate, because Revelation 2:9 notably lacks the definite article. Those who are criticized are labeled as "**a** synagogue of Satan," and as previously described, are only one part of *all* of the Adversary's forces.

Various interpretations of what "the synagogue of Satan" is, or was, throughout history, have been used at times to defame Judaism and all Jewish people. In extreme cases it has been used as theological justification by anti-Semites to persecute Jews.[152] A widespread evangelical Christian interpretation of the "synagogue of Satan" is that it represents the First Century Judaizers, possibly being those of the nations who converted to Judaism as proselytes, and then received the gospel message. It is thought that these Judaizers held a hard disdain toward non-Jewish Believers who did not have to "convert" as they did, and they demanded a legalistic Torah observance from them.

Some of the challenges to this view is that in early Christian history, in Smyrna at least (Revelation 2:8-11), there was a sector of the Jewish community that had a serious problem with the Believers. "The Martyrdom of Polycarp...records that Jews brought wood for his pyre even though it was a sabbath" (*ISBE*).[153] G.R. Beasley-Murray is right to indicate, though, "Naturally this is not to be generalized, as though John believed that the whole Jewish nation had become the people of Satan. His description applies to a {specific} synagogue which implacably opposed the people of Christ."[154]

---

[152] Cf. Craig S. Keener, *NIV Application Commentary: Revelation* (Grand Rapids: Zondervan, 2000), 118.

[153] R. North, "Smyrna," in *ISBE*, 4:556.

[154] G.R. Beasley-Murray, *New Century Bible Commentary: Revelation* (Grand Rapids: Eerdmans, 1974), 82.

It is true that there are some "who claim to be Jews though they are not, but are liars" (Revelation 3:9, NIV). One needs to properly weigh the words of the Apostle Paul, who when directing specific instruction to the Jews among the assembly at Rome, wrote some very stringent words on what it means to truly be a "Jew":

"For he is not a Jew who is one outwardly, nor is circumcision that which is outward in the flesh. But he is a Jew who is one inwardly; and circumcision is that which is of the heart, by the Spirit, not by the letter; and his praise is not from men, but from God" (Romans 2:28-29).

Here, writing some specific words to the Jewish Believers in Rome, he says that being a "Jew" is ultimately something that is determined by the heart. This indicates that from the Apostle's perspective, even though some people could be born Jewish, in the end because of rejecting the good news of Messiah Yeshua, they may not be considered as such by God.[155] In the case of Revelation 2:9 and 3:9, it would seem that the work of the Believers in Smyrna and Philadelphia was opposed by a sector of Jews who were determined to stop them. As far as Yeshua the Messiah was concerned, they will not be considered Jews in the end, if they remain unrepentant. They are to be counted as **"the gathering of the Adversary."**

To say that all Jews in history since have been part of such a "gathering of the Adversary" goes too far, and is unjustifiable. The terminology "the synagogue of Satan" concerns a certain sector of Jewish people who opposed the Messiah as associated with the ancient congregations at Smyrna and Philadelphia, and by extension whatever those two congregations might represent for various sectors of the Body of Messiah subsequent to Yeshua's return.

From what angle is it claimed that those who may affirm the prophecies of a larger restoration of Israel, involving the descendants of the exiled Northern Kingdom of Israel, are actually "the synagogue of Satan"? This point of view has found some ancillary support in Stern's remarks on Revelation 2:9, in his *Jewish New Testament Commentary:*

"Should it nevertheless be thought improbable that Gentiles would call themselves Jews, Hebrews or Israelites, consider the following modern examples. The 'British Israelites' regard the British as the Ten Lost Tribes. The Mormons not only consider themselves to be the Ten Lost Tribes but regard themselves as Jews and everyone else (real Jews included) as Gentiles! A sect of mostly American-born blacks consider themselves the true Hebrews; several thousand of them are living in Israel. All of these are outside the pale of Christianity. In addition, scattered about are well-meaning Gentile Christians whose strong identification with and love for the Jewish people has made them believe—without a shred of evidence—that they are actually Jewish themselves."[156]

---

[155] For a further evaluation, consult the author's examinations of Romans 2:28-29 and 9:3-6, in his publication *Are Non-Jewish Believers Really a Part of Israel?*

[156] Stern, *Jewish New Testament Commentary*, 796.

Stern is right to direct our attention to how there have always been those groups who have always claimed that they are the "true Israel" or "new Israel," be it through replacement theology or phenomena such as British-Israelism. There are also various non-Jews, who are a part of the contemporary Messianic Jewish movement, who think via some sort of supposed dream or vision, that they are distant descendants of the Jewish people via some sort of Medieval European assimilation. These groups can often disclude the historical Jewish people—those who are legitimate descendants of the Patriarchs Abraham, Isaac, Jacob—claiming that only they are the "true Jews." Such groups are, without a doubt, accomplishing the Adversary's tasks and purposes.

Can it be concluded with any degree of accuracy that those who affirm—from a series of prophecies in the Tanach (Isaiah 11:12-16; Jeremiah 31:6-10; Ezekiel 37:15-28; Zechariah 10:6-10)—that a greater restoration of Israel is to be anticipated, that such specific persons are somehow of "the synagogue of Satan"? Given the possibility that some Messianic Jews might rebukingly say that those who believe in a futuristic fulfillment of these prophecies are of "the synagogue of Satan," a larger reunion of Israel still to occur needs to be placed *well within* the Jewish eschatological expectation (as well as in line with a basic, evangelical Christian pre-millennial model). Concurrent with this, there needs to be great respect and honor issued for the Jewish people, Judaism, and Jewish tradition and culture. A great number of leaders and teachers in the Two-House sub-movement **have been entirely impotent to see this accomplished.**

British-Israel Dangers and Concerns

When the Two-House teaching began to grow in adherence in various Messianic sectors in the late 1990s to 2000s, many leaders and teachers within Messianic Judaism were understandably very disturbed. They were disturbed because it appeared that many of the components of the Two-House teaching were not only disrespectful and unfair to Judaism and evangelical Christianity, but that various concepts and ideas had been appropriated, somehow, from Nineteenth/Twentieth Century British-Israelism.[157] Perhaps some adherents and proponents did not know that various points of view or interpretations of some Tanach passages were quite similar to those of British-Israel advocates. Others, however, in promoting a dispersion of the exiled Northern Kingdom of Israel into Northwestern Europe and the British Isles, strongly believed that British-Israel proposals had various, if not many, components of presumed "truth."

British-Israelism gained a wide degree of adherence during the Victorian Era of the Nineteenth Century, when the British Empire was at its zenith, and when, as can be historically recognized, "The sun never sat on the British Empire." Many in Britain and its colonies felt that the Empire was some kind of new manifestation of

---

[157] British-Israel doctrine is particularly marked by a work like J.H. Allen, *Judah's Sceptre and Joseph's Birthright* (Merrimac, MA: Destiny Publishers, 1902), many of whose ideas have filtered down into the popular literature of certain leaders within the Two-House sub-movement.

the Kingdom of Israel on Earth, with the British monarchy in actuality being the throne of King David. Heraldic symbols such as the lion of England, the unicorn of Scotland, and the harp of Ireland—quickly got associated with representing the lion of Judah, a unicorn of Ephraim or Manasseh, and the preferred musical instrument of King David. British-Israel doctrine later influenced the Twentieth Century work of Herbert Armstrong's Worldwide Church of God (WWCOG).

Being a Law- and festival-keeping, Sabbatarian group, many from the former WWCOG were left without a home following Armstrong's death in 1986 and his organization's subsequent collapse. Many of these people have gone on to other religious pursuits, but many have found a new home within not only the Two-House sub-movement, but even within Messianic Judaism itself. For many former members of the WWCOG, entering into the Messianic movement has been a positive experience, and they have been able to jettison some of Armstrong's problematic theological views about the nature of the Messiah and human destiny, among others. At the same time, other former members of the WWCOG have entered into Messianic congregations, and have brought their problematic doctrines with them. Within the Two-House sub-movement and its pseudo-denominations, these kinds of people (who may have even thought Armstrong to be a kind of "prophet" or "apostle"), have been allowed to have a voice of, at least semi-major influence.

British-Israel doctrine is very easy to poke fun at. Most of us just get a good laugh out of thinking that King Edward VIII, who abdicated the throne for Wallis Simpson in 1936 *and* who was actually called "David" by his family,[158] could honestly be a legitimate royal heir to the rather godly King David. British-Israel doctrine attempts to make many connections between the symbols of Great Britain and things witnessed in the Bible, which are also present in other European countries, and most importantly originate from the Middle Ages. But these things are not at all the result of Ancient Israelite migration; they are the result of people adapting Biblical imagery for themselves, their families, and their leaders. (The two keys on the Vatican flag, for example, are most likely based on the words of Revelation 1:18.)[159] When one visits the city of London and goes to have a pint at the George Inn, the sign depicts St. George slaying a dragon, which is a known legend going back to the Crusades. What kind of Biblical imagery is this? It is Medieval lore, even if we might be respectful of it in *a somewhat* less-than-serious way.

This is not why British-Israel doctrine is so much of a problem. There are many offshoots of the WWCOG, and associated Christian Identity groups, who think that deportees from the exiled Northern Kingdom of Israel migrated into Northwestern Europe, and that white people or Caucasians are the only "true Israelites" on Planet Earth today. It is these groups who largely deny that the Jewish people are

---

[158] The full name of King Edward VIII was Edward Albert Christian George Andrew Patrick David.

[159] "When I saw Him, I fell at His feet like a dead man. And He placed His right hand on me, saying, 'Do not be afraid; I am the first and the last, and the living One; and I was dead, and behold, I am alive forevermore, and I have the keys of death and of Hades'" (Revelation 1:17-18).

legitimate Israelites, have a right to the Holy Land of *Eretz Yisrael*, and they are extremely anti-Semitic. These are the kinds of people who would actually think that the known forgery, *The Protocols of the Elders of Zion*, is real history, and that there is a secret Jewish conspiracy of some kind of "Satan worshippers" to control the world and its banking system. British-Israelism has often been closely linked to the Christian Identity movement, many of whose members are opposed to the American government, with some of them actually having participated in domestic terrorism. Bruce Hoffman summarizes the following in his book *Inside Terrorism* (which was among the course materials I had to read for Prof. Stephen Sloan's Study of Terrorism class at the University of Oklahoma in 2003):

> The connecting thread in this seemingly diverse and disparate collection of citizens' militias, tax resisters, anti-federalists, bigots and racists is the white supremacist religious dogma espoused by the Christian Identity movement, itself based on the 'Anglo-Israelism' movement that emerged in Britain during the mid-nineteenth century. The core belief of Anglo-Israelism was that the ten lost tribes of ancient Israel were composed of Anglo-Saxons, not Jews. However, in marked contrast to the present-day Christian Identity movement in the United States, nineteenth-century Anglo-Israelism embraced an entirely pacifist doctrine. The basic tenants of the contemporary American version of the Identity movement include the beliefs that:
> - Jesus Christ was not a Semite; but an Aryan;
> - the lost tribes of Israel are not composed of Jews, but of 'blue eyed Aryans';
> - white Anglo-Saxons and not Jews are the true 'Chosen People';
> - the United States is the 'Promised Land'.
>
> In this context, Jews are viewed as imposters and Children of Satan who must be exterminated.
>
> Identity theology, combined with militant tax resistance and a form of regressive populism, figures prominently in Christian Patriotism doctrine subscribed to by the 'marching' militia groups today. The ideological hermit to the Posse Comitatus with its hard-line anti-federalist principles, Christian Patriotism goes one step further by embracing a salient theological component that combines Identity interpretation of scripture with the myth of the Illuminati—the global conspiracy theory, first promulgated in the late eighteenth century in respect of Freemasons and later adapted to include Jews, worldwide banking interests and other dark, mystical forces. According to its modern-day American interpretation, the so-called 'two seed' theory embraced by Christian Patriotism, there are two races on earth: one godly and one satanic—the former comprised of white, Anglo-Saxon Christians and the latter of Jews and all non-whites...[160]

The kinds of statements made above should make anyone who approaches the subject matter of the prophesied reunion of the Northern and Southern Kingdoms of Israel, be very conscientious about the connections that some people will make between hearing about Judah and Ephraim, British-Israel, Christian Identity, and

---

[160] Bruce Hoffman, *Inside Terrorism* (New York: Columbia University Press, 1998), 112.

then Christian Patriotism with its anti-government and anti-Semitic viewpoints. The only way that anyone can quantitatively break out any false connections that people might make, is by non-Jewish Believers who examine this subject matter **closely cooperating with Jewish Believers, supporting the State of Israel, and being respectful to mainline Jewish customs.** The message needs to be kept *well within* the confines of the Jewish theological expectation of the restoration of Israel, and highly regard and value mainline Jewish traditions (i.e., Matthew 23:2-3, Grk.; Romans 3:2; 11:29).

Does any teaching on the Northern and Southern Kingdoms of Israel to be reunited in the future, actually mimic those who believe that the British Crown has some supernatural connection to the throne of David, and that the British Empire and Commonwealth is really the Kingdom of Israel? When you encounter various teachers and people within the Two-House sub-movement, who were a part of Armstrong's WWCOG, then you may be very likely to hear things such as English, Scottish, and/or Irish royal heraldry being "Israelite" to some degree, or that the Empire had a destiny to play in history far beyond that recognized by fair-minded and secular historians (i.e., opposing Nazi Germany long before the United States did).

One of the major points that is made by British-Israel proponents, is the widespread claim that the term **British** is actually a Hebrew word. In actuality, the national designation British is derived from the Roman name for what is modern-day England and Wales: Britannia (modern-day Scotland was actually called Caledonia by the Romans; Great Britain is considered to be the whole island). British-Israel proponents actually claim that the term "British" is a combination of the Hebrew words *b'rit* (בְּרִית) or "covenant," and *ish* (אִישׁ) meaning "man," likely implying that God's covenant is with those of British ancestry. In his book *The "Lost" Ten Tribes of Israel...Found!*, Steven M. Collins confirms for us their view: "The ancient Hebrew word for 'covenant' still forms the root word for the modern English word 'British.' Since 'ish' is also a Hebrew word meaning 'man,' the word 'Brit-ish' is also Hebrew for 'covenant-man.'"[161] Collins' publication is one which has most lamentably had an influence on a wide number of people within the Two-House sub-movement.

Quite contrary to the claim that the word "British" is somehow of Semitic origin, Walter Martin appropriately details in his classic work *Kingdom of the Cults*,

"It is sufficient to point out...that the Hebrew words *berith* [בְּרִית] and *ish* [אִישׁ] literally mean 'covenant and man,' not, 'men of the covenant,' as Armstrong and Anglo-Israelites maintain. When to this is added the unbiased and impeccably researched conclusions of the venerable *Oxford English Dictionary* and every other major English work on etymology, there is absolutely no connection between the Anglo-Saxon tongue and the Hebrew language."[162]

---

[161] Steven M. Collins, *The "Lost" Ten Tribes of Israel...Found!* (Boring, OR: CPA Books, 1995), 392.

[162] Walter Martin, *Kingdom of the Cults* (Minneapolis: Bethany House, 1985), 309.

It is worth noting, perhaps in response to Martin's comments that English and Hebrew are completely unrelated, that a resource released by a Jewish teacher named Isaac E. Mozeson, *The Word: The Dictionary That Reveals The Hebrew Source Of English*—which does float around a variety of Messianic groups—proposes there are connections between English via Greek and Latin to Hebrew. In Mozeson's view, "Greek and Latin are merely grandfathers, while Hebrew is the patriarch."[163] Whether or not Mozeson's work is at all credible can be vigorously debated. Yet, it is important that *nowhere* in Mozeson's book does he make a connection between the English term "British" and the Hebrew words *b'rit* (בְּרִית) and *ish* (אִישׁ). I personally would not put too much stock in Mozeson's *The Word* or his theories,[164] but it is quite poignant that he does not claim that "British" is a Semitic word. The modern Hebrew term for "British" is actually *Briti* (ברימי; br*ee*tee),[165] which is hardly what one would expect if "British" were indeed a Hebrew word.

British-Israel proponents, as should be expected, propose that various other nationalistic terms also originate from Biblical Hebrew, when in actuality they do not. I am in full agreement with William Varner, who notes the following in his book *Jacob's Dozen*:

"British-Israelism maintains that the *lost* tribes left landmarks on their trek across Europe. Thus, the Dan and Danube Rivers, as well as the city of Danzig and country of Denmark are clear indications to them of the tribe of Dan! The term 'Saxons' is supposedly a contradiction of 'Isaac's Sons'…These linguistic arguments have been rejected by every reputable Hebrew scholar as absolutely groundless."[166]

Toward a More Biblically Rooted Approach of a Larger Restoration of Israel

It is easily observed that throughout the past few centuries, that when the subject matter of what happened to the descendants of the exiled Northern Kingdom of Israel/Ephraim, or the "Ten Lost Tribes," has been examined—**that there has been a significant risk or gamble evident.** Some Bible teachers refuse to even touch the issue, because of various associations that can be made from past dealings, most frequently the historical errors of British-Israelism and theological abuses of Armstrongism. Even when a Bible teacher is intent to largely stay focused on Scripture, a safe window of extra-Biblical literature and respected Jewish and Christian scholarship, and be very cautious about the conclusions drawn—too many laypersons are likely to go off and explore things on their own,

---

[163] Isaac E. Mozeson, *The Word: The Dictionary That Reveals The Hebrew Source Of* English (New York: SPI Books, 2000), 5.

[164] Concurrent with this, I would also frown extensively on so-called Hebrew letter pictures, which are affluent through the broad Messianic world, including much of "safe" Messianic Judaism.

Consult the FAQ on the TNN website, "Hebrew, Letter Pictures."

[165] Hayim Baltsan, *Webster's NewWorld Hebrew Dictionary* (Cleveland: Wiley Publishing, Inc., 1992), 497.

[166] Varner, 94; cf. Martin, 308.

and go into places where they have no business going. Too many people are simply not disciplined or mature enough to keep themselves within the world of the Biblical text and let the prophecies of those of the Northern and Southern Kingdoms of Israel naturally take care of themselves, and they cannot resist the temptation to speculate.

For a variety of complicated reasons, when one surveys the Two-House sub-movement, it is not difficult to detect how much of it is a rather fertile field for a wide and broad number of urban legends that are present within the broad Messianic movement.[167] *Why this is* specifically *the case we may never know.* But, it is easily discerned from what is witnessed in the writings, recordings, and conference events of various popular/populist teachers and leaders, that they have gone beyond the Biblical expectations of the restoration of Israel's Kingdom, and have (significantly) added their own baggage to the issue.

The approach, of a ministry like Outreach Israel and TNN Online, has always been to view the reunification of Judah and Israel/Ephraim, **and the significant majority of companions from the nations at large**—as a larger restoration of Israel, and/or expansion of Israel's Kingdom realm, that has been prophesied in Holy Writ. If one approaches this issue as end-time prophecy or eschatology—with God Himself knowing all of the finer details—then the issue largely becomes one of interpretation regarding future events. Many of the popular voices which you will hear who promote teaching about this issue, have made things a bit too simplistic, under-developed, and have cut corners. They have not put enough time into seeing the issue of a larger restoration of Israel refined and defined further from the Biblical text, and have rightly opened themselves up to some legitimate criticism.

Only future examinations of the Historical Books and Prophetic literature of the Tanach will bring many of the answers which we all need—but acquiring such specific answers will take time, which far too many are unwilling to commit, on this—and, *for a fact,* many other issues of hundreds of times more importance.[168]

---

[167] It cannot be at all be overlooked, that one publication with a great deal of exaggeration and non-credible history (which even promotes some presumed Ancient Israelite settlement in North America, referencing discredited people like E. Raymond Capt), Victor Schlatter, *Genetically Modified Prophecies: Whatever Happened to all the Sand and Stars God Promised to Abraham?* (Mobile: Evergreen Press, 2012), is actually advertised for sale on p 8 of the 2012-2013 *Messianic Jewish Resources Catalog* published by Lederer <messianicjewish.net/docs/MJRCatalog2012.pdf >.

Lost Tribes speculation, even while opposed by various Messianic Jewish leaders, is alive and well beyond the Two-House sub-movement. Schlatter's book actually received an endorsement from Frank Lowinger, who is listed as a former president of the Messianic Jewish Alliance of America (MJAA).

[168] It is advised that you generally consult the author's workbooks *A Survey of the Tanach for the Practical Messianic* and *A Survey of the Apostolic Scriptures for the Practical Messianic,* for some preliminary, conservative approaches to the books of the Bible, from an inclusivist Messianic perspective.

As the author of this publication, I dare say that there are many unanswered, yet critical issues, regarding the material of Genesis chs. 1-11, which most of today's Messianic leaders and/or people at large, while knowing that they need to examine in greater detail per various astronomical and cosmological issues, will likely never really bother to consider. So, for some further consideration, consult the useful books J.P. Moreland and John Mark Reynolds, eds., *Three Views on Creation and Evolution* (Grand Rapids: Zondervan, 1999) representing a general perspective of the positions; and Hugh Ross, *The Genesis Question: Scientific Advances and the Accuracy of Genesis,* second expanded edition (Colorado Springs: NavPress, 2001);

And as this is conducted, there will need to be a significant amount of *reigning in* of various over-statements and exaggerations—to what can actually be proven—Biblically and historically—which a great number of Two-House adherents likely have no intention of doing at present...[169]

A Matter of Days: Resolving a Creation Controversy (Colorado Springs: NavPress, 2004) representing an Old Earth Creationist perspective.

    Also consult the FAQ entries on the TNN website, "Creationism" and "6,000 Year Teaching," which generally represent an emerging Messianic, Old Earth Creationist position.

    Another useful resource for consideration is C. John Collins, *Genesis 1-4: A Linguistic, Literary, and Theological Commentary* (Phillipsburg, NJ: P&R Publishing, 2006).

    [169] Consult the author's YouTube video podcast from 06 January 2013, "Old Controversies, New Controversies," accessible via <youtube.com/tnnonline>.

-4-

Anti-Semitism
in the Two-House Movement

Anti-Semitism or anti-Judaism is a significant crime, with devastating prejudices and a poisonous ideology, which has been present in our world since long before the time of Yeshua the Messiah. While manifested in many forms throughout the ages, anti-Semitism undeniably reached its lowest point in the 1930s and 1940s with Hitler's Holocaust and the attempted annihilation of the Jewish people by Nazi Germany. While it can be said that out of the Holocaust and World War II, the State of Israel was birthed *and* Jewish-Christian relations have improved—making sure that non-Jewish followers of Israel's Messiah have a relatively positive and well-informed view of Jewish religion, Jewish tradition, Jewish history, and the Jewish people in general, **is indeed a major undertaking.**

One of the pleasant highlights of my time as an undergraduate at the University of Oklahoma (1999-2003) was being able to attend an evening lecture delivered by Sir Martin Gilbert, the official biographer of Winston Churchill, hosted by the Hillel Foundation. Gilbert is a British Jew, and the 2001 lecture I attended was on the subject of "Winston Churchill and the Jews."[1] Also in attendance were both my modern Hebrew and British history professors, who were both Jewish. We shared a few thoughts afterward about Nineteenth and Twentieth Century Jewish history, and I was able to make a few remarks to both of my classes the following week, when they both noted those whom they saw from class who were there. I did not tell them that I was Messianic, but they could surely tell that I was an inquiring Christian person with an appreciation for the Jewish people, their unique contributions to global civilization, and the establishment of Israel as a sovereign country in the modern Middle East.

My own family's involvement in the Messianic community since 1995 has been predicated upon the basis of two primary things. **(1)** In embracing our Hebraic Roots in a very real and tangible way, we desire to live in fuller obedience to God's Torah, and we really do want to live as Yeshua and His original disciples lived. **(2)** We wish to sincerely and honorably recognize the Biblical facts that "salvation is from the Jews" (John 4:22), that Jesus was Jewish, and that our Messiah did indeed

---

[1] Much of the material Gilbert spoke about was later incorporated into his book *Churchill and the Jews: A Lifelong Friendship* (New York: Henry Holt and Company, 2007).

pray, "...that they may be one, just as We are one" (John 17:22). We know that with the emergence of today's Messianic movement, that much of the centuries-old hatred, bigotry, venom, and mutual distrust and loathing of Jewish and Christian persons toward one another *has been left in the past.* A future of working together, joining in common cause, and using all of our special gifts and talents for the furtherance of God's Kingdom should instead be witnessed. Understanding where past generations of Jews and Christians had misunderstanding, and rectifying this, **must be present.**

Obviously, there is still much to work through—because people are people. Today's broad Messianic movement is still trying to figure out what Jewish and non-Jewish Believers composing a "one new humanity" (Ephesians 2:15, NRSV/CJB) really means. While there are many Messianic Jewish congregations and assemblies that are fully welcoming of non-Jewish Believers in their midst, in many other settings such people are not equal members or are at all that welcome. In various sectors of Messianic Judaism, non-Jewish Believers who have entered in and have expected to be welcome with open arms as past injustices have hopefully been repented of, have found themselves turned away. Our own family can attest that in the time we have spent in the Messianic community, that we have visited a few Messianic Jewish congregations which would much rather prefer that people like us not be there. There are a number of groups, for whatever reasons, which treat non-Jews as being second class....

What happens when non-Jewish Believers are told that not only is Messianic Judaism not really for them, **but they are really not wanted in some Messianic Jewish congregations?** Do they just leave happily? Do they leave upset? Does an anti-Semitism that has been confessed and repented of *return* to them in some way? What happens when such people have been convinced from Scripture that they are a part of the Commonwealth of Israel too (Ephesians 2:11-12), and they find themselves somehow ejected from it?

Why the Two-House Teaching Has Gained Attention

For many non-Jewish Messianics, the Two-House sub-movement has provided an alternative, welcome place, for those who have not really found themselves with a welcome place in Messianic Judaism. Aside from some of its many shortcomings and tall tales about the descendants of the exiled Northern Kingdom of Israel/Ephraim, the Two-House sub-movement does rightly tend to be welcoming of all people as a part of the Commonwealth of Israel (Ephesians 2:11-13) or the Israel of God (Galatians 6:16), a trait it tends to share with those in the One Law/One Torah sub-movement as well.[2] Even with various (significant)

---

[2] It is a bit inappropriate though, as has been witnessed in some literature, to basically synthesize the One Law/One Torah sub-movement and Two-House sub-movement, as basically being the same. The former has a far more healthy and appropriate view of mainline Jewish traditions—such as those examined in this article—even if it can seem, at times, to force a Torah *halachah* on non-Jewish Messianic Believers, which would essentially see them live as though they were ethnically and culturally Jewish, when they are not, as opposed to them being sizably enriched by their Hebraic and Jewish Roots.

complimentarian limitations, it does tend to emphasize some degree of equality among all Believers (cf. Galatians 3:28; Colossians 3:11) a little better than today's Messianic Judaism. Much of Messianic Judaism maintains a status-quo of "Jew and Gentile" being unified, but with distinctions to be rigidly maintained. What this means in practice is that Jewish Believers end up being superior, or at the very least in a higher status, to non-Jewish Believers. It does not often mean that both are on equal footing before the Lord, working together in mutual honor and respect (cf. Romans 12:10; Philippians 2:3-4). Suspicions and rivalry among those who are supposed to be fellow brothers and sisters in Messiah Yeshua, can certainly be detectable.

Hopefully, among those seeking true equality and fairness for all of God's people in the Messianic community, *all* are allowed to be reckoned as a part of "the Israel of God" (Galatians 6:16)—and not multiple parts of an enlarged community of Israel (cf. Acts 15:15-18; Amos 9:11-12, LXX) which is rigidly factionalized. There are various fellowships, congregations, and ministries which endorse various forms of a Two-House teaching, and do their best to emphasize a high degree of equality and a place of being welcome among all people in today's Messianic community.[3] There are those who recognize that we all have something to offer the community of faith, but at the same time that we all have been blinded because of our various human limitations. The Jewish people have largely been blind to the Messiah, and Christians have largely been blind to the importance of God's Torah. Both have been right and wrong—all at the same time. Regardless of the finer details, these are the groups whom we obviously have to believe God will primarily use to bring about the complete restoration of His Kingdom.

Many non-Jewish Believers who have become a part of Messianic Judaism have rightfully repented of attitudes and prejudices rooted in anti-Semitism. Even if "unwelcomed" from some Messianic Jewish congregations, they have done their absolute best to guard themselves against such sins. If they find themselves in one of the many independent Messianic assemblies, they make sure that the Jewish people and their heritage are appropriately honored.

At the same time, many of the same non-Jewish Believers who feel like they have been "booted out" of Messianic Judaism, revisit some old negativity they may have felt toward Judaism. This does not necessarily regard support for the State of Israel or standing against hate crimes directed toward Jews. The kind of anti-Jewish attitudes which manifest from non-Jewish Believers who felt unwelcome in Messianic Judaism and who left, mostly concern a widescale misunderstanding of

---

This is explored in further detail, in the forthcoming *Messianic Torah Helper* by TNN Press, as well s the author's forthcoming work *Torah In the Balance, Volume II.*

[3] Consult the author's exegesis paper on Galatians 3:28, "Biblical Equality and Today's Messianic Movement." It should be stressed that even among various independent Messianic groups, many of which are "Two-House" to some degree, that they are often unwilling to let the full egalitarian implications of Galatians 3:28 to take root. This not only includes "There is neither Jew nor Greek," **but also** "there is neither male nor female."

Consult the FAQ entry on the TNN website, "Women in Ministry," and the various sections of his commentaries *Ephesians for the Practical Messianic* and *The Pastoral Epistles for the Practical Messianic.*

Jewish religion, tradition, and Torah *halachah* (הֲלָכָה). Mainline practices, which are found in Orthodox, Conservative, Reform, *and* Messianic Jewish synagogues, are widely rejected by a great deal of today's Two-House sub-movement.

There are many assembly groups today who compose the Two-House sub-movement, and whose fellowships are almost exclusively non-Jewish. (Many of these almost-exclusively non-Jewish groups just *assume* they are descendants of the exiled Northern Kingdom of Israel/Ephraim, when most of these people are just of the nations.) Rather than emulating to a wide degree, the orthopraxy of much of contemporary Messianic Judaism—the Jewish people, and virtually anything religiously Jewish, is quantitatively left out of the picture.[4] Even more sadly, in many cases those who put our Jewish brethren in this position, and identify themselves, perhaps rather stridently, as being Two-House advocates, are promoting a noticeable form of anti-Semitism *and do not tend to even realize it*. While there are many Messianic Jews, who continue to look out at their own congregations, and see the numbers of non-Jewish attendees rise—and they are honestly asking the Lord what is happening, perhaps realizing that more is going on than meets the eye—much of the anti-Jewish attitudes present in the Two-House sub-movement and its populism, have made dialoguing about a larger restoration of Israel in future prophecy *most difficult.*

We need to certainly address some of the controversial problems that currently exist with forms of anti-Semitism in the Two-House movement. **You can have no genuine restoration of the Kingdom to Israel without the Jewish people, after all!** Attitudes and misunderstandings allowed to continue for too long have kept many reasonable-thinking Messianic Jews from thinking about more on the horizon. We will analyze some of the issues which stand before us, and how more balanced and fair-minded people can counter this.

Why Many People Just Dismiss What Happened to the Northern Kingdom of Israel

Before we consider some of the specifics of the anti-Semitism present in the Two-House sub-movement—it is important that we address a specific reason why many in Messianic Judaism, and many evangelical Christians for that same matter, tend to reject *any* emphasis upon a future reunion of the Southern Kingdom of Judah and the descendants of the exiled Northern Kingdom of Israel/Ephraim. Many Messianic Jews and Christians reject it **because they believe the subject matter is anti-Semitic.** This is largely the result of considering the behavior and attitudes of people who have addressed the Lost Tribes of the Northern Kingdom before in religious history. Most recently in the Twentieth Century, the phenomenon of British-Israelism gained considerable popularity through the efforts of Herbert W. Armstrong and his Worldwide Church of God.

---

[4] Among such groups is also a great deal of disrespect and dishonor toward Christianity, and its positive contributions on global civilization.

In his book *Jacob's Dozen*, author William Varner makes an important observation about the problems customarily associated with British-Israelism.[5] He correctly directs our attention to how, "A number of groups, affirming the Satanic character of Zionism and the so-called worldwide Jewish conspiracy, have adopted British-Israelism to prove the superiority of the white race over Jews, Asiatics and Negroes. These groups have often led demonstrations against the supposed Jewish control of money and the media, as well as engaging in violent actions against so-called Jewish 'enemies.'"[6] His conclusion on this heinous occurrence is,

"Satan's attempts to destroy the Jewish people have taken various forms in history, from the days of Antiochus Epiphanes to the murderous plan of Hitler. Now the evil one is promoting the lie that the Jews are not truly the Jews, thus robbing Israel of its promises and covenants and transferring them to the Anglo-Saxon race."[7]

Another Christian author, Dave Hunt, expresses a particular view in his book *How Close Are We?*, concluding,

"[T]he theory of the 'ten lost tribes' is an antisemitic myth. Space does not permit the detailed discussion which this subject perhaps deserves. However, a careful reading of the history of Israel in Scripture denies what must be considered a Satanic doctrine, for it destroys in theory (as others have sought to do in practice) the continuity of Israel. That continuity was repeatedly assured by God and is essential for the major prophecies of Scripture to be fulfilled in the last days."[8]

If we have read Hunt correctly, he has presumably claimed that *any kind* of belief in people descended from the exiled Northern Kingdom, "out there" in the world, and not a part of the established Jewish community, is not only "an antisemitic myth" but even "Satanic." Why would he make such assessments?

Neither Varner nor Hunt have given appropriate attention to the main Tanach prophecies regarding a larger restoration of Israel in their books (i.e., Isaiah 11:12-16; Jeremiah 31:6-10; Ezekiel 37:15-28; Zechariah 10:6-10). They largely dismiss the whole subject matter because of the bad behavior—the anti-Semitism and anti-Judaism—of those who have attempted in the past to address it, and address it *very poorly.*

Many of those who have addressed the subject matter of people from the exiled Northern Kingdom of Israel/Ephraim, being "out there" in the world, have incorrectly—and we should recognize have *damnably thought*—that today's Jewish people are not true descendants of the Patriarchs Abraham, Isaac, and Jacob. At best, such persons have been thought to be usurpers of some kind. At worst, such persons are some kind of literal seed or offspring of the Devil.

These kinds of attitudes are most especially insulting to our Creator God, and they demonstrate absolutely no understanding or empathy toward the terrible tragedies, humiliations, and persecutions that the Jewish people have had to

---

[5] Varner, pp 94-95.
[6] Ibid., 95.
[7] Ibid., 99.
[8] Dave Hunt, *How Close Are We?* (Eugene, OR: Harvest House Publishers, 1993), 30.

experience throughout history. To deny that the Jewish people—who Two-House advocates largely regard as representing the Southern Kingdom of Judah in restoration of Israel prophecies—are not legitimate Israelites, categorically denies that our Heavenly Father has guarded, protected, and preserved them through many hardships, difficulties, and tribulations. (Much of this has unfortunately been at the hands of institutional Christianity.) **Any attempt to degrade the position of the Jewish people in God's eternal plan, or deny that He has protected and guided them, is anti-Semitic and must be viewed as suspect.**[9]

In spite of the manifold abuses from those who have addressed the exiled Northern Kingdom of Israel in previous history, there are still legitimate questions to be raised from statements like: "So Israel was carried away into exile from their own land to Assyria until this day" (2 Kings 17:23; 1 Chronicles 5:26). It is quite notable, though, that the deportees from the Northern Kingdom were largely dispersed *eastward*, and would have remained within the sphere of influence of the old Assyrian, Babylonian, and Persian Empires. One can legitimately acknowledge that there are people groups "out there" in the world in those places, who are descended from the Ten Tribes of the old Northern Kingdom of Israel/Ephraim.

One can hardly claim that a relatively liberal source like *JPS Guide: The Jewish Bible* is anti-Semitic, when it notes that "The 10 tribes of **Israel**...disappeared from biblical accounts after the Northern Kingdom of Israel was conquered by the Assyrians in 722/1 B.C.E. The tribes lost their separate identity during their exile and captivity and are thought by some to have intermarried with the Assyrians."[10] When Jewish figures like Simcha Jacobovici travel to remote corners of the world, searching for the descendants of the Northern Kingdom, releasing programs like "Quest for the Lost Tribes" for A&E—going to dangerous corners of India and Afghanistan—this is far from being anti-Semitic. Messianic Jews like Jonathan Bernis are hardly anti-Semitic when they think, "exactly what happened to the 10 Northern Tribes is not known,"[11] affirming some level of future return beyond the known Jewish community. His own biographical description in the book *Awakening the One New Man* actually says, "The Lost Tribes of the House of Israel are of particular interest to Jonathan."[12]

The point that should be understood, which too many who consider the fate of the Northern Kingdom have not taken to serious heart, is how "He who scattered

---

[9] Concurrent with disparaging today's Jewish people as not being legitimate Israelites, is the specific denial that today's Ashkenazic Jews—the children and grand-children of the ones who suffered the most during the Holocaust—are actual Semites. These people make up the majority of the Jewish population in Israel and the Diaspora, and also the Messianic Jewish community.

A relative scholastic work like Philip F. Esler, *Conflict and Identity in Romans: The Social Setting of Paul's Letter* (Minneapolis: Fortress Press, 2003), 67 actually claims, "[T]he Khazars (a Turkic group from southern Russia)...became ancestors of Ashkenazi Jews..."

This was a book that I had to use for my Exegesis of Romans class at Asbury Theological Seminary (Fall 2008). I did ask my instructor, James C. Miller, about this. He informed me that Esler did go a little far in this assessment and has been reprimanded about it from other academics.

[10] *JPS Guide: The Jewish Bible*, 231.

[11] Bernis, *The Scattering of the Tribes of Israel*.

[12] Robert F. Wolff, ed., *Awakening the One New Man* (Shippensburg, PA: Destiny Image, 2011), 228.

Israel will gather him" (Jeremiah 31:10). Even with some clues given to us in Scripture, **God Himself ultimately knows where the main descendants of the exiles of the Northern Kingdom have gone.**

Are today's Messianic non-Jewish Believers, who feel a strong connection and feeling of comradeship to the Jewish people (especially Messianic Jews)—*and* who affirm a larger restoration of Israel to occur, involving Judah and Israel/Ephraim as participants—at all promoting anti-Semitism?

Clearly, it would be very difficult to argue that one is anti-Semitic on the basis of saying that a variety of prophecies are unfulfilled (Isaiah 11:12-16; Jeremiah 31:6-10; Ezekiel 37:15-28; Zechariah 10:6-10); such is an issue best left to the realm of eschatology and prophetic accomplishment as we get closer to the return of the Messiah. It would also be hard to say that if there are particular family lines and pockets of people out there in the nations (in places such as Southeast Asia, South Asia, the Middle East, Eastern Mediterranean basin, and into Central Africa) who are descendants of the exiled Northern Kingdom—and they have an oral tradition that traces their origins back to the fallen Kingdom of Israel/Ephraim—that such a thought is anti-Semitic. *This is no more anti-Semitic than recognizing how various people of European ancestry might have a Jewish ancestor or two, who assimilated into Christianity of the Middle Ages!* From an eschatological vantage point, not quite knowing who all of the descendants of the exiled Northern Kingdom are—or even if one has lost Jewish ancestry—is quantitatively indifferent from not knowing the identity of the antimessiah/antichrist or the false prophet, who the two witnesses of Revelation will be, or what the mark of the beast will ultimately be.

What would not be difficult to argue as being anti-Semitic, is if a wide majority of the Two-House sub-movement—largely non-Jewish, white Caucasian people, who forcibly claim that they are descendants of the exiled Northern Kingdom—is ever caught making unfair claims about Jewish religion, tradition, and culture. If the challenges, difficulties, and humiliations the Jewish people have experienced throughout history are totally disregarded and not understood, then the Two-House sub-movement could be considered anti-Semitic. If one continually pokes fun at Judaism and demonstrates no empathy or sympathy for the Jewish struggle witnessed throughout the centuries, then claims of anti-Semitism will be made. **And it is these things that a great deal of the Two-House sub-movement has certainly done, and does not tend to discourage.**

If there is no separate group of elect called "the Church,"[13] and the Commonwealth of Israel or Israel of God[14] may ultimately be considered a multi-ethnic faith community, an expanded Kingdom realm of Israel if you will[15]—then an extreme amount of care, honor, and respect needs to be expressed toward the Jewish people by non-Jewish Believers. Adding to the numbers of the community of Israel, be one a descendant of the exiled Northern of Israel/Ephraim, or far more

---

[13] Consult the author's article "When Did 'the Church' Begin?"

[14] Ephesians 2:11-12; Galatians 6:16.

[15] Consult the author's publication *Are Non-Jewish Believers Really a Part of Israel?*

probable a sojourner from the nations at large, should never be **tantamount to replacing or disbursing the Jewish people**, or shoving them into the proverbial corner to be silenced. Caution and discretion should be demonstrated when any non-Jew claims to be a part of an enlarged community of Israel, which has incorporated the righteous from the nations into its polity. When honor and dignity are expressed toward Judaism and the Jewish people, then true progress should be able to be made. When Judaism is disrespected, the plight of the Jewish people throughout history is not understood, and the challenges of today's Messianic Jews are not recognized—by non-Jewish Messianics—then the proper forum for discussing and evaluating the prophesied restoration of Israel cannot be facilitated.

When the Northern Kingdom of Israel/Ephraim was conquered by Assyria, by all rights, the Southern Kingdom of Judah then fully inherited the title of "Israel" as the legitimate, albeit smaller, successor state. There should be absolutely no doubt in anyone's mind that the Jewish people have been the legitimate torchbearers of "Israel" since that point in the ancient past. If the Jewish people and Judaism are demeaned, and made a less-than-legitimate part of Israel, what is that to say about a larger restoration of Israel prophesied? *Should this not instead bring more unity and appreciation among God's people?* If Jewish people are given a second-class treatment in the Two-House sub-movement, just as many non-Jews are in Messianic Judaism, then should the Two-House teaching that has been popularized, be considered insulting to God and anti-Semitic?

I very much understand why many of today's Messianic Jews reject even wanting to discuss prophecies of a larger restoration of Israel, when they witness the behavior of many Two-House advocates who have little or no regard for Judaism. These are not the kind of Messianic Jews who want to see non-Jewish Believers removed from their assemblies, but those who consider *all* to basically be an equal part of the Commonwealth of Israel. They genuinely want all to be welcome in their assemblies. When Judaism is (grossly) disrespected by various Two-House people, especially various individuals reckoned as "leaders" or "spokespersons," such Messianic Jews do not really want to hear about the possibility of more being on the agenda of salvation history.

The Two-House Sub-Movement and Its Approach to "Tradition"

Why is it that a large part of the Two-House sub-movement has definitely gained a reputation for being negative toward Judaism? In a great deal of the popular/populist Two-House literature,[16] more time and energy are actually expelled criticizing Jewish tradition and mainline Jewish practices, than in trying to formulate practical solutions of how all of God's people can be brought together *and* how various mainline Jewish traditions can benefit and enrich all of us.

Too much negativity is witnessed in the Two-House sub-movement surrounding little sound bytes thrown here and there, laced with "tradition(s) of men"[17] rhetoric. Little care is taken for how, while Yeshua the Messiah did condemn some human traditions adopted by the Rabbis of His day, the majority of these pertained to how various practices subtracted from the Torah's ethical and moral imperatives. A clear example would be claiming to use family finances as an offering unto God, while failing to use those monies and provide for the well being of one's aged parents (Mark 7:8-13).

Why is there such a noticeable degree of anti-Judaism present within the Two-House sub-movement? One would think that in a faith community which is actively trying to see a larger restoration of Israel take place, by raising the awareness of unfulfilled prophecies which may otherwise go unnoticed—that more forbearance and understanding of people, and their presumed limitations, would instead be emphasized. But since the mid-to-late 1990s when the Two-House teaching became popularized, *populism* and not reason have been more easily detectable. Some of this may be a direct result of some of the early voices asking questions about prophecies involving the Southern and Northern Kingdoms of Israel being reunited, being rejected by Messianic Judaism. And so, it is quite possible that in being rejected by Messianic Judaism, such people have responded with a quantitative rejection in turn of mainline Jewish tradition, as a kind of personal quest *or* even vendetta. This is now something that has spread as a not-so-subtle infestation, and even a venomous poison, throughout the Two-House sub-movement.

What are some of the things specifically being said or disseminated, to perhaps give the impression that the Two-House sub-movement is anti-Semitic? Surely it

---

[16] The writings representing this perspective include, but are not limited to:

Batya Ruth Wootten, *Who Is Israel? And Why You Need to Know* (St. Cloud, FL: Key of David, 1998); *Who Is Israel?*, enlarged edition (St. Cloud, FL: Key of David, 2000); *Redeemed Israel—Restored and Reunited* (St. Cloud, FL: Key of David, 2006); *Israel's Feasts and their Fullness*, expanded edition (St. Cloud, FL: Key of David Publishing, 2008); *Who Is Israel? Redeemed Israel—A Primer* (St. Cloud, FL: Key of David, 2011); Angus Wootten, *Restoring Israel's Kingdom* (St. Cloud, FL: Key of David, 2000); Eddie Chumney, *Restoring the Two Houses of Israel* (Hagerstown, MD, Serenity Books, 1999); Moshe Koniuchowsky, *The Truth About All Israel: A Refutation of the I.M.J.A. Position Paper on the Two Houses of Israel* (Miami Beach: Your Arms to Israel, 2000); Sandy Bloomfield, *The Errors of "The Ephraimite Error": Disposing of the Lies and Hatred* (Lebanon, TN: Messianic Israel Alliance, 2008).

[17] Grk. *tēn paradosin tōn anthrōpōn* (τὴν παράδοσιν τῶν ἀνθρώπων); the inclusive language "human tradition(s)" (NRSV/CJB/TNIV) should be more preferable.

should not be an emphasis on overlooked Bible prophecies that include the exiled Northern Kingdom as a participant.

The anti-Semitism, that one finds manifest in sectors of the Two-House sub-movement, surrounds an entire host of issues often pertaining to Jewish interpretations and traditions relating to the Torah. (Much of this often manifests itself during the yearly commemoration of the Spring and Fall high holidays.[18]) The most common statement that is made today goes along the lines of something like,

You do not want to come out of the Church, only to trade errant Christian tradition in for errant Jewish tradition.

This statement is one that is at least, partially accurate. There is non-Biblical Christian tradition and theology which needs to be jettisoned. A non-Jewish Believer who enters into the Messianic community, should not trade Christian error for Jewish error. Judaism has its problems too, just like Christianity. However, Christianity does have its truths, just as Judaism has its truths. Both Christianity and Judaism have had it right, and they have had it wrong, as those communities which have sought after the One True Creator God of the Holy Scriptures. But rather than having nothing to do with Jewish tradition, as is the preference of some, we must exhibit wisdom, discernment, and Holy Spirit-powered innovation—being able to recognize those things that are spiritually edifying to Messiah followers. (Likewise, we must recognize what is spiritually edifying about Christianity, at least since the Protestant Reformation.)

Obviously, there are going to be some things that are not spiritually edifying from Judaism, like practices which clearly originate from the Jewish mystical tradition or the Kabbalah.[19] Wearing a red bracelet to ward off the so-called "evil eye," via ancient superstition, would be something appropriately opposed. Encountering someone who is following an ultra-Orthodox Jewish custom of not shaking hands with a woman, for a polite greeting of one to another, should be considered a bit insulting. Yet, a considerable majority of mainline Jewish traditions, seen even in the most progressive and liberal branches of today's Synagogue, can be quite beneficial to those trying to live a Torah obedient walk of faith. Tradition need not be an enemy to non-Jewish Believers who desire to be "one" with their fellow Jewish Believers.

The statement previously quoted is made with some honorable intentions by those who emphasize it. Some non-Jewish Believers who have been convicted that the Torah is valid instruction for God's people today, and who realize that much of historic Christianity has an anti-Semitic past, have later denied Yeshua as the Messiah and have converted to Judaism. These people have become enamored with Jewish religion to such an extent where they have become more concerned

---

[18] This is explored in more detail in various parts of the *Messianic Spring Holiday Helper* and *Messianic Fall Holiday Helper* by TNN Press.

[19] Consult the useful summary by Todd Baker, "Kabbalah and the God of the Bible" Levitt Letter May 2011:21.

about extra-Biblical tradition, and they have taken their eyes off Scripture, its imperatives to live holy, and the Messiah Himself. This is extremely problematic, and anything that leads to apostasy from the faith **must be prevented.**

However, there are many other factors which can cause people to deny Yeshua the Messiah. The most serious of these is forgetting to place Yeshua at the center of one's life experience (cf. 1 Corinthians 2:2), and ahead of all human achievements (cf. Philippians 3:4-7). Apostasy can take place in Messianic environments where everyone is generally welcome as an equal part of the assembly, but people have an insecure faith in the Lord because something *other than He* is uplifted as more important. Even among various Two-House (as well as One Law/One Torah) fellowships, anti-missionary arguments issued against the Messiahship of Yeshua have been able to wreak havoc, because the spirituality of the people is not focused *first* around the One who came to be sacrificed as a permanent atonement for human sins.[20]

There are valid concerns raised by various voices in the Two-House sub-movement, in that non-Jewish Messianic Believers are not to become "Jewish" at the expense of their own ethnic or cultural heritage—especially if such an ethnic or cultural heritage has made some sort of sizeable contribution to Protestant, Western Christian civilization.[21] Many of us from evangelical Christian backgrounds have perspectives which today's Jewish Believers in Messiah Yeshua need to surely hear—just as much as we need to hear what they have to sincerely offer from their background in the traditional Synagogue. There are non-Biblical elements of Judaism, just as there are non-Biblical elements of Christianity. *But,* there are many godly and most edifying virtues in Judaism, just as there are many godly virtues in Christianity.[22]

Non-Jewish Messianics *need not at all* become hostile to Judaism. Yet, as many have recognized themselves as a part of the Commonwealth, or an enlarged Kingdom realm of Israel, and have rightfully sought to become Torah observant and live as Messiah Yeshua lived—many within the Two-House sub-movement have completely overlooked that the Northern Kingdom fell to the Assyrians, not only because of disobedience to the Torah and idolatry, but rebellion against the House of David (1 Kings 12:19; 2 Chronicles 10:19). The monarchy of the Northern Kingdom was *never considered* to be something legitimate and blessed by God. The

---

[20] Consult the author's article "The Faithfulness of Yeshua the Messiah."

[21] This is a place where the author would be personally, and somewhat familialy, compelled, to appeal to the various sentiments seen in works such as Duncan A. Bruce, *The Mark of the Scots: Their Astonishing Contributions to History, Science, Democracy, Literature and the Arts* (New York: Citadel Press, 1998); and Arthur Herman, *How the Scots Invented the Modern World: The True Story of How Western Europe's Poorest Nation Created Our World & Everything in It* (New York: Three Rivers Press, 2001).

By far, though, the author is most impressed to mention the work of his own late, third cousin, Charles L. Allen, *God's Psychiatry* (Grand Rapids: Fleming H. Revell, 1953).

[22] In spite of their many unfortunate, complimentarian limitations, Michael & Fronczak, *Twelve Gates*, 71, were gracious enough to recognize, in their estimation, that the material contained in this chapter, included "corrections to some of the worst offenses of the Two-House movement," and were actually "significant, wide-ranging, and refreshing."

first thing that occurred, after the Northern Kingdom of Israel/Ephraim seceded away from the Southern Kingdom of Judah, was that King Jeroboam established false gods, counterfeit holidays, and a counterfeit priesthood against what the Lord established in the Torah:

"If this people go up to offer sacrifices in the house of the LORD at Jerusalem, then the heart of this people will return to their lord, *even* to Rehoboam king of Judah; and they will kill me and return to Rehoboam king of Judah. So the king consulted, and made two golden calves, and he said to them, 'It is too much for you to go up to Jerusalem; behold your gods, O Israel, that brought you up from the land of Egypt.' He set one in Bethel, and the other he put in Dan. Now this thing became a sin, for the people went *to worship* before the one as far as Dan. And he made houses on high places, and made priests from among all the people who were not of the sons of Levi. Jeroboam instituted a feast in the eighth month on the fifteenth day of the month, like the feast which is in Judah, and he went up to the altar; thus he did in Bethel, sacrificing to the calves which he had made. And he stationed in Bethel the priests of the high places which he had made. Then he went up to the altar which he had made in Bethel on the fifteenth day in the eighth month, even in the month which he had devised in his own heart; and he instituted a feast for the sons of Israel and went up to the altar to burn incense" (1 Kings 12:27-33).

Everything that Jeroboam did was in direct opposition to what the God of Israel had prescribed in the Torah. He first made two golden calves for the people to worship, claiming that these were in actuality Israel's gods. He built temples on the high places, one in the southern parts of the Northern Kingdom and the other in the northern parts of the Northern Kingdom, for the "convenience" of the people, so they would not go to Jerusalem and seek reunification with the Southern Kingdom. He likewise instituted substitute festivals for the holidays that the Lord prescribed in the Torah, and he created a priesthood that was not of the line of Levi.

Biblical history records what came about as a result of these sins. The Northern Kingdom of Israel/Ephraim later fell to the Assyrian Empire, and was corporately deported into the nations.

Do not establish proper rulings?

Many non-Jewish Believers in today's Messianic community, rightly look to the example of the Jewish people for insight into following God's Torah. This is good, because Judaism indeed has much valuable insight and understanding concerning God's commandments.[23] However, Biblical history also shows that the Southern Kingdom of Judah was taken into its own captivity by the Babylonians for its idolatry and rebellion against God, and likewise Judaism has its own errors.

---

[23] It should be observed, in total fairness, that the two main Protestant strands of Calvinism and Wesleyanism, which have always viewed the so-called "moral law" of the Torah as valid instruction for Christians to follow—surely also have much to teach and guide today's Messianic Believers.

Consult the relevant sections of the author's book *The New Testament Validates Torah.*

The Jewish people, while not rejecting the validity of the Torah or Moses' Teaching, have placed a fence around many of the commandments (m.*Avot* 1:1),[24] adding customs and traditions that have enhanced the keeping of God's commandments, *but* then various others that have skewed or negated some. The most significant and grievous mistake is that most Jews, unfortunately, have rejected Messiah Yeshua as the Eternal Savior.

When looking to Judaism for spiritual insight, *every Messianic Believer* must use some degree of discernment and caution. The Jewish people have accumulated over two millennia of study, obedience, and communal experience surrounding the Torah. **To reject all Jewish interpretations and insight is wrong.** Jewish perspectives on the Tanach Scriptures are surely considered and consulted in Biblical Studies, along with Christian perspectives, when a viable interpretation is needed. This is even more true of areas of Torah instruction that have been largely kept by Judaism, and largely ignored by Christianity, throughout the centuries. While Jewish perspectives and traditions should not be considered authoritative *as Scripture*, recognizing that they have a **_consultative_ authority** for the Messianic community is something that will do far more to bring God's people together than keep them apart. *Learning how to do this*, though, *is an absolute art and science.* Unfortunately, a significant number within today's Two-House sub-movement are not up to this task, and lack the proper abilities, skills, temperament, and mental acumen to do so.

Why do many non-Jewish Believers in the Messianic community, *specifically* in the Two-House sub-movement, think that they can widely reject a majority of Jewish interpretations of the Torah, and associated tradition?

Much of what one encounters, in the teachings of various Two-House advocates, is a great deal of significance given to a passage of the Torah like Deuteronomy 4:2. Within this verse, Moses told the Ancient Israelites, "You shall not add to the word which I am commanding you, nor take away from it, that you may keep the commandments of the LORD your God which I command you." The primary emphasis of this commandment, more than anything else, is that God Himself was the only One who could tell the community of Israel what to do and not to do. This was most serious given the overall message of Deuteronomy opposing idolatry and sexual immorality in the Promised Land, which the people were preparing to enter.[25] Yet, a noticeable number of individuals who are outspoken Two-House proponents, also think that Deuteronomy 4:2 quantitatively rules out *any* Jewish tradition from being recognized as a legitimate expression of Torah observance, to be followed by (any of) God's people.

However, if we were to hold to a strict interpretation of Deuteronomy 4:2, then this likely means that when situations arise which require the faith community to make judgments on various issues or circumstances which are not directly or

---

[24] "Be deliberate in judgment, raise up many disciples, and make a fence around the Torah" (m.*Avot* 1:1b; Leonard, and Kerry M. Olitzky, eds. and trans., *Pirke Avot: A Modern Commentary on Jewish Ethics* [New York: UAHC Press, 1993], 1).

[25] Consult the author's article "The Message of Deuteronomy."

indirectly addressed in the Torah, or any part of Scripture, that *any decision* could possibly be acceptable. In the independent Messianic community today this has led to many interpretations of the Torah that are foreign to mainline Judaism, and can be quite offensive to Jewish people. It can lead to everyone doing what he or she feels is right (cf. Judges 17:6; 21:25), with confusion about what to do often abounding. (Even various evangelical Christians on the outside wonder about what they witness.)

It can be irresponsible to strongly assert that traditions are not at all commanded by God, when the Torah itself later says that if a matter arises within Israel, that His people are to follow the rulings of the priests and judges who He has recognized as occupying positions of authority:

"If any case is too difficult for you to decide, between one kind of homicide or another, between one kind of lawsuit or another, and between one kind of assault or another, being cases of dispute in your courts, then you shall arise and go up to the place which the LORD your God chooses. So you shall come to the Levitical priest or the judge who is *in office* in those days, and you shall inquire *of them* and they will declare to you the verdict in the case. You shall do according to the terms of the verdict which they declare to you from that place which the LORD chooses; **and you shall be careful to observe according to all that they teach you. According to the terms of the law which they teach you, and according to the verdict which they tell you, you shall do; you shall not turn aside from the word which they declare to you, to the right or the left**" (Deuteronomy 17:8-11).

The clause of interest is *al-pi ha'Torah* (עַל־פִּי הַתּוֹרָה), "According to the tenor of the law" (YLT),[26] which is given to those needing a definite judgment issued regarding a matter.

Some would make the argument that *every Rabbinical ruling* made in Orthodox Judaism today needs to be followed by the Messianic community at large—but this definitely goes too far. At the same time, though, Deuteronomy 17:11 does give a berth of authority to those in Jewish religious leadership which needs to be considered—as at least with what we should consider to be a **consultative authority**. Many within today's Messianic Judaism believe that its Torah observance should parallel the major *halachic* matters which bind the broad Jewish community together (Orthodox, Conservative, and Reform). This would include those areas of when it celebrates the appointed times (including *Chanukah* and *Purim*), how people would generally dress in a congregational environment, how people generally eat kosher, and other traditions which are beneficial to the broad community at large. Of course, there is certainly internal variance witnessed in Messianic Judaism, just as there is variance among various Jewish sects today.

If a person in the independent Messianic movement has never been exposed to Messianic Judaism, or if someone is naturally predisposed to "do his own thing" (or even worse, "buck the {proverbial} system") and not respect any established order, then it should not be surprising to see a strong impetus to develop

---

[26] "according to the mouth of the law" (LITV); "According to the sentence of the law" (KJV).

applications of the Torah that are (absolutely) foreign to mainstream Judaism (or at least Reform and Conservative Judaism). For many complicated reasons, both psychological and spiritual, outward un-conformity is something easily discerned within much of the Two-House sub-movement—*and it is a notable, and most significant problem.*

The instruction in Deuteronomy 17:11 is that God's people are to, "According to the teaching that they will teach you and according to the judgment that they will say to you, shall you do; you shall not deviate from the word that they will tell you, right or left" (ATS). We should not all believe that what is implied here is a blind obedience to the ancient rulings left by all of the Sages and Rabbis of Judaism. Messianic Believers have to ultimately evaluate their rulings against the canonical Word of God—and via the impetus of the Holy Spirit—to see if something aligns with the ethos or general tenor of Scripture, as most major rulings relate to ethical value judgments which the written Scriptures may not directly address. With all things, we have to see whether it parallels God's written Word, and enhances our relationship and walk with Yeshua. There are clearly things that have come down through history that can deter our walk with Him, but then there are many things which can surely enhance it. *Each of us must use proper discernment and consideration—in our appeal to God for His Divine will.*

What is perhaps most important more than anything else is that the rulings anticipated by Deuteronomy 17:8-11 have to often be made by recognized, qualified spiritual leaders of the community of faith at large. The Torah is designed to be lived out in a community, as opposed to an exclusive "one-on-one" basis between oneself and God. A prime example of this witnessed today is that when you see kosher-for-Passover food items, they often say "consult your rabbi" on the packaging. This indicates in some way that there is debate over whether or not an item is kosher for Passover, and that the ultimate determination should go to your local rabbi, who can evaluate what your personal or family circumstances are.

This can be a difficult concept for many who come from evangelical Christian backgrounds to accept, because many are often not used to their pastor making "rulings" on what Believers should do or not do concerning God's commandments. Many non-Jewish Believers are taught in church that our relationship with God is just between us and Him. While this is *ultimately* true, each of us is also in corporate, covenant association with other members of the faith community. Just like many probably went to a pastor for spiritual guidance, prayer, counseling, or just help regarding an issue, and took his advice and followed it, so can the rulings of the Jewish Rabbis apply. Just as many of us would expect an evangelical Christian pastor to be anointed by the Lord, and for his words to carry authoritative weight, so can the rulings of the Jewish Rabbis.

Of course, as with all things, we should never follow the opinions of a Christian pastor blindly, nor should we ever follow the rulings of the Jewish Rabbis blindly, either. We have to test everything against God's Word, to make sure that it aligns with the character of our Heavenly Father, and we have to see if it is something that enhances our walk with Him, rather than takes us away from Him.

More than anything else, *we have to deal with things on <u>a case-by-case basis</u>,* and recognize the fact that there is a great deal of "grey" when it comes to interpretation and application. In today's emerging Messianic community, hopefully we can find a proper balance between Scripture and tradition, where neither is considered unimportant.[27] We should also pray to have good local Messianic leaders be raised up by the Lord, who can issue sound decisions for their own communities and the issues they face (cf. Matthew 16:19).

Unbalanced and Unfair Criticisms of Major Jewish Torah Interpretations

Much of what may be considered anti-Semitic rhetoric in the Two-House sub-movement regards a series of Jewish interpretations surrounding various Torah commandments and mainline *halachic* practices. In respectable society, when there may be misunderstandings present between diverse groups of people, then those seeking fair-minded solutions will hopefully take the necessary time to investigate those areas not understood and seek some answers. As it regards some of the things we need to discuss here: **Why do today's Jews live the way they do?**

The criticism directed by a wide variety of non-Jewish Believers, in the Two-House sub-movement, is issued toward some specific mainline Jewish interpretations of the Torah. Some of this is simply the result of being under-informed, but some of this is also the sad, and most sorry consequence, of thinking that the Jewish people have nothing legitimate to offer to the Body of Messiah at large. I know that in my own dialogue with various open-minded Messianic Jews over the years about the Northern Kingdom of Israel in Biblical history and prophecies of its reunion with the Southern Kingdom of Judah, they largely approach the issue with disdain *not* necessarily because of the idea of various groups of people from the Northern Kingdom "out there" in the world offends them—but because they find the attitudes of many self-claiming "Ephraimites" in the Two-House sub-movement toward mainline Jewish tradition to be quite offensive.

Whether you agree with some of the Torah interpretations or *halachic* positions present in Judaism, which we are preparing to discuss, is not as important as *the attitudes* in which these things are criticized. Has there been any criticism issued, with little or no understanding—or even an effort to understand? Some of these things regard the "finer issues" of the Torah, and they are to a certain degree open to interpretation. **You will actually see some variance within Judaism itself.** The key to having constructive dialogue, though, is being informed and not being ignorant about an issue, acting as though we were some kind of "flaming-fundie." All of us must be very careful when critiquing the varied Jewish positions on the issues detailed below, as obedience to these commandments is quite foundational

---

[27] For a further discussion of related topics, consult the author's exegetical paper on Matthew 23:2-3, "Who Sits in the Seat of Moses?" in the *Messianic Torah Helper* (forthcoming).

to many Jews and their identity. We need not *unnecessarily offend* anyone, but exhibit an appropriate level of respect and forbearance.

(One highly useful resource for you to possess as a home reference about a great deal of Jewish custom and practice found today in the Twenty-First Century is Ronald L. Eisenberg, *The JPS Guide to Jewish Traditions* [Philadelphia: Jewish Publication Society, 2004]).

The Proper Name of God, and Titles Issued Toward the Creator

For some reason or another, since the mid-to-late 1990s, the circulation of questions about the Northern and Southern Kingdoms of Israel, being reunited in future prophecy, have been closely associated with questions about the proper name of God. Much of the Two-House sub-movement, or at least its popular literature, is closely connected to some degree with the perspectives of **the Sacred Name movement.** The Sacred Name movement, which has been around in various seventh-day and Sabbatarian groups for over a century, since the early 1900s, largely advocates that people must know the proper name of the Creator in the Hebrew Scriptures, YHWH/YHVH (יהוה), in order to possess eternal salvation. It is quite difficult to find Two-House publications and literature which directly refers to the Supreme Deity as either "God" or "Lord."

Much like how the false doctrines of psychopannychy and annihilation[28] have been closely tied to denominations like the Seventh-Day Adventist Church (neither of which has anything to do with keeping the Sabbath), so have the abuses of Sacred Name Onlyism been closely tied to various populist voices present within the Two-House sub-movement.

One of the major criticisms that quite a few Two-House advocates have of Judaism in general, is Judaism's avoidance of using the proper name of God. This same widescale non-usage is present in Messianic Judaism as well, and is also followed by the majority in the One Law/One Torah sub-movement. Many in the Two-House sub-movement, contrary to this, freely use and widely speak God's proper name of YHWH, often pronounced either Yahweh or Yahveh, and believe that Judaism is in significant error for failing to use it. Some have even accused the Jewish people of "hiding the name of God" from them, and believe that failure to speak the proper name of God is a "gross error" of Judaism.[29]

While it is absolutely true that our Heavenly Father has a name, we should agree as Believers that whatever Yeshua and the Apostles did concerning its usage should be what we do. In contrast to what those who advocate its usage may say, **there is not a single instance in the Apostolic Scriptures of Yeshua or the Apostles ever speaking the Divine Name.** By the period of Second Temple Judaism, the name of God was only spoken on *Yom Kippur* or the Day of

---

[28] Consult the author's publications *To Be Absent From the Body* and *Why Hell Must Be Eternal.*

[29] Academic Jewish resources do not hide the Divine Name from common knowledge.
Cf. *Jewish Study Bible*, 2141; *JPS Guide: The Jewish Bible*, 242.

Atonement in the Temple. The Mishnah reflects these traditions that existed in the Judaism of Yeshua's day:

"And the priests and people standing in the courtyard, when they would hear the Expressed Name [of the Lord] come out of the mouth of the high priest, would kneel and bow down and fall on their faces and say, 'Blessed be the name of the glory of his kingdom forever and ever'" (m.*Yoma* 6:2).[30]

Within the Judaism of Yeshua's day, the people used terms such as "the Temple," "the Place," "the Kingdom," "Heaven," or even "the Name" to refer to God, a custom we see employed throughout the Gospel of Matthew. This extended into early Christianity as well with Christians using "God" and "Lord" to refer to the Supreme Deity. Neither Yeshua nor the Apostles made using the Divine Name an issue, and they fully adhered to the Jewish custom which was prevalent in the First Century. If they had ever spoken the Divine Name, then claims of blasphemy would have been issued against them by the Jewish religious leaders, something which does not appear in the Gospels or the Book of Acts.

We would do well to follow Yeshua's non-usage of the Father's name. Using the proper name of God, as is too commonplace throughout the Two-House sub-movement, significantly offends our Jewish *and* Messianic Jewish brethren, and is not something that Yeshua did during His ministry. The Jewish people of the First Century and the Jewish people today hold the name of God in such high regard and holiness that they consider it to be blasphemous to pronounce it with human lips. While pronouncing God's name might not be "blasphemy," per se, we must treat it with holiness and respect *by not speaking it casually*. At most, we might be able to get away with speaking the name YHWH a few times in an academic sense.

But why does it seem that the issue of God's proper name has become such a problem? Many people who use the Divine Name in sectors of the Messianic movement tend to forget that our Father has many titles that are used complimentary *and independently* of the name YHWH. In the Hebrew Scriptures, the most notable titles that are used are *Elohim* (אֱלֹהִים) and *Adonai* (אֲדֹנָי). In the Greek Scriptures, their counterparts are *Theos* (θεός) and *Kurios* (κύριος). These titles in English correspond to "God" and "Lord."

Sacred Name Only advocates often have a field day in attacking people who use the titles God and Lord. It is often said that these words are of pagan origin and should have no place whatsoever in the vocabulary of a Believer. This claim is made on the basis that God and Lord have also been titles of pagan deities. This claim is made even more so for the Greek titles *Kurios* and *Theos*, which were used in Ancient Greek as titles for the deities of Mount Olympus. However, arguments against *Kurios* and *Theos* significantly lose weight when we see that the Jewish Rabbis who translated the Hebrew Tanach into Greek had no problem using them in reference to the Holy One of Israel. In fact, when the Apostles went into Greek-

---

[30] Jacob Neusner, trans., *The Mishnah: A New Translation* (New Haven and London: Yale University Press, 1988), 275.

speaking lands, this is *exactly* what they called the God of Israel—just as Greek-speaking Diaspora Judaism had done for several centuries before them.

It is not uncommon at all for many in today's Messianic movement to perceive of the Hebrew language as being the "holy tongue." This is based on a misunderstanding of Zephaniah 3:9, where the Prophet says "I will give to the peoples purified lips" or *safar beruah* (שָׂפָה בְרוּרָה). To assume that this means that the peoples will be given an ability to speak the Hebrew language is not an honest assessment of the Book of Zephaniah, as the previous verses tell us exactly what the problem of Ancient Israel has been:

"Woe to her who is rebellious and defiled, the tyrannical city! She heeded no voice, she accepted no instruction. She did not trust in the LORD, she did not draw near to her God. Her princes within her are roaring lions, her judges are wolves at evening; they leave nothing for the morning. Her prophets are reckless, treacherous men; her priests have profaned the sanctuary. They have done violence to the law. The LORD is righteous within her; He will do no injustice. Every morning He brings His justice to light; He does not fail. But the unjust knows no shame. I have cut off nations; their corner towers are in ruins. I have made their streets desolate, with no one passing by; their cities are laid waste, without a man, without an inhabitant. I said, 'Surely you will revere Me, accept instruction.' So her dwelling will not be cut off *according to* all that I have appointed concerning her. But they were eager to corrupt all their deeds" (Zephaniah 3:1-7).

Being given "purified lips" is undoubtedly connected with moving from a state of sinfulness to a state of holiness—from a state of profanity to a state of purity. Zephaniah's prophecy of "I will make the peoples pure of speech" (NJPS) is akin to the Apostle Paul's later instruction, "Let no unwholesome word proceed from your mouth, but only such *a word* as is good for edification according to the need *of the moment*, so that it will give grace to those who hear" (Ephesians 4:29). The "purified lips" pertains to *a manner of speech* by which the Father's people will be able to serve Him.[31]

While the Hebrew language certainly has great beauty—it is still *a human language* (and in many cases a primitive language, with limited vocabulary, at that). And perhaps most significantly, Hebrew is an Ancient Near Eastern language with relatives such as Aramaic, Akkadian, and Ugaritic. Yet this is not understood by many within the broad Messianic community, who assume that Hebrew is a holy language and that every other language is to some degree unholy. Such a misunderstanding can lead to ridiculous conclusions such as,

"The Set-apart Spirit, inspiring all Scripture, would most certainly not have transgressed the Law of Yahuweh by 'inspiring' the Messianic Scriptures in a language riddled with the names of Greek deities and freely using the names of

---

[31] For further consideration, consult the author's article "The Message of Zephaniah."

these deities in the text, no way!" (C.J. Koster, from the book *Come Out of Her, My People*).[32]

Here, because common nouns in Greek are also attested to be used as names of Greek deities, the Greek Scriptures are assumed to obviously not be inspired of the Almighty. This has led to a number of people doubting the message of the gospel, and leaving faith in Yeshua the Messiah.

But what happens if we were to apply this logic equally to the Hebrew Scriptures? Terms common to Hebrew, used as the proper names of pagan gods in languages such as Ugaritic—including the terms *El* (אֵל) and *Elohim* (אֱלֹהִים)—are applied to YHWH in the Tanach. If such a standard as proposed were applied to the whole of Scripture, **neither the Hebrew Tanach nor Greek Messianic Writings could really be considered as inspired**, as both languages include common vocabulary words used to refer to pagan deities. Are today's Messianics ready to start reading the Tanach against its Ancient Near Eastern context? This has certainly been a significantly deficient area of our collective Biblical Studies.

If we are to reject titles such as God and Lord because they might be used to refer to pagan deities, then we must hold the Hebrew titles of *Elohim* and *Adonai* to the exact same standard. Not surprisingly, both of these titles have been used to refer to *pagan deities* every bit as much as the deity YHWH. *TWOT* explains that *El* (אֵל), the singular form of *Elohim*, "is a very ancient Semitic term. It is also the most widely distributed name among Semitic-speaking peoples for the deity, occurring in some form in every Semitic language, except Ethiopic."[33] So, if we are to reject God and Lord as titles, we must do the same for *Elohim* because *Elohim* is used to refer to pagan deities, and *El* is used in almost every Semitic language to refer to deities other than YHWH.

But it even goes beyond this. A shortened poetic form of "Yahweh," *Yah* (יָהּ), which appears in the Hebrew Tanach, was possibly used by pagan societies that pre-dated the Israelites. The *IVPBBC* tells us, "There are a number of possible occurrences of Yahweh or Yah as a deity's name outside of Israel, though all are debatable."[34] Yet even if true, we certainly should not conclude that YHWH is a pagan name because the pagans may have used derivations of it. Furthermore, in 2 Samuel 5:20, David describes the God of Israel as *Ba'al* (בַּעַל), which was the name of a Canaanite deity! But note that, "In the early years the title Baal seems to have been used for the Lord (Yahweh)" (*NIDB*).[35] Is this an error on David's part? We should not believe so.

There is no substantial evidence that makes "God" and "Lord" pagan titles. Otherwise, titles such as the Hebrew *Elohim*, and possibly even the name YHWH itself, would be pagan. A failure to use standard terms for the Supreme Deity, by a wide variety of people within the Two-House sub-movement, has severely limited

---

[32] C.J. Koster, *Come Out of Her, My People* (Northriding, South Africa: Institute for Scripture Research, 1998), vi.

[33] Jack B. Scott, "'ēl," in *TWOT*, 1:42.

[34] Walton, Matthews, and Chavalas, 80.

[35] Steven Barabas, "Baal," in *NIDB*, 113.

the audience of those who have been able to listen to proposals about a larger restoration of Israel prophesied in Scripture. Because of the widespread Sacred Name Only agenda seen within the Two-House sub-movement, many Messianic Jews do not want to fairly consider the subject matter of the Northern and Southern Kingdoms of Israel to be reunited according to Bible prophecy—and Messianic Jewish leaders are certainly not going to allow Sacred Name Onlyism into their congregations. And, claiming that people who do not speak the name YHWH are not saved, is actually one of an entire host of highly problematic beliefs that one finds often adhered to by Sacred Name Onlyists.[36]

Tzit-tzits and Tallits

Within the Torah, one of the most interesting instructions that is given to the Ancient Israelites is, "Speak to the sons of Israel, and tell them that they shall make for themselves tassels on the corners of their garments throughout their generations, and that they shall put on the tassel of each corner a cord of blue" (Numbers 15:38; cf. Deuteronomy 22:12). When many non-Jewish Believers have their first exposure to the Messianic movement, it is usually by attending a *Shabbat* service on Saturday morning at a Messianic Jewish congregation. Like the traditional Synagogue, one will witness that many men, and even a few women, will be wearing some kind of four-cornered garment, called a *tallit* (טַלִּית), with tassels or fringes on it.[37]

When one sees a *tallit* (טַלִּית), or prayer shawl, onto which four *tzit-tzits* are attached, one at each of the corners, a person is undeniably connected to the ancient past. *Tallit*s vary in size from a small shawl to a large garment that can be used as a kind of cloak, and they usually have colored stripes, often blue or black. These prayer shawls are customarily worn during prayer times, and often in congregational services. In traditional Judaism, the *tallit* is only worn during the daytime, except for the evening of the high holidays of *Rosh HaShanah* and *Yom Kippur*.

Wearing tassels, fringes, or *tzit-tzityot* (צִיצִיוֹת) is easily observed on the clothing of many Orthodox Jews today. A garment that is usually worn is the *tallit katan* (טַלִּית קָטָן), a four-cornered undergarment worn by men onto which *tzit-tzits* are attached and then can be pulled out to be seen at the waist. Conservative and Reform Jews will often only wear a *tallit* with *tzit-tzityot* during the

---

[36] Concurrent with the Sacred Name Only agenda regarding the Father's name, are claims made about the name of the Son. It is frequently claimed that the name Jesus is pagan and derived from the name Zeus, but this is without viable linguistic support. Iēsous (Ἰησοῦς) and Zeus (Ζεύς) have two totally different Greek spellings and different pronunciations. Likewise, if the Greek name Iēsous were of pagan origin, and not a Jewish transliteration of the Hebrew name Yeshua (יֵשׁוּעַ) to be employed among Greek speakers, then it would not have been used for the title of the Book of Joshua (appearing as ΙΗΣΟΥΣ) in the Septuagint.

For more information and detail, consult the author's article "Sacred Name Concerns."

[37] Consult Ronald L. Eisenberg, *The JPS Guide to Jewish Traditions* (Philadelphia: Jewish Publication Society, 2004), pp 377-382 for a summary of how the *tallit* is employed in the mainline Jewish Synagogue.

Shabbat service, the Fall high holidays, and personal, private prayer times.

Largely in Judaism, the *tzit-tzit*s that are witnessed on the *tallit* or *tallit katan* are all white. Why is this the case? The blue dye or *techelet* (תְּכֵלֶת) that was used for the single fringe on the *tzit-tzit* was traditionally taken from a small sea snail (b.*Menachot* 42b), and following the destruction of the Second Temple the process was largely lost to history. There are organizations in Israel today which have claimed to rediscover the original blue dye, or a close substitute, and there are various observant Jews who will now wear *tzit-tzityot* with a thread of blue. There are also those who do not do this, and continue to simply wear all white fringes.

Generally speaking, today's Messianic Jews will fall somewhere within how Orthodox, Conservative, and Reform Jews observe the commandments to wear *tzit-tzityot*. Some of today's Messianic Jews wear the tassels or fringes with the cord of blue, but others do not.

Many non-Jewish Messianic Believers today who have entered into the Messianic movement have gone along with their Messianic Jewish counterparts, in observing the instruction to wear *tzit-tzityot*. This more often includes having the cord of blue. This may involve using *tzit-tzit*s imported from Israel using the apparently-rediscovered *techelet* blue dye. It is also quite frequent, however, to encounter many homemade *tzit-tzit*s with a synthetic blue dye. In a great deal of the independent Messianic world, especially in the Two-House sub-movement, while *tzit-tzit*s can be witnessed on a traditional *tallit*, more frequently homemade *tzit-tzit*s with a synthetic blue cord are attached to belt loops. (It is also true that there are some Messianic Jews who have taken to wearing their own *tzit-tzit*s with a synthetic blue dye, on their belt loops.[38])

Beyond this, there is a large cottage industry that has developed, with various multi-colored *tzit-tzit*s with a synthetic blue cord present. Some of these *tzit-tzit*s are white, with a synthetic blue cord, *and* a synthetic red cord to presumably represent the blood of Yeshua. Other types of *tzit-tzit*s are even more creative, appearing in multiple colors of the rainbow. Yet, unless *tzit-tzit*s are either white with the *techelet* cord of blue, or all white, they stand outside of the window of what would be recognized as legitimate Torah *halachah* by most of today's observant Jews.

Problems abound when we see various non-Jewish Believers in the Two-House sub-movement, forcibly identifying themselves as "returning Ephraim," who have said that the Jewish *tallit* is something that is unimportant and is an invalid tradition. Too many, in seeing how the *tallit* has been employed throughout the centuries in the Synagogue, have claimed that it is an invalid application of the Torah instruction. More frequently, though, what is witnessed is not an invalidation of the Jewish *tallit*, but rather *tallit*s being employed in a disrespectful manner, and in ways for which the *tallit* was never originally intended. It is apparently not enough for various people in the Two-House sub-movement to be

---

[38] They are advertised on p 23 of the 2010-2011 *Messianic Jewish Resources Catalog* published by Lederer.

aware of the diversity of views present in Orthodox, Conservative, and Reform Judaism—which for the latter two includes the acceptance of females wearing a *tallit* (or at least a feminine pastel *tallit*)—picking an already established manner and using it.

While everyone has a free will, the Jewish reaction—especially in the Land of Israel—to independent interpretations of wearing *tzit-tzits* speaks for itself, and tends to be anything but positive. *Tzit-tzits* with a synthetic cord of blue look very odd when associating with non-believing Jews (although they do not incur anger, as much as they do mocking). Picking up a *tallit* for anything other than personal morning prayers or congregational worship on Saturday morning, can be a bit out of place.

Tefillin (Phylacteries)

A steadfastly important admonition in the Torah is to remember not only how the Lord led Ancient Israel out of Egypt with His powerful hand and arm, but also how His people are to have His Word placed upon their own hands and foreheads:

- "So it shall serve as a sign on your hand and as phylacteries on your forehead, for with a powerful hand the LORD brought us out of Egypt" (Exodus 13:16).
- "You shall bind them as a sign on your hand and they shall be as frontals on your forehead" (Deuteronomy 6:8).

How these instructions have been interpreted by much of historical Judaism is viewed with a great deal of suspicion *and* mistrust by many non-Jewish Believers in the Messianic community—but most significantly in the Two-House sub-movement. Observant Jews who observe this direction, bind leather boxes known as *tefillin* (תְּפִלִּין) or phylacteries (derived from the Greek *phulaktērion*, φυλακτήριον) onto their arms and heads, remembering that the Lord led His people out of Egypt with an outstretched arm, and that they are to have His Word in their minds. *Tefillin* are used as an important part of a Jewish person's daily prayers.[39]

 In Orthodox Judaism, wrapping *tefillin* is considered to not only be one of the most important commandments of the Torah, but one of the most key rituals that identifies oneself as a Jew. Within the broad Jewish tradition, the instruction to bind God's Word on the hand and forehead has been taken literally, as the phylacteries include small parchments inside that have transcribed these Torah instructions (Exodus 13:1-10, 11-16; Deuteronomy 6:4-9; 11:13-21). Conservative and Reform Jews will also frequently wrap *tefillin*, but probably not as frequently as the Orthodox. These latter two Jewish sects will also allow women to use *tefillin*, whereas in Orthodox Judaism only men use them.

The custom of wrapping *tefillin* is not that commonplace within the daily prayer activities of today's Messianic Jews, although there are some trends which

---

[39] Consult Eisenberg, pp 382-386 for a summary of how *tefillin* is employed in the mainline Jewish Synagogue.

indicate that this is changing, with more open to the tradition. Many non-Jewish Messianics take this instruction as meaning that God's people are to *only* have His Word present in what they do with their hands and with their minds.

While remembering what God's Word says about what we do with our hands and minds is surely important, this does not make the practice of wrapping *tefillin* wrong or invalid. That the custom of employing phylacteries in Jewish prayer was present several centuries before the ministry of Yeshua is non-disputable.[40] The common rejection of using *tefillin* or phylacteries, for any kind of personal prayer, is often disputed from the basis that Yeshua the Messiah spoke against them in His criticism of the Pharisaical leaders:

"All their works they do to be noticed by men. They make their *tefillin* wide and their *tzitziyot* long" (Matthew 23:5, TLV).

Did Yeshua speak against wrapping *tefillin*/phylacteries in this verse? In His criticism of the Pharisaical leaders, Yeshua also criticized these individuals for their wearing of tassels or *tzit-tzityot*. Yet, elsewhere we see that Yeshua Himself wore fringes attached to the corners of His garments:

"Wherever He entered villages, or cities, or countryside, they were laying the sick in the market places, and imploring Him that they might just touch the fringe of His cloak; and as many as touched it were being cured…And a woman who had a hemorrhage for twelve years, and could not be healed by anyone, came up behind Him and touched the fringe of His cloak, and immediately her hemorrhage stopped" (Mark 6:56; cf. Luke 8:43-44).

Yeshua's word of Matthew 23:5 is clear: "They do everything to be observed by others" (HCSB). Yeshua actually criticizes these Pharisees for the manner in which they wore *tzit-tzits* and wrapped *tefillin*, in order to draw attention to themselves. The Messiah did not say that the custom of wrapping *tefillin* or phylacteries is wrong and ungodly. It is quite feasible that Yeshua Himself had employed *tefillin* within His own personal prayer times. The very purpose of taking the time in the morning, and binding a physical, ritual object like the *tefillin* or phylacteries—is so that one can be disciplined and focused in one's prayers and entreaties to the Heavenly Father.

There are Messianic Jews today who recognize the practice of wrapping *tefillin* as one of several interpretive options of how to have God's Word placed upon the hand and forehead. It is certainly an exercise that can direct one's attention upon God's Word.

Now if you do not wish to wrap *tefillin* and consider it an invalid interpretation of the Torah, you are entitled to your opinion. Some of you may not wrap *tefillin* because they can very expensive, or you are unprepared to make the commitment to use them on some kind of regular basis. None of us needs to find ourselves criticizing Judaism, though, for adhering to a custom that long pre-dates the Messiah's ministry. Wrapping *tefillin* in prayer times—not to be seen by

---

[40] Cf. R.L. Omanson, "Phylactery," in *ISBE*, 3:864-865; Ruth Santinover Fagen, "Phylacteries," in *ABD*, 5:368-370.

others—is something which is to enhance the intimacy and communication between a person who uses them, and his (or her) Creator.

Kippahs (Yarmulkes) and Headcovering Garments

One of the most obvious elements of modern Jewish identity witnessed in the world today, is men wearing the *kippah* (or *yarmulke*, יארמולקע) or skullcap. The idea behind wearing this small skullcap is that it shows submission to God. The term *kippah* (כִּפָּה) is derived from the Hebrew verb *kafar* (כָּפַר), meaning "to cover, to forgive, to expiate, to reconcile" (*AMG*).[41] The *kippah* is believed to be a "covering" which represents a man's submission to God.

It is notable that the headcovering garment of a *kippah* is not an explicit commandment of Scripture. This is a Jewish tradition which has developed over time. Alfred J. Kolatch explains this in *The Jewish Book of Why*:

> "A *yarmulke*, called a *kipa* in Hebrew, is a skullcap worn by Jews. Some wear one at all times, others only during prayer and at mealtime.
>
> "….The custom of covering the head received wide acceptance, but not by all. Historian Israel Abrahams points out that in the thirteenth century 'boys in Germany and adults in France were called to the Tora in the synagogue bareheaded.'
>
> "In the Middle Ages, French and Spanish rabbinical authorities regarded the practice of covering the head during prayer and when studying the Tora to be no more than mere custom. Some rabbis were known to pray bareheaded.
>
> "Today, Orthodox Jews and many Conservative Jews believe that covering the head is an expression of *yirat Shama'yim* ('fear of God' or 'reverence for God')…."[42]

Wearing a *kippah* is quite commonplace throughout the diverse social strata of modern Israel. Jews of all types throughout the Diaspora commonly wear them as well, sometimes as a part of their everyday dress. While wearing a *kippah* is more frequently associated with Synagogue worship or personal prayers, wearing a *kippah* at the home dinner table of a Jewish family is also witnessed. It is quite commonplace to see a majority of men in today's Messianic Jewish congregations wear *kippah*s in *Shabbat* worship. Various Messianic Jews also wear a *kippah* as a part of their normal, everyday dress.

It is not uncommon in many Messianic congregations to see non-Jewish men wear *kippah*s. This is largely so that they can respect the protocol of the assembly, as generally all men are expected to wear a *kippah* if they were to attend a service at any non-Messianic synagogue.

---

[41] Baker and Carpenter, 521.

[42] Alfred J. Kolatch, *The Jewish Book of Why* (Middle Village, NY: Jonathan David Publishers, 1981), pp 121-122.

Consult Eisenberg, pp 374-377 for a summary of how the *kippah* and related headcovering garments, are employed in the mainline Jewish Synagogue.

It is not difficult, though, to find a substantial amount of criticism, in some parts of the Messianic community—most especially the Two-House sub-movement—on whether or not the *kippah* is something appropriate to wear. It is usually based on the Apostle Paul's instructions witnessed in 1 Corinthians 11:4-16. As we will proceed to describe, there are some translation issues present in these verses in various English Bible versions, as well as some ancient background issues germane to First Century Corinth, which need to be seriously considered.

Paul says in 1 Corinthians 11:4, *pas anēr proseuchomenos ē prophēteuōn kata kephalēs* (πᾶς ἀνὴρ προσευχόμενος ἢ προφητεύων κατὰ κεφαλῆς), "Every man praying or prophesying, having *something* down *from* the head..." (my translation). Many versions add something like "with his head covered" (NIV) or "who has *something* on his head" (NASU), but does this really due justice to the clause *kata kephalēs* (κατὰ κεφαλῆς)? Would it have really been disgraceful for a First Century Jewish man, or even a Greek or Roman man, to wear a garment upon his head during a time of prayer or prophecy? *No.* Paul specifies later in 1 Corinthians 11:14 that there is something which could be down from a man's head that would disgrace him: "if a man has long hair, it is a dishonor to him." Long hair on a man hanging down, could have communicated something in Corinth that might not have been very good for the Believers. At the very least, some males with long hair hanging down, from certain angles, could possibly be confused as being female. Philip B. Payne further describes,

> "Something 'down from' (κατά [*kata*] with the genitive, 'lit. hanging down fr. the head,' BDAG 511 A.1.a) or 'over' the head of men leading in worship was disgraceful. Paul does not in this verse identify what was down from the head, so any explanation, to be convincing, needs to cite evidence from this passage and its cultural context. What hanging down from a man's head would be disgraceful for men leading worship in Corinth, a Greek city and a Roman colony? Many assume it is a toga (*himation*). It was not, however, disgraceful in the cultural context of Corinth or in Jewish culture for a man to drape a garment over his head. The *capite velato* custom of pulling a toga over one's head in Roman religious contexts symbolized devotion and piety, not disgrace. Jewish custom and the Hebrew Scriptures also approved head-covering garments for men leading in worship[43]...Thankfully, Paul identifies in verse 15 what 'hanging down from the dead' causes disgrace: 'If a man has long hair, it is a disgrace to him [1 Corinthians 11:14, NIV].'"[44]

Continuing in 1 Corinthians 11:5a, Paul issues instruction regarding *pasa de gunē proseuchomenē ē prophēteuousa akatakaluptō tē kephalē* (πᾶσα δὲ γυνὴ προσευχομένη ἢ προφητεύουσα ἀκατακαλύπτῳ τῇ κεφαλῇ), "every woman praying or prophesying, with the head uncovered..." (my translation) is to be regarded as having dishonored her head, even as though her head were shaved (1 Corinthians 11:5b).

---

[43] E.g., Exodus 28:4, 37, 39; 29:6; 39:28, 31; Leviticus 8:9; 16:4; Ezekiel 24:17; 44:18; Zechariah 3:5.

[44] Philip B. Payne, *Man and Woman, One in Christ: An Exegetical and Theological Study of Paul's Letters* (Grand Rapids: Zondervan, 2009), pp 141-142.

Having a shaved (Grk. verb *xureō*, ξυρέω) head in ancient times, whether in Ancient Israel, Second Temple Judaism, or even Greco-Roman culture, was frequently a sign of mourning and/or humiliation. The challenge for interpreting a "head uncovered," is that it is frequently read from the perspective of it meaning that a woman praying or prophesying must have some kind of a garment present. Is wearing a headcovering garment really the issue?

A significant usage of the adjective *akataluptos* (ἀκατακάλυπτος), in the Septuagint, is Leviticus 13:45, speaking of "the leper who has the plague in him, his garments shall be torn, and his head shall be **uncovered** [*akataluptos*]" (LXE).[45] *Akataluptos* actually renders the Hebrew verb *para* (פָּרַע), meaning "to let the hair on the head hang loosely" (*HALOT*),[46] as "The leper who has the disease shall wear torn clothes and let the hair of his head **hang loose** [*para*]..." (Leviticus 13:45, RSV).[47]If this background is kept in view, than a Corinthian woman who had her head "uncovered," is one who actually had her long hair hanging loose for all in the assembly to see. It is true that when modern readers encounter a term like "uncovered," it is more natural for us to think that the Corinthian woman was to probably be wearing some sort of head garment. But wearing or not wearing a head garment would not have been as problematic as a female having loosed hair flowing freely. In a largely progressive and so-called "sexually liberated" city like First Century Corinth, a woman with free-flowing loose hair **was anything but respectable.** In fact, such a hairstyle would be like a prostitute advertising her wares! Payne details,

"Loosed hair was disgraceful (11:5) and symbolized sexual looseness in Roman, Greek, and Jewish culture....Loosed hair fits the cultural influence and specific practice of the Dionysiac cult, which was popular in Corinth and explains why women in Corinth might have let their hair down."[48]

Contrary to women with "uncovered" heads—heads with hair freely flowing down—respectable women would have "covered heads" with their hair arranged in a kind of bun, something attested in the artwork of the broad First Century.[49] A Corinthian woman with an "uncovered" head meaning free-flowing long hair, hair

---

[45] NETS similarly has: "let his clothes the loosened and his head be uncovered [*akataluptos*]."

[46] *HALOT*, 2:970.

[47] Payne, 167 further states,

"The only occurrence in the text Paul cited the most, the LXX [Septuagint], of 'uncovered' (11:5; ἀκατακάλυπτος [*akatakaluptos*] in Lev 13:45) translates פָּרֻעַ [*paru'a*], from פרע, which Hebrew scholars agree means 'to let the hair on the head hang loosely.' It is the earliest instance of the word 'cover' (κατακάλυπτος [*katakaluptos*]) occurring with 'head' in the *TLG* database...'Uncovered' is explained twice in verses 5-6, using 'for' (γάρ [*gar*]). Both reasons explain the uncovering as equivalent to hair being clipped or shaved. This associates the covering as hair and fits most naturally if 'uncovered' refers to a woman with her hair let down."

[48] Ibid., 166.

[49] "What about having one's head 'uncovered' would cause shame to a woman leading in worship in the cultural setting of Corinth? The extensive evidence from portraiture, frescoes, sculptures, and vase paintings in Greek and Roman cities of Paul's day almost universally depicts respectable women with their hair done up. Women in everyday public settings are not depicted with their hair hanging loose over their shoulders" (Ibid., 151).

that has not been arranged in a proper manner, makes sense of Paul's prescription that such an "uncovered" woman's hair be cut or shaved off—which was definitely a sign of dishonor (1 Corinthians 11:6). A proper recognition of the genders is in view here (1 Corinthians 11:7-8), including being aware of how at a previous time in Biblical history (e.g., Genesis 6:4) women may have been able to tempt the angels (1 Corinthians 11:10).

Both man and woman—especially if they are married—are to understand that they are not independent of one another, with all originating from God (1 Corinthians 11:11-12). With the realization that "covered" and "uncovered" probably relates to hairstyles of short hair or hair pulled up, and free-flowing long hair, how does this change our reading of Paul's further direction? When people would attend home gatherings of the Corinthians, *including* any visiting pagans, what impression would it give of the Messiah followers and the Lord Yeshua? As 1 Corinthians 11:13-16 details,

"Judge for yourselves: is it proper for a woman to pray to God *with her head* uncovered {**meaning:** with free-flowing long hair}? Does not even nature itself teach you that if a man has long hair, it is a dishonor to him, but if a woman has long hair, it is a glory to her? For her hair is given to her for a covering [mantle; Grk. *peribolaion*, περιβόλαιον]. But if one is inclined to be contentious, we have no other practice, nor have the [assemblies] of God."

It is difficult at first for us to consider covered/uncovered to relate to hairstyles, which either communicated lewdness or promiscuity or just general disrespectfulness to wider society—but it is a much better way for us to understand the issues of 1 Corinthians 11:1-16. The actual issue in Ancient Corinth regarding male and female heads that are "covered" and "uncovered" **actually pertained to specific hairstyles.** Men should not have long hair hanging down. Women should have their long hair put up, being "covered," as being "uncovered" would mean letting the hair go. The association that such hairstyles would have, could not only communicate a degree of prostitution-promotion (female *and* male) to outsiders, but perhaps also associate the Corinthians as participating with local pagan religious activities. The Apostle Paul clearly did not want something like this communicated to outsiders in the gatherings and worship activities of the Messiah followers!

I have never seen the perspective of "covered" and "uncovered" relating to Ancient Corinthian hairstyles ever really considered in any sector of today's Messianic movement. Many believe that "covered" and "uncovered" relates to head garments like the *kippah/yarmulke*, various uses of the *tallit*, or some kind of female head garment. While not all of these items as we know them were in use in the Biblical period, ultimately the issue of headcovering garments for men and women is one that is **entirely traditional and cultural.** It is something that all Messianic Believers need to be sensitive about in their *halachah* to be certain (like men wearing a *yarmulke* at the Western Wall in Jerusalem), **but headcovering garments are not the real issue** of 1 Corinthians 11:1-16. The main thrust of this part of Paul's letter to the Corinthians pertains to how various grooming styles can damage the credibility of the faith community. In First Century Corinth, women who let their hair go "uncovered"—long and loose—were communicating something bad. Today, long hair on a woman (perhaps in a pony tail or other style) in some places might instead communicate conservativeness.[50] As far as shorter or longer degrees of hair length on a woman *or* man are concerned: they regard the general evaluation of their (Twenty-First Century [Western]) cultural context, and what may be considered respectable.

I have personally been in widescale favor of all Messianic men wearing a *kippah/yarmulke* during weekly *Shabbat* services **and most especially** during the high holy days of *Rosh HaShanah* and *Yom Kippur*. Likewise, all of those who also don a *tallit* for prayer and worship should not do so without a *kippah/yarmulke*. While it is a tradition, the wearing of the skullcap is nonetheless considered to be a sign of a man's reverence for God in mainline Judaism. The protocol observed in a Messianic congregation should be similar to that in the Jewish Synagogue.[51]

At the same time, the wearing of the *kippah* cannot be construed as any kind of Biblically-prescribed commandment, nor something that should be forced upon anyone. I urge sensitivity concerning the Jewish custom of wearing the *kippah*, especially considering how widespread it is. No non-Jewish Believer should ever be caught trying to degrade the role that the *kippah/yarmulke* has played in many centuries of Jewish culture. Yet, unbalanced interpretations of 1 Corinthians 11:1-16, slurs such as calling the *kippah/yarmulke* some kind of "beanie," and disrespect for the custom in general—has definitely been witnessed by those in the Two-House sub-movement. How can such people ever hope to see a larger restoration of Israel's Kingdom come to pass, if they cannot respect one of the most basic and widespread traditions of the Jewish people?

The Mixing of Meat and Dairy

Generally speaking, across the broad Messianic movement, some level of kosher eating is followed, and it is not believed that the dietary laws of the Torah were abolished by either Yeshua or the Apostles. There is considerable variance, though, of how such kosher eating is to be observed. This minimally involves an abstention from unclean meats like pork and shellfish. In many cases, clean meats such as beef, lamb, chicken, turkey, and various fish are only purchased (or at least preferred to be purchased) from authorized Jewish sources. Beyond this, a wide array of Jewish traditions regarding food storage and preparation, are encountered. While a bulk of the Messianic movement may only be found to keep what it considers to be "Biblically kosher" or "kosher style," there are a considerable

---

[50] Indeed, in our family's experience in the Messianic movement since 1995, most of the average men and women in our faith community have little problems as it concerns our proposed reading of 1 Corinthians 11:1-16. They tend to have hairstyles and a mode of dress which communicate a rather conservative demeanor to society at large, consistent with much of respectable Judaism and Christianity, not at all being associated with much popular culture.

[51] This section has adapted quotations from the author's article "The Message of 1 Corinthians."

number of those who observe the many Rabbinical rulings on *kashrut* law (כַּשְׁרוּת), which are principally observed in today's Orthodox Judaism.

One of the recognizable features, of much Jewish kosher observance throughout history, has been the separation of meat and dairy products.[52] This has been largely based on the Torah's instruction, "You are not to boil a young goat in the milk of its mother" (Exodus 23:19; cf. 34:26; Deuteronomy 14:21). Orthodox Jews today, especially, do not eat meat and dairy products together. This not only involves not drinking milk or eating cheese along with meat, but also how various baked goods that might be served with meat, will not include dairy ingredients. Among different communities, meat or dairy will only be eaten after a sufficient time of digestion, which varies from group to group. Some of the main theological reasons for not mixing meat and dairy products, as based from the Torah, are summarized in the *ArtScroll Chumash*:

"Meat represents the animal portion of life, the muscle and sinew. Milk represents the reproductive capacity of animal life, for milk is the nourishment that supports new life. In animals, these two aspects of life are inseparable; animals instinctively eat and reproduce. Man has a higher calling. He must not mingle these aspects of his nature. To the contrary, he must learn to differentiate between his activities and—primarily—to subjugate them all to his duty to grow in the service of God and to put Godliness into all his activities. The higher duty is symbolized in the prohibition against mixing milk and meat. Its proximity to the law of the festivals and the first of first fruits coveys the teaching that one who succumbs to his animal instincts destroys the holy nature of the seasons and God's blessings of prosperity."[53]

The Hebrew verb translated as "boil" is *bashal* (בָּשַׁל), which appearing in the Piel stem (intensive action, active voice) means "**cook, boil, roast**" (*CHALOT*).[54] But what is the reasoning behind, "Do not cook a young goat in its mother's milk" (Exodus 23:19, NIV)? It might be explained on humanitarian grounds, and how it could be perceived as cruel to actually cook the meat of a calf or kid in the very milk that once fed it. Likewise, it has been suggested that cooking such meat in milk is a prohibition against an Ancient Canaanite religious ritual, possibly related to fertility.[55] It is true that the practice of separating meat and dairy was a debate present within the Second Temple Judaism in which Yeshua's ministry functioned (m.*Chullin* 8:3-4; b.*Chullin* 104a; cf. b.*Shabbat* 130a), which makes it possible that the family of Joseph and Mary did not really eat meat and dairy products together.

There are a wide number of people within the Messianic community, including much of Messianic Judaism, who do not agree with the separation of

---

[52] Consult Eisenberg, pp 662-664 for a summary of how prohibition on mixing milk and meat is practiced in the mainline Jewish Synagogue.

[53] Scherman, *Chumash*, 437.

[54] *CHALOT*, 51.

[55] Brevard S. Childs, *The Book of Exodus* (Philadelphia: Westminster Press, 1974), pp 485-486; John I. Durham, *Word Biblical Commentary: Exodus*, Vol. 3 (Waco, TX: Word Books, 1987), 334; Walton, Matthews, and Chavalas, 103.

meat and dairy as is principally witnessed in much of Orthodox Judaism's practice of keeping kosher. Separating meat and dairy is, of course, an interpretation of the Torah's instructions about not boiling or cooking a kid in its mother's milk. The challenge is not when we recognize how the historical Jewish practice of separating meat and dairy is a noticeable part of the traditional Synagogue's observance of keeping kosher; problems are seen when people choose to totally disregard the right of a Jewish person to separate meat and dairy as a part of his or her *legitimate* Torah application and heritage.

The Two-House sub-movement has quite a few people who are rather disrespectful of the common Jewish separation of meat and dairy products. These are largely non-Jewish Believers who have expelled no effort, to at least understand in an historical sense, how the kosher dietary laws have been followed by the Synagogue. These are people who are largely insensitive to Jewish views and interpretations of *kashrut*, and in a few cases actually includes people who will just flat make fun of Jews who do not eat cheeseburgers or lasagna. Yet, even if it can be observed that various Jews are a bit overly-ambitious about their kosher eating, they have at least been trying to keep the dietary laws. Ironically, many of the non-Jews within the Two-House sub-movement, (improperly) believing themselves to be of "returning Ephraim," have perhaps ironically overlooked the prophetic sentiment of Hosea 9:3:

"Ephraim shall return to Egypt, **and they shall eat unclean things in Assyria**" (LITV).

The Hebrew text specifically says *u'v'Ashur tamei yokeilu* (וּבְאַשּׁוּר טָמֵא יֹאכֵלוּ), "in Asshur an unclean thing they eat" (YLT). Those within the Two-House sub-movement, who choose to criticize mainline Jewish interpretations and applications for observing *kashrut*, often do not consider the fact that those of the exiled Northern Kingdom were actually prophesied to eat unclean things, not considered food, in their exile.

While it is unlikely that we are going to see a huge number of today's Messianic people, non-Jewish *or* Jewish, keep a level of kosher the same as Orthodox Judaism—more understanding and appreciation, of the different aspects and levels of kosher observance by the Synagogue, is surely needed. None of us needs to ever find ourselves in a restaurant in Israel, or a place like New York City or Los Angeles with its large Jewish populations, making snide remarks about separating meat and dairy, and instead arrogantly insist the rightness of being "Biblically kosher."[56]

Beards and Facial Hair

It is not difficult for people to acknowledge how wearing beards (Heb. sing. *zaqan*, זָקָן), or facial hair in general, is quite commonplace among many male Jews. Many Jewish cultural features have been rooted within the instruction of Leviticus

---

[56] For more information on this subject matter and related issues, consult the *Messianic Kosher Helper* by TNN Press (forthcoming).

19:27, "You shall not round off the side-growth of your heads nor harm the edges of your beard" (Leviticus 19:27). There has been internal debate within Judaism what "the side-growth of your beard" (NJPS) actually means, though, with varied applications of this present among modern Jews.[57]

Some interpret this command as relating to a man's full beard, others only his sideburns, and others the extremities of the beard. Some believe that a man's facial hair has actual "boundaries," more or less defined, and others believe that the hair on a man's face should just grow without any type of grooming. Some believe that a man can trim and groom his beard. Others believe that a man can shave his beard, provided it is with an electric razor. And, others even think that a man can shave his beard with a conventional depilatory razor, provided that it has at least two blades, and not a single cutting edge. Consequently, the same variance of interpretations has made its way into the Messianic movement, and one will see a wide array of applications.

In approaching the word of Leviticus 19:27, we should acknowledge the diversity of opinions within Judaism. Whatever interpretation you hold to about beards, you should respect others. It is notable that there is a distinct Messianic subculture that insists that all men wear beards, and there are those who will often be judgmental and quite harsh of men who do not have them. Having or not having a full beard is not an issue of a man's spirituality, as one's relationship with the Lord is contingent on having a heart and mind which have been transformed by the Holy Spirit, demonstrating God's love to others in the world. As God had to remind the Prophet Samuel, "for the LORD does not see as mortals see; they look on the outward appearance, but the LORD looks on the heart" (1 Samuel 16:7, NRSV).

Some men are incapable of growing beards, or even a moustache or goatee, and that is the way God made them. Are they less spiritual because they cannot have a beard? Others have beards as a matter of personal preference, and not necessarily because they think the Bible requires them. In some Messianic congregations, you will find that facial hair on men is not an issue, where in others it is an issue. Speaking for myself, I do not choose to make the facial hair I see or do not see on any man into an issue, although men who wear beards can obviously be easily distinguished from women.

Concurrent with the variance of views, concerning beards and facial hair within Judaism, is how much of Orthodox Judaism practices the custom of wearing *payot* (פֵּאוֹת). This interpretation stems from the meaning of the Hebrew word for "corner" in Leviticus 19:27, *peah* (פֵּאָה), "side, edge, border" (BDB).[58] *Payot* are often curls that extend down from the area of the sideburns, and they vary in length from a few inches, to even eighteen inches. Kolatch explains that "many Jews, particularly members of *chassidic* sects, will not trim the sidelocks even of children. Long, curled sidelocks (*payot*) on the children of *chassidim* is a common sight."[59]

---

[57] Consult Eisenberg, pp 590-592 for a summary of how the issue of beards, grooming beards, and shaving is approached in the mainline Jewish Synagogue.

[58] *BDB*, 802.

[59] Kolatch, 122.

Not very many in the Messianic community practice the custom of having *payot*. No one, though, should ever be found harassing Jews who do wear them. Simply consider the many Orthodox Jews during World War II, who had Nazi troops shame them by cutting off their *payot*. Even with the wearing of *payot* something that is not too common in the worldwide Jewish community, it is certainly an interpretation of Leviticus 19:27 that has a longstanding practice throughout Jewish history, and is a part of the heritage of unique sectors of the Orthodox Synagogue.

The Biblical Calendar

The new month, as originally specified by the Torah, was to be determined by the changing of the moon or *chodesh* (חֹדֶשׁ). Genesis 1:14 states how God originally made the lights of the sky, as the means by which His people were to keep time: "Let there be lights in the expanse of the heavens to separate the day from the night, and let them be for signs and for seasons and for days and years." Numbers 29:6[60] records how there were to be a variety of special offerings presented to the Lord, during the time of the New Moon.

Since the Biblical period of ancient times up until modern times, there has been a diversity of opinion present within Judaism as to how time is to be reckoned. For practical purposes, this most often concerns the days on which the appointed times are to be observed. While residing within the Land of Israel in either the First or Second Temple periods, it would be quite easy for an enclosed group of Ancient Israelites or Ancient Jews to maintain a calendrical system via a visible sighting of the New Moon, things definitely changed in history with the destruction of Jerusalem in 70 C.E. and widespread expulsion from the Holy Land. How was the Jewish community, the vast majority of which was spread abroad in Diaspora, to keep the appointed times and maintain some level of cohesion and unity? George Robinson offers the following fair summation in his book *Essential Judaism*, of how the Hillel II calendar was developed in the Fourth Century C.E.:

> "In the time of the Temple in Jerusalem (the First Temple was destroyed in 586 B.C.E., the Second Temple, built in 538 B.C.E. was razed in 70 C.E.), communication over long distances was problematic. It was imperative, if all Jewish communities were to celebrate at the same time, that everyone know when the new moon occurred, since the date of a festival would be based on when the first of the month fell…Until 358 C.E., when Rabbi Hillel II introduced a permanent fixed calendar, it was up to the Sanhedrin, the governing body of rabbis in Jerusalem, to decide when the new moon fell, based on eyewitness testimony. They in turn would send a signal to a man on a neighboring hilltop who would light a signal fire; another fire would be lit on a nearby hilltop and so on, until a chain of signal fires was flickering through the known Jewish world, telling the Jews that the new month had begun.

---

[60] "[T]he burnt offering of the new moon and its grain offering, and the continual burnt offering and its grain offering, and their drink offerings, according to their ordinance, for a soothing aroma, an offering by fire to the LORD" (Numbers 29:6).

"This was, needless to say, an inexact system. The rabbis of the Sanhedrin worried that communities outside the Holy Land would not know the exact date on which to celebrate a festival. In response to this problem, they instituted a second day for each festival in the Diaspora so that there could be no mistake. The second day is preserved in the practice of Orthodox and Conservative Jews in the Diaspora of celebrating a second day of major holidays. In Israel and the Reform movement, only one day of each festival is observed."[61]

With a few modifications since, the Hillel II calendar—which is all *pre-calculated* for the beginning of the month and days for the appointed times—is followed by the worldwide Jewish community today, as well as the considerable majority of Messianic Judaism. One of the biggest areas of divergence, that is easily detectable between much of the Two-House sub-movement and Messianic Judaism, is that the former largely rejects the validity of the mainline Jewish calendar. When various "Two-House" assemblies and fellowships gather to remember the appointed times, such as Passover, it is usually not at the same time that mainline Messianic Jewish congregations will gather.

The issue of the calendar in general, is often regarded as one of authority. Do the Rabbis of Judaism have *any* significant place in the *halachah* of today's Messianic community and Messianic Believers? It is not difficult for a Messianic Jewish person, in respecting his or her heritage, to conclude that the Hillel II calendar should be followed, since it provides common dates for all Jews the world over to observe the appointed times. Believing in Messiah Yeshua does not all of a sudden make such a person un-Jewish or significantly disconnected from the wider Jewish world, especially in matters like the calendar followed. Even if the Rabbis have been wrong in many theological areas, this does not mean that they are completely ignorant and totally devoid of basic wisdom.

Within much of the Two-House sub-movement, rather than the pre-calculated Hillel II calendar being followed, many instead prefer to follow the calendrical determinations by the Karaite movement. The Karaites were an ancient sect of Judaism that arose in the Middle Ages, that quantitatively rejected Rabbinical authority and the value of works like the Mishnah or Talmud. The Karaite movement in Israel, while extremely small, has its own calendar based on their visible sighting of the New Moon.

(It does have to be noted that a small number of people within the Two-House sub-movement do still follow the mainline Jewish calendar. But even in doing so, there are disagreements often present with the date for keeping *Shavuot*, or referring to the Feast of Trumpets as *Rosh HaShanah*.[62])

Within the Two-House sub-movement and at many its popular conference events, it is not uncommon to find various outspoken teachers who advocate things along the lines of, "The Father is restoring the Biblical calendar to us…" Within

---

[61] George Robinson, *Essential Judaism: A Complete Guide to Beliefs, Customs, and Rituals* (New York: Pocket Books, 2000), pp 79-80.

[62] Consult the relevant sections of the *Messianic Spring Holiday Helper* and *Messianic Fall Holiday Helper* by TNN Press for a further discussion of these issues.

such teachings, one does not often find that much regard expressed for the complexities of ancient Jewish history, and the need for the Rabbinic authorities to develop a calendar that *the worldwide Jewish community* could use to keep them unified together as a people. Unfair accusations and disgust toward the Synagogue, and Jewish religion in general, are instead more easily detected.

Too much of the independent Messianic movement has many "restored Biblical calendars" littering its ranks. While various persons have taken it upon themselves to produce their own "restored Biblical calendar," this has tended to only cause *more confusion* and division, as one does not know which calendar is to be followed from congregation to assembly to fellowship. Not all agree with the determination of the Karaite movement in Israel, or when the New Moon begins and ends. The default calendar choice, for any Messianic, is understandably the mainline Rabbinical calendar used by Judaism today.

What really needs to be recognized, about why there is so much diversity circulating in the independent Messianic world about the Biblical calendar, is that a group's so-called "restored Biblical calendar" is really not a means by which to determine the "real date" for remembering Passover or *Yom Kippur*. Many have produced their own calendars as a means to promote their own predictions and calculations regarding the end-times and Second Coming. With this, the most amount of attention focused is not upon the determination of the New Moon, but rather **the year.** Many assumptions are made from mathematics, astronomy, chronology, and science. It is not too infrequent that someone's "restored Biblical calendar" gets proven wrong, and suggested dates and times have to be adjusted and recalculated when predictions come and go when nothing happens.

There is likely a season coming when some of the presuppositions that have gone into the different "restored Biblical calendars," will need to be radically reevaluated. Recalculating and recalculating the presumed year of Yeshua's return (2000, 2007, 2012, 2017, etc.) cannot be allowed to continue indefinitely. The severe challenge to people reconsidering the various presuppositions that are associated with highly-packaged teachings like the so-called 6,000-year doctrine,[63] is that it will open up areas of theological discussion which have largely remained closed to all sectors of the Messianic movement, particularly as it concerns the material of Genesis chs. 1-11.[64] Anthropologically speaking, we see human cave paintings, such as those in Lascaux, France from an estimated 16,000 years ago[65] (with some of the other cave paintings in France and Spain dating to as many as 32,000 years ago). One need not be an evolutionist to legitimately recognize that the popular

---

[63] Consult the FAQ on the TNN website, "6,000 Year Teaching."

[64] For a worthwhile review, I recommend that you consider the views of Creationist Hugh Ross, *The Genesis Question: Scientific Advances and the Accuracy of Genesis*, second expanded edition (Colorado Springs: NavPress, 2001) and *A Matter of Days: Resolving a Creation Controversy* (Colorado Springs: NavPress, 2004).

[65] Information on visiting the cave of Lascaux can be accessed on the French Ministry of Culture website: <http://www.culture.gouv.fr/culture/arcnat/lascaux/en/>.

6,000-year doctrine has made some assumptions, about both eschatology and Biblical genealogies (i.e., Genesis 5, 11),[66] that do not bear out in human history.

Yeshua will only return **when His people are ready.** The Apostle Peter says we "ought...to be in holy conduct and godliness, looking for and hastening the coming of the day of God" (2 Peter 3:11-12). He employs the present active participle *speudontas* (σπεύδοντας)—"hastening"—to describe this action. The righteous behavior of Believers affects "the coming of the day of God,"[67] not any human being's mistaken calculation of it.

Outreach Israel Ministries and TNN Online see absolutely no reason why today's Messianic movement should not be observing the appointed times *on all of the same dates* as the rest of the worldwide Jewish community. The areas where the Rabbinical authorities should be rejected concern matters like Yeshua's Messiahship, or Jewish and non-Jewish equality in the people of God. Matters, like making sure that the assembly follows the same calendar, are in a quantitatively different category. Significant, unnecessary divisions have been caused by all of the "restored Biblical calendars" out there—and various, presumed "leaders" of note in the Two-House sub-movement have been caught going after Jewish customs, which have not at all helped reasonable dialogue about Biblical prophecies concerning a larger restoration of the Kingdom to Israel (Isaiah 11:12-16; Jeremiah 31:6-10; Ezekiel 37:15-28; Zechariah 10:6-10).

Torah Halachah for Messianic Believers

Having been involved in the Messianic movement since 1995, my family and I have seen and witnessed a great deal firsthand that many of you have not experienced. We have been involved with several Messianic Jewish congregations, and have been exposed to many "independent" forms of Messianic expression as well. We have seen individuals who largely embrace an Orthodox or even ultra-Orthodox style of Torah application for their lives, and then others who completely shun any form of mainline Jewish tradition. *How do we weather the extremes?*

In the previous sections describing various aspects of Jewish custom and tradition, derived from Torah instructions, there has not been a huge amount of understanding—or even a desire for understanding—among far too many people in the Two-House sub-movement. Why have the Jewish people separated meat and dairy, worn *tallit*s, or prayed with *tefillin* throughout history? When people criticize things they do not express any interest in understanding, not only do they show themselves to be ignorant, but in too many times they show themselves to be arrogant. Some of the aspects of Jewish Torah practice, such as employing a *tallit* and/or *tefillin* in regular times of prayer, can definitely be used—if I may call it something from my Wesleyan heritage—as a **means of grace.** Using these elements of faith, undeniably derived from interpretations of Holy Writ, can be a physical way for individuals to partake of God's goodness, learning tangible lessons.

---

[66] Consult the FAQ on the TNN website, "Genesis 5, 11 Genealogies."

[67] Consult the author's blog editorial, "The Hastening of Righteousness."

(Quantitatively speaking, using *tefillin* for regular prayer times is no different than remembering the Lord's Supper or being baptized, as is practiced in much of evangelical Christianity.)

I understand why some non-Jewish Messianics shy away from a great deal Jewish custom and tradition, because they see the pitfalls of various people in the Messianic movement who embrace it all with little discernment, and whose relationship is far more with Jewish tradition than it is with the God of Israel. There are Messianic Jews who are over-zealous for Judaism, and there are non-Jews in the Messianic movement who sometimes want to be "more Jewish" than most Jewish Believers themselves. These are the ones, sadly, who can be easily persuaded against the Messiahship of Yeshua, because embracing tradition is more important to them than knowing and having a supernatural experience with the Creator God via His Son. In various cases, a few of these people want most non-Jewish Believers removed from the Messianic movement. Unfortunately, the presence of a number of people with bad attitudes, has gone a long way at influencing a wide number of non-Jews in the Two-House sub-movement, in their being strongly opposed to mainline Jewish ways of following the Torah.

Can tradition *and* history be totally discarded as one attempts to keep God's Torah? *It would be naïve of anyone to think so.* The Messianic movement would not be here, unless someone had started examining the Gospels and the letters of the New Testament with more Jewish resources at their disposal than generations past. We recognize that Yeshua and His Disciples lived like the average Jews of the First Century. They adhered to many of the customs and traditions of their time, and instructed their followers to likewise keep them. If they were living today, they would do their best to be living, (at least somewhat) as active members of the worldwide Jewish community.

What Jewish community the Disciples might, or would, be a part of today is a vigorous debate. Many believe that they would be Orthodox. Many believe that they would be Conservative or Reform. I believe that they would be part of the Jewish community that interacts the most with the world at large, being concerned with social justice and fairness for all. To me, I do not believe Yeshua or the Apostles would be a part of an Orthodox Jewish community largely off to itself, but instead that they would be part of the more Centrist branches of Judaism.

No religious practice, be it of Judaism or Christianity, is beyond criticism. No one's own personal faith is beyond criticism, as we must reevaluate where we stand before God every day. Constructive criticism is a good thing, as it helps us grow and learn. In mainline Judaism, the majority of the traditions and customs that have developed are supposed to help one's relationship with God, and they are based in the Scriptures. At the same time, no one Jew is going to apply it all the same, and non-Jewish Believers in the Messianic movement are likewise not going to apply these things the same way.

But should the Torah be applied in a manner that is not consistent with any branch of Judaism? Some say yes, **but I would say no.** Even though the vast majority of Judaism today is not Orthodox, those who are observant still wear a *yarmulke* to a religious service, they know what *tefillin* and what a *tallit* are, and they will nominally separate meat and dairy for much of what they eat. I believe that a moderate approach to these issues is best, where we can recognize the value in them, while at the same time respect one's personal choice. Arrogantly coming against them is wrong, but equally so, no one should be forced or coerced to follow them.[68]

The Jewish Leadership of Israel, and Mutual Honor and Respect

Why does it seem, to many observers, that a large number of people within the Two-House sub-movement have a problem with mainline Jewish traditions and customs, which are often based in the Torah and were observed in the Biblical period? Why do people who commonly claim to be doing their best to see a larger restoration of Israel come to pass, **actually seem to be doing more to see it deterred?**

The word of Isaiah 11:13 should be well taken: "...the jealousy of Ephraim will depart...Ephraim will not be jealous of Judah, and Judah will not harass Ephraim." This did involve the political rivalry that existed between the ancient Northern and Southern Kingdoms of Israel. By extension, there tends to be strong hostility, tension, and even some hatred, which can flame up among Jewish and non-Jewish people in today's Messianic movement, when the prophecies of the Northern and Southern Kingdoms yet to be reunited are discussed.

Most of the non-Jews, who forcibly claim to be "returning Ephraim," are not all descendants of the exiled Northern Kingdom—and they do not have a distant Jewish ancestor or two, either. Yet, it is absolutely true that purposefully fomenting more bitterness, resentment, and misunderstanding among people in the broad Messianic community **has to stop.** Someone, when approaching the subject matter, has to make sure that the bickering depicted by Isaiah 11:13 can be **steadfastly avoided.** Even with the significant number of self-claiming "Ephraimites" being only of the nations, many of these people have definitely opened themselves up to the same, negative spiritual influences which operated via the different monarchs and leaders of the Northern Kingdom of Israel (discussed further in **Chapter 5**).

While it is true that there are Messianic Jewish leaders and teachers who have contributed to the problem, and they have little interest in discussing the relevant prophecies, it is most unfortunate to observe how *the majority of the problems* are most often found among those of the Two-House sub-movement itself. When many people within today's Two-House sub-movement are told that they need to respect Judaism and the Jewish people, they frequently scoff, mock, and reject it. (And, they typically do the same to evangelical Christianity as well.) The Holy Scriptures themselves, however, bid all Messiah followers to respect the Jewish

---

[68] The various aspects of Torah *halachah* mentioned in this article, and related issues, are going to be examined in further detail in the author's forthcoming book *Torah In the Balance, Volume II.*

people, who gave humanity at large the Messiah Yeshua. Yeshua Himself said, "for salvation is of the Jews" (John 4:22).

What does the Torah communicate to us about the position of the Jewish people within the community of Israel? Prior to blessing Ephraim and Manasseh, the Patriarch Jacob/Israel blessed his fourth son, Judah:

"Judah, your brothers shall praise you; your hand shall be on the neck of your enemies; your father's sons shall bow down to you. Judah is a lion's whelp; from the prey, my son, you have gone up. He couches, he lies down as a lion, and as a lion, who dares rouse him up? The scepter shall not depart from Judah, nor the ruler's staff from between his feet, until Shiloh comes, and to him *shall be* the obedience of the peoples" (Genesis 49:8-10).

The prophetic word, *ki-yavo Shiloh v'lo yiqehat ammim* (יָבֹא שִׁילֹה וְלוֹ יִקְּהַת עַמִּים כִּי), is often thought to be some kind of reference not only to the Davidic monarchy, but to the eventual arrival of Yeshua the Messiah (Jesus Christ) on the scene of world history. It is He, the Lion of the tribe of Judah (Revelation 5:5), who will be granted the ultimate scepter or *shevet* (שֵׁבֶט),[69] and to whom all the peoples of Planet Earth must acknowledge as supreme (i.e., Psalm 2:8; 72:8, 11; Isaiah 11:10, 12; Micah 5:4; Zechariah 9:10).[70] The association with the tribe of Judah, which would become the dominant force in the Southern Kingdom of Israel, with the Messiah Himself—requires any person who recognizes Yeshua as Savior to highly respect His fellow Jews. The Rabbinical commentary on this, as offered by the *ArtScroll Chumash*, should be well taken:

"The word *until* does not mean that Judah's ascendancy will end with the coming of Messiah. To the contrary, the sense of the verse is that once Messiah begins to reign, Judah's blessing of kingship will become fully realized and go to an even higher plateau (*Sh'lah*). At that time, all the nations will assemble to acknowledge his greatness and pay homage to him."[71]

The teaching of Yeshua and the Apostles does not imply that once the Messiah arrives on the scene of world history, that the scepter of leadership will somehow be completely removed from the Jewish people. It will undoubtedly be transformed, and altered to a degree, by the arrival of the Messiah and the salvation historical work He will perform—but it is not to be cast aside, dishonored, and revoked. In Yeshua's word of Matthew 25:45-46, it is rightly concluded that those who did not offer care for those in need, *most especially Yeshua's Jewish brethren*,[72] will suffer the same penalties as Satan and the demonic host:

"Then He will answer them, 'Truly I say to you, to the extent that you did not do it to one of the least of these, you did not do it to Me.' These **will go away into eternal punishment,** but the righteous into eternal life."

---

[69] "rod, staff, club, scepter" (*BDB*, 986).
[70] Mathews, pp 894-896.
[71] Scherman, *Chumash*, 279.
[72] Cf. Stern, *Jewish New Testament Commentary*, 77.

When you see something like this, while it undeniably concerns care for strangers or prisoners in general, it must also concern Yeshua's own Jewish brothers and sisters. These are people who throughout history have suffered great humiliation, and even near genocide (on more than one occasion, no less). Anyone in the Messianic community—especially purporting a larger restoration of Israel yet to occur in prophecy—cannot afford to fall into the trap of treating the historic Jewish people with any degree of unfairness or lack of understanding. Yet, in dismissing a great deal of mainline Jewish Torah practice and *halachah*, and even acting as though "Judah needs correction" for a variety of mainline traditions and customs, a wide variety number of people in the Two-House sub-movement have really thought that the Jewish leadership of the Kingdom of Israel has been nullified.

The Apostle Paul asks, "what advantage has the Jew? Or what is the benefit of circumcision? Great in every respect. First of all, that they were entrusted with **the oracles of God**" (Romans 3:1-2). What are *ta logia tou Theou* (τὰ λόγια τοῦ θεοῦ)? Many readers think that these are the Tanach Scriptures. But, the singular term *logos* (λόγος) has a wide variety of applications, including things that are "chiefly oral" (*BDAG*).[73] What if Paul has actually included in his statements of Romans 3:1-2, that the Jewish people were entrusted with the *oral explanations* of how much of God's Instruction is to be properly followed? Many of these traditional explanations could have made their way into Jewish literature like the Mishnah, Tosefta, Talmud, Midrashim, and even Dead Sea Scrolls—which Bible scholars today generally all consult as containing important background material, as at least historical witnesses to ancient opinions.

We see later in on Romans 9:3-4, how Paul speaks of "my kinsmen according to the flesh, who are Israelites, to whom belongs the adoption as sons, and the glory and the covenants and the giving of the Law and **the temple service** and the promises." The term *latreia* (λατρεία) largely relates to cultic worship.[74] Historically speaking, the Synagogue has certainly preserved many traditional liturgies, hymns, and psalms (not necessarily present in the Book of Psalms) originally used in Temple worship that have made their way into the *siddur* (סדור) or prayer book.[75]

Taken together, the Jewish people have historically been given the responsibility of preserving the protocol of proper worship and mainline Torah *halachah*. Yeshua Himself actually bid His disciples to follow the lead of the Pharisees (Matthew 23:1-2), even though He did warn them about some of the leaders' hypocrisy (Matthew 23:3). Because of Judah's leadership affirmed in the Torah (Genesis 49:10), the Jewish people do get to determine a wide degree of the

---

[73] *BDAG*, 599.

[74] Cf. Ibid., 587.

[75] The valid statements of Daniel C. Juster, *Growing to Maturity* (Denver: The Union of Messianic Jewish Congregations Press, 1987), 228 on the *siddur* need to be recognized here:

"Eighty percent is either direct Scriptural quotation or creative intertwining of Scripture passages....Fifteen percent is prayer material inspired by Scripture....Only a small portion contains anything contrary to Biblical faith."

proper way of how the commandments of the Torah are to be interpreted. Today's Messianics should follow—and certainly expel efforts to be knowledgeable—of many of the Jewish interpretations of Moses' Teaching.

Does this mean that the Rabbinical authorities are to be *blindly followed* in all matters? **Of course not.** No astute and intelligent Bible reader thinks that Paul instructing Believers to follow the government in Romans ch. 13, means that man-made laws that are in flat defiance of God's will are to be followed. Similarly, any applications of God's Torah seen in the Jewish theological tradition need to be spiritually edifying—as Philippians 4:8 would say, "whatever is true, whatever is honorable, whatever is right, whatever is pure, whatever is lovely, whatever is of good repute, if there is any excellence and if anything worthy of praise, dwell on these things"—and be compatible with His mandate of Israel making a difference in the world (Genesis 12:2-3; Deuteronomy 4:5-8). There are Jewish views of the Tanach Scriptures which clearly do subtract from the gospel, and which disregard the Messiahship of Yeshua, that are to surely be disregarded.[76] Yet, one can clearly recognize that the Apostles affirmed that the Jewish religious leadership of their day had an authority—what today we should best call a **consultative authority**, alongside that of leaders in the Body of Messiah (cf. Matthew 16:19)—not to be so casually dismissed. Many of the traditions Judaism has preserved can be considered "Spirit-inspired," and doubtlessly aid non-Jews in the Messianic movement, being enriched by their Hebraic and Jewish Roots.

As with all issues, though, discernment and wisdom from the Holy Spirit should be able to identify those things which subtract from Yeshua and His atoning work.[77] Much of today's Messianic Judaism has rightfully recognized various areas of Jewish Torah practice, where Yeshua's ministry and teachings and the thrust of the gospel clearly stand in contrast. The majority of Messianic Judaism does not follow an Orthodox level of Torah observance, but one closer to contemporary Conservative or Reform Judaism.

We all have a great debt to Judaism and the Jewish people, and while *it will take time* for many of today's Messianic Jews that there is a larger restoration of Israel to occur via prophecy, incorporating the righteous from the nations into an expanded Kingdom realm of Israel—**non-Jewish Believers in the Messianic movement should not be causing problems.**

But why are there problems? This can happen when one witnesses non-Jewish Believers *inappropriately assuming* some sort of identity as "returning Ephraim" (as opposed to just affirming prophecies that speak of the reunification of the Northern and Southern Kingdoms of Israel, yet to occur). Too many place the Jewish people in a distant junior role in widely speaking of "Ephraim and Judah," so that the distinct contributions that Judaism and the Synagogue have to make to the people of God get effectively nullified. While today's Two-House teachers will widely

---

[76] For a notable example of this, consult the FAQ on the TNN website, "Ephesians 2:14-15."

[77] For a further discussion on this and related issues, consult the author's article "The Role of History in Messianic Biblical Interpretation."

claim they do not promote replacement theology, in dismissing a great deal of the value of mainline Jewish tradition—even that which is widely seen in much of today's (Left of Center) Messianic Judaism—they definitely tend to practice a form of social supersessionism, when it comes to the Jewish Synagogue. (And, they practice just outright dismissal and dishonor when it comes to the sizeable, legitimate spiritual contributions of evangelical Protestant Christianity.)

The instruction of Romans 12:10 points us in a direction much different than that commonly witnessed in today's broad Messianic community: "love one another with mutual affection; outdo one another in showing honor" (NRSV). The instruction of Philippians 2:3-4 can be added to this: "Do nothing from selfishness or empty conceit, but with humility of mind regard one another as more important than yourselves; do not *merely* look out for your own personal interests, but also for the interests of others." When approaching the subject matter of a prophesied larger restoration of Israel, the unity among God's people that should be present can only be manifested when we all learn to respect and honor one another. *Far too few have asked the Lord to give them these abilities.* It is required, though, of all Believers to "be subject to one another in the fear of Messiah" (Ephesians 5:21).

This does not mean that non-Jewish Messianic Believers have to become culturally or ethnically Jewish in all of their Torah observance, and have Jewish tradition and custom permeate *every single area* of their lives. (It is my personal opinion that there is a difference between traditional observances like lighting *Shabbat* candles or employing the *haggadah* for Passover, which normally take place within a local faith community, and more cultural practices like having a *chuppah* during a wedding ceremony, which is more of a family affair.)[78] In fact, non-Jewish Believers in the Messianic movement, often have many edifying perspectives and views from their evangelical Christian backgrounds that our faith community should benefit from. A position of mutual respect, as encouraged by the Apostolic Scriptures, allows for multiple parties to come together and for their best virtues, talents, and abilities to be used to accomplish the mission of God (cf. Ephesians 4:11-13).

Anti-Semitism In the Two-House Movement

How do any of us learn to put another's needs before our own (cf. Philippians 2:3-4)? Many of today's Messianic Jews have undergone a great deal of rejection from their families and communities for expressing faith in Yeshua (Jesus). They are essentially ostracized from the Synagogue, and many are prohibited from becoming citizens of the State of Israel. All these Messianic Jews tend to have, is the fellowship of their fellow Jewish Believers, and the (distant) hope that one day their extended families and many more in the worldwide Jewish community *may* recognize the Savior. Non-Jewish Believers who make up a great deal of the Two-House sub-movement, *do not often realize this.* They are actually (and most

---

[78] This is discussed in further detail in the author's article, "Considering Messianic Jewish Fears of Replacement and Irrelevance," appearing in the *Messianic Torah Helper* by TNN Press (forthcoming).

inappropriately, and sometimes even delusionally) expecting to be recognized as "Ephraim," when they seldom realize that they have interjected themselves into a Messianic community where many Messianic Jews are still trying to handle the basic religious and social issues of being Jewish and believing in Yeshua.

There is a distinct sector of today's Messianic Jews which is definitely of the position that the Messianic movement is not something for non-Jewish Believers to be that involved in. *They want to see most of them go back to church.* When they see non-Jewish Believers keeping *Shabbat*, the appointed times, or eating kosher, they feel that their heritage is possibly being robbed from them. A wide number of forceful accusations are likely to be made in the (not so distant) future, by such a group, in regard to replacement theology or supersessionism. These are people who do not consider non-Jewish Believers to be a real part of the Commonwealth of Israel (cf. Ephesians 2:11-13), much less are that interested in entertaining a larger restoration of Israel beyond the rebirth of the Jewish State and the salvation of a generation of Jews. A Two-House populism which advocates that most non-Jews in the Messianic movement are some sort of lost "Ephraimites," coupled with a high level of opposition to mainline Jewish tradition, is **an easy target** for such Messianic Jewish teachers and leaders to go after.

It cannot be avoided that many movements in past history, which to some degree or another have approached the "lost tribes of Israel" subject matter, have often had (extreme) levels of anti-Semitism (eventually) associated with them. Making some observations on British-Israelism of the Nineteenth Century, author Zvi Ben-Dor Benite, of the book *The Ten Lost Tribes: A World History*, indicates how "There were several advantages to focusing on the ten tribes: as part of Israel, they were chosen, blessed by God, and—most important—they were not Jews. Exiled seven centuries before Jesus, they could not be guilty for the Crucifixion." Noting this one example, he further explains, "This idea [of British-Israelism], despite its philo-Jewish beginnings, would later pave the way for some radical forms of anti-Semitism within the various Anglo-Israelist offshoots."[79] While possibly starting out as being pro-Jewish on various levels, Nineteenth Century British-Israelism helped give rise to other groups like that of Christian Identity and their white supremacism. (They may have fallen prey to the errant idea that the Jewish people were "Christ killers," when **all of sinful, fallen humanity** is actually responsible for Yeshua's execution.)

As things stand today, the various Two-House pseudo-denominations should not be regarded as being blatantly anti-Semitic, although they have not exactly taken any quantitative positions of being philo-Jewish, either. These are groups which tend to spur mainline Jewish positions as they regard usage of the Divine Name of God, customs like men wearing *yarmulke*s in worship services and places of reverence, and most notably they disregard the Hillel II Rabbinical calendar. There is a wide degree of theological fundamentalism and rigidity also present,

---

[79] Zvi Ben-Dor Benite, *The Ten Lost Tribes: A World History* (New York: Oxford University Press, 2009), 193.

which if not reigned in, could very well lead to problems much worse than simply disregarding mainline Jewish traditions. Unfortunately, some of the main leaders and teachers of the Two-House sub-movement, due to their own personal fundamentalism and over-simplicity, are widely unwilling to implement the necessary changes to see some of the claims against them thwarted.

-5-

The Biblical, Rebellious Legacy of the Northern Kingdom of Ephraim
truly considering the instability of the Northern Kingdom of Israel

The Two-House teaching of Judah and Ephraim, being reunited in the period prior to the Messiah's return, is one which has certainly stirred a great deal of controversy across the broad Messianic community. Why has this been the case? A ministry like Outreach Israel and TNN Online has always thought that the safest approach to this difficult issue, is to focus the attention of Bible readers to a series of unfulfilled prophecies (i.e., Isaiah 11:12-16; Jeremiah 31:6-10; Ezekiel 37:15-28; Zechariah 10:6-10), which point to a larger restoration of Israel occurring subsequent to the Second Coming of Yeshua the Messiah. Such an eschatological approach to the subject matter, with many of its finer details only known by a Sovereign and Eternal God, should not really be that controversial. At the very most, such an approach is about as controversial as pre-tribulationism versus post-tribulationism.[1] Things can get a bit heated from time to time, but ultimately it comes down to one's vantage point regarding various prophecies, events that have yet to occur in future history, and how much we let God be God.

What has drawn a great deal of the controversy over the past two decades, or so (1990s-2000s), is what is often labeled to be the "Ephraimite movement." Such a group of people, aside from emphasizing commonly overlooked prophecies regarding the restoration of Israel involving the descendants of the exiled Northern Kingdom as a player, *go much further* than the Biblical text itself. They commonly claim that the considerable, or even vast majority, of non-Jewish Believers in the broad, contemporary Messianic movement today, absolutely must be those descendants. Far from adhering to the Scriptural word, "He who scattered Israel will gather him" (Jeremiah 31:10), with God only knowing all of the details of where the Northern Kingdom has gone (cf. Hosea 8:8; Amos 9:9), those non-Jewish Believers who commonly and/or forcibly label themselves "Ephraimites," feel that their identity as descendants of the exiled Northern Kingdom of Israel/Ephraim is

---

[1] For the tenor of how this discussion often ends up, consult Gleason L. Archer, Jr., and Paul D. Feinberg, Douglas J. Moo, Richard R. Reiter, *Three Views on the Rapture* (Grand Rapids: Zondervan, 1996).

absolutely certain. It does not matter if such people have no documentation proving this or not; they have a "feeling" that they are, and that is good enough.

For a non-Jewish Believer like myself, my ancestry is not at all what motivates me to serve and worship and obey the Lord; what motivates me to serve and worship and obey the Lord is the salvation of Yeshua, and how the Holy Spirit is to continually mold my heart and mind to be more like Him. I am a human being who is subject to the fallenness of sin; I need redemption from eternal punishment like everyone on Planet Earth; I have received it via the Messiah of Israel, and am incorporated into the Kingdom realm of Israel via my trust in Him.

Given the fact that the actual pockets of people in today's world, who claim to be descended from the exiled Northern Kingdom, are found in Southeast Asia, South Asia, Central Africa, and the Mediterranean basin—I have a much better chance at having Jewish ancestry from someone who assimilated into Medieval European Christianity, than being some sort of descendant of "Ephraim." Regardless of who I am in the flesh, I am by my faith in Israel's Messiah, a part of the Commonwealth of Israel (Ephesians 2:11-13) or the Israel of God (Galatians 6:16), grafted-in to the olive tree (Romans 11:17-18). I possess citizenship in Israel via Yeshua. The larger restoration of Israel anticipated by the Scriptures is going to affect me as a participant, regardless of who I am in the flesh—because it involves Judah, Israel/Ephraim, and far many more companions from the nations themselves (cf. Ezekiel 37:15-28).

I have interacted with many people over the years who claim to be some sort of "Ephraimites." Usually, their claims to such an identity are rooted in sentiment, and not in any kind of documentable fact. *Some of these people base their belief on supposed dreams and visions.* A selection of these people, unfortunately, have latched onto various tall tales and stories about the exiles of the Northern Kingdom migrating to various countries, and that whole, modern ethnicities in Europe today can actually trace their origins to Tribe XYZ of Ancient Israel. What is most disturbing, though, is that very few of those, who claim to be "Ephraimites," have taken a good, honest look at what the Tanach (Old Testament) really says about the Northern Kingdom of Israel. **The legacy of Ephraim, as seen in the Scriptures, is not at all a positive one**—and why anyone would really want to claim this as their own, is more than a bit confounded. The well-known epithet on the fallen Northern Kingdom seen in 2 Kings, squarely places their downfall and exile with sin and rebellion committed against God:

"The LORD rejected all the descendants of Israel and afflicted them and gave them into the hand of plunderers, until He had cast them out of His sight. When He had torn Israel from the house of David, they made Jeroboam the son of Nebat king. Then Jeroboam drove Israel away from following the LORD and made them commit a great sin. The sons of Israel walked in all the sins of Jeroboam which he did; they did not depart from them until the LORD removed Israel from His sight, as He spoke through all His servants the prophets. So Israel was carried away into exile from their own land to Assyria until this day" (2 Kings 17:20-23).

This is not the only part of the legacy of Ephraim that Bible readers encounter in the Tanach. We see a disdain that the Northern Kingdom of Israel had for the Southern Kingdom of Judah, we see a series of different ruling houses present in the Northern Kingdom contrasted to the singular line of David in the Southern Kingdom, and we see significant prophetic rebukes issued against the Northern Kingdom. In too much of the Two-House sub-movement, when one encounters people who are self-claiming "Ephraimites," this is not the heritage that a non-Jewish Believer tends to claim. On the contrary to dealing honestly with the Biblical record of the Northern Kingdom of Israel, such "Ephraimites" tend to instead want to claim some of the pseudo-history of people like Steven Collins or Yair Davidy, which stem from British-Israelism and its associated mythology. *Few want to actually deal with the Scriptural legacy of Ephraim, and the great sins committed against the LORD God that caused the Northern Kingdom to be judged.*

Ephraim Breaks Away From Judah

The Northern Kingdom of Israel was an illegitimate entity from its very beginning. It is true that in the narrative of 1 Kings, as Solomon fell further and further into idolatry (1 Kings 11:1-10), the decree is issued by the Lord that following his death the United Kingdom of Israel will split into two (1 Kings 11:11-13). Jeroboam, one of Solomon's servants, and from the tribe of Ephraim, is promised ten of Israel's tribes by God (1 Kings 11:30-40). In order for him to have an enduring legacy like that of David, there is a condition from God that Jeroboam remain faithful to him:

"Then it will be, that if you listen to all that I command you and walk in My ways, and do what is right in My sight by observing My statutes and My commandments, as My servant David did, then I will be with you and build you an enduring house [a dynasty as enduring, NIV; a lasting dynasty, NJPS][2] as I built for David, and I will give Israel to you. Thus I will afflict the descendants of David for this, but not always" (1 Kings 11:38-39).

Following the death of King Solomon (1 Kings 11:41-43), his son Rehoboam succeeds him, and fails to heed the advice of his counselors in making the yoke of the people lighter (1 Kings 12:1-15). This only fueled the fire of secession for the ten northern tribes (1 Kings 12:16-20). While there were some legitimate grievances issued by the people to King Rehoboam's exclamation, "My father made your yoke heavy, but I will add to your yoke; my father disciplined you with whips, but I will discipline you with scorpions" (1 Kings 12:14), the authors/editors of Kings observed, "So Israel has been in rebellion against the house of David to this day" (1 Kings 12:19). When the Books of Samuel-Kings reached their final form after the end of the Babylonian exile in the Sixth-Fifth Centuries B.C.E., the Northern Kingdom of Israel was still regarded as corporately being in rebellion. We are capriciously reminded, however, that when Rehoboam tried to recapture the

---

[2] Heb. *bayit-ne'e'man* (בֵּית־נֶאֱמָן).

northern tribes with a great army, that the division of Israel into the Northern and Southern Kingdoms was from the Lord, and it was prevented (1 Kings 12:21-24).

While the Lord had promised the new King Jeroboam an enduring legacy if he remained faithful to Him and His Instruction, from the very beginning of the Northern Kingdom of Israel/Ephraim—**this is what we do not see.** In establishing his base of power, King Jeroboam was very concerned that the people would demand reunification with the Southern Kingdom, because they would have to go to Jerusalem to offer sacrifices and commemorate the appointed times as instructed by the Torah. Jeroboam installed his own centers of worship in Bethel and Dan, he made golden calves for the people to serve, and he instituted a separate priesthood and separate holidays for the people to remember:

"Jeroboam said in his heart, 'Now the kingdom will return to the house of David. If this people go up to offer sacrifices in the house of the LORD at Jerusalem, then the heart of this people will return to their lord, *even* to Rehoboam king of Judah; and they will kill me and return to Rehoboam king of Judah.' So the king consulted, and made two golden calves, and he said to them, 'It is too much for you to go up to Jerusalem; behold your gods, O Israel, that brought you up from the land of Egypt.' He set one in Bethel, and the other he put in Dan. Now this thing became a sin, for the people went *to worship* before the one as far as Dan. And he made houses on high places, and made priests from among all the people who were not of the sons of Levi. Jeroboam instituted a feast in the eighth month on the fifteenth day of the month, like the feast which is in Judah, and he went up to the altar; thus he did in Bethel, sacrificing to the calves which he had made. And he stationed in Bethel the priests of the high places which he had made. Then he went up to the altar which he had made in Bethel on the fifteenth day in the eighth month, even in the month which he had devised in his own heart; and he instituted a feast for the sons of Israel and went up to the altar to burn incense" (1 Kings 12:26-33).

The Lord had promised an enduring legacy for the kingship of Jeroboam, if he would remain faithful to Him and to His ways. This did not happen, and so it should not be surprising that rebukes were issued against Jeroboam. A prophet from Judah went to Bethel and denounced the pagan altar that had been established (1 Kings 13:1-4). King Jeroboam's hand withered up, and then was restored by the prophet (1 Kings 13:5-6), and with it is witnessed a momentary recognition of Israel's One True God by Jeroboam. But, the prophet said that he must leave without any food or drink (1 Kings 13:7-10). This prophet encountered another prophet, who lied to him by saying that the Lord would allow him to eat and drink at his house (1 Kings 13:11-18). Because of this deception, the prophet who denounced Jeroboam was later killed by a lion (1 Kings 13:19-31). Hearing that the prophet who spoke out against him had fallen, Jeroboam's temporary lapse back into fidelity with God stopped, and so anyone who wanted to be a priest in the religion of the Northern Kingdom could be: "the lowest of the people[3]" (1 Kings 13:33, KJV). This could have been those not even remotely qualified to help service the specific Levitical priesthood, in a secondary or tertiary capacity. *Those who would abuse religious service now became priests.* This sin sealed the fate of Jerobaom's legacy, and as it is stated, "This event became sin to the house of Jeroboam, even to blot *it* out and destroy *it* from off the face of the earth" (1 Kings 13:34).

A scene later arose when Abijah, Jeroboam's son, became deathly ill. The original prophet, Ahijah, who had told Jeroboam that God was intending to give him the northern tribes, is visited by Jeroboam's wife at Shiloh (1 Kings 14:1-5). Jeroboam's wife tried to hide herself, but her trickery did not work (1 Kings 14:6). All Ahijah had for Jeroboam's wife was a negative word of rebuke for the Northern Kingdom, and Jeroboam's family, in particular:

"Go, say to Jeroboam, 'Thus says the LORD God of Israel, "Because I exalted you from among the people and made you leader over My people Israel, and tore the kingdom away from the house of David and gave it to you—yet you have not been like My servant David, who kept My commandments and who followed Me with all his heart, to do only that which was right in My sight; you also have done more evil than all who were before you, and have gone and made for yourself other gods and molten images to provoke Me to anger, and have cast Me behind your back—therefore behold, I am bringing calamity on the house of Jeroboam, and will cut off from Jeroboam every male person, both bond and free in Israel, and I will make a clean sweep of the house of Jeroboam, as one sweeps away dung until it is all gone"'" (1 Kings 14:7-10).

Far from Jeroboam's son just dying (1 Kings 14:12-13, 18), the dynasty of Jeroboam in the fledgling Northern Kingdom would fall fast: "Anyone belonging to Jeroboam who dies in the city the dogs will eat. And he who dies in the field the birds of the heavens will eat; for the LORD has spoken *it*...Moreover, the LORD will raise up for Himself a king over Israel who will cut off the house of Jeroboam this day and from now on" (1 Kings 14:12, 14). Ahijah not only decreed that the reign of Jeroboam and his family would not last long over the Northern Kingdom of Israel/Ephraim, but that eventually Jeroboam's sin would cause the people to be exiled:

"For the LORD will strike Israel, as a reed is shaken in the water; and He will uproot Israel from this good land which He gave to their fathers, and will scatter them beyond the *Euphrates* River[4], because they have made their Asherim, provoking the LORD to anger. He will give up Israel on account of the sins of Jeroboam, which he committed and with which he made Israel to sin" (1 Kings 14:15-16).

When one reviews the history of the Northern and Southern Kingdoms of Israel, no honest reader can deny that sin and idolatry were present among all of

---

[3] Heb. *m'qetzot ha'am* (מִקְצוֹת הָעָם); "all classes of the people" (NEB); "commoners of the peoples" (ATS).

[4] Heb. *v'zeira m'eiver l'nahar* (וְזֵרָם מֵעֵבֶר לַנָּהָר).

the people. There was idolatry and rebellion against God present in Judah just as there was in Ephraim. Yet, Judah still had an operating Temple, at least superficially loyal to the God of Israel. Upon its secession, Ephraim established a different religious system, and one that would haunt it for the remainder of its time as a state.

The Northern Kingdom was Not a Model of Stability

Speaking for the Lord, the observation of the Prophet Hosea regarding the legacy of Ephraim was, "They have set up kings, but not by Me; they have appointed princes, but I did not know *it*. With their silver and gold they have made idols for themselves, that they might be cut off" (Hosea 8:4). While the idolatry and paganism of the Northern Kingdom of Israel tend to rightfully garner a great deal of attention from Bible readers, not enough attention is probably given to the fact that not only would the ruling line of Jeroboam fall, but that it would give rise to a wide number of succeeding ruling lines. Far be it from no legitimate heirs being present for a ruling family in Ephraim, the change in royal dynasties was often instigated by rivalry, a conspiracy, and a violent coup.

In the history of the Southern Kingdom of Judah, only the House of David ruled. In the history of the Northern Kingdom of Israel/Ephraim, a total of **nine royal dynasties** ruled, along with one period where there was a pretender to the throne also ruling.[5] While a bit abbreviated from the history seen in 1&2 Kings, the following summary of the rulers of the Northern Kingdom should give you a good enough idea about how many problems were present among those of Ephraim, simply because of how one royal dynasty fell due to intrigue, and/or the weight of its own corruption and mistakes, and then another arose in its place:

House of Jeroboam
Jeroboam (928-907 B.C.E.)
Nadab (907-906 B.C.E.)

Nadab falls because of evil (1 Kings 15:25-26). Baasha rises up against him in a conspiracy, killing him at Gibbethon (1 Kings 15:27).

House of Baasha
Baasha (906-883 B.C.E.)
Elah (883-882 B.C.E.)

Elah rules for two years (1 Kings 16:8), and then is overthrown by Zimri, a chariot commander. Zimri eliminates all of the House of Baasha, with no male heir or any relative or even a friend left over (1 Kings 16:9-11).

---

[5] This information has been adapted from "Chronology of the Monarchies," in *JPS Guide: The Jewish Bible*, 259.

The Biblical, Rebellious Legacy of the Northern Kingdom of Ephraim

House of Zimri
Zimri (882 B.C.E.)

The reign of Zimri is very short lived, having lasted a total of only seven days. Those in the army at Gibbethon hear of this. Omri, the army commander is made king. Zimri dies in a fire that he sets himself in the king's palace (1 Kings 16:16-19). The people of the Northern Kingdom were divided on who to follow as their next monarch. Half of them follow after Tibni, and the other half follow after Omri (1 Kings 16:21-22).

Tibni (882-872 B.C.E.)

House of Omri
Omri (882-871 B.C.E.)
Ahab (871-850 B.C.E.)
Ahaziah (850-848 B.C.E.)
Jehoram (848-842 B.C.E.)

The House of Omri is one of the most infamous in the history of the Northern Kingdom, because of the presence of the evil Queen Jezebel, wife of King Ahab.

Having come back from battle, defending Ramoth-gilead against the Arameans, King Jehoram is killed with an arrow by Jehu (2 Kings 9:14-26). Jehu also assassinates King Ahaziah of the Southern Kingdom (2 Kings 9:27-32). Most significantly, Jehu sees to the downfall of Jezebel herself (2 Kings 9:33-37), and judgment is enacted upon Ahab's family (2 Kings 10:1-17) and the Baal worshippers (2 Kings 10:18-19). The Lord promises Jehu that his family will rule over the Northern Kingdom through four generations (2 Kings 10:20-33).

House of Jehu
Jehu (842-814 B.C.E.)
Jehoahaz (814-800 B.C.E.)
Jehoash (800-784 B.C.E.)
Jeroboam II (784-748 B.C.E.)
Zechariah (748 B.C.E.)

Following the death of his father, Zechariah becomes ruler of the Northern Kingdom, and rules from Samaria for only six months (2 Kings 15:8-9). Due to his evil, Shallum conspires against him, killing him in public, and takes over (2 Kings 15:10).

House of Shallum
Shallum (748 B.C.E.)

Shallum rules for one month in Samaria, and then Menahem overthrows him, becoming king in his place (2 Kings 15:13-14).

House of Menahem
Menahem (748-737 B.C.E.)
Pekahiah (737-735 B.C.E.)

Pekahiah becomes king after his father's death, but because of doing evil, his officer Pekah strikes him down and becomes king in his place (2 Kings 15:23-25).

House of Pekah
Pekah (735-732 B.C.E.)

Pekah did evil (2 Kings 15:28), and so because of this Hoshea conspires against him and becomes king in his place (2 Kings 15:30).

House of Hoshea
Hoshea (732-725 B.C.E.)

Hoshea does evil against the Lord (2 Kings 17:2), and is captured by Shalmaneser of Assyria, for failing to send tribute (2 Kings 17:3-4).

The Fall of Samaria to the Assyrians and the Fall of Israel (722-721 B.C.E.)

There is obviously more to the history of Ephraim that Bible readers should investigate, by digging into what actually took place during the reigns of each of the Northern Kingdom monarchs. Much can be learned, though, by simply seeing how many rulers Ephraim actually had, and the collective legacy that they have left for us in Scripture.

One does not have to seek out any kind of numerological connection between the nine royal houses and the one pretender to the throne, which ruled in the Northern Kingdom, **to know that this was a less-than-stable or ideal country.** There was internal rivalry and insurrection, and one could legitimately wonder what would have happened if the Assyrian Empire did not encroach upon Ephraim. Would the Northern Kingdom have fallen into its own civil war? Would a demand for reunification with the Southern Kingdom occur, in order to bring more political stability? We do not know.

What we do know is that any person in today's Two-House sub-movement, forcibly claiming some kind of an "Ephraimite" status—claims *this utterly ridiculous mess* as his or her national heritage—as opposed to any of the hype as put out by some Lost Tribes seekers. The legacy of Ephraim seen here is not something worth boasting about, nor should anyone take any sort of pride in it. Anyone who reads the Biblical narrative is to learn valuable lessons on how not to rule or be ruled, from the internal political rivalries present in the Northern Kingdom of Israel/Ephraim. One can legitimately wonder if, among the many self-claiming "Ephraimites" in today's Two-House sub-movement—if in their strident insistence that they must be descended from the exiled Northern Kingdom—whether they are or not, if they have actually opened themselves up to the same insidious spiritual influences, which were quite active in the Northern Kingdom of Israel/Ephraim. In many cases, given the strong feelings of resentment that many people in the Two-House sub-movement have for those in Messianic Judaism, the possibility that they could be influenced by the same demonic principalities which ultimately led the Northern Kingdom—even if many of these people are not descendants of the exiled Northern Kingdom—is something to seriously contemplate.

Some Prophetic Rebukes Issued Against the Northern Kingdom

While the political issues surrounding the leadership of the Northern Kingdom of Israel/Ephraim often elude many people in today's Two-House sub-movement, what should not elude any of us are the prophetic declarations issued against it. The Books of Amos and Hosea, in particular, are often cited as containing many important rebukes against the legacy of Ephraim. Common sins that the people of the Northern Kingdom are faulted for include idolatry, child sacrifice, and oppression of the rich upon the poor. Here is a selection of key prophetic rebukes that anyone approaching the debated subject matter of the "Two-House teaching" needs to be quite consciously aware of:

"Hear this word, you cows of Bashan who are on the mountain of Samaria, who oppress the poor, who crush the needy, who say to your husbands, 'Bring now, that we may drink!' The Lord GOD has sworn by His holiness, 'Behold, the days are coming upon you when they will take you away with meat hooks, and the last of you with fish hooks. You will go out *through* breaches *in the walls*, each one straight before her, and you will be cast to Harmon,' declares the LORD" (Amos 4:1-3).

"*For* those who turn justice into wormwood and cast righteousness down to the earth. He who made the Pleiades and Orion and changes deep darkness into morning, who also darkens day *into* night, who calls for the waters of the sea and pours them out on the surface of the earth, the LORD is His name. It is He who flashes forth *with* destruction upon the strong, so that destruction comes upon the fortress. They hate him who reproves in the gate, and they abhor him who speaks *with* integrity. Therefore because you impose heavy rent on the poor and exact a tribute of grain from them, *though* you have built houses of well-hewn stone, yet you will not live in them; you have planted pleasant vineyards, yet you will not drink their wine. For I know your transgressions are many and your sins are great, *you* who distress the righteous *and* accept bribes and turn aside the poor in the gate. Therefore at such a time the prudent person keeps silent, for it is an evil time. Seek good and not evil, that you may live; and thus may the LORD God of hosts be with you, just as you have said! Hate evil, love good, and establish justice in the gate! Perhaps the LORD God of hosts may be gracious to the remnant of Joseph" (Amos 5:7-15).

"Do you put off the day of calamity, and would you bring near the seat of violence? Those who recline on beds of ivory and sprawl on their couches, and eat lambs from the flock and calves from the midst of the stall, who improvise to the sound of the harp, *and* like David have composed songs for themselves, who drink wine from sacrificial bowls while they anoint themselves with the finest of oils, yet they have not grieved over the ruin of Joseph. Therefore, they will now go into exile at the head of the exiles, and the sprawlers' banqueting will pass away. The Lord GOD has sworn by Himself, the LORD God of hosts has declared: 'I loathe the arrogance of Jacob, and detest his citadels; therefore I will deliver up *the* city and all it contains'" (Amos 6:3-8).

"Listen to the word of the LORD, O sons of Israel, for the LORD has a case against the inhabitants of the land, because there is no faithfulness or kindness or knowledge of God in the land. *There is* swearing, deception, murder, stealing and adultery. They employ violence, so that bloodshed follows bloodshed. Therefore the land mourns, and everyone who lives in it languishes along with the beasts of the field and the birds of the sky, and also the fish of the sea disappear. Yet let no one find fault, and let none offer reproof; for your people are like those who contend with the priest. So you will stumble by day, and the prophet also will stumble with you by night; and I will destroy your mother. My people are destroyed for lack of knowledge. Because you have rejected knowledge, I also will reject you from being My priest. Since you have forgotten the law of your God, I also will forget your children" (Hosea 4:1-6).

"When I would heal Israel, the iniquity of Ephraim is uncovered, and the evil deeds of Samaria, for they deal falsely; the thief enters in, bandits raid outside, and they do not consider in their hearts that I remember all their wickedness. Now their deeds are all around them; they are before My face. With their wickedness they make the king glad, and the princes with their lies. They are all adulterers, like an oven heated by the baker who ceases to stir up *the fire* from the kneading of the dough until it is leavened. On the day of our king, the princes became sick with the heat of wine; he stretched out his hand with scoffers, for their hearts are like an oven *as* they approach their plotting; their anger smolders all night, in the morning it burns like a flaming fire. All of them are hot like an oven, and they consume their rulers; all their kings have fallen. None of them calls on Me" (Hosea 7:1-7).

These five passages from Amos and Hosea, respectively, should be enough of a snapshot to get a good idea about how bad the Northern Kingdom of Israel/Ephraim actually was.[6] It is observed how in judgment, "Strangers devour his strength, yet he does not know *it*; gray hairs also are sprinkled on him, yet he does not know *it*" (Hosea 7:9). The Northern Kingdom might be described as a person aging too quickly, with old age setting in before its time—all due to the presence of sin. We should not be surprised how it is said of them, "they have transgressed My covenant and rebelled against My law[7]...Though I wrote for him

---

[6] For a further review, consult the author's articles "The Message of Amos" and "The Message of Hosea."

[7] "rebelled against My Torah" (ATS); "faithless to My teaching" (NJPS).

ten thousand *precepts* of My law, they are regarded as a strange thing" (Hosea 8:1, 12).

Still, in spite of the collective, sinful legacy of Ephraim, there is hope. Thankfully, when the prophesied restoration of Israel finally consummates, there is a recognition on the part of Ephraim of its sinful legacy and its waywardness toward God's Instruction:

"I have surely heard Ephraim grieving, 'You have chastised me, and I was chastised, like an untrained calf; bring me back that I may be restored, for You are the LORD my God. For after I turned back, I repented; and after I was instructed, I smote on *my* thigh; I was ashamed and also humiliated because I bore the reproach of my youth'" (Jeremiah 31:18-19).

It is at such a point that all of the corporate dimensions of the New Covenant can then be realized, with a permanent cleansing of sin, forgiveness, and realization of Moses' Teaching enacted (cf. Jeremiah 31:31-34).[8] While there are rebukes issued against those of the Northern Kingdom of Israel/Ephraim, at a future point in history, its legacy of sin, idolatry, rebellion, and insurrection will be a thing of the past.

Approaching the Legacy of Ephraim

In much of the popular literature that has circulated throughout the 1990s and 2000s about the "Two-House teaching," there has not been a huge amount of attention really focused on what actually took place in the Northern Kingdom of Israel—as recorded in the Bible. One cannot totally blame some of these materials for not focusing too much on the political instability present in the Northern Kingdom, or the prophetic denunciations encountered—because the negative legacy left by Ephraim in the Biblical record (or even just a brief survey of it) is something that is to surely teach the succeeding generations of God's people on how *not to behave.*

Anyone who believes that there is still resolution to be brought to the issue of the exiled Northern Kingdom of Israel/Ephraim, by necessity has to recognize that there will be a corporate repentance of the sins committed in ancient times by the Northern Kingdom. Unfortunately for many people in the Two-House sub-movement, there has not at all been a significant, and more further review of the legacy of Ephraim as witnessed in the Tanach. The sinful problems the Northern Kingdom had, have not at all been probed and considered, for the key lessons that they contain—for anyone who wants to take instruction from the Holy Scriptures. Unlike the Southern Kingdom of Judah, which was similarly judged for sins of idolatry and rebellion against it, the Northern Kingdom of Israel/Ephraim never corporately returned from its exile. We still await for its return as salvation history looms closer and closer to the return of the Messiah—even if the vast and considerable majority of self-claiming "Ephraimites," are going to actually be

---

[8] For a further discussion, consult the author's article "What is the New Covenant?"

companions from the nations themselves, involved in Israel's restoration (cf. Ezekiel 37:16).

When I look through some of the royal history of the Northern Kingdom, I can only be reminded of a question that a good Messianic Jewish friend of mine once asked: *Why would anyone want to be Jewish?* Serving in the leadership of a Messianic congregation, he encountered many non-Jewish Believers who thought that they were in the assembly because of having a lost Jewish ancestor several generations removed. When seeing this, he could only think back on the complicated history of his own Jewish ancestors over the past few centuries, including the pogroms of the Russian Empire and various levels of anti-Semitism he had witnessed in his life in America. (Thankfully, his Jewish family was not caught in the Holocaust.) My friend honestly wondered why some non-Jews in the Messianic world would urgently, or even desperately search, for a Jewish relative. In his own Jewish experience, at least, he did not think it was really "worth it."

With this in mind, we should legitimately wonder why any non-Jewish Believer in the Messianic movement **would really want to be** some sort of "Ephraimite." While the Jewish struggle throughout history has been quite significant, the Northern Kingdom's sinful legacy of rebellion against the Lord, should not be something that any Believer would want to eagerly claim as his or her own. Why would anyone want to claim figures like King Ahab and Queen Jezebel, as his or her national "heroes," as it were? *I know that I do not want to be associated with these two grossly evil people, who lived in utter rebellion toward God.* Some non-Jewish Messianics are looking for an identity beyond being in Yeshua[9]—falsely thinking that only those physically descended from Abraham, Isaac, and Jacob are truly God's own—and claiming to be a descendant of the exiled Northern Kingdom is the option they have chosen. Many claim an identity of being "Ephraim," without truly knowing what they have claimed.

When we see the prophecies of a larger restoration of Israel in the Tanach, if it were not **for the sheer grace of God** and His love for the Patriarchs—then the exiled Northern Kingdom of Israel/Ephraim should have just been assimilated into the nations of the Ancient Near East, and then become a forgotten part of ancient history. This is not what we see in the Prophets, however. Zechariah 10:6, 10 tells us, "I will strengthen the house of Judah, and I will save the house of Joseph, and I will bring them back, because I have had compassion[10] on them; and they will be as though I had not rejected them, for I am the LORD their God and I will answer them...I will bring them back from the land of Egypt and gather them from Assyria; and I will bring them into the land of Gilead and Lebanon until no *room* can be found for them." While there are many specific details yet to be known regarding a prophetic word like this, there is every indication that the sinful legacy seen of Ephraim in the Tanach, will one day be replaced by a new legacy of

---

[9] Consult the author's article "The Faithfulness of Yeshua the Messiah."
[10] Heb. verb *racham* (רָחַם).

corporate fidelity and reconciliation with not only Judah—but most importantly with the LORD God of Israel.

The testimony of the Apostolic Scriptures is that the greater restoration of Israel has already begun. At the Jerusalem Council, James the Just indicated that the restoration of David's Tabernacle had already started, with the nations coming to faith in Israel's Messiah (Acts 15:15-18; cf. Amos 9:11-12). Whether the early non-Jewish Believers in the Mediterranean basin had a small few among them descended from the deportees of the Northern Kingdom or not, was humanly unknown to the Apostles. What is known from the Scriptures, is that restoration of Israel prophecies are applied to the nations—meaning that the salvation of Yeshua is available to all people, and all followers of the Messiah will be involved in the process of the Kingdom being restored to Israel (cf. Acts 1:6).

The Kingdom of Israel that is to be restored, is not at all the Northern Kingdom of Israel/Ephraim. The Kingdom of Israel that is to be restored, is that realm which is ruled by Great David's Greater Son, Yeshua the Messiah (Jesus Christ). In much of today's Two-House sub-movement, there are non-Jewish Believers who stridently claim the legacy of the Northern Kingdom of Israel/Ephraim as their own. Yet, how many have overlooked *the utter illegitimacy* of any of the monarchs or ruling lines of Ephraim?

There is much more to be investigated regarding the legacy of Ephraim, from the Tanach Scriptures. If a larger restoration of Israel is something to be genuinely anticipated in the future, and we have started to see it in our day—then why have we not seen an understanding of Ephraim's heritage of sin, rebellion, insurrection, intrigue, and even coups merit more attention? Perhaps the greater restoration of Israel many anticipate, will not occur until some more Bible studies are conducted on the Divided Kingdom era? If so, let us not be *too afraid* about some of the things that may be uncovered, and how many self-claiming "Ephraimites" really are indeed *of the nations themselves…*

-6-

Have the Two Sticks Been Reunited?

What is commonly called the two-stick prophecy, appearing in Ezekiel 37:15-28, has generated a great deal of attention since the late 1990s. This, in no small part, has been due to the large numbers of non-Jewish Believers entering into the Messianic movement, embracing their Hebraic Roots, and setting out on a life of Torah observance like Messiah Yeshua (Christ Jesus). Inevitably asked, or at least wondered by such people, is how much of a part of Israel they truly are. Do they just have citizenship in Israel's Kingdom because of their faith in Israel's Messiah (Ephesians 2:11-12; 3:6), being a part of the Israel of God (Galatians 6:16), being grafted-in to the olive tree (Romans 11:17-18)—*or* could such people at all be Israel on a physical level? Do these people have a lost Jewish ancestor, and that is why they are drawn into Messianic things—or are they even a part of what is commonly called the "Lost Tribes"? *Questions have certainly been asked, which have generated a wide number of responses.*

At the center of many of these questions is the oracle of **Ezekiel 37:15-28**. This short selection of fourteen verses has generated a huge amount of discussion for proponents, opponents, and skeptics of what has been widely touted as "the Two-House teaching." Many of today's Messianic Jews believe that all Israel was gathered together and restored in ancient times, and that nothing more really awaits. Many other people believe that a larger restoration of Israel awaits in the future eschaton. Many people do not want to touch the subject matter, considering it to be too flammable. Many people do not know what to do, especially with all of the opinions floating around, and are confused.

- What is the truth? Has all of Israel been restored, or is it something with more to be experienced in the future?
- Who is involved with this restoration? Only Jews? Only physical Israelites? Or all who acknowledge the God of Israel?

The only way we can know for certain is **by going to the text.** If we do this, we do not have any excuse to overlook or dismiss it with some kind of hyped-up rhetoric about the "two schticks." And if we do this, we also have to acknowledge that the overriding message of Ezekiel 37:15-28 is about bringing all of God's people together, and that we should not unnecessarily be driving people apart with either this prophetic word, anything we might relate to it, or some kind of associate agenda.

Are we really ready to see whether the two sticks of Ezekiel 37:15-28 have been reunited? I think that an exegetical paper on this passage of Scripture, engaged with scholastic proposals from the past half-century or so, **is long overdue.** *I have been quite curious for a while, as to what this investigation will uncover.* Why some of the biggest and most well-known leaders and teachers in the Two-House sub-movement have yet to write anything detailed on this prophecy, makes very little sense to me. Would they at least be interested in how other people have interpreted it: Jews, Christians, conservatives, and liberals? Or, could there be some things seen in the prophecy that they do not wish to recognize, because they have made this subject matter something a bit too simplistic and under-developed? Have some of today's popular/populist Two-House proponents actually failed to follow some of this prophecy's clear directives?

I have been interested in this prophecy for quite a while. I think that when we weigh not only the claims of the text, but also the different views that are out there, **we can safely say that the two sticks of Judah and Israel/Ephraim have not yet been reunited.** Yet this prophecy also has an important message of fostering unity among God's people, which many of today's popular Two-House teachers, who you are likely to encounter, have seriously overlooked or just absolutely not implemented.

EZEKIEL 37:15-28 – HEBREW

[15] *v'yehi devar-ADONAI elai l'emor*

[16] *v'attah ben-adam qach-lekha etz echad u'ketov alayv l'Yehudah v'livnei Yisrael (chavero) [chaverayv] u'leqach etz echad u'ketov alayv l'Yosef etz Efraim v'kol-Beit Yisrael (chavero) [chaverayv]*

[17] *v'qarav otam echad el-echad lekha l'etz echad v'hayu l'achadim b'yadekha*

[18] *v'k'asher yom'ru eleykha benei amekha l'emor ha'lo-taggid l'nu ma-elleh llak*

[19] *daveir alei'hem koh-amar Adonai ELOHIM hinneih ani loqeiach et-etz Yosef asher b'yad-Efraim v'shiv'tei Yisrael (chavero) [chaverayv] v'natatti otam alayv et-etz Yehudah v'asitim l'etz echad v'hayu echad b'yadi*

[20] *v'hayu ha'etztim asher-tiktov alei'yhem b'yadkha l'eineihem*

[21] *v'daveir alei'hem koh-amar Adonai ELOHIM hinneih ani loqeach et-benei Yisrael mi'bbein ha'goyim asher halku-sham v'qibbatz'ti otam mi'saviv v'heiveiti otam el-admatam*

[22] *v'asiti otam l'goy echad b'eretz b'harei Yisrael u'melek echad yih'yeh l'kulam l'melek v'lo (yih'yeh-)[yihyu]-od l'shnei goyim v'lo yeichatzu od l'shtei mamlakot od*

[23] *v'lo yitamm'u od b'gillulei'hem u'b'shiqqutzei'hem u'v'kol pish'eihem v'hosha'ti otam m'kol moshvotei'hem asher chatu b'hem v'tiharti otam v'hayu-li l'am v'ani ehyeh l'hem l'Elohim*

[24] *v'avdi David melek alei'hem v'roeh echad yih'yeh l'kulam u'v'mishpatai yeileiku v'chuqotai yish'meru v'asu otam*

[25] *v'yashvu al-ha'eretz asher natatti l'avdi l'Ya'akov asher yashvu-bah avoteikhem v'yashvu aleyah heimmah u'beneihem u'benei beneihem ad-olam v'David avdi nasi l'hem l'olam*

[26] *v'karati l'hem b'rit shalom b'rit olam yih'yeh otam u'netattim v'hir'beiti otam v'nattati et-*

miqdashi b'tokam l'olam

[27] v'hayah mishkani alei'hem v'hayiti l'hem l'Elohim v'heimmah yih'yu-li l'am

[28] v'yad'u ha'goyim ki ani ADONAI meqadeish et-Yisrael b'heyot miqdashi b'tokam l'olam

[15] וַיְהִי דְבַר־יְהֹוָה אֵלַי לֵאמֹר:

[16] וְאַתָּה בֶן־אָדָם קַח־לְךָ עֵץ אֶחָד וּכְתֹב עָלָיו לִיהוּדָה וְלִבְנֵי יִשְׂרָאֵל (חֲבֵרוֹ) [חֲבֵרָיו] וּלְקַח עֵץ אֶחָד וּכְתוֹב עָלָיו לְיוֹסֵף עֵץ אֶפְרַיִם וְכָל־בֵּית יִשְׂרָאֵל (חֲבֵרוֹ) [חֲבֵרָיו]

[17] וְקָרַב אֹתָם אֶחָד אֶל־אֶחָד לְךָ לְעֵץ אֶחָד וְהָיוּ לַאֲחָדִים בְּיָדֶךָ

[18] וְכַאֲשֶׁר יֹאמְרוּ אֵלֶיךָ בְּנֵי עַמְּךָ לֵאמֹר הֲלוֹא־תַגִּיד לָנוּ מָה־אֵלֶּה לָךְ

[19] דַּבֵּר אֲלֵהֶם כֹּה־אָמַר אֲדֹנָי יְהוִה הִנֵּה אֲנִי לֹקֵחַ אֶת־עֵץ יוֹסֵף אֲשֶׁר בְּיַד־אֶפְרַיִם וְשִׁבְטֵי יִשְׂרָאֵל (חֲבֵרוֹ) [חֲבֵרָיו] וְנָתַתִּי אוֹתָם עָלָיו אֶת־עֵץ יְהוּדָה וַעֲשִׂיתִם לְעֵץ אֶחָד וְהָיוּ אֶחָד בְּיָדִי

[20] וְהָיוּ הָעֵצִים אֲשֶׁר־תִּכְתֹּב עֲלֵיהֶם בְּיָדְךָ לְעֵינֵיהֶם

[21] וְדַבֵּר אֲלֵיהֶם כֹּה־אָמַר אֲדֹנָי יְהוִה הִנֵּה אֲנִי לֹקֵחַ אֶת־בְּנֵי יִשְׂרָאֵל מִבֵּין הַגּוֹיִם אֲשֶׁר הָלְכוּ־שָׁם וְקִבַּצְתִּי אֹתָם מִסָּבִיב וְהֵבֵאתִי אוֹתָם אֶל־אַדְמָתָם

[22] וְעָשִׂיתִי אֹתָם לְגוֹי אֶחָד בָּאָרֶץ בְּהָרֵי יִשְׂרָאֵל וּמֶלֶךְ אֶחָד יִהְיֶה לְכֻלָּם לְמֶלֶךְ וְלֹא (יְהְיֶה)[יִהְיוּ]־עוֹד לִשְׁנֵי גוֹיִם וְלֹא יֵחָצוּ עוֹד לִשְׁתֵּי מַמְלָכוֹת עוֹד

[23] וְלֹא יִטַמְּאוּ עוֹד בְּגִלּוּלֵיהֶם וּבְשִׁקּוּצֵיהֶם וּבְכֹל פִּשְׁעֵיהֶם וְהוֹשַׁעְתִּי אֹתָם מִכֹּל מוֹשְׁבֹתֵיהֶם אֲשֶׁר חָטְאוּ בָהֶם וְטִהַרְתִּי אוֹתָם וְהָיוּ־לִי לְעָם וַאֲנִי אֶהְיֶה לָהֶם לֵאלֹהִים

[24] וְעַבְדִּי דָוִד מֶלֶךְ עֲלֵיהֶם וְרוֹעֶה אֶחָד יִהְיֶה לְכֻלָּם וּבְמִשְׁפָּטַי יֵלֵכוּ וְחֻקֹּתַי יִשְׁמְרוּ וְעָשׂוּ אוֹתָם

[25] וְיָשְׁבוּ עַל־הָאָרֶץ אֲשֶׁר נָתַתִּי לְעַבְדִּי לְיַעֲקֹב אֲשֶׁר יָשְׁבוּ־בָהּ אֲבוֹתֵיכֶם וְיָשְׁבוּ עָלֶיהָ הֵמָּה וּבְנֵיהֶם וּבְנֵי בְנֵיהֶם עַד־עוֹלָם וְדָוִד עַבְדִּי נָשִׂיא לָהֶם לְעוֹלָם

[26] וְכָרַתִּי לָהֶם בְּרִית שָׁלוֹם בְּרִית עוֹלָם יִהְיֶה אוֹתָם וּנְתַתִּים וְהִרְבֵּיתִי אוֹתָם וְנָתַתִּי אֶת־מִקְדָּשִׁי בְּתוֹכָם לְעוֹלָם

[27] וְהָיָה מִשְׁכָּנִי עֲלֵיהֶם וְהָיִיתִי לָהֶם לֵאלֹהִים וְהֵמָּה יִהְיוּ־לִי לְעָם

[28] וְיָדְעוּ הַגּוֹיִם כִּי אֲנִי יְהוָה מְקַדֵּשׁ אֶת־יִשְׂרָאֵל בִּהְיוֹת מִקְדָּשִׁי בְּתוֹכָם לְעוֹלָם

EZEKIEL 37:15-28 – ENGLISH

NASU	NJPS
[15] The word of the LORD came again to me saying, [16] "And you, son of man, take for yourself one stick and write on it, 'For Judah and for the sons of Israel, his companions'; then take another stick and write on it, 'For Joseph, the stick of Ephraim and all the house of Israel, his companions.' [17] Then join them for	[15] The word of the LORD came to me: [16] And you, O mortal, take a stick and write on it, "Of Judah and the Israelites associated with him"; and take another stick and write on it, "Of Joseph -- the stick of Ephraim -- and all the House of Israel associated with him." [17] Bring them close to each

yourself one to another into one stick, that they may become one in your hand. [18] "When the sons of your people speak to you saying, 'Will you not declare to us what you mean by these?' [19] say to them, 'Thus says the Lord GOD, "Behold, I will take the stick of Joseph, which is in the hand of Ephraim, and the tribes of Israel, his companions; and I will put them with it, with the stick of Judah, and make them one stick, and they will be one in My hand."' [20] "The sticks on which you write will be in your hand before their eyes. [21] Say to them, 'Thus says the Lord GOD, "Behold, I will take the sons of Israel from among the nations where they have gone, and I will gather them from every side and bring them into their own land; [22] and I will make them one nation in the land, on the mountains of Israel; and one king will be king for all of them; and they will no longer be two nations and no longer be divided into two kingdoms. [23] "They will no longer defile themselves with their idols, or with their detestable things, or with any of their transgressions; but I will deliver them from all their dwelling places in which they have sinned, and will cleanse them. And they will be My people, and I will be their God. [24] "My servant David will be king over them, and they will all have one shepherd; and they will walk in My ordinances and keep My statutes and observe them. [25] They will live on the land that I gave to Jacob My servant, in which your fathers lived; and they will live on it, they, and their sons and their sons' sons, forever; and David My servant will be their prince forever. [26] I will make a covenant of peace with them; it will be an everlasting covenant with them. And I will place them and multiply them, and will set My sanctuary in their midst forever. [27] "My dwelling place also will be with them; and I will be their God, and they will be My people. [28]

other, so that they become one stick, joined together in your hand. [18] And when any of your people ask you, "Won't you tell us what these actions of yours mean?" [19] answer them, "Thus said the Lord GOD: I am going to take the stick of Joseph -- which is in the hand of Ephraim -- and of the tribes of Israel associated with him, and I will place the stick of Judah upon it and make them into one stick; they shall be joined in My hand." [20] You shall hold up before their eyes the sticks which you have inscribed, [21] and you shall declare to them: Thus said the Lord GOD: I am going to take the Israelite people from among the nations they have gone to, and gather them from every quarter, and bring them to their own land. [22] I will make them a single nation in the land, on the hills of Israel, and one king shall be king of them all. Never again shall they be two nations, and never again shall they be divided into two kingdoms. [23] Nor shall they ever again defile themselves by their fetishes and their abhorrent things, and by their other transgressions. I will save them in all their settlements where they sinned, and I will cleanse them. Then they shall be My people, and I will be their God. [24] My servant David shall be king over them; there shall be one shepherd for all of them. They shall follow My rules and faithfully obey My laws. [25] Thus they shall remain in the land which I gave to My servant Jacob and in which your fathers dwelt; they and their children and their children's children shall dwell there forever, with My servant David as their prince for all time [26] I will make a covenant of friendship with them -- it shall be an everlasting covenant with them -- I will establish them and multiply them, and I will

And the nations will know that I am the LORD who sanctifies Israel, when My sanctuary is in their midst forever."'''	place My Sanctuary among them forever. [27] My Presence shall rest over them; I will be their God and they shall be My people. [28] And when My Sanctuary abides among them forever, the nations shall know that I the LORD do sanctify Israel.

The Context and the Purpose of the Prophecy

The prophecies contained in the Book of Ezekiel were delivered to the Jewish exiles in Babylon, likely sometime between 593-573 B.C.E., with the Book of Ezekiel probably reaching its final textual form sometime after the exile in the later 500s B.C.E. Many of the messages that we see in Ezekiel were given to motivate the Jewish exiles, so that they would know that in spite of their sins which caused their expulsion to Babylon, God had not totally forgotten about them, nor was it His intention to never restore Israel. He would erase their record of sin and return them to their Land.

The two-stick prophecy of Ezekiel 37:15-28 occurs within a much larger narrative of various messages of hope (33:1-48:35). It is wedged between a description of the Prophet Ezekiel as a watchman (33:1-20), an explanation of Jerusalem's fall (33:21-33), a prophetic word delivered against false shepherds (ch. 34), judgment declared against Mount Seir and Edom (ch. 35), a prophetic word on how the mountains of Israel will be fruitful and how God's people will be given new hearts (ch. 36), and the valley of dry bones depicting the resurrection of Israel (37:1-14). After the two-stick prophecy, prophetic oracles are delivered against Gog and Magog (chs. 38-39), and the remainder of the Book of Ezekiel is spent discussing the reconstruction of the Temple, and the inauguration of a new spiritual order (chs. 40-48).

It is not at all surprising, seeing the various themes of Ezekiel, why many people are confused, and why many do not really know how to handle the various symbols and images employed by the Prophet. Are these images to be taken literally or figuratively? Will there be a real restoration of Israel to the Promised Land, or should we allegorize these passages? Does this concern an ancient Sixth Century B.C.E. scene, or something to occur in the distant future? Will there be a physical Temple reconstructed (for a future Millennial Kingdom), where God's presence will manifest itself on Earth, or is this just symbolic of the *ekklēsia* and God's people possessing His Spirit? Anyone who chooses to give some kind of significance to the two-stick prophecy of Ezekiel 37:15-28 is admittedly walking into a place where this Divine oracle is actually one of the least controversial words, given what is seen in the surrounding chapters.[1]

---

[1] For some further discussion, consult the author's entry for the Book of Ezekiel in *A Survey of the Tanach for the Practical Messianic.*

The two-stick prophecy of Ezekiel 37:15-28, no different than the other prophetic words seen in chs. 33-48, is seriously meant to inspire the Jewish exiles in Babylon. God had not abandoned them, and by His power He was going to accomplish some awesome works. The Prophet Ezekiel, in his unique style, uses physical objects such as *etzim* (עֵצִים)—pieces of wood—to visually show his audience that the Lord is going to perform important activity. Daniel I. Block observes how "There are no convincing reasons, historical or otherwise, to deny Ezekiel credit for both the visual and oral presentation of this prophecy. In a text that affirms his literacy, he may even have been responsible for its transcription"[2] (i.e., 37:16, 20).

The circumstance that the two-stick prophecy intends to reverse is the division of the Ancient Kingdom of Israel, which had been split since King Solomon's death, in 921-922 B.C.E. (1 Kings 12). The theme of the two-stick prophecy not only concerns the general restoration of Israel, but the reunion of Israel's *divided* Kingdom. The Southern Kingdom, which had remained loyal to the Davidic monarchy, was known as Judah (1 Kings 12:22-44), with the Northern Kingdom known as either Israel, or by the name of its largest tribe, Ephraim (i.e., Hosea 5:3, 5, 11-14). Ephraim is also used as the name of the Northern Kingdom, possibly because its first monarch, Jeroboam, was from the tribe of Ephraim (1 Kings 11:26). The Northern Kingdom of Israel/Ephraim had been corporately taken away into captivity by the Assyrian Empire in 722-721 B.C.E., with Judah being taken away in a series of exiles by the Babylon Empire in 606, 597, and 586 B.C.E.[3] Somehow and in some way, God is going to miraculously bring all of Israel back together.

Ezekiel has been prophesying on what is to come to Israel (chs. 34-39), most notably including a resurrection of dry bones (37:1-14). When we arrive at the two-stick prophecy, we see how the reunion of Judah and exiled Israel/Ephraim is the critical point where everything crescendos, the fulfillment of which can then lead to the succeeding events and establishment of the new Temple. Iain M. Duguid considers how this oracle "acts as a hinge, both summing up the oracles of hope in chapters 34-37 and looking forward to the establishment of the new sanctuary (chs. 40-48) after the...convulsion of evil in chapters 38-39."[4] From a literary standpoint, one cannot avoid the significance that the two-stick prophecy of Ezekiel 37:15-28 plays within the larger narrative of events seen in Ezekiel chs. 33-34 all the way to ch. 48.

Because of the importance of the two-stick prophecy within the expectation of Israel's restoration, it should not be surprising that there does exist the very real possibility of being burned when trying to read and interpret it. Charles H. Dyer has to mention one view of how, "Some have claimed that the two sticks represent the Bible (the stick of Judah) and the Book of Mormon (the stick of Joseph).

---

[2] Daniel I. Block, *New International Commentary on the Old Testament: The Book of Ezekiel, Chapters 25-48* (Grand Rapids: Eerdmans, 1998), 394.

[3] Cf. Charles H. Dyer, "Ezekiel," in John F. Walvoord and Roy B. Zuck, eds., *The Bible Knowledge Commentary: Old Testament* (Wheaton, IL: Victor Books, 1985), 1299.

[4] Iain M. Duguid, *NIV Application Commentary: Ezekiel* (Grand Rapids: Zondervan, 1999), 435.

However, this assertion ignores the clear interpretation in verses 18-28 and seeks to impose a foreign meaning on the sticks."[5] One only need to add to this mix various speculations made by both British-Israel and Christian Identity people, and their many offshoots, and the significant anti-Semitism they promote. For some, the association of these groups to this prophecy is just too much, and so they think that it is best to avoid the prophecy of Ezekiel 37:15-28 altogether. But even though there have been abuses with the two-stick prophecy, and no one can deny how aberrant groups have interpreted it throughout recent religious history—it is **nevertheless a part of the Biblical canon that cannot be avoided.**

At the exact opposite end of the theological spectrum, one encounters the thoughts and sentiments of liberal interpreters who engage with Ezekiel 37:15-28. Katheryn Pfisterer Darr makes the remark of how God's "plan for the people encompasses not only those who survived the collapse of Judah and their offspring, but also the descendants of those northern Israelites who, in the wake of Assyria's defeat of their kingdom in 721 BCE, were dispersed across the Assyrian empire a century and a half earlier. Farfetched as this might sound, it was a pulsating hope at the time."[6] Yet, liberals think that this is not something we are to really take that serious today. Darr further notes various challenges that have existed, concerning the authenticity of Ezekiel's prophecy, specifically in how "from the perspective of many modern-day commentators...[there is] evidence to suggest that in addition to clarifying glosses interspersed here and there, the original sign-act account was subsequently expanded..."[7] by later redactors. So, liberals say how much of the two-stick prophecy is real cannot be known for certain, and we need not give it too much significance.

While most proponents of a larger restoration of Israel yet to come, adhere to the view that the prophecy of Ezekiel 37:15-28 is yet to be fulfilled—few are actually aware of the wide diversity of interpretations that exist in contemporary theology today. Jewish and Christian commentators have had more time to deal with the Book of Ezekiel than any of today's Messianics. Even though one can correctly assume that laypersons have been largely ignorant of the two-stick prophecy, it is not right for us to assume that Rabbis and theologians have been totally ignorant. Anyone, who has had to write a commentary on the Book of Ezekiel, has had to interpret it on some level. This most especially includes conservative evangelical interpreters, who consider 37:15-28 to be an authentic Ezekielian prophecy that somehow concerns the future—with whom we will be engaging the most. As John B. Taylor summarizes it,

"[I]n the restored Israel, the old divisions of north and south will be abolished and the nation will be united in God's hand. The interpretation of this, however, raises a number of controversial issues. If the inhabitants of Israel/Samaria were scattered throughout the Assyrian Empire, is there any prospect of their

---

[5] Dyer, in *BKCOT*, 1299.

[6] Katheryn Pfisterer Darr, "The Book of Ezekiel," in Leander E. Keck, ed., et. al., *New Interpreter's Bible*, Vol. 6 (Nashville: Abingdon, 2001), 1505.

[7] Ibid.

descendants being literally brought back, with the exiles from Judah, into the promised land? Or are we to understand 'Israel' as consisting simply of those men of northern tribal origin who had associated themselves wth [sic] Judah from time to time? Do we allegorize it all and see it simply as a picture of the church, the new Israel, united in the future kingdom of God?"[8]

These are only a few of the interpretations of Ezekiel 37:15-28 which are present in today's theology. Taylor is right to recognize, though, that the vision foresees the removal of divisions between Northern and Southern Israel, and the establishment of a single sanctuary, reversing the split enacted after Solomon's death (1 Kings 12:25-33). And, not to be overlooked is how Ezekiel's word is to be applied to the daily mission and focus of today's Believers, where we strive to see the Lord's people all brought together as one in Him.

In our examination of this prophetic oracle, we will assume that the material is more-or-less authentic to Ezekiel himself, but that Ezekiel was probably not the one who transcribed it in its final form. Our responsibility is to deal with the text in its final, canonical form, recognizing how all of what is seen in Ezekiel 37:15-28 is concurrent with the will of God and overall message of the Prophets, even if a few points here or there might have been added by a later editor. Leslie C. Allen specifically describes how "vv 15-28 represent a basic text that has been subsequently amplified, as is the case with very many of the literary units in the book. Its early part derives from Ezekiel, but seems to be later than vv 1-13, which still reflect the shock of the catastrophe in 587 B.C. It looks back at the crisis reflectively...and ponders deeply upon its reversal."[9] He notes his view that whether vs. 23-24a are original to what Ezekiel first delivered, or are a further reflection on Israel's restoration, "is not easily decided."[10]

I think that if those ultimately responsible for compiling Ezekiel's prophecies may have noted some additional things, not explicitly stated by Ezekiel in his act of putting the two sticks together—we need not think that Ezekiel's prophecy has been "tampered" with. Such redactors had to be just as Divinely inspired as the Prophet Ezekiel himself was, in their work of preserving his oracles for future generations of God's people.

---

[8] John B. Taylor, *Tyndale Old Testament Commentaries: Ezekiel* (Downers Grove, IL: InterVarsity, 1969), 239.

[9] Leslie C. Allen, *Word Biblical Commentary: Ezekiel 20-48*, Vol 29 (Dallas: Word Books, 1990), 192.

[10] Ibid.

The Prophecy

15 The word of the LORD came again to me saying, 16 "And you, son of man, take for yourself one stick and write on it, 'For Judah and for the sons of Israel, his companions'; then take another stick and write on it, 'For Joseph, the stick of Ephraim and all the house of Israel, his companions.' 17 Then join them for yourself one to another into one stick, that they may become one in your hand.

37:15 The two-stick prophecy begins with the important indicator of its origin. Ezekiel says "a message came to me from the LORD" (NLT). The term *davar* (דָּבָר) simply relates to "**word**," or quite possibly also an "**affair, thing**" (*CHALOT*).[11] This *devar-ADONAI* (דְּבַר־יְהוָה) coming to Ezekiel is simply a recognition of the prophecy's Divine origin, as "The revelatory work of God is often expressed by 'the word of the Lord came' to or upon a person" (*TWOT*).[12] Being such a Divine matter, any interpreter of Ezekiel's prophecy that follows has to make sure that he or she is sure to render due honor to the Source from which it came, and His intention for His people. It is a very important matter to our Heavenly Father, which is not to be mocked, misappropriated, or abused.

37:16 The Prophet Ezekiel is instructed by the Lord to take a physical object and perform a symbolic act. He tells him, "son of man, take for yourself one stick and write on it." When reading this prophecy, we are not at all unjustified to ask ourselves who this *ben-adam* (בֶן־אָדָם) is. Is it simply describing Ezekiel as a "mortal" (NRSV/NJPS), or is more intended? In v. 19 we later see how it is God Himself who fuses Israel together. While Ezekiel might be the one called to pick up a piece of wood and write on it, is it at all inappropriate to recognize this *ben-adam* as ultimately being the Son of Man, Yeshua the Messiah? Scholars largely recognize how "Son of Man" is the one term that the Messiah refers to Himself as in the Gospels more than any other, originating from the various Danielic references to the *bar enash* (בַּר אֱנָשׁ) who is given ultimate power and dominion (Daniel 7:13-14).[13] It would certainly not be a stretch to conclude that even though Ezekiel takes the stick and presents it to his audience of Jewish exiles, that it is ultimately God's Messiah who must be the actual One who restores Israel.

What does the physical object or stick represent? Ezekiel says how the Lord instructed him, "take for yourself one stick and write on it, 'For Judah and for the sons of Israel, his companions'; then take another stick and write on it, 'For Joseph, the stick of Ephraim and all the house of Israel, his companions.'" The first stick represents the Southern Kingdom of Judah, and the second stick represents the Northern Kingdom of Israel/Ephraim. *But is it really a "stick"?*

The Hebrew term *etz* (עֵץ) has a variety of possible meanings, including both the plural and singular "**trees**" and "**tree**," as well as "**wood**" and "**timber**"

---

[11] *CHALOT*, 67.
[12] Earl S. Kalland, "dābār," in *TWOT*, 1:180.
[13] Cf. I. Howard Marshall, "Son of Man," in *Dictionary of Jesus and the Gospels*, pp 775-781.

(*CHALOT*).[14] The two objects that Ezekiel holds in his hands can very well be considered sticks, but they could just be some generic pieces of wood that he picked up off the ground. S. Fisch considers the *etz* to be an "emblem of the royal sceptre."[15] One of the most intriguing views of what the *etz* represents, compared to the rest of them, is reflected in the NEB extrapolation: "take one leaf of a wooden tablet."

Are the two pieces of wood that the Prophet Ezekiel is called to take some kind of a wooden tablet or board? This position is especially argued by Block, with supports given from various Ancient Near Eastern sources.[16] His viewpoint is highlighted by the fact that the prophecy does not envision the reunification of the monarchies of the Northern and Southern Kingdoms—with the *etz* representing some kind of regal staff—but of the Kingdoms themselves:

"Nowhere is the union of the northern dynasty with the Davidic house contemplated; on the contrary, the northern kingdom was considered an aberration from the beginning and all its kings illegitimate...Here [Ezekiel] takes extra pains to link these wooden objects with their respective nations rather than their kings, and in the interpretation to follow he will highlight Yahweh's activity of bringing the 'descendants of Israel' to their own land and making them one nation."[17]

The necessity of the pieces of wood that Ezekiel is to join together being writing tablets, in the view of his audience, at least to Block,[18] is substantiated by some other prophetic words:

"Now go, write it on a tablet [*luach*, לוּחַ] before them and inscribe it on a scroll, that it may serve in the time to come as a witness forever" (Isaiah 30:8).

"Then the LORD answered me and said, 'Record the vision and inscribe *it* on tablets [*luchot*, לֻחוֹת], that the one who reads it may run'" (Habakkuk 2:2).

With these other prophecies in view, it is certainly not outside of the realm of possibilities for the two pieces of wood for Ezekiel to be holding to be some kind of ancient writing tablets. This could be a bit more significant for the Prophet's audience than just two generic sticks, which he might have difficulty writing on. From this angle, Christopher J.H. Wright connects this to what might make the most sense to Twenty-First Century people, paraphrasing v. 16 with, "Take a single sheet of notepaper and write this on it...Then take another single sheet of notepaper and write this on it...Now glue them together down the middle to make the two sheets into one new single sheet."[19]

The reason for some that writing tablets or boards, as opposed to just generic pieces of wood, are to be preferred, is because upon them the redemptive work of

---

[14] *CHALOT*, 279.

[15] S. Fisch, *Soncino Books of the Bible: Ezekiel* (London: Soncino, 1950, 1994), 249.

[16] Block, pp 397-400.

[17] Ibid., 399.

[18] Ibid., 401.

[19] Christopher J.H. Wright, *The Message of Ezekiel* (Downers Grove, IL: InterVarsity, 2001), 312.

God can be transcribed. For some interpreters it is insufficient for just *Yehudah* (יְהוּדָה), *Yosef* (יוֹסֵף) or *Efraim* (אֶפְרַיִם), and then some other scribbling, to be whittled onto a common stick, which may not even possess enough space to contain more than a few words. In Block's estimation, "the boards offer visual affirmation of the truth declared in the following promises that *all* Israel would participate in the envisioned restoration. No tribe or clan would be missing....once Ezekiel had presented his interpretation in the sign action (vv. 21-28), he would have used these tablets to record the oracle."[20] This reason is certainly compelling, because the Prophet Ezekiel would have been unable to record the reunification oracle on a stick that only gave him a few inches to carve into. Furthermore, writing tablets or boards could be used later as a primary source to compile Ezekiel's prophecies into their canonical form.

Block's view of the wooden objects to be fused together, as writing tablets or boards, is both interesting and compelling, although it is speculative. It is possible that the Prophet Ezekiel used some kind of ancient writing board, but then again it may be unlikely as Ezekiel has used more common objects to make previous points to his audience.[21] The Septuagint renders *etz* as *hrabdos* (ῥάβδος), itself having a variety of possible meanings, including "*a rod, wand, stick, switch,*" but here most likely pertaining to "*a staff of office*" (*LS*).[22] Allen, but more because of the wider themes of kingship (v. 24), opts for the *etz* being some kind of regal staff. He remarks, "The sticks have a national significance insofar as they suggest the institution of monarchy that represents the nation."[23]

Using staffs is also an important feature seen throughout the Tanach. The rod or *matteh* (מַטֶּה) of Aaron actually sprouted almond blossoms:

"Moses therefore spoke to the sons of Israel, and all their leaders gave him a rod apiece, for each leader according to their fathers' households, twelve rods, with the rod of Aaron among their rods. So Moses deposited the rods before the LORD in the tent of the testimony. Now on the next day Moses went into the tent of the testimony; and behold, the rod of Aaron for the house of Levi had sprouted and put forth buds and produced blossoms, and it bore ripe almonds. Moses then brought out all the rods from the presence of the LORD to all the sons of Israel; and they looked, and each man took his rod. But the LORD said to Moses, 'Put back the rod of Aaron before the testimony to be kept as a sign against the rebels, that you may put an end to their grumblings against Me, so that they will not die'" (Numbers 17:6-10).

The post-exilic word of Zechariah 11:7, believed by many to be based on this oracle in Ezekiel, uses a staff or *maqqeil* (מַקֵּל) to make an important point:

"So I pastured the flock *doomed* to slaughter, hence the afflicted of the flock. And I took for myself two staffs: the one I called Favor and the other I called Union; so I pastured the flock."

---

[20] Block, pp 404-405.
[21] Cf. Ibid., 399; Darr, in *NIB*, 6:1507.
[22] *LS*, 714.
[23] Allen, 193.

Also not to be overlooked, per what *etz* may mean in Ezekiel, is how the Apostle Paul describes Israel as an olive tree, with natural branches broken off, and with wild branches grafted in (Romans chs. 9-11).

Weighing all the options together—whether we are to view Ezekiel's *etz* as a writing tablet, a regal staff or scepter, or just a stick or generic piece of wood—the default option is to just call it a **stick.** We can safely disregard *etz* as being a tree, simply because of the fact that unless Ezekiel possessed superhuman strength, or there were some really small bonsai-like trees convenient, it would be difficult to see him pick up two trees and try to join them together. While I personally find Block's writing tablet hypothesis intriguing, as have others, for the sake of our examination we will simply refer to what Ezekiel joins together as sticks or pieces of wood. The prophetic point being made more than anything else is that they are to become one. The term *echad* (אֶחָד) or "one" is used a total of ten times in this passage—an emphasis on the theme of unity that God will bring to Israel.

Anyone who reads the two-stick prophecy of Ezekiel 37:15-28 recognizes how, on the whole, it is a message of the unity that is to take place between Judah and Israel/Ephraim. Everyone agrees that the stick marked "*Yehudah*," and the stick marked "*Yosef*" or "*Efraim*," represents the people of either the Southern Kingdom or the Northern Kingdom. But there is no agreement about how to render the wider two clauses *l'Yehudah v'livnei Yisrael (chavero) [chaverayv]* (חֲבֵרָיו] (חֲבֵרוֹ) יִשְׂרָאֵל וְלִבְנֵי לִיהוּדָה), and *l'Yosef etz Efraim v'kol-Beit Yisrael (chavero) [chaverayv]* (חֲבֵרָיו] לְיוֹסֵף עֵץ אֶפְרַיִם וְכָל-בֵּית יִשְׂרָאֵל (חֲבֵרוֹ). There are some textual variants in the manuscript traditions that have to be weighed, and we may also have to consider a slightly wider window of restoration of Israel prophecies in order to make a determination.

First of all, how is the preposition *l'* (לְ) to be viewed in what the two sticks represent? It can mean to, for, concerning, or indicate some kind of possession,[24] as in "belonging to" (NIV). Does each stick represent either Judah and Israel as a group of people, or does each stick represent a power that each possesses? Does it at all regard something that either Judah and Israel must give up to be reunited, or are these just symbols? Block argues that we should view *l'* "as a *lamed* of reference,"[25] meaning that *l'Yehudah* and *l'Yosef* mean "Pertaining to Judah....pertaining to Joseph..."

Secondly, if one is comparing Bible translations, it is not too difficult to discern a difference between versions like the NASU, when compared against either the RSV or NIV. One speaks of Judah and Israel having some kind of "companions." The other two (and also NRSV, NJPS, ESV, HCSB, etc.) have something like "and the Israelites associated with him...and all the house of Israel associated with him" (NIV). From this point of view, rather than the people of the House of Judah, and the people of the House of Israel/Ephraim, both possessing some kind of associated

[24] *BDB*, pp 510-518.
[25] Block, 403.

companions from outside themselves—the only "companions" seen are the natural born Israelites who make up either House.

We cannot overlook the fact that there is a difference between the Qere (what is read) and Ketiv (what is written) of v. 16.[26] What is read is *chaverayv* (חֲבֵרָיו), which is implied to be "the Israelites/all the House of Israel associated with him" (NJPS), only members of either Judah and Israel/Ephraim. What is written is *chavero* (חֲבֵרוֹ), simply meaning "his companion(s)," which can be viewed as a third group of people connected to Judah and Israel/Ephraim, but still a third group of people. Most interpreters choose to follow the Ketiv rendering.[27]

The prophecy of the two sticks was originally directed to a Jewish audience in Babylonian exile. They would probably have thought that a reunion with the scattered Northern Kingdom was utterly impossible, and so we certainly cannot deny how the two sticks the Prophet Ezekiel is directed to present to them principally represent these two divided kingdoms. Those of the exiled Southern Kingdom, who made up the tribes of Judah and Benjamin, were intended to be encouraged by this oracle. The *ArtScroll Chumash* notes for us,

"[T]he prophecy of this *Haftarah* [connected to *V'yigash*, Genesis 44:18-47:27] was a source of great comfort to the tribes of Judah and Benjamin, for even if their long-lost comrades of the Northern Kingdom were assured that they would again become part of the nation, surely the two southern tribes could be certain that God was not forsaking them."[28]

The (assimilated) exiles of the Northern Kingdom were not in Babylon to hear Ezekiel make his prophecies, but those from the exiled Southern Kingdom certainly were. All are agreed that at least two groups of people—Judah and Israel/Ephraim—are involved in this restoration.

But is there really a third group, a group of "companions"? Is the Qere or Ketiv right? The singular term *chaver* (חָבֵר) can mean "united, associate, companion" (*BDB*).[29] It appears in Judges 20:11, where the people of Israel are gathered together "as one man—companions"[30] (YLT). Those of Jerusalem are chastised in Isaiah 1:23 with "Your rulers are rebels and companions of thieves."[31] In Song of Songs we see references to "the flocks of your companions"[32] and "O you who sit in the gardens, *My* companions[33] are listening for your voice" (Song of Songs 1:7; 8:13). *Chaver* has a variance of usages, which although can be a reference to all of those people who compose either Judah or Israel/Ephraim, could also be a reference to people who have joined alongside Judah or Israel/Ephraim, and are involved along with them in the restoration process.

---

[26] Aron Dotan, ed., *Biblia Hebraica Leningradensia* (Peabody, MA: Hendrickson, 2001), 784.

[27] Cf. Block, 396 fn#11.

[28] Scherman, *Chumash*, 1145.

[29] *BDB*, 288.

[30] Heb. *k'ish echad chaverim* (כְּאִישׁ אֶחָד חֲבֵרִים).

[31] Heb. *v'chaverei gannavim* (וְחַבְרֵי גַּנָּבִים).

[32] Heb. *chaverekha* (חֲבֵרֶיךָ).

[33] Heb. *chaverim* (חֲבֵרִים).

If one chooses to follow the Ketiv of v. 16, *chavero* (חֲבֵרוֹ), then the singular *chaver* (חָבֵר) would need to be rendered somewhere along the lines of "*an associate, a companion, fellow*" (*Gesenius' Hebrew-Chaldee Lexicon to the Old Testament*).[34] While "his companions" (NASU) is seen, "his associates" would also be a proper translation as well.

That there is some group of people associated with Judah and Israel/Ephraim is certainly implied by v. 16. But, are these people those of the Israelite tribes that made up the Northern or Southern Kingdoms *or* associated companions from the nations, to be likened unto the *gerim* (גֵּרִים) or sojourners seen in the Torah?[35] It would seem a bit redundant to include either the Qere *chaverayv* or Ketiv *chavero*, when both Judah and Joseph/Ephraim referenced, would be an indicator enough for the people of the two divided Kingdoms. The presence of *chavero*, "his companions" or "his associates," points us in the direction of more people than just the descendants of either the Southern Kingdom of Judah or Northern Kingdom of Israel/Ephraim, being involved in the restoration process.

The Greek LXX has some very interesting renderings that need to be considered in our deliberations. The first rod concerns *Ioudan kai tous huious Israēl tous proskeimenous ep' auton* (Ιουδαν καὶ τοὺς υἱοὺς Ισραηλ τοὺς προσκειμένους ἐπ' αὐτόν), and the second rod concerns *tō Iōsēph rhabdon Ephraim kai pantas tous huious Israēl tous prostethentas* (τῷ Ιωσηφ ῥάβδον Εφραιμ καὶ πάντας τοὺς υἱοὺς Ισραηλ τοὺς προστεθέντας). This is a fairly literal translation of the Hebrew. Both Judah and Israel/Ephraim here have a group of people attached to them, designated by the plural participles *proskeimenous* and *prostethentas*.

The first participle (verb functioning as a noun), *proskeimenous*, a group associated with Judah, is derived from the verb *proskeimai* (πρόσκειμαι), meaning "*to be attached* or *devoted to*" (*LS*),[36] "his adherents" (LXE). The second participle, *prostethentas*, a group associated with Israel/Ephraim, is derived from the verb *prostithēmi* (προστίθημι), which *BDAG* first defines as "**to add to someth. that is already present or exists,**"[37] either those "that belong to him" (LXE) or "that are added to him."[38]

The opening message of the two sticks, representing Judah and Israel/Ephraim, and who the companions are—whether they are Israelites who make up either House, or companions from the nations at large—can only really be known by weighing in other prophecies of Israel's restoration. What I actually consider to be *the most important prophecy*, that is to guide our overall exegesis and understanding of the Father's mission, is Isaiah 49:6, where He says of the Messiah,

---

[34] H.F.W. Gesenius: *Gesenius' Hebrew-Chaldee Lexicon to the Old Testament*, trans. Samuel Prideaux Tregelles (Grand Rapids: Baker, 1979), 259.

[35] Cf. Gerard Van Groningen, "hābēr," in *TWOT*, 1:260.

[36] Cf. Exodus 22:21; 23:9; Leviticus 19:33-34; 24:22.

[37] *LS*, 692.

[38] *BDAG*, 885.

[38] Sir Lancelot C. L. Brenton, ed & trans, *The Septuagint With Apocrypha* (Peabody, MA: Hendrickson, 1999), 1029 fn δ.

"It is too small a thing that You should be My Servant to raise up the tribes of Jacob and to restore the preserved ones of Israel; I will also make You a light of the nations so that My salvation may reach to the end of the earth."[39] The Lord is not only planning to bring Judah and Ephraim together — **His salvation is going to go out to the entire world.** We are thus on a safe footing to conclude that the "companions" of v. 16 are largely not people who compose either Judah or Israel/Ephraim, but are instead non-Israelites from the nations at large, who are involved in the restoration of Israel, and are to be incorporated into an enlarged Kingdom realm of Israel in the eschaton.

The restoration of Judah and Israel/Ephraim really does involve *three*, and not two groups, of people. This could just about qualify anyone who acknowledges the God of Abraham, Isaac, and Jacob. And, it is most probable that the significant majority of people involved in the two-stick reunion are actually welcome companions from the nations themselves.

37:17 The Prophet Ezekiel is instructed by God to do something with the two sticks: "Then bring them close to yourself, one to the other, like one piece of wood, and they will become united in your hand" (ATS). The two sticks are to be made into *etz echad* (עֵץ אֶחָד), representing a reassembling together. We can certainly recall here the similar word of Hosea 1:11, "the sons of Judah and the sons of Israel will be gathered together." Perhaps most significant and reflective would be the previous oracle of Ezekiel 37:1-14 and the reassembling of the dry bones. Just as Judah and Israel are to be brought together in the day of Jezreel (Hosea 1:11b; cf. Revelation 16:16), so does the revivifying of the dry bones indicate the future resurrection (1 Thessalonians 4:16-17). This is a very good indicator that this word of Judah and Israel becoming a united *etz* occurs subsequent to the eschaton. Most of what is communicated by Ezekiel thus concerns the future eschaton, and not necessarily the Jewish exiles to whom he was speaking in Babylon.

18 **"When the sons of your people speak to you saying, 'Will you not declare to us what you mean by these?'** 19 **say to them, 'Thus says the Lord GOD, "Behold, I will take the stick of Joseph, which is in the hand of Ephraim, and the tribes of Israel, his companions; and I will put them with it, with the stick of Judah, and make them one stick, and they will be one in My hand."'**

37:18 Seeing Ezekiel join two pieces of wood together, the curiosity of the people is aroused, something that is not uncommon (12:9; 21:7; 24:19). They ask him, "Won't you tell us what these things have to do with us?" (NIV). To these exiles, they would be confounded at what all this symbolism would mean. Was the Prophet Ezekiel just mentally disturbed in picking up two pieces of wood off the ground, joining them together? Block indicates, "If the restoration of Judah

---

[39] Heb. *u'netattikha l'or goyim l'heyot yeshuati ad-qetzeih ha'eretz* (לְאוֹר גּוֹיִם לִהְיוֹת יְשׁוּעָתִי עַד־קְצֵה הָאָרֶץ וּנְתַתִּיךָ).

represented a major problem in the people's minds, how much more would they have stumbled over the idea of the restoration of the northern kingdom"?[40] They would have likely thought this was a sheer impossibility.

Moving forward to today, we are a generation that has actually witnessed a fair number of prophecies regarding Israel's restoration. Most notably, we have seen the fulfillment of Isaiah 66:8, "Can a land be born in one day? Can a nation be brought forth all at once?" via the establishment of the State of Israel in 1948. Yet many evangelical Christians *and* Messianic Jews, though, are surprisingly unfamiliar with a word like Ezekiel 37:15-28. Perhaps various leaders have stayed away from talking about a prophecy like this, because of controversies in history over the Lost Tribes of Israel. At the same time, if there is more to be expected in salvation history regarding the restoration of Israel in the Last Days, a word like this deserves to be considered and probed for significance.

When people approach the two-stick oracle of Ezekiel 37:15-28, the question "Will you not show us what you mean by these?" (RSV) is not only tended to be asked by many who encounter it and are asking questions; **it is prayed to God.** People really want to entreat the Lord for answers!

There are many people who see the growth of today's Messianic community, particularly Jewish and non-Jewish Believers being brought together in common cause and unity, and do instinctively know by the presence of the Holy Spirit inside of them that more is going on. The basic question of "What does all this mean?" is being asked, but the possibility of the answer involving the two-stick oracle of Ezekiel 37:15-28, is more than frightening for a few.

What is really going on in today's Messianic movement? Is it just a movement designed to see a form of Jewish Christianity come forth, that will not really include anybody but Jewish Believers? The question of v. 18 has notably been answered in a variety of ways, some of which have, and some of which have not, been in alignment with the Lord's objectives. Jews, Christians, and Messianic Jews have all approached the subject, at times, with an agenda.

37:19 The Prophet Ezekiel might have been the one called to take two pieces of wood, and visually show his fellow exiles that the divided, scattered, and exiled Northern and Southern Kingdoms would reunite—**yet it is God Himself who performs the reunion.** Ezekiel is to just declare, "Thus says the Lord GOD, 'Behold, I will take the stick of Joseph, which is in the hand of Ephraim, and the tribes of Israel, his companions; and I will put them with it, with the stick of Judah, and make them one stick, and they will be one in My hand.'" God is the One who says, *ani loqeiach* (אֲנִי לֹקֵחַ), "I am going to take..." (NIV/NJPS).

This is a very special, Divine action that is to be performed. The Kingdom of Israel had been split since after Solomon's death (1 Kings 12), and attempts made by Southern Kingdom monarchs like Hezekiah or Josiah to reunite with people from the Northern Kingdom (2 Chronicles 30; 34:6, 9; 35:18), had really not succeeded. Duguid notes, "The solution to Israel's lengthy history of internal

---

[40] Block, 395.

division is not to be found in the appointment of a binational committee to develop a 'peace process' but in the divine act of reuniting his people."[41] And examining the prophecy, it will really take an act of God to reunite Judah, Israel/Ephraim, and companions from the nations into a single community chosen not only for Him, but for His end-time service to the world (Daniel 12:3; Titus 2:14; et. al.)

Those who give any significance in their theology or praxis to the two-stick prophecy *have to recognize* how the job of ultimately restoring Israel's Kingdom is to be left in the hands of the Lord. While people may recognize various things in motion, and rightly have a much bigger vision for the Messianic movement—than it just becoming another branch of Judaism—**the final orchestration of events is to occur in His perfect timing.** It is certainly not the job of any Messianic ministry or (pseudo-)denomination to try to declare the reunion of Judah and Ephraim from the halls of some conference, which would actually contribute to seeing people driven apart. Nor is it the job of any interfaith Jewish-Christian organization that might downplay the place of Yeshua in a person's salvation. Only God can orchestrate this reunion! He might use flawed people to do it, but the responsibility is ultimately His.

It is quite important to remember how King Rehoboam would not do what was right to serve the people, contrary to the advice of his counselors (1 Kings 12:7). He had an opportunistic agenda, and the division between the Northern and Southern Kingdoms was finalized. Today, it is not difficult to see how sectors like the Two-House sub-movement are utterly riddled with similar opportunists, who have not fully heeded the warnings given in the Historical Books of the Tanach. Thankfully, though, we can have confidence that **God will see His promises come to pass.**

20 **"The sticks on which you write will be in your hand before their eyes.** 21 **Say to them, 'Thus says the Lord GOD, "Behold, I will take the sons of Israel from among the nations where they have gone, and I will gather them from every side and bring them into their own land;** 22 **and I will make them one nation in the land, on the mountains of Israel; and one king will be king for all of them; and they will no longer be two nations and no longer be divided into two kingdoms.**

37:20 The *etzim* (עֵצִים) that the Prophet Ezekiel must bear, possibly being wooden writing tablets and not just sticks, has its strongest support from v. 20. Here, he is instructed, "the leaves on which you write are there in your hand for all to see" (REB). The message of Israel's reunification, or even the complete prophecy itself, is to be laid before the eyes of the people. Thus, the people can be held accountable for what they do with the prophecy, most especially in terms of whether they mock it, disregard it, or ignore it—all of which has happened in various parts of the Messianic community today.

---

[41] Duguid, 436.

37:21 The work of the Lord in bringing Israel together does not only involve a reunification of the people of Judah and Israel/Ephraim, but also bringing them home to the Promised Land. The Prophet Ezekiel declares, "Thus said the Lord HASHEM/ELOHIM: Behold I am taking the Children of Israel from among the nations to which they have gone; I will gather them from all around and I will bring them to their soil" (ATS). Ezekiel has previously alluded to a theme of a Second Exodus (34:13; 36:12, 24; 37:12), some of it even with a harsh tone (20:33-44). We should also be reminded of the Prophet Jeremiah's previous oracle,

"In those days the house of Judah will walk with the house of Israel, and they will come together from the land of the north to the land that I gave your fathers as an inheritance" (Jeremiah 3:18).

It is important to remember that Ezekiel's prophecy was delivered almost five centuries *after* the split of Israel into the Northern and Southern Kingdoms, meaning that the return of the people was going to fix a significant breach present in God's chosen nation. Yet the *b'nei Yisrael* (בְּנֵי יִשְׂרָאֵל) here is a reference to all of Israel, and not just those of the exiled Northern Kingdom. The Jewish exiles in Babylon were just as exiled as those of the Northern Kingdom before it, and they would take this as a promise for some kind of a return home, regardless of what would happen with those of Israel/Ephraim.

Yet from the vantage point of the Jewish exiles in Babylon, the most important fact that is often overlooked is that God *would even bother* to gather those of the exiled Northern Kingdom. In Block's words, "Ezekiel's Judean audience learns that the scope of the anticipated restoration extends far beyond their own exilic situation in Babylon; Yahweh will regather the descendants of Israel from all around (*missābîb* [מִסָּבִיב])."[42] Peter C. Craigie also observes how the Jewish exiles in Babylon "had ceased to wonder whether or not there was a future for their relatives in the northern kingdom, which had been defeated in war in 722 B.C. But where human memory ceases, often through selfish lack of concern for others, the divine memory is still at work."[43]

One challenge, not to be overlooked in contemplating God's promise to gather the Israelites, is that He says He will bring them *mi'bbein ha'goyim asher halku-sham* (מִבֵּין הַגּוֹיִם אֲשֶׁר הָלְכוּ-שָׁם), "from among the nations where they have gone" or "from among the nations they have gone to" (NJPS). Is this speaking of where Israel had been scattered during the time of Ezekiel, in which case a futuristic regathering of people will pretty much be limited to extent of the sphere of influence of the Assyrian and Babylonian Empires (and later the Persian Empire)? Or, is it speaking of the past tense time—in the future—when this prophecy will be accomplished, subsequent to the eschaton? While the Jewish exiles in Babylon probably thought that God had completely written off the Northern Kingdom, how extensive is the regathering of these people from the nations?

---

[42] Block, 411.
[43] Peter C. Craigie, *Daily Study Bible Series: Ezekiel* (Philadelphia: Westminster Press, 1983), 264.

Much of this is determinant on not just the Jewish exile to Babylon, or the dispersion of the Jewish people following the destruction of the Temple in 70 C.E. Much of it is determinant on how broad the Northern Kingdom Israelites were, or would be, scattered. This is where many people stop reading the prophecy, in no small part due to the abuses that have ensued when the subject of the "Lost Tribes" comes up,[44] and is only compounded by a misdiagnosis of what is being addressed. A regathering of all Israel, including a scattered group from the Northern Kingdom out there in the world, is only necessary for the fulfillment of prophecy and the participation of a certain player in prophecy. The involvement of this "Ephraim" is only important because it is one of the three players who participate in Israel's restoration, along with Judah and the many associated companions from the nations. No physical ancestry from the exiled and relatively lost Northern Kingdom of Israel/Ephraim, is at all a guarantee of eternal salvation.

What happened in the punishment and scattering of Israel? The *Dictionary of Judaism in the Biblical Period* aptly summarizes, "The prophets threatened the nation with the loss of the land if they were unfaithful to the covenant; after several centuries their words came true, when Assyria exiled many residents of the northern kingdom in 722 B.C.E. and the Babylonians deported thousands from the southern kingdom in 587 and 586 B.C.E...Though not all residents left the land, the return to the land of a sizeable number of Jewish people from Babylon and points east began in 538 B.C.E. and continued in different waves for some time thereafter,"[45] suggesting that this was in fulfillment of Jeremiah 32. Any careful interpreter of the two-stick prophecy is stuck having to wonder about the scattered Northern Kingdom of Israel/Ephraim, and really weigh how serious this message might be, beyond the hope of an ancient Jewish return to the Land of Israel from Babylon.

Allen is one who poignantly indicates, "We know comparatively little about the history of the exiled northerners, but there is no evidence of any return. There was Jewish awareness of northern tribes in Assyria: the apocryphal book of Tobit has such a setting. In Judah's early post-exilic period it is clear that barriers were erected from the southern side, and time seems to have done nothing to demolish them."[46] The Book of Tobit is a very interesting case study to be aware of, because if we consider it to have any degree of accurate history, it does indicate that there were Northern Kingdom exiles in Assyria, who not only were not assimilated into the dominant culture, but maintained a degree of loyalty to the God of Israel.

Tobit was of the tribe of Naphtali, exiled to Assyria, but who lamented how his people were separated from the House of David and the Temple worship in Jerusalem (Tobit 1:3-4). While in Assyrian exile, he instructs his son not to marry a

---

[44] For an assortment of many of these abuses, which today's Two-House sub-movement has widely done a very poor job at staying away from, consult the relevant sections of Tudor Parfitt, *The Lost Tribes of Israel: The History of a Myth* (London: Phoenix, 2002) and Zvi Ben-Dor Benite, *The Ten Lost Tribes: A World History* (New York: Oxford University Press, 2009).

[45] "Israel, Land of," in *Dictionary of Judaism in the Biblical Period*, pp 322-323.

[46] Allen, 195.

foreign woman, but instead marry from his own people, like the Patriarchs before them (Tobit 4:12). It is possible that Tobit's family remained faithful to the God of Israel for multiple generations, and after Babylon conquered Assyria, and then after Persia conquered Babylon, his descendants joined with the Jewish returnees in the Land of Israel, becoming a part of the Jewish community.

Tobit appears to be an exception, though, rather than the rule. Various Northern Kingdom Israelites here and there, being integrated into the Southern Kingdom—either before or after the exile—is not the issue of Ezekiel's prophecy. **The issue of Ezekiel's prophecy is the corporate restoration of Israel.** Block observes,

"From a human perspective, Ezekiel's vision of remnants of the original twelve-tribe nation streaming back to their hereditary homeland seems impossible. The northern population had been dispersed in upper Mesopotamia by an entirely different regime, the Assyrians, one and one-half centuries earlier; further Assyrian imperial policy deliberately aimed to assimilate them into the population."[47]

Block notes some references present in 2 Kings to be aware of, detailing the scattering of the Northern Kingdom Israelites:

- "In the ninth year of Hoshea, the king of Assyria captured Samaria and carried Israel away into exile to Assyria, and settled them in Halah and Habor, *on* the river of Gozan, and in the cities of the Medes" (2 Kings 17:6).
- "Then the king of Assyria carried Israel away into exile to Assyria, and put them in Halah and on the Habor, the river of Gozan, and in the cities of the Medes" (2 Kings 18:11).

These two verses indicate a dispersion of people into Mesopotamia. Assimilation into the Assyrian Empire was imposed, either through some kind of forced intermarriage, forced religious and cultural changes, or simply displacing the people from their homeland so far away that future generations would largely forget who they were. Block goes on to say, though, "the presence of distinctly Israelite names in documents from their exilic settlements generations after the collapse of Samaria suggest that many retained a distinctive ethnic self-consciousness."[48] It is possible that from this group of people, families like that of Tobit eventually integrated themselves into Judaism. But Ezekiel's prophecy of reunification does not speak to individual groups like these—**it speaks to the corporate division of Israel that needs to be repaired.** Block further indicates, "religious and political jealousies were too deeply entrenched to contemplate

---

[47] Block, pp 411-412.

[48] Ibid., 412.

For a further discussion, consult B.E. Kelle and B.A. Strawn, "History of Israel 5: Assyrian Period," in *Dictionary of the Old Testament Historical Books*, pp 468-469.

Kelle and Strawn note how "The presence of Israelite exiles in Mesopotamia after 720 BCE is attested also by the appearance of West Semitic personal names in Assyrian texts, but the occasional references suggests that Israelite ethnic and national identity was lost within a few generations" (Ibid., 469).

rapprochement between the northern Israelite exiles and their southern Judean counterparts."[49]

Block concludes that only Divine intervention, likened unto a heart transplant (36:27-28) or the dead bones coming back to life (37:1-14), would be sufficient to enact such a miracle. In his words, "ethnic reunion alone was insufficient to restore the national integrity of Israel."[50] While various families and groups from the scattered Northern Kingdom, remaining loyal to the God of Israel, were likely to have integrated themselves into Judaism, perhaps like the First Century Anna from the tribe of Asher (Luke 2:36), this does not constitute the kind of reunion foreseen by Ezekiel. Aside from those Northern Kingdom Israelites who later became part of the Jewish community, what is to be made of the summarizing remark of 2 Kings 17:23? It says,

"[T]he LORD removed Israel from His sight, as He spoke through all His servants the prophets. So Israel was carried away into exile from their own land to Assyria until this day" (cf. 1 Chronicles 5:26).

The authors or editors of 1&2 Kings say that the people of the Northern Kingdom were exiled to Assyria *ad ha'yom ha'zeh* (עַד הַיּוֹם הַזֶּה), extrapolated by the NIV as, "and they are still there." The real challenge to understanding this remark is that while Samuel-Kings is undoubtedly a product of the historians of the Southern Kingdom, when did the text reach its final form? Is this a pre-exilic remark made, or a post-exilic remark?[51] Arguments can probably be made from both sides, but if the latter is the case, it would indicate that there were exiled Northern Kingdom Israelites still in the land of Assyria, and associated territories, even if there had been a significant return of exiled Southern Kingdom Israelites back to the environs of Jerusalem in the Persian era.

The view that the Northern Kingdom was still corporately in exile is reflected in the writings of the First Century C.E. Jewish historian Josephus. Reflecting on his time, he makes the observation that "the ten tribes are beyond Euphrates till now, and are an immense multitude, and not to be estimated by numbers" (*Antiquities of the Jews* 11.133).[52] He does not at all intend to fill in any specific details, but just asserts that people from the scattered Northern Kingdom were out there in the world. "God only knows who and where they are..." seems to be the thought.

A largely pessimistic thought on what we encounter in v. 21 is offered by Charles L. Feinberg, when he says, "The prophets all recognized the northern tribes as still in existence and knew of no such error as 'lost' tribes (cf. Isa. 43:5-7, 'every one'; 49:5-6; Jer. 3:12-15)."[53] These remarks are not so much focused on the statement "I will take the sons of Israel from among the nations where they have gone," however extensive this may be at the moment of restoration in the end-

---

[49] Block, 412.

[50] Ibid.

[51] For further consideration, consult the author's entry for the Books of Kings in *A Survey of the Tanach for the Practical Messianic*.

[52] *The Works of Josephus: Complete and Unabridged*, 294.

[53] Charles L. Feinberg, *The Prophecy of Ezekiel: The Glory of The Lord* (Chicago: Moody Press, 1969), 215.

times, but instead are an overreaction to the mid-Twentieth Century abuses with British-Israelism.[54] The conservative scholastic position in Old Testament scholarship, on the exiled Northern Kingdom, has always been concurrent with the Assyrian practice of displaced persons being forced to assimilate,[55] so that they would not rebel against the regime. The traditional places where the descendants of the deported exiles of the Northern Kingdom have always been sought out, have been in Southeast Asia, South Asia, the Middle East, Central Africa, and the Eastern Mediterranean basin—*not* Northwestern Europe and the British Isles. In terms of prophetic fulfillment, God scattered Israel, and thus it is God's responsibility to gather the people back (cf. Jeremiah 31:10).

I do not believe it would be entirely appropriate for us to consider the end-time gathering together of Israel to only be limited to the extent of the modern Middle East. It will take place from however extended the descendants from both the Northern *and* Southern Kingdoms have gone out, when the Lord sovereignly brings them back together and restores the broken Kingdom of Israel. I look to the general sphere of influence of the old Assyrian, Babylonian, and Persian Empires, for those geographic areas where the exiles of the Northern Kingdom of Israel/Ephraim would have migrated and/or been assimilated. As Lamar Eugene Cooper says, "God will personally find Israel and gather the people from among the nations."[56] Deuteronomy 30:1-4 is commonly applied to the Jewish people returning to the Promised Land, yet in consideration of other prophecies, it also concerns the descendants of the exiled Northern Kingdom as well:

"So it shall be when all of these things have come upon you, the blessing and the curse which I have set before you, and you call *them* to mind in all nations where the LORD your God has banished you, and you return to the LORD your God and obey Him with all your heart and soul according to all that I command you today, you and your sons, then the LORD your God will restore you from captivity, and have compassion on you, and will gather you again from all the peoples where the LORD your God has scattered you. If your outcasts are at the ends of the earth, from there the LORD your God will gather you, and from there He will bring you back."

Here, Moses communicates that the exiles of Israel will actually return to their home country b'qetzeih ha'shamayim (בִּקְצֵה הַשָּׁמָיִם), from "the uttermost parts of heaven" (ESV), which would be a much further radius than the exiles being scattered to what is today the modern Middle East. It implies something that is a little more global in scope. It surely involves the Jewish people returning to the Promised Land, but it also involves more. The Jewish people have certainly been dispersed since the fall of the Second Temple in 70 C.E. If we consider the sphere of influence of the Ancient Assyrian, Babylonian, and Persian Empires in view for the areas where exiled Israel/Ephraim has gone—presumed descendants of those

---

[54] Ibid. speaks earlier of "the folly of the Anglo-Israel delusion."
[55] Cf. C.F. Pfeiffer, "Israel, History of the People of," in *ISBE*, 2:917.
[56] Lamar Eugene Cooper, *New American Commentary: Ezekiel* (Nashville: Broadman & Holman, 1994), 327.

people have certainly moved around since the European powers decolonized after the Second World War, pulling out of Southeast Asia, the Indian sub-continent, the Middle East, and Africa.

(This would mean, for example, that various people of Indian or Pakistani nationality living in the United Kingdom, have a much better chance at being a descendant of the Northern Kingdom of Israel/Ephraim, than a native Briton [English, Scottish, Irish, or Welsh] has. A native British person, would actually have a much better chance at having a Jewish ancestor or two, who assimilated into Christianity of the Middle Ages.)

Taylor recognizes how "The explanation given in 21-28 is futuristic," but he is also right to describe, "The answer of the New Testament to this future hope of Israel is that it has come about, but has not been fulfilled. The golden age has dawned in the coming of Jesus the Messiah; fulfillment has begun, but it has not yet been completed."[57] It is correct that on some level, the unity that God wanted to see restored to a divided Judah and Israel/Ephraim, can be experienced among His people today who are filled with His Spirit and bound together in the gospel. But this is not the corporate, futuristic restoration of the Kingdom to Israel. We might experience some of the elements what this prophecy, and many others, depict in our individual lives—**but more is yet to come.**

Reflecting a more liberal perspective of Israel being brought together, Joseph Blenkinsopp does note, "Perhaps Ezekiel had in mind the survivors of the mixed population to the north of whom we hear from time to time (e.g., Jer. 41:4-8)." This would be an indication that they will be gathered together some time in the future. But for him, given the tenor of the whole prophecy, Blenkinsopp concludes, "Ezekiel is acting out and proclaiming an eschatological goal the fulfillment of which, would be brought about by God."[58] Blenkinsopp leaves any kind of restoration of Israel's Kingdom as something that only concerns God, and not any of us today, following a much more allegorized view of the prophecy (quoted further).

For those of us who read prophecy through a much more literal lens, the scope of Israel—either of Judah or scattered Israel/Ephraim—being brought together, is wider in extent than those who were initially exiled to the vicinity of the Ancient Near East. *It is surely only by the sovereign hand of God that they are brought together.* We might know where there are large Jewish communities outside of the Land of Israel, but only He may know where the various pockets of Israel/Ephraim are ultimately scattered. It would go too far to think that such lines are in every corner and country on Planet Earth. It does not go too far to think that it involves groups of people adjacent to where the exiles of the Northern Kingdom were originally scattered, whose main leaders or elders have preserved some kind of oral tradition tracing their descent back to the Assyrian exile.

---

[57] Taylor, pp 239-240.

[58] Joseph Blenkinsopp, *Interpretation, A Bible Commentary for Teaching and Preaching: Ezekiel* (Louisville, KY: John Knox Press, 1990), 176.

Furthermore, as the restoration of Israel is initiated by God and proceeds ahead, companions from the nations at large will hear of this and will naturally join—fully concurrent with God's mission to see the light of truth reach the entire world (Isaiah 42:6; 60:3)—and they will most probably make up *the majority* of those who are involved. The worldwide effects of the two-stick prophecy, beyond just Judah and Ephraim, are too often downplayed by today's popular Two-House advocates (v. 28). Likewise, at least experiencing the motif of unity depicted, by the two-stick prophecy in the workings of the Body of Messiah, is too widely overlooked.

37:22 What the Prophet Ezekiel actually declares is a time of not only restoration of the Twelve Tribes to the Promised Land, but a political reunification that is far different from the period of the Divided Kingdom. He says, "I will make them a single nation in the land, on the hills of Israel, and one king shall be king of them all. Never again shall they be two nations, and never again shall they be divided into two kingdoms" (NJPS). A single king will rule over this Israel. Did this ever happen in ancient times when the Jewish exiles returned from Babylon, and a few stragglers from the Northern Kingdom, who had remained loyal to the Lord, joined them? Or is this really a futuristic oracle describing a reunited Israel ruled by the Messiah?

23 **"They will no longer defile themselves with their idols, or with their detestable things, or with any of their transgressions; but I will deliver them from all their dwelling places in which they have sinned, and will cleanse them. And they will be My people, and I will be their God.**

37:23 A return of Judah and Israel/Ephraim to the Promised Land, and a healing of the division between the Southern and Northern Kingdoms, is important. **But it is not as important as Israel's corporate relationship with God being fully restored.** The long-term affects of two exiles, not only one exile, have to be reversed. And, punishment was issued upon the people of the Northern and Southern Kingdoms not only for sin and idolatry committed in the Land of Israel. When the grand return and restoration occurs, Ezekiel declares,

"[N]or shall they defile themselves any more with their idols, nor with their detestable things, nor with any of their transgressions: but I will save them in all their dwelling places, where they have sinned, and will cleanse them: so shall they be my people and I will be their God" (Jerusalem Bible-Koren).

Take notice of how the people committed sin against God even in their exiles—from where He must deliver them home—*m'kol moshvotei'hem asher chatu* (מִכֹּל מוֹשְׁבֹתֵיהֶם אֲשֶׁר חָטְאוּ): "from all their dwelling places in which they had sinned" (ATS).[59] Deliverance for the sins Israel committed in their places of exile

---

[59] The LXX has instead *apo pasōn tōn anomiōn autōn hōn hēmartosan* (ἀπὸ πασῶν τῶν ἀνομιῶν αὐτῶν ὧν ἡμάρτοσαν), which the NRSV tries to conform with, "from all the apostasies into which they have fallen."

(Deuteronomy 28:64-65) will be offered. Corporate redemption from these previous sins, which caused the exile into the nations and has been compounded, will end.

Do remember and **never forget** that individuals may be redeemed from all their sins and possess eternal life *in Messiah Yeshua* long before the complete restoration of Israel culminates. Yet the community of Israel as a whole—composed of Judah, Israel/Ephraim, and many companions—has to acknowledge its sin, confess, and be corporately restored to God and to His purpose. Thankfully, God is able to hear such cries for mercy, and He does offer forgiveness (cf. Romans 5:6-9)!

While there has been a great deal of discussion about our Heavenly Father restoring Judah and Ephraim in the Two-House sub-movement and its popular conference events—how much of this discussion has really taken into consideration a serious reflection on Israel's corporate sins? These sins are not necessarily having Christmas trees in ignorance, going to church on Sunday instead of remembering *Shabbat*, nor are they eating pork thinking that it is food—as has been too commonly asserted. These sins are detailed in the historical record of the Tanach in 2 Kings, and include not only idolatrous worship and gross sexual immorality, **but child sacrifice** to Canaanite deities like Molech. The historical record of the different Northern Kingdom dynasties, in particular, should not go overlooked.

If any non-Jewish Messianic Believer really wants to claim "Ephraim" as his or her heritage, *this sin heritage has to be claimed as well*, and a corporate repentance before the Creator God must follow. It is not at all surprising why this is not a subject of interest at many of the popular Two-House conference gatherings, a likely indicator that it will be a good long while before Israel will be fully restored, among other reasons. And, the continuation of such sins, perhaps up even into the more modern period, are far more consistent with the religious and cultural groups of the East—as the exiles of the Northern Kingdom were progressively spread eastward—than they are with the more relative Judeo-Christian West.

24 **"My servant David will be king over them, and they will all have one shepherd; and they will walk in My ordinances and keep My statutes and observe them. 25 They will live on the land that I gave to Jacob My servant, in which your fathers lived; and they will live on it, they, and their sons and their sons' sons, forever; and David My servant will be their prince forever. 26 I will make a covenant of peace with them; it will be an everlasting covenant with them. And I will place them and multiply them, and will set My sanctuary in their midst forever.**

37:24 As Israel is brought together, and experiences a corporate ceasing from the sins that caused the exile of both the Southern *and* Northern Kingdoms, a special king, *melek* (מֶלֶךְ), will come forth to rule. It is decreed, "My servant David will be king over them." We can certainly see a reiteration here of the Davidic Covenant (2 Samuel 23:5), as well as the promises detailed in Isaiah 11. Many Christian interpreters, and I believe quite rightly, have proposed that "David" is a reference to Yeshua the Messiah. Ralph H. Alexander summarizes,

"The Messiah, David's greater Son, would be the only King, Shepherd, and Prince and Israel would ever have in accord with the Davidic covenant (vv. 22b, 24a, 25b; cf. 34:10b-31; 2 Sam 7:13, 16). This united people of God would be cleansed from their former idolatry and transgressions through the complete forgiveness provided by the Messiah's death and the ministry of the Spirit promised in the new covenant (v. 23a; 36:16-32; Jer 31:31-34)."[60]

The result of being ruled by the Messiah, as Davidic King, will be one of total obedience—reversing the state of the disobedience and idolatry: "They will follow my laws and be careful to keep my decrees" (NIV). This is an obvious reiteration of the previous word Ezekiel delivered about the work of God's Spirit (36:27), but also of Jeremiah's oracle about God writing His Torah onto the hearts of Judah and Israel (Jeremiah 31:31-34). As this word reaches its complete fulfillment, an obedience to God's Torah will lead a regathered Judah and Israel/Ephraim to dwell once again in the Promised Land—something that will not be stopped as it is the will of God. Allen indicates,

"The people's obedience would make possible continued occupation of the promised land envisaged in 28:25-26 and 36:28. The disobedience that had been the cause of the exile would haunt them no longer."[61]

What is this obedience to the Torah primarily related to? A *complete overturning* of the idolatry and paganism that had permeated both the Northern and Southern Kingdoms (v. 23). This involves a corporate acknowledgment of guilt and repentance, for abominable practices like child sacrifice committed by Ancient Israel, going well beyond just having various high places or idolatrous shrines alongside worship of HaShem. Consequently, if anyone is really serious about

---

[60] Ralph H. Alexander, "Ezekiel," in *EXP*, 6:927.
[61] Allen, 194.

Israel being restored, not only will a conscious recognition of these sins need to be accomplished (preceded by an examination of the record of 2 Kings)—but also a **corporate and public confession of them.**[62] As to my knowledge, none of the popular Two-House advocates one is likely to have encountered, have ever really noted the importance of this for Israel's restoration.[63]

37:25 In order to give the Jewish exiles a real sense of hope for a grand restoration of Israel in the future, Ezekiel's word includes an appeal made to the distant past: "they shall remain in the land which I gave to My servant Jacob and in which your fathers dwelt; they and their children and their children's children shall dwell there forever, with My servant David as their prince for all time" (NJPS). Jacob, as we know, was the father of all of Israel's twelve tribes. The result of the two-stick prophecy being fulfilled, and those of Judah and Israel/Ephraim brought together, is that David as their leader will rule over them in the Promised Land *l'olam* (לְעוֹלָם).[64] This indicates a high degree of permanency—not at all experienced after the Jewish return from Babylonian exile. This is a Messianic rule over Israel, and thusly the world as a whole, that can only be trumped by the inauguration of the Eternal State after the Millennium, and the ushering in of the New Creation.

Is there any particular reason why in v. 24 this leader is referred to as a *melek*, but in v. 25 is referred to as a *nasi* (נָשִׂיא) or prince? Is there a contradiction with the assertion in v. 22, *u'melek echad yih'yeh l'kulam l'melek* (וּמֶלֶךְ אֶחָד יִהְיֶה לְכֻלָּם לְמֶלֶךְ), "and one king will be king for all of them"? I do not believe that there are contradictions, as the different roles of the Davidic ruler—also including that of shepherd (Heb. verb *ra'ah*, רָעָה)—are being summarized. Fisch concludes, "While *king* signifies a political ruler, *shepherd* denotes a spiritual leader. The Messiah will combine both offices."[65] Another Jewish commentator, A. Cohen, remarks, "The Messiah will be called David, because he will be descended from him; or perhaps, it hints at the resurrection."[66]

Various Jewish interpreters of the two-stick prophecy do recognize that it is yet to be fulfilled, even though the Davidic King to which they are looking might not be Yeshua the Messiah, but perhaps a resurrected King David. Interestingly enough, even John F. Walvoord, a dispensational pre-tribulationist, concurs with the Jewish view that a resurrected King David will reign over Israel in the Millennium:

---

[62] Please note that as heinous a sin as abortion is today, this kind of public confession is for past sins that are contained in the Biblical record.

[63] On the contrary, many Two-House advocates and teachers do not even really know what to do with *Yom Kippur* or the Day of Atonement. This should be a time for Messianic congregations to come together and corporately confess sins, but it should also be a time of serious intercession for the lost and unsaved of Planet Earth—most especially our Jewish brethren who do not know Yeshua.

For further consideration, consult the relevant sections of the *Messianic Fall Holiday Helper* by TNN Press.

[64] Cf. Darr, in *NIB*, 6:1510.

[65] Fisch, 251.

[66] A. Cohen, *Soncino Chumash* (Brooklyn: Soncino Press, 1983), 294.

"[T]he clear statement is that David, who is now dead and whose body is in his tomb in Jerusalem (Acts 2:29), will be resurrected. This will occur at the Second Coming (Dan. 12:1-3), indicating plainly that the restoration of Israel will be subsequent to, not before, the Second Coming...The promise that David would be her prince forever must be interpreted as being fulfilled in the 1,000-year reign."[67]

Walvoord's dispensational bias does come through, which requires him to view a resurrected King David as ruling over Israel, with the Messiah Himself reigning over the whole Earth and the Church having returned from Heaven after the seven-year Tribulation. The valid point that is made, though, is that Walvoord recognizes how Israel's restoration **is not yet completed.** Walvoord is entirely right to chastise how "some have attempted to take this prophecy in less than its literal meaning."[68]

David avdi (דָּוִד עַבְדִּי), "My servant David," ruling over Israel "forever," can be taken as a clear implication of this being a supernatural ruler,[69] and not necessarily a resurrected King David, but Messiah the Prince of Peace (i.e, Isaiah 9:6). And this King Messiah, while certainly being the Leader of a restored Judah and Israel/Ephraim, is King of the whole world.

Having noted that companions from the nations are involved in the restoration process, when the Land of Israel is divided in the Millennium, it is notable that various aliens are included and they are welcomed into the community of Israel on an equal footing with the native born:

"'So you shall divide this land among yourselves according to the tribes of Israel. You shall divide it by lot for an inheritance among yourselves and among the aliens who stay in your midst, who bring forth sons in your midst. And they shall be to you as the native-born among the sons of Israel; they shall be allotted an inheritance with you among the tribes of Israel. And in the tribe with which the alien stays, there you shall give *him* his inheritance,' declares the Lord GOD" (Ezekiel 47:21-23).

This group is considered by me, at least, to be a very small, specialized group of non-Israelites—who have no physical descent from Abraham, Isaac, and Jacob— yet who during the Millennial reign of Yeshua the Messiah are, for various unique reasons, likely as a reward given to them by the Lord, permitted permanent residence in the Land of Israel.

37:26 The Prophet Ezekiel's declarations about Judah, Israel, and various companions coming together as one people, while surely important, is not as important as the spiritual effects of what this involves. The Lord promises, "I will seal a covenant of peace with them; it will be an eternal covenant with them; and I will emplace them and increase them, and I will place My Sanctuary among them forever" (ATS). The Lord will establish a *b'rit shalom b'rit olam* (שָׁלוֹם בְּרִית עוֹלָם בְּרִית), an eternal peace covenant, with His corporate people as the eschaton

---

[67] Walvoord, *Every Prophecy of the Bible*, 187.
[68] Ibid.
[69] Cf. Taylor, 240.

culminates. This eternal peace covenant signals a complete end of hostilities between God and Israel that were created by the sin committed by the Northern and Southern Kingdoms, requiring the exile.

We can certainly see some echoes of God's covenant of peace with Phinehas (Numbers 25:10-13), and how Isaiah declared "My lovingkindness will not be removed from you, and My covenant of peace will not be shaken" (Isaiah 54:10). Ezekiel himself had previously decreed, "I will not let you hear insults from the nations anymore, nor will you bear disgrace from the peoples any longer, nor will you cause your nation to stumble any longer" (36:15). This is to be contrasted with the departure of God's glory seen in Ezekiel chs. 9-11.

Because of the sacrifice of Yeshua, and Believers partaking of salvation and eternal life, we already experience the reality of an eternal covenant of peace in our individual lives. By repenting of our sins and partaking of salvation, each one of us has (or should have!) made our peace with God. What Ezekiel declares is a corporate covenant with peace with a reunited Israel. It also involves God's sanctuary or *miqdash* (מִקְדָּשׁ) being present in the midst of the Earth, discussed further in the Temple visions of Ezekiel chs. 40-48, and not necessarily just His presence in our individual selves. While this message speaks very readily to concepts of realized eschatology—future realities of the age to come partaken of in the present evil age—the eternal covenant of peace is something yet to be fully enacted. Fisch correctly concludes, "This assurance indicates that the prophecy of the restoration and reunion of the Kingdoms relates to the Messianic era."[70]

27 **"My dwelling place also will be with them; and I will be their God, and they will be My people. 28 And the nations will know that I am the LORD who sanctifies Israel, when My sanctuary is in their midst forever."'**

37:27 Israel being restored not only as an exiled and scattered people, and not only being forgiven of sins, but also with God's presence visibly among them, **is a theme that cannot be overlooked.** All of this speaks to the *futuristic aspects* of the two-stick prophecy. When Judah and Israel/Ephraim are finally brought together, and returned back to the Promised Land, it is decreed "My dwelling place also will be with them; and I will be their God, and they will be My people." The clause *v'hayah mishkani alei'hem* (וְהָיָה מִשְׁכָּנִי עֲלֵיהֶם) is actually rendered by the NJPS with "My Presence shall rest over them." *Mishkan* (מִשְׁכָּן), however, would most especially concern God's "tabernacle" (*CHALOT*; Exodus 25:9).[71] A full, corporate restoration of Israel is in view—where they are specifically designated as "My people."

In order to be God's people, one has to be cleansed from sin, a theme seen throughout Ezekiel (11:20; 14:11; 36:28). Being a member of God's people also

---

[70] Fisch, 252.
[71] *CHALOT*, 219.

requires a great deal of responsibility, *beyond just obedience* to His Instruction. J.H. Hertz points out, "God's Divine Presence will be clearly among them when they are true to their vocation as a Holy People. And thus too will Israel be the means of revealing God to the nations."[72] Keep in mind that these are the remarks of an early Twentieth Century, Orthodox Jewish academic, and not the words of a Twenty-First Century evangelical Christian missiologist. Yet, they are absolutely true **because a cleansed and restored people of God will accomplish His mission of testifying to the world of His goodness.** For us as Believers, this is only intensified as God's restored people must be able to declare forth the message of the Davidic Messiah, our Savior Yeshua!

37:28 The effects of the restoration of Israel, or perhaps even an in-process restoration of Israel, are surely to be worldwide. Ezekiel ends this oracle with the promise, "the nations will know that I the LORD make Israel holy, when my sanctuary is among them forever" (NIV). This is a reiteration of the Torah's promise of how the nations at large will know how God sanctifies Israel, seeing His sanctuary in their midst (cf. Leviticus 26:4-13).

The end-time restoration of Israel will include the reconstruction of His sanctuary. Dyer comments, "This literal structure will serve as a visual object lesson to Israel and **the nations** of God's presence in the midst of His people."[73] He may consider this to be the Third Temple, to be desecrated by the antimessiah/antichrist (Daniel 9:27; 2 Thessalonians 2:4), whereas I am more inclined (at least right now) to think of this as the Ezekiel 40-48 Millennial Temple. *Perhaps these are just finer points that we have to leave open-ended.* Block reminds us of the overall importance of this word, asserting, "Ezekiel's statement expresses Yahweh's definitive rejection of any threat ever to abandon his people again, as he had in 586 B.C., and as was so graphically portrayed in the temple vision of chs. 8-11."[74]

As the two-stick prophecy, decreeing the reunification and restoration of Judah and Israel/Ephraim, comes to a close, what would this have meant to the Jewish exiles of Babylon? If they had faith in the Lord, it would have given them the confidence to know that the wrongs both the Northern and Southern Kingdoms had committed would be righted. Israel would be brought back into its fullness, and recognizing God's hand in this restoration (v. 21), it would take place sometime in the future. **This restoration would be a significant Divine act, with eternal effects.** We should be able to easily agree with Jewish commentator Michael Fishbane,

"[This text] focuses on settlement in the Land, and the new sanctuary. The elements of ingathering, monarchy, repurification, and Temple building constitute the main configuration of messianic hope for ancient Israel and for subsequent Jewish generations....[A] recurrent theme is 'permanence,' expressed as a

---

[72] Hertz, *Pentateuch & Haftorahs*, 179.
[73] Dyer, in *BKCOT*, 1299.
[74] Block, 421.

permanent change from the past and as a vision of a permanent future. The idioms used are *lo od* [לֹא עוֹד] (never again, vv. 22,23) and *l'olam* [לְעוֹלָם] (forever, vv.25,26,28)."[75]

Have the Two Sticks Been Reunited?
A Review of Opinions

Most of today's Messianic Believers read prophecies of the Tanach or Old Testament through a literal lens, especially prophetic words applying to Israel. While we may be able to learn principles about God's goodness toward individuals, and even be informed about the dynamics of the salvation we possess in Messiah Yeshua, nevertheless a word like Ezekiel 37:15-28 should be read as a futuristic prophecy that is yet to be fulfilled. Looking at the two-stick prophecy as a future prophetic oracle, what is to take place when it is completed?

1. We see this united Israel with a single King reigning over it (v. 22).
2. We see this restored Israel cleansed of its corporate sins and defilements (v. 23).
3. We see the inauguration of a new Davidic King, the Messiah, where obedience and God's blessings can flourish (vs. 24-25).
4. We see an eternal covenant of peace enacted (v. 26).

All of the promises of the two-stick prophecy of Ezekiel 37:15-28 envision a complete reversal of what is depicted in Ezekiel chs. 8-11, and the bringing in of what is summarized by Ezekiel 20:40: "'For on My holy mountain, on the high mountain of Israel,' declares the Lord GOD, 'there the whole house of Israel, all of them,[76] will serve Me in the land; there I will accept them and there I will seek your contributions and the choicest of your gifts, with all your holy things.'"

The main issue we need to be considering is whether the two-stick prophecy was, in fact, really fulfilled in ancient times. When the exiles returned from Babylon, and "Ezra rose and made the leading priests, the Levites and all Israel, take oath" (Ezra 10:5), who are we to understand *kol-Yisrael* (כָּל־יִשְׂרָאֵל) to be? Were the expectations seen in Ezekiel's two-stick oracle fully completed in the Sixth Century B.C.E., with the Second Temple constructed? Or, is "all Israel" simply a recognition of how the Jewish returnees certainly constituted the remaining people of Israel, those who were responsible for the rebuilding of the nation? From this perspective, "all Israel" would simply be *all Israel present*, or perhaps even, *all Israel that had survived and returned*.

(We probably need to take a cue here from how 1 Kings 12:20 speaks of "all Israel," and it is not "all Israel" in the sense of *both* the Northern and Southern Kingdoms: "It came about when all Israel heard that Jeroboam had returned, that they sent and called him to the assembly and made him king over all Israel. None but the tribe of Judah followed the house of David." In this verse "all Israel" referred to is the Northern Kingdom of Israel/Ephraim. In a similar manner, a verse

---

[75] Fishbane, "Haftarah for Va-Yiggash," in *Etz Hayim*, 290.
[76] Heb. *kol-Beit Yisrael kulloh* (כָּל־בֵּית יִשְׂרָאֵל כֻּלֹּה).

like Ezra 10:5 does not refer to "all Israel" reunited, but only those of the Southern Kingdom who had returned. Context should always determine who is being talked about, when "all Israel" is used.)

It is not easy to consider the two-stick prophecy of Ezekiel 37:15-28 sometimes, because of all the "Who is an 'Ephraimite'?" rhetoric out there in the various Two-House pseudo-denominations and their popular/populist conference events. Rather than trying to speculate on whether today's Messianic non-Jews really are some sort of scattered Israelites, which populist voices tend to push—what we need to do instead is look at the expectations the Prophet Ezekiel spoke directly from the Lord. *We have to let the text guide us.* Israel's regathering and restoration is a sovereign act of God, and as such it is His job to sort out the finer details of this prophecy. **It is our job to recognize whether this prophetic oracle is fulfilled or not.**

When one weighs into the equation the different scope of interpretations available for Ezekiel 37:15-28, the options are actually not as simple as it being fulfilled in past history *versus* to be fulfilled in the future. There are actually four primary interpretations we encounter, to be considered:

1. This is a prophecy of Israel's restoration, either accomplished in the past or to be accomplished in the future.
2. This is an allegorical depiction of the unity required in today's Christian Church, and/or the unity required between Christians and Jews.
3. This is an idealistic vision with no particular application.
4. This is an idealistic vision that is so ideal, it will never be accomplished (and perhaps even Ezekiel has misled us).

The following chart has summarized a selection of various opinions present among an array of commentators and scholars today:

Ezekiel 37:15-28	
A REVIEW OF OPINIONS	
IDEALISTIC VISION	**PROPHECY WILL NOT BE FULFILLED**
"One conclusion that can be drawn by the Christian reader of the Old Testament is that the ecumenical movement, which has lost some of its urgency in recent years, has its biblical basis in the unity of Israel acted out and proclaimed by Ezekiel after the fall of Jerusalem...And, as Karl Barth pointed out during the Second Vatican Council, beyond the issue of church unity there lies the one basic and immensely problematic issue of Christian-Jewish relations...The attainment of a lost unity may be an eschatological goal but one that no Christian body professing allegiance to the biblical tradition can afford to neglect."[77] Joseph Blenkinsopp, *liberal Catholic*	"Ezek.'s theme of reconciliation was shared by some (cf. Isa. 56:3-8) but ignored by many of the returning exiles (cf. Ezra 4:1-3). A complete reversal of this pantomime is found in Zech. 11:7-14, where 'the brotherhood between Judah and Israel' is annulled."[78] William Hugh Brownlee, *liberal Christian*
"The New Testament proclaimed a new Christ-centered unity between Jew and Samaritan (John 4:7-42; Acts 1:8; 8:5-25) and indeed an overarching unity between Jew and Gentile that created a metaphorical 'holy people' (Eph 2:11-12) and posited the idea of 'one flock, one shepherd' (John 10:16). The ideal, like that which Ezekiel set before his Judean audience, presents a challenge to work toward."[79] Leslie C. Allen, *British Bible scholar*	
"Christ has broken down the old wall between Jews and Gentiles through his death on the cross, building both together into a new, holy temple to the Lord (Eph. 2:14-22). There is but one temple of God in this age, the church, the body of Jesus Christ, in which Jews, Samaritans, and Gentiles are all brought together as one...[quotes Galatians 3:28]."[80] Iain M. Duguid, *Reformed Christian*	

---

[77] Blenkinsopp, 175.

[78] William Hugh Brownlee, "The Book of Ezekiel," in Charles M. Laymon, ed., *The Interpreter's One-Volume Commentary on the Bible* (Nashville: Abingdon, 1971), pp 430-431.

[79] Allen, 196.

[80] Duguid, pp 440-441.

"...Ezekiel's point...is not so much ethnic and geographical, but theological, or perhaps we might say ecclesiological. He is determined to insist that the future of God's people is a future for *one* people. One God, one people, one covenant...God's work in Israel would have implications beyond Israel and affect the rest of the nations...God's ultimate purpose is 'one new humanity', of believing Gentiles and Jews, united through the cross of Christ and acceptable to God."[81]
Christopher J.H. Wright, *evangelical Christian*

"This may be a highly idealized prophecy, since it is unlikely that significant remnants of the ten northern tribes survived until this period."[82]
Marvin A. Sweeney, *liberal Jewish*

FUTURE PROPHECY AWAITING FULFILLMENT

"It is sometimes pointed out that this never happened in the post-exilic history of Israel; but the prophet is looking for nothing less than the advent of the Messianic kingdom, when the Tabernacle of God shall be with His people (v. 27; see Rev. 21:3). At that time the nations shall recognize the power of Yahweh through His redemption of His people (v. 28)."[83]
G.R. Beasley-Murray, *evangelical Christian*

"It is difficult to know how to apply or interpret the oracle. The northern kingdom no longer existed, and many of its peoples had been scattered and long absorbed by other cultures. How could it be restored to the land? Recognising this mystery, several cults and sects in recent centuries have sought to identify themselves with the lost tribes of Israel, and thus find a place in prophecy. But it is safer to recognise the necessary element of mystery involved in any language addressing the future. The main thrust of the prophecy is that *all* of God's people would somehow participate in the future restoration; how this could be is not known, yet it is the essence of the prophet's affirmation....It is clear, with the benefit of hindsight, that the prophecy concerns a distant future. The preceding passage, concerning the dry bones, could be interpreted simply in terms of exiles returning to their homeland. But this oracle moves out of the realm of history, as we commonly understand it, and anticipates a future time in which God will bring a new kind of reality into being. While the precise significance of each part of the prophecy may elude us, the broad thrust in clear: God had not forgotten his people and had determined their restoration."[84]
Peter C. Craigie, *evangelical Christian*

---

[81] Wright, *The Message of Ezekiel*, pp 313, 314.
[82] Marvin A. Sweeney, "Ezekiel," in *Jewish Study Bible*, 1114.
[83] G.R. Beasley-Murray, "Ezekiel," in *NBCR*, 681.
[84] Craigie, pp 263-264.

"It is clear from our vantage point that all of these promises were not fulfilled after the first return from Babylon. Prophecy often had an immediate, limited fulfillment but also a long-range, more complete fulfillment. If this was the case, it meant that Ezekiel was describing details, many of which would be fulfilled in a future permanent return beyond the immediate purview of the return from Babylon. This explains why so many symbols, figures, and verses from Ezekiel were incorporated into John's view of the last days in Revelation. The truth is that both were describing the same events....The passage anticipates the future work of God with Israel in bringing about a complete restoration of the nation."[85]
Lamar Eugene Cooper, *dispensational Christian*

"This regathering cannot be the one conducted by Zerubbabel in 536 B.C., or the one overseen by Ezra in 457, or the one led by Nehemiah in 445, for these three are only a prelude to a worldwide gathering that God himself will conduct in that final era of history when there will be 'one king' over his people and they will again be 'one nation' (v. 22), without the northern and southern divisions that have existed since 931 B.C.....This promise of a reunited nation in the land of Canaan was not fulfilled according to the terms of this prophecy in David and Solomon's day, any more than it was fulfilled in the days of Zerubbabel, Ezra, and Nehemiah—unless someone wants to argue for an unusual period of obedience to God's law in Israel and for a temporary unification of the nation when presumably the Messiah came down to rule and reign in the postexilic days—an event that never took place!"[86]
Walter C. Kaiser, *evangelical Christian*

"The prophecy speaks not of a mere political union, free from the wars and rivalry that marred the era of the First Temple. Rather, it speaks of an era under a king from the House of David, who will be a servant of God and who will unify the people in allegiance to the Torah. Idolatry will be gone and the Temple will stand; the standard of life will be obedience to the laws of the Torah and the result will be that the entire world will know that HASHEM is God."[87]
ArtScroll Chumash, *Orthodox Jewish*

"After Solomon, the ten tribes following Jeroboam became the kingdom of Israel, the two remaining tribes in Jerusalem, Judah and Benjamin, became the kingdom of Judah. The ten tribes were carried off to Assyria in 722 B.C., and the two remaining tribes were carried off by Babylon between 605 and 586 B.C. The situation where these two kingdoms were divided will end, and as this and other prophecies predict, the two kingdoms will become one nation (cf. Jer. 3:18; 23:5-6; 30:3; Hosea 1:11; Amos 9:11). No fulfillment has ever been recorded in history, and the future regathering of Israel will occur in the Millennium."[88]
John F. Walvoord, *dispensational Christian*

---

[85] Cooper, 327, 327 fn#80.

[86] Walter C. Kaiser, *The Messiah in the Old Testament* (Grand Rapids: Zondervan, 1995), 198.

[87] Scherman, *Chumash*, 1445.

[88] John F. Walvoord, *Every Prophecy of the Bible* (Colorado Springs: Chariot Victor Publishing, 1999), pp 186-187.

> "The Kingdom of David and Solomon split in 931 B.C., becoming Israel and Judah. In restored Israel, all tribes are represented and the nation will be united, as the sign of the fused stick reveals."[89]
> Tim LaHaye Prophecy Study Bible, *dispensational Christian*

While there is an array of points of view to be considered, as shown from the diversity of views quoted above, most Messianics' interpretation of Ezekiel 37:15-28 will fall into the literal scope of fulfilled in the past/to be fulfilled in the future. The primary Jewish orientation of the regathering of all Israel, even though there was certainly debate in ancient times, is reflected in the Talmud:

> "'The ten tribes are not destined to return, since it is said, "And he cast them into another land, as on this day" (Deu. 29:28). Just as the day passes and does not return, so they have gone their way and will not return,' the words of R. Aqiba. R. Eliezer says, 'Just as this day is dark and then grows light, so the ten tribes for whom it now is dark — thus in the future it is destined to grow light for them.'
>
> *"Our rabbis have taught on Tannaite authority:* 'The ten tribes have no portion in the world to come [T.: and will not live in the world to come], as it is said, "And the Lord drove them out of their land with anger and heat and great wrath" (Deu. 29: 8) — in this world; and cast them forth into another land' (Deu. 29:28) — in the world to come,' the words of R. Aqiba. R. Simeon b. Judah of Kefar Akkum says in the name of R. Simeon, 'Scripture said, "As at this day" — if their deeds remains as they are this day, they will [not] reach it, and if not, they will (not) reach it.' Rabbi says, '[Both these and those] have a portion in the world to come, as it is said, "And it shall come to pass in that day that the trumpet shall be blown [and those who are perishing in the land of Assyria and those who are driven away in to the Land of Egypt shall come and worship the Lord in the holy mountain, in Jerusalem]" (Isa. 27:13).' [T. San. 13:12]." (b.*Sanhedrin* 110b).[90]

Some of the Jewish Sages, while acknowledging that the Northern Kingdom was exiled, denied that its descendants would ever return to the fold of Israel. At the same time, other Jewish Sages affirmed the Prophets' expectation that the Northern Kingdom would be restored within a wider restoration of Israel. Within later history, we see how historian Zvi Ben-Dor Benite can make reference to the Italian Jewish Rabbi Isaac Lampronti (1679-1756), commenting how "whatever others might be debating about the tribes and their location, what the Jews really ought to do is stick to the prophecy promising their return. This reunion, [Lampronti] assures his readers, is going to be the work of God, not of modern

---

[89] LaHaye, 873.
[90] *The Babylonian Talmud: A Translation and Commentary.*

geography, and will happen 'according principally to the prophecy of Ezekiel in chapter 37' (*principalmente di quella d'Ezechiel cap. 37*)."[91]

Today's Orthodox Jewish expectation, concurrent with what is communicated in the Talmud regarding Israel's restoration, and among some later voices, does seem to be a little bigger than the construction of the Second Temple by Zerubbabel, and affirmation statements regarding "all Israel present" after the Babylonian exile. Every day in the *Shacharit* or the weekday morning service, Orthodox Jews pray that the Lord will come to Jerusalem and establish His Kingdom once again. This also includes the reestablishment of the Davidic Kingdom, which did not happen following the return of the Jews from Babylon:

> "And to Jerusalem, Your city, may You return in compassion, and may You rest within it, as You have spoken. May You rebuild it soon in our days as an eternal structure, and may You speedily establish the throne of David within it. Blessed are You HASHEM, the Builder of Jerusalem....The offspring of your servant David may You speedily cause to flourish, and enhance his pride for Your salvation all day long. Blessed are You, HASHEM, Who causes the pride of salvation to flourish."[92]

Holding to a futuristic fulfillment of Ezekiel 37:15-28 is surely compatible with Jewish views of Israel's restoration. Yet quite surprisingly, and even a bit disturbingly, some of today's Messianic Jews try to honestly argue that Israel was reunited and restored in past history, which is often flippantly based on surface references to "all Israel" in Ezra-Nehemiah.[93] The two sticks are believed to have already been reunited, because along with the survivors of the Babylonian exile, various survivors from the Northern Kingdom, had been already been joined with Judah. Well, if this is true and the Northern and Southern Kingdoms of Israel have been corporately reunited in all their fullness, then we should assume that *all of the expectations* of Ezekiel's two-stick prophecy have now been accomplished. This is a position, we should believe, that is widely unsustainable when remarks like "the nations shall know that I the LORD sanctify Israel, when my sanctuary is among them forevermore" (37:28, NRSV) are made.

Daniel C. Juster has been among those Messianic Jews who have affirmed a past fulfillment of Ezekiel 37:15-28 in the Sixth Century B.C.E., as he detailed in his 1994 report "Is the Church Ephraim?", "When the nation of Israel came back from captivity, Northerners were included and there was one country. The two sticks became one and will yet receive the covenant of peace after their present regathering is complete. Perhaps over time, more Northerners found their way back to the land of Israel and into the Jewish community in Israel and Babylon than

---

[91] Ben-Dor Benite, 208.

[92] Scherman and Zlotowitz, *Complete ArtScroll Siddur*, 109.

[93] Ezra 2:70; 6:17; 8:25, 35; 10:5; Nehemiah 7:73; 12:47; 13:26.

we realize."[94] Juster then added the conditional statement, which is a bit revealing: "The Messiah could identify and gather the lost tribes after his return."[95]

Juster appears, here in 1994, to admit to the possibility of a future fulfillment of the two-stick prophecy, but is largely pessimistic to it, and relegated almost all of it to the past. While he is, of course, free to hold to such a position, a majority of pre-millennial interpreters in contrast, hold to an almost entirely futuristic fulfillment of Ezekiel 37:15-28 (especially Craigie, Kaiser), even if they do not know all of the finer details of it. There are some other voices within contemporary Messianic Judaism, in contrast to this, who affirm a more futuristic orientation of Ezekiel 37:15-28:

- Arnold G. Fructenbaum: "One of the major features of the final restoration is that Israel will be reunited as a nation, never to be divided into separate kingdoms again....[I]n Ezekiel 37:15-23, the prophet is commanded to take two sticks. On one stick he is to write *Judah* and on the other *Joseph*, and then put the two sticks together sot that they become one stick in his hand (vv. 15-17). The interpretation is that the two kingdoms will someday be reunited into one nation (vv. 18-20). When the regathering of Israel comes (v. 21), they will not be regathered into two nations, but only into one, for they will be under one king in one kingdom (v. 22). At that time they will be thoroughly cleansed of their sins which were the root cause of the original division."[96]

- Jeffrey Enoch Feinberg: "[T]he prophet Y'chezkel (*Ezekiel*), in exile with his people, promises complete restoration between the tribes led by Y'hudah and the ten lost tribes led by Yosef's son Efrayim. Indeed, the two kingdoms will be united under a king from Y'hudah (Ez. 37:22, 24)....The LORD promises to purify his people into a holy kingdom (Ez. 37:23). He promises a covenant of peace, and a Sanctuary in which He will dwell among His people. Only then will the nation find its place among the nations of the world."[97]

- Michael L. Brown: "[T]here is one good thing that has been accomplished by the Two House theory, and that is to draw attention to passages such as Ezekiel 37:15-25, where God speaks of the reunification of Judah with Ephraim. The Two House proponents do get these texts wrong, but the question must be asked: Were verses such as these fulfilled in the return of the Jews from Babylonian exile, since among them were Israelite exiles as

---

[94] Daniel C. Juster, in *Is the Church Ephraim? A Requested Response to the Union of Messianic Jewish Congregations*, 10.

[95] Ibid., 11.

[96] Arnold G. Fructenbaum, *Israelology: The Missing Link in Systematic Theology*, revised edition (Tustin, CA: Ariel Ministries, 1996), 806.

[97] Jeffrey Enoch Feinberg, *Walk Genesis: A Messianic Jewish Devotional Commentary* (Clarksville, MD: Lederer, 1998), 204.

well, or do they point to a yet future restoration, one that could be ongoing this very day, in which scattered remnants of the so-called Ten Lost Tribes—from India and Africa—are returning to the Land?"[98]

- Boaz Michael & Jacob Fronczak: "The prophets repeatedly prophesy to both houses even after the deportation of both kingdoms. One passage in particular clearly speaks of their reunification as one indivisible body (Ezekiel 37:15-28), and it is a passage that, at least toward its end, is clearly referring to the Messianic Age. This seems to imply that the reunification of the people of Israel has not yet been accomplished and will not be until Messiah returns...Ezekiel's prophecy certainly has elements that are unfulfilled..."[99]

The problem with claiming that Ezekiel 37:15-28 is an essentially fulfilled prophecy today, as encountered in some parts of Messianic Judaism, is obvious: if the two-stick prophecy was accomplished in past history, then one has to entirely allegorize the requirement for God's Sanctuary to be present in the Earth. Likewise problematic is why the Jewish people were again dispersed from the Land of Israel after 70 C.E., with "all Israel" supposedly having returned to the Promised Land with David as king *l'olam* or "for eternity" (37:25). Should we be surprised that in his 2013 edition of *Jewish Roots*, Juster has had to now acknowledge, "there is evidence that Orthodox Rabbis and Messianic Jewish leaders are finding real lost tribes people in Pakistan, India, South Africa, and Zimbabwe"?[100]

Not unlike prophecies such as those of the New Covenant (Jeremiah 31:31-34; Ezekiel 36:25-27), or the nations coming to Zion to be taught God's Law (Micah 4:1-3; Isaiah 2:2-4), given the corporate restoration of Israel here to the Promised Land, a fulfillment of the two-stick oracle of Ezekiel 37:15-28 would be most impossible for the pre-resurrection era. If we choose to take a realized eschatology approach to this oracle, where many of its realities can be experienced now among God's people, then *only* when the complete cleansing (37:20) would be available via the work of Yeshua the Messiah in the post-resurrection era, could this prophecy really begin to take shape. Only from the First Century C.E. to the present could Israel truly be in the process of restoration.

I think that much of today's Messianic Judaism simply does not want to consider the serious ramifications of the two-stick prophecy, and on the whole wants to stay away from an issue that is bound to get non-Jewish Believers in their

---

[98] Michael L. Brown, *60 Questions Christians Ask About Jewish Beliefs and Practices* (Minneapolis: Chosen Books, 2011), 244.

[99] Boaz Michael, with Jacob Fronczak, *Twelve Gates: Where Do the Nations Enter?* (Marshfield, MO: First Fruits of Zion, 2012), pp 26, 27.

Also to be noted are the thoughts of D. Thomas Lancaster, *Grafted In: Israel, Gentiles, and the Mystery of the Gospel* (Marshfield, MO: First Fruits of Zion, 2009), 167:

"Judaism anticipates that when Messiah comes, he will sound a great trumpet and gather the Jewish people back to the land of Israel. Even the ten lost tribes will be included in this end-times gathering."

[100] Daniel Juster, *Jewish Roots: Understanding Your Jewish Faith*, revised edition (Shippensburg, PA: Destiny Image, 2013), 326.

midst stirred up, as many are likely to think that they "must be" descendants of the exiled Northern Kingdom. Various leaders within today's Messianic Judaism will devise as many ways as they can to get out of addressing the verses of Ezekiel 37:15-28 in detail, and with that fail to weigh the opinions of commentators and interpreters who direct us to a futuristic perspective of fulfillment.

A futuristic view of the two-stick prophecy fits well within an appropriate window of interpretational possibilities of Ezekiel 37:15-28, especially those who hold to a pre-millennial eschatology. Ironically enough, dispensational Christian theologians—who think that the so-called "Church" will be raptured out prior to the Tribulation—even recognize that the two-stick prophecy is yet to be fulfilled.

An interpreter like John Goldingay will not avoid the two-stick prophecy the same way as some of today's Messianic Jews. He actually labels the oracle of Ezekiel 37:15-28 to be "A Conjuring Trick Whereby Two Sticks Become One."[101] He considers Ezekiel to be like a "contextual theologian," recognizing "that Yahweh cannot have finished with...northern Israel as an entity."[102] However, not quite knowing what to do, Goldingay is left comparing the two-stick prophecy to religious divisions that exist between Jews and Christians, and within the broad spectrum of Christianity, summarizing,

"It was not clear then and it is not clear 2,500 years later how....[this] can be worked out for the Jewish people or for the Christian church. Both are riven by divisions: orthodox, conservative, liberal; Orthodox, Catholic, Protestant, Pentecostal; liberal, fundamentalist. One group refuses to accept the validity of another's religious practices. As some divisions fade away, others develop."[103]

In Goldingay's estimation, the two-stick prophecy of Ezekiel 37:15-28 is no more fulfillable than Yeshua's prayer in John 17 for unity among His followers. The more mainline allegorized views of this oracle, though, are from interpreters who simply consider the two-stick prophecy as a motivation for expressing faith in God, as the Jewish exiles to Babylon would have required overwhelming faith to see their nation fully restored. Darr remarks, "We cannot know how Ezekiel's fellow exiles responded to his perfect portrait of Israel's future...Surely some thought the prophet to be crazy..."[104]

Other than interpreters who really do allegorize the Ezekiel 37:15-28 prophecy, or consider it to be so impossible that it will never happen, it is really sad that a wide number of today's Messianic Jews are those who pretty much avoid the futuristic reality of the text. Or, when holding to a pre-millennial eschatology, some of today's Messianic Jews actually argue that this prophecy was largely accomplished in ancient times. This is notably quite contrary to some mainline Jewish interpretations of the two-stick prophecy, which even though do not

---

[101] John Goldingay, "Ezekiel," in James D.G. Dunn and John W. Rogerson, eds., *Eerdmans Commentary on the Bible* (Grand Rapids: Eerdmans, 2003), 657.

[102] Ibid.

[103] Ibid.

[104] Darr, in *NIB*, 6:1511.

recognize Yeshua the Messiah as the Davidic King, **do recognize future fulfillment.**

What do these things mean to them?

One of the most significant things, that the Lord Himself actually anticipates, as the Prophet Ezekiel held up two pieces of wood to the Jewish exiles in Babylon, is that they would ask, "Will you not show us what you mean by these?" (Ezekiel 37:18, RSV). Hopefully for Ezekiel's original audience, they took the message of Israel's future restoration to be one of promise—recognizing that God would surely end the period of exile. Today in much of the Messianic movement, the same basic question of "What do these things mean?" is being asked. People who read the two-stick prophecy of Ezekiel 37:15-28 are answering this question in a variety of ways. Some of these answers have been good, and some of them have not at all been that good. Answering this question properly—concurrent with the Lord's desire to see His people brought together—will be very important for the future.

A cursory examination of the Messianic world will reveal that today's Messianic Jews have largely chosen to ignore or discount this prophecy. Likewise, there has arisen a large number of Two-House populists, who make a prophecy like Ezekiel 37:15-28 the very center of their spiritual being, sometimes even more important than the personal salvation that we are to all possess in Messiah Yeshua. These populists see the message as one of physical identity, rather than unfulfilled Bible prophecy. Finding a third alternative, which respects the eschatological focus of the two-stick oracle, but keeps it within the right perspective of who we are to be first and foremost as redeemed people in Yeshua the Messiah, may be a challenge for the short term.

Many of today's Messianic Jews and adherents of a populist Two-House teaching are actually not that different in their approach to spirituality, with each unable to see the real focus of what our Father wants the Messianic movement to become. Much of today's Messianic Judaism has the vision of becoming another formal, recognized branch of Judaism. Those who adhere to this ideological drive want to build a faith community that is almost exclusively composed of Jewish Believers in Yeshua, (reluctantly) with a few intermarrieds, but without the large numbers of non-Jews that currently make up and (financially) support much of Messianic Judaism. Their desire is to build a "safe," almost totally ethnic Jewish environment, where Yeshua can be honored, but where non-Jewish Believers pretty much remain in the Christian Church and away from them. This is supposed to be a vision of what ultimately may be considered two sub-peoples of God.

For far too many in the Two-House sub-movement, a person's identity is similarly focused on just being a member of physical people. It is automatically assumed, quite presumptuously, that if a non-Jewish person is a part of the Messianic movement, that he or she must automatically be a member of the "Lost Tribes." One will hear an overblown emphasis on the reunion of "Ephraim and Judah," so much so that many Jewish Believers are quite turned off to considering the wider scope of prophecies of Israel's restoration, with themselves often being placed as significantly secondary to this "Ephraim." Furthermore, the two-stick prophecy's emphasis on companions from the nations being a part of this reunion, is a fact often quickly left by the wayside—especially if it is proven that as many as eighty to ninety percent or more of those involved in the restoration of Israel's Kingdom, are going to be companions from the nations at large. The populist Two-House teaching also employs a great deal of theological eisegesis, whereas many accounts of "two" in the Scriptures are all of a sudden about the Two Houses of Israel, when they may not be (i.e., Luke 15:11-32). Much of the long term focus of what is to become of this is just all over the board at present.

While many of the populist Two-House advocates will simply claim that all non-Jewish Believers are "Ephraim," this is much more of a "touchy feely" thing more than anything else, guided by a semi-charismatic approach to spirituality. A more extreme variety of this goes beyond simply claiming that most every non-Jew in the Messianic movement is a scattered "Ephraimite," but would actually identify various people of specific nationalities as being of Tribe XYZ (perhaps even with the necessity of DNA studies to be conducted in the future). Concurrent with this is a great deal of pseudo-history, the most significant encountered being British-Israelism. The fact that there are pseudo-historical claims sometimes associated with those who interpret Ezekiel 37:15-28, has not gone unnoticed by evangelical scholars. Of particular importance are the thoughts of Wright, originally from Northern Ireland, who comments,

"The view, which is still adamantly held in some quarters, that the 'ten lost tribes' of the destroyed northern kingdom somehow migrated to northwestern Europe and became the ancestors of the Anglo-Saxon peoples (primarily Britain and America) has no basis in reputable historical research....and the theological implication that it is built upon...flies in the face of the New Testament teaching which affirms Ezekiel's vision of the unity of Israel in the Messiah Jesus, and generates an ethnocentric (and virtually racist) contradiction to the biblical picture of the multinational nature of the people of God in Christ."[105]

If there are truly groups of people out in the nations, descended from the exiles of Israel/Ephraim, then the prophecy clearly states that God is the One who restores them to corporate Israel in the eschaton (Ezekiel 37:19). It is not the job of any human person to be so presumptuous so as to absolutely think that this or that tribe went here or there, and promote ridiculous assertions like the term "British" being of Hebrew origin, or fantastical claims that the Ancient Israelites somehow settled North America. The imperative of Amos 9:9 is, "I will shake the house of Israel among all nations as *grain* is shaken in a sieve, but not a kernel will fall to the ground." God's sovereignty alone will gather scattered Israel (of either Judah or Ephraim) back, not any human arrogance—as best epitomized by the false claims of British-Israelism and its offshoots. He alone knows where they went, He will gather them back, and the *only importance* is that scattered Israel/Ephraim is one of the three groups to be reunited as a part of restored Israel in prophecy. Even if one

---

[105] Wright, *The Message of Ezekiel*, 313 fn# 108.

is of scattered Ephraim, that by no means guarantees him or her eternal salvation. All are human, and all need the same salvation available in Yeshua (cf. Romans chs. 1-3).

On the whole, the vision of much of Messianic Judaism or Two-House sub-movement cannot really affect **significant spiritual change in people's lives,** where the mandate of God is entirely fulfilled. This involves understanding what Israel was called to be as a missional community, a kingdom of priests called to serve the people of Planet Earth, by spreading the light and goodness of the Creator God (Exodus 19:6; Isaiah 42:6), and now by extension Messiah Yeshua. If today's Messianic Jews or Two-House adherents could really grasp the significance of this simple, yet complex requirement that the Lord has given us, *we could be a real force of positive change for the world.* The Messianic emphasis on the Torah, for example, is desperately needed in an hour of moral relativism and growing licentiousness.[106]

Israel's restoration is much bigger than just the Jewish people, or even Judah and Israel/Ephraim; **it is something that affects the entire world.** If today's Two-House sub-movement actually bothered to really emphasize the associated "companions" (Ezekiel 37:16, 19; cf. Isaiah 49:6) from the nations at large a little more frequently, then some of the (valid) accusations of "racism" that get levied against it would have no basis at all. Alas, often because of the limitations of these still early years of the Messianic movement, the restoration of Israel's Kingdom presented as a *very inclusive process* might take a while to see come to the forefront.

Concurrent with this is the debate that is raging right now in the Messianic movement about the relevance of God's Torah for (all of) God's people.[107] In the context of the two-stick prophecy of Ezekiel 37:15-28, all those who are brought together—Judah, exiled Israel/Ephraim, and companions from the nations—will be fully obedient to the Lord when it is completed (Ezekiel 37:24). Yet, such an obedience is to be surely compelled by the transformative work of God's Spirit on the hearts and minds of His people (Ezekiel 36:25-27).

Yet this has its own unique set of challenges. Many people in today's Messianic world have a very close relationship with the Law, but they do not have a very close relationship with the Lawgiver, failing to see how the Torah is to point people to Yeshua (Galatians 3:24, Grk.; Romans 10:4, Grk.). Some consider the Torah to be part of the time prior to Messiah, perhaps important for Jewish identity, but not that important as the foundational instructions that inform God's people how to live holy lives. Many people in today's Two-House sub-movement, while rightfully believing that the Torah is for today, disregard too many mainline Jewish interpretations and viewpoints concerning its application.

The issue of the Torah's relevance, but perhaps more specifically how it is to be followed, has been a major wedge that divides many Two-House advocates

---

[106] Consult the author's McHuey Blog post from 14 September, 2009, "A Low Hamartology," appearing in the *Messianic Torah Helper.*

[107] Consult the author's publication *One Law for All: From the Mosaic Texts to the Work of the Holy Spirit.*

with Messianic Jews. The Two-House sub-movement, in particular, has various leaders who speak in favor of uniting "all Israel," but absolutely thumb their nose at mainline Jewish traditions that would be honored in either the Conservative or Reform Synagogue, or most Messianic Jewish congregations (not fringe things like the Kabbalah or some of the Orthodox Jewish extremities). Very little sensitivity has been encouraged toward understanding Christian theology, and so the same bad approach has similarly been encouraged toward Jewish theology. So while claiming to want to see people brought together, particularly Jews and Christians, very little is able to be accomplished *at actually bringing them together.*

This is not to say that many of today's Messianic Jews have not been immature and childish when it comes to examining a Biblical passage like Ezekiel 37:15-28. *On the contrary, they have!* Some of today's Messianic Jews expect a blind obedience to many Jewish traditions that violate the ethos of Scripture, in particular as it comes to the equality of all people in the Lord. But rather than take Messianic Judaism to task over a serious issue like this, and how many non-Jews may sometimes be treated as second or third-class people by them, Two-House advocates often go after Messianic Jews for issues like not using the Divine Name of God or following the Hillel II Rabbinical calendar. This does not help, and it only makes things more complicated.

While populist Two-House advocates at least try to address the two-stick prophecy of Ezekiel 37:15-28, even if they go to some extremes here and there, many of today's Messianic Jews cannot even handle it without having some kind of heart palpitations. The fact remains that unless one wants to allegorize the two-stick prophecy, it is a *yet-to-be-fulfilled* prophecy. And we might not know all the details right now, but that is perfectly alright if we have faith in the Lord. We do not know many of the specific details of the eschaton—especially that of the resurrection—yet we still believe!

People like myself have no problem thinking that significant numbers of non-Jewish Believers being led into the Messianic movement is quite important, in fulfillment of the prophetic words such as the nations streaming toward Zion and toward God's Torah (Isaiah 2:2-4; Micah 4:1-3). But unlike most of the popular Two-House proponents out there, as a non-Jewish Messianic Believer I definitely feel a strong need to honor the positive difference that Messianic Judaism has made in my life. I have to recognize that on the whole Messianic Judaism is far more spiritually and theologically stable (in spite of its flaws) than a Two-House sub-movement that is often riddled with a great deal of unprofessionalism and grossly unqualified leaders.

I think the main answer in getting Messianic Jews to really consider Biblical passages like Ezekiel 37:15-28 will be found in whether or not those in the more independent Messianic movement will continue to place any unnecessary barriers between itself and Messianic Judaism. We need to position ourselves to grow and mature in a close parallel to Messianic Judaism, so that when a future time comes, we can hope to have greater dialogue about what is transpiring. Unfortunately, though, too many barriers probably exist for such progress to really be made today.

What do these things mean to me?

While the question of Ezekiel 37:18, "Will you not show us what you mean by these?" (RSV), has been answered in various ways by today's Messianic Jews and Two-House advocates, **I have my own views as to how this question should be properly answered.** I think that when stuck between the extremes of people avoiding the subject matter of the two-stick prophecy, or then placing their lives at the very center of the issue, that a third alternative must emerge.

The only "safe" way that we can really address the whole issue of a larger restoration of Israel, is as **futuristic end-time prophecy.** Because this is futuristic prophecy, it automatically is not placed at the center of who we are as Believers, because who we are as Believers is to know and emulate the Lord Yeshua. Likewise, because the two-stick oracle is recognized as futuristic prophecy, we may not know all of the details of how it is to come to pass. This does not mean that we ignore it, but it does mean that we have to place a great deal of trust in God. Any interpretation we have cannot by any means be branded as "heresy," especially if we are in common agreement with both Jewish and evangelical Christian interpreters who recognize Ezekiel 37:15-28 as yet-to-be-fulfilled.

Something that I have also had to consider very seriously about the two-stick prophecy, especially when evaluating the wide spectrum of opinions, is its significant theme of unity. While I may not totally approve of those who allegorize or spiritualize Ezekiel's word, commentators who do so are absolutely right about how the Prophet Ezekiel communicates a broad message of required unity to God's people. How often do we really sit down as Messianic Believers, and consider what Paul says in 1 Corinthians 1:10?

"Now I exhort you, brethren, by the name of our Lord Yeshua the Messiah, that you all agree and that there be no divisions among you, but that you be made complete in the same mind and in the same judgment."

Applying the themes of Ezekiel 37:15-28 to an evangelical Christian audience, Duguid's thoughts should be well taken:

"Churches and denominations ought not to be 'homogeneous units,' where Christians choose to meet together with others exactly like them. Rather, each church should strive to be a heterogeneous mixture of those for whom Christ died, an entity that transcends racial, ethnic, cultural, and class barriers, giving expression as a worshipping community to the unity that is ours in our common adoption into God's family."[108]

Even though much of today's Messianic Judaism may have the long term vision of its congregations being relatively homogeneous, with a few intermarrieds, I have seldom attended a Messianic congregation that is not ethnically and culturally diverse. There is very much a "mixed salad" present in today's Messianic movement. Given the themes of Israel's olive tree in Romans 9-11, this may be an olive salad with some very dominant Jewish flavors, but there are enough associated flavors for it to still be a rather unique olive salad.

---

[108] Duguid, 441.

As I have searched the Scriptures, read the words of trusted scholars and theologians, and experienced much in my Messianic walk—I have a vision of the Messianic movement, albeit developing, that is rather unique. It is not the multi-class system of today's Messianic Judaism, nor is it the populism of much of today's Two-House sub-movement. It is a view that will build on the work of our Jewish and Christian forbearers, which I would hope has the capacity to bring those who believe in the God of Israel, and our Messiah Yeshua, together as one group of people empowered to fulfill the Divine mandate. It will recognize us all as a part of the Commonwealth of Israel (Ephesians 2:11-13), and that what is to befall Israel in the end-times—including prophecies like Ezekiel 37:15-28—will involve all of us in some way. Most of today's non-Jewish Messianic Believers are not at all going to be descendants of the exiled Northern Kingdom in the end, **but we will all end up being a part of the same community, or enlarged Kingdom realm, of Israel.**

I do very much believe that a Jewish leadership in matters of Torah *halachah* is to be respected (Genesis 49:10; Matthew 23:2-3; Romans 3:2; 11:29), and that many of the independent forms of Torah observance present in the Two-House sub-movement have not helped. This does not mean that I advocate that we blindly follow all Jewish traditions, but we certainly need to have a traditionally Jewish style of Torah observance consistent with the Conservative or Reform Synagogue today. I also very much believe that we need to give what is properly due to our shared Jewish and Christian theological heritage, as our engagement with the Scriptures improves, and we learn to join into a larger conversation of Biblical Studies. We need to learn to focus on what we have in common with others first (Ephesians 4:1-6), and then respectfully and constructively work through our differences. If we cannot learn how to fairly dialogue with our evangelical Christian brethren who know the Messiah, how will we be able to fairly dialogue with our Jewish brethren who do not know the Messiah? Some of these questions may always be *in process*, but the word of Ephesians 4:29 cannot be forgotten:

"Let no unwholesome word proceed from your mouth, but only such *a word* as is good for edification according to the need *of the moment*, so that it will give grace to those who hear."[109]

I have also learned via some experience that one of the main reasons why today's Messianic movement, while wishing to have unity—does not have it—is because we are not fully prepared to consider the three categories of people who have been made equal via the atoning work of Messiah Yeshua. According to Galatians 3:28, where Paul directly subverted an ancient Rabbinical prayer (t.*Berachot* 6:18) appearing in the Orthodox Jewish *siddur* even until today,[110] not only are Jews and Greeks and slaves and free equal, but so are males and females. There is actually a **three-class**, and not a two-class system, that needs to be

---

[109] Consult the author's exegetical paper on Ephesians 4:29, "How Are Messianics to Properly Communicate?"

[110] Hertz, *Authorised Daily Prayer Book*, pp 19, 21; Scherman and Zlotowitz, *Complete ArtScroll Siddur*, 19.

jettisoned from too much of the broad Messianic movement. Yet, considering the full implications of the kind of Biblical equality restored by the Lord, is one that today's Messianic generation, regardless of what position people take regarding a larger restoration of Israel, is not that ready or willing to consider. I personally do not believe that God will grant us unity, though, until we not only consider it, but do something about it. We need to work toward the "one new humanity" (Ephesians 2:15, NRSV/CJB)[111] that He desires us to be, **not** some "one new man/male."[112]

By no means do I think that the Messianic movement needs to embrace some kind of broad ecumenical vision, but it is a bit too parochial at the present time. We have difficulty looking at the bigger picture, the world beyond Israel, and God's desire to see the good news of salvation reach the ends of the Earth. We are only now beginning to consider the great potential we have, beyond the awesomeness of reaching out to Jews and Christians, in an effort to see Jewish people saved and Christians embrace their Hebraic Roots. Perhaps not too unlike how some of the Prophet Ezekiel's fellow Jewish exiles disregarded or mocked what he said when he held two pieces of wood before them, some of my own thoughts of what the Messianic movement needs to be considering (although on a far lesser plain than Ezekiel), are disregarded by some of the Messianic leaders I have interacted with.

While it is certainly important for us to encourage Messianic congregations and fellowships to be places where all are welcomed in the Lord and spiritually edified, and we need to be far more united than we are—there are justifiable reasons to be divided. Duguid refers to 2 John 10-11 and 1 Corinthians 5:1-5 as some examples to be considered, specifically recognizing how some people may need to show that they have God's approval on the basis of 1 Corinthians 11:19: "For there must also be factions among you, so that those who are approved may become evident among you."[113] Unfortunately, due to the small size and relatively young age of today's emerging Messianic movement, there are some necessary divisions over significant theological issues. Since I have already addressed these in various articles and other publications, I see no need in this paper to refer you to some long list of theological and spiritual issues to be remedied, which you may find a bit depressing.

As someone who chooses to engage with the issues of Ezekiel 37:15-28, J.K. McKee is placed between two extremes: one ignores the subject matter, and then another over-emphasizes the subject matter. One group does not really want to align itself with God's mission of having a single albeit internally diverse people united in Him, and the other bears all the signs of a still-maturing movement that is under-developed in too many areas.

I am basically an advocate for a Messianic faith, similar to what has been seen in much of Messianic Judaism—but definitely with equality for all of God's people.

---

[111] Grk. *kainon anthrōpon* (καινὸν ἄνθρωπον).

[112] For a further discussion, consult the author's exegetical paper on Galatians 3:28, "Biblical Equality and Today's Messianic Movement."

[113] Duguid, 442.

It would affirm that a larger restoration of Israel is something in process, but it would leave many of the details in His hands to be sorted out. I am a conundrum to many I interact with, because I could easily be classified as being the most "Messianic Jewish" of the various people out there who address passages like Ezekiel 37:15-28 in a positive manner. I have no problem with the healthy role that a Conservative degree of Jewish tradition can play in Torah observance—yet as a Bible teacher true to the text, I have to actually deal with passages like Ezekiel 37:15-28, unlike what many Messianic Jews have chosen to do. I likewise know that today's Messianic movement positively benefits in too many ways from our evangelical Christian heritage, not to just be discarded as well. On the whole, this tactful approach represents a third stream of Messianic faith that has yet to really be seen in today's generation—yet it probably represents the best way we can be all the things that the Lord wants us to be. It will certainly be growing in the 2010s!

Already knowing that my identity in the Lord is secure, because of how Yeshua has saved me from my sins and made me a new person via the transforming power of the gospel—I personally do not care whether or not I am a physical descendant of Abraham, Isaac, and Jacob. *I am a human being made in God's image, with extreme value to my Creator.* Everyone who calls on the same Messiah Yeshua (Christ Jesus) is welcome to be a part of Israel's restoration, as God's people are brought together in the sovereign hand of the Son of Man.

While many non-Jewish Believers who adhere to the Two-House teaching speculate that they could actually be scattered Israelites from Tribe XYZ, I think such speculation is utterly **off limits** from what we see in the Scriptures. The Apostle Paul instructed Titus on the island of Crete to "avoid foolish controversies and genealogies and strife" (Titus 3:9).[114] When people spend more time trying to figure out who they are physically, **than who they are in Messiah Yeshua,** God's objective of seeing people saved and discipled is not easily achieved. The Apostles never identified non-Jewish Believers as being of Tribe XYZ, but they did affirm the expectation of the Prophets, and how Israel would be restored by God's sovereign hand. They certainly had no difficulty applying various prophecies about Israel's restoration to the salvation of the nations in the ancient Mediterranean (i.e., Acts 15:15-18; Amos 9:11-12), but they stopped at trying to figure out "who was who." That people were being redeemed from their sins, and being granted eternal salvation, **was by far the most important thing!**

A significantly moderate approach to this subject matter does need to emerge that focuses more on the eschatological side of the matter, rather than on some kind of physical identity. Some people are really not going to like the idea—and I say

---

[114] The perspective of Titus 3:9 is directly concerned with "those of the circumcision" (Titus 1:10), likely some kind of Jewish troublemakers who were using their pedigree to act superior to everyone else. In 1 Timothy 1:4, which also refers to genealogies, this is most probably associated with the misuse of the Torah that Paul confronts (1 Timothy 1:6-7), and involved speculations by the false teachers on the genealogy listings of obscure Tanach figures (i.e., Genesis chs. 5, 11).

For a further discussion on this and related issues, consult the author's commentary *The Pastoral Epistles for the Practical Messianic.*

this as an Arminian and a Wesleyan—that much of the issue of who scattered Israel/Ephraim is, should be left to the sovereign working of God as prophecies like Ezekiel 37:15-28 are fulfilled in future time and naturally play out. *This means that we may not know all the details until Yeshua returns.* Craigie has properly directed us, "it is safer to recognise the necessary element of mystery involved in any language addressing the future. The main thrust of the prophecy is that *all* of God's people would somehow participate in the future restoration; how this could be is not known."[115]

Most importantly and above all, what has to emerge regarding a larger restoration of Israel, will *really be concerned* about bringing people together as one in Messiah Yeshua. **All of God's people get to be involved in the restoration of God's Kingdom!** Unfortunately, the modus operandi that we find in many sectors of the current Two-House sub-movement of giving the Christian Church and Jewish Synagogue a proverbial "kick in the ass" (*tuccus* for you Yiddish speakers), has deterred this significantly. Mutual respect and honor needs to be encouraged, and the Messianic movement needs to grow up into adulthood and become a unifying force of God's holiness and righteousness.

As important as the Ezekiel 37:15-28 prophecy is for giving us a glimpse into the restoration of God's Kingdom, the unity of Judah and Israel/Ephraim is by no means enough, as it is not the consummation of God's plan for humanity. Block's view of the two-stick prophecy is, "The prophet's vision concerns not so much the consummation, the end of history, as its climax."[116] The unity of Jewish and non-Jewish Believers as one, is depicted in Ephesians 3:10,[117] as a foretaste of the ultimate consummation coming to the cosmos (Ephesians 1:21-23). The consummation of the ages will only take place when the redeemed enter into the New Creation that is coming. It just so happens, though, that the restoration of Israel's Kingdom realm is the major event seen in the Bible that is going to help leapfrog us closer to the Eternal State.

How do we see God's people unite?

I suspect that most of you who have read this analysis of Ezekiel 37:15-28, who have been in the Messianic movement for a while, and who have been exposed to the Two-House sub-movement and its teachings in some form—had no idea that there were this many opinions floating around about the two-stick prophecy. Having had to see some of these opinions, how do you think we are to move forward? How can we let the thoughts of both Jewish and Christian scholars inform us as to future Messianic development, as we seek answers to the questions posed by the Prophet Ezekiel? Taylor points out some things that we need not forget:

---

[115] Craigie, 263.

[116] Block, 417.

[117] "[S]o that the manifold wisdom of God might now be made known through the [assembly] to the rulers and the authorities in the heavenly *places*" (Ephesians 3:10).

"An over-literal interpretation of one aspect of this future hope prevents one from seeing that the prophet is mainly concerned with the ideal of unity in the Messianic kingdom."[118]

No one who honestly reads the oracle of Ezekiel 37:15-28 can avoid its message of unity. *God wants to see His people brought together.* Wright appeals to Ephesians 3:6 as being an appropriate New Testament equivalent of Ezekiel's message, concluding how "Nothing less than this great declaration will satisfy the chords of Ezekiel's great symphonic prophecy of one people under the Lord."[119] The Apostle Paul's assertion that the nations "are fellow heirs and fellow members of the body, and fellow partakers of the promise in Messiah Yeshua through the gospel" (Ephesians 3:6), is often not that welcomed in various parts of today's Messianic Judaism. Many Messianic Jews do not want to see non-Jewish Believers as "co-heirs" (HCSB) and equal citizens of an enlarged Kingdom realm of Israel with them. Whether they really do stand against God's intention to unite all of His people, as laid forth by prophetic passages like Ezekiel 37:15-28, is a matter that we should leave entirely to His determination.

Today's Two-House sub-movement needs to be about improving itself, refining what the subject matter it advocates is Biblically, and reorienting itself to fulfilling God's mission of being a blessing to the world at large. Sadly, it does seem that most of the Two-House sub-movement is completely impotent to doing this, as it has become a sideshow in recent days for an entire array of urban legends and myths.[120] The most recent, and I believe most problematic of these thus far, has been the promotion of polygamy by a particular Two-House teacher.[121] The enemy knows the power that can be manifest in God's people being united together. This is not some ecumenical unity that waters down foundational doctrines, but Jewish and non-Jewish Believers coming together as one people in Messiah Yeshua, laying the groundwork for the eventual restoration of Israel's Kingdom **that will indeed change the world.**

Messianic Judaism may be immature in completely avoiding things like the two-stick prophecy, "whiting out" as it were, Ezekiel 37:15-28. But, various voices in the Two-House sub-movement have not given their cause a great deal of credibility, either. How we get beyond this, and emphasize the kind of unity envisioned by Ezekiel's prophecy, will be a significant goal for us to work toward in the days ahead. It will surely have to be accomplished in a different way from what we have seen in the recent past. It is not something impossible to reach for,

---

[118] Taylor, 240.

[119] Wright, *The Message of Ezekiel*, 314.

[120] Consult the author's articles "The Quest for Credibility" and "The Top Ten Urban Myths of Today's Messianic Movement," appearing in his book *Confronting Critical Issues: An Analysis of Subjects that Affects the Growth and Stability of the Emerging Messianic Movement.*

[121] Moshe Koniuchowsky, *Sex and the Believer: Shocking Freedom of Sexuality in Torah* (Margate, FL: Your Arms to Israel Publishing, 2008).

For an analysis and refutation of the concept of polygamy, consult the author's article "Is Polygamy for Today?"

but will not happen overnight. Some painful changes needing to be implemented are most probably on the near horizon.

We may not know all of the details of how the two-stick prophecy of Ezekiel 37:15-28 comes together. Some of the people who assume themselves to be of "Ephraim" are just companions from the nations at large. Yet the restoration of Israel is to be an inclusive process, and the worldwide affects of it cannot be avoided or underemphasized. It is also very much a message tied to the gospel of the Kingdom, a message of personal salvation and inclusion within Israel to be declared in the Last Days (Matthew 24:14).

Block holds that there is no built in timeframe for the Ezekiel 37:15-28 prophecy, observing, "no hints concerning the time of fulfillment are given. Accordingly, these events are deemed eschatological not because they are expected to transpire at the end of history but because they are new and they are final—their effects are guaranteed to continue forever."[122] It may very well be, that there is no "In that day...." clue mentioned in the two-stick oracle, **because the Lord is the One who really does bring it to pass.** He will only accomplish it when His people are mature and ready.

So how do we make sure that we are facilitating the restoration of God's Kingdom? Such a unity begins when we can recognize the high value that God had placed on each and every one of us as His human creations. We must learn to work together to achieve the mandate He originally gave to Ancient Israel, and be a blessing to all we encounter. *Let us get ready for great things ahead!*

---

[122] Block, pp 416-417.

Israel In Future Prophecy

Afterward

Most likely, if you have been diligently reading *Israel in Future Prophecy*, it is fair to say that you are a non-Jewish Messianic Believer who has been curious as to what my perspective is regarding the whole "Two-House" controversy—*or* you might be a Messianic Jewish Believer who knows that our broad faith community needs some resolution to this issue, as time proceeds forward, and as theological and spiritual challenges of much more major substance and importance present themselves (i.e., debates over the Divinity of Yeshua and His Messiahship). There have been a number of sensational and hype-laden books circulate throughout the broad Messianic movement over the past ten to fifteen years, promoting the Two-House issue, which have caused an unnecessary amount of confusion and discord. It is, to be sure, one thing to raise the awareness level of the issue of the exiled Northern Kingdom of Israel/Ephraim in Biblical history, as well as unfulfilled prophecies concerning its descendants. It is another thing to just assume that just about every non-Jewish Believer in the Messianic movement is a descendant of those people, without any substantial proof other than a "feeling."

If you presently consider yourself a member or a part of the Two-House sub-movement—or are even a non-Jewish Believer who has classified himself or herself as some kind of "Ephraimite"—after reading this publication you should see that I am in agreement with you that prophetic oracles like Jeremiah 31:6-10 or Ezekiel 37:15-28 are obviously unfulfilled. I also agree with you that there are people groups on Planet Earth today who are descended from the exiled Northern Kingdom. *More is on the agenda of history regarding Israel in future prophecy.* At the same time, though, I think that the numbers of those people are far, far less than you likely do, because the Torah itself has said that a significant lessening of Israel's numbers would come as a consequence of disobedience (Deuteronomy 28:62).[1] There are no billions, or even hundreds of millions, of physical descendants of Abraham, Isaac, and Jacob on Planet Earth. If you are a white, Caucasian Messianic Believer who has thought of himself or herself as some kind of "Ephraimite," you need to come to the stark reality that you probably bear no genetic ancestry to those of either the Northern or Southern Kingdoms of Israel.

Various non-Jewish people in today's Two-House sub-movement have been led astray to think that they *must be* descendants of the exiled Northern Kingdom, but not because they think they are descendants of the exiled Northern Kingdom; they have been led astray because these people tend to believe that *only* a physical connection with the progenitors of Israel makes them acceptable in the eyes of God, and that someone from the nations generally is not that close to his or her Creator. Such a concept is absolutely deplorable, and many of the popular/populist leaders

---

[1] "Then you shall be left few in number, whereas you were as numerous as the stars of heaven, because you did not obey the LORD your God" (Deuteronomy 28:62).

of the Two-House sub-movement will have to answer before the Lord for placing an unbalanced and grossly inappropriate emphasis on physical bloodline.[2] This is not just because it causes people to look down on others, but mostly because it causes people to think that if they are physical descendants of Abraham, Isaac, and Jacob that they are entitled to some sort of special favors before God. The errant thinking expressed by many ancient Jews in the Second Temple period was, "All Israelites have a share in the world to come" (m.*Sanhedrin* 10:1),[3] meaning that physical descendants of the Patriarchs were guaranteed eternal salvation. Quite contrary to this, the Apostle Paul was clear to say, about his own fellow Jews, "For not all Israelites truly belong to Israel" (Romans 9:6, NRSV), and how the natural branches of Israel's olive tree could be cut off (Romans 11:17). Without the eternal redemption available in Messiah Yeshua, "both Jews and Greeks are all under sin" (Romans 3:9).

Will those who compose the Two-House sub-movement be willing and able to pull back the reigns where necessary? For the immediate future, there is a desperate need for many of today's Two-House people to become far more respectful to Judaism and Christianity, than is commonly seen. Improvements need to definitely be made by Two-House people in how they approach Torah application, and much of the anti-traditionalism and anti-Judaism witnessed from them. Getting many people who have been involved in the Two-House sub-movement to stop using the Divine Name of God (YHWH/YHVH) as flippantly as they tend to, and to use the standard, Hillel II Rabbinical calendar employed by both mainstream Judaism and Messianic Judaism, would be two places for some positive changes to begin. While many of today's Two-House leaders and teachers claim they want to bring unity between non-Jewish Messianic Believers and those in Messianic Judaism, many Two-House advocates have done more to keep these groups of people divided, because of the various rogue tendencies that manifest when it comes to mainline Jewish tradition and custom. (It is not as though non-Jewish Messianics have to live as though they are ethnically and culturally Jewish, but more understanding and respect are surely needed.)[4]

For the longer term future, there are definite clashes of ecclesiology which are coming,[5] which are going to be lobbied from many in Messianic Judaism, at a largely independent, non-Jewish Messianic community, which substantially sits outside of *the control* of the major Messianic Jewish denominations and associations. Two wide groups are going to emerge: **(1)** those who believe that the Commonwealth of Israel (Ephesians 2:11-13) is composed of the two sub-groups of the ethnic Jewish people and Christian Church, and that non-Jewish Believers need not concern themselves that much with their Hebraic Roots or the Torah, and **(2)**

---

[2] Cf. Wootten, *Who Is Israel? Redeemed Israel—A Primer*, 43 and the various references to so-called "genetic memory."

[3] Neusner, *Mishnah*, 604.

[4] Consult the author's article "Considering Messianic Jewish Fears of Replacement and Irrelevance" appearing in the *Messianic Torah Helper* by TNN Press (forthcoming).

[5] Cf. Michael & Fronczak, pp 50-52 for a preview.

those who believe that with the arrival of Yeshua the Messiah, David's Tabernacle will be restored, resultant in an enlarged Kingdom realm of Israel (Amos 9:11-12; Acts 15:15-18) that welcomes in the righteous from the nations. In this latter scenario, there will be resolution brought to the issue of the exiled Northern Kingdom for sure, but at the same time, with Israel expanding its borders—like it did with David's rule extending to Edom—so will the reign of King Yeshua result in an expanded polity of Israel welcoming in the nations.[6]

Claims of replacement theology or supersessionism are going to come from many leaders in today's Messianic Judaism, if you do not embrace a bilateral ecclesiology of the Commonwealth of Israel composing the Jewish people and Christian Church, with distinctions and differences among people to be rigidly emphasized. Yet traditionally, replacement theology has advocated that the Jewish people have no more Biblical right to live in the Holy Land, and that the rebirth of the State of Israel was according to political self-determination and not God's promises. Non-Jewish Believers such as myself, while foreseeing more Jews and pockets of people descended from the exiled Northern Kingdom, migrating to the Land of Israel in fulfillment of prophecy, **will not claim some kind of ownership over territory that is exclusively reserved for Israel's twelve tribes.** But there are many non-Jewish Messianics in the Two-House sub-movement who think that they have a Biblical right to permanently live in the Holy Land. Non-Jewish Messianic Believers need to become more familiar with the strident word, "The heavens are Yours, the earth also is Yours; the world and all it contains, You have founded them" (Psalm 89:11). *All Messianics decisively need a more global vision, which places a much higher estimation and value on all of the people and natural wonders of this great planet.*

Much of the extremism, sensationalism, hype, and bad behavior manifested by much of the Two-House sub-movement—we should all likely think—is going to naturally moderate itself out, and be burned off, over time. (Much of this will occur, as it becomes more and more apparent how some of the popular/populist Two-House leaders are not as astute with their Biblical Studies as they may present themselves.) But in order to see this occur, there is a need for patience, more Bible studies, and a more reflective and self-critical manner of spirituality which needs to be embraced by many in the Two-House sub-movement (which many will choose to reject). As this is done, many non-Jewish Two-House people will stop seeing themselves as some sort of "Ephraimites," and instead will see themselves as being a part of the Commonwealth of Israel, rightly understood to be an enlarged Kingdom realm of Israel. They do not need to think of only the physical descendants of Abraham, Isaac, and Jacob as being special to God; all of God's human creations, made in His image (Genesis 1:27), are special to Him.

With important changes doubtless to come to many people who have composed the Two-House sub-movement, many non-Jewish Believers who have been caught up in some of the "Ephraimite" sensationalism, will be likely to

---

[6] Consult the author's publication *Are Non-Jewish Believers Really a Part of Israel?*

transition more to a One Law/One Torah style of position, when it comes to the people of God.[7] While the One Law sub-movement has its own spiritual issues to be sure (particularly in terms of diagnosing the significance of Yeshua's sacrifice for the post-resurrection era), it has been far more respectful and honoring of Judaism and Christianity, and it tends to value Biblical scholarship and reason much more.[8] Non-Jewish Believers should be much more content in who they mainly are as those from the nations, whom God loves dearly, and who according to prophecy will come to Zion to be taught from His Torah or Law (Micah 4:1-3; Isaiah 2:2-4), joining with the Jewish people (Zechariah 8:23). Even with many non-Jewish Believers having been caught up in some Two-House hype and sensationalism—they have still made some significant, important, and positive changes in adopting a Messianic, Torah obedient lifestyle, striving to live more like Yeshua and the First Century Believers.

How we all learn, whether we are Jewish or non-Jewish, to recognize ourselves as a part of the "Israel of God" (Galatians 6:16), in mutual honor and submission (Ephesians 5:21; Philippians 2:3-4), is going to be a challenge in the short term, due to the shortsightedness of many leaders and those they have influenced. *I do not think it is going to be a challenge in the long term, though, as a larger restoration of Israel begins to really take shape.* For, in spite of the short sightedness and limitations of mortals, God's future plans will inevitably transpire!

---

[7] Consult the author's publication *One Law for All: From the Mosaic Texts to the Work of the Holy Spirit.*

[8] The various features of this are examined and explored in the *Messianic Torah Helper* by TNN Press (forthcoming 2013).

About the Author

John Kimball McKee is the founder and principal writer for TNN Online, an Internet website that specializes in a wide variety of Biblical topics. He has grown up in a family that has been in constant pursuit of God's truth, and has been exposed to things of the Lord since infancy. Since 1995 he has come to the realization of the post-tribulational return of the Messiah for His own and the importance of our Hebraic Roots. He is a graduate of the University of Oklahoma (Class of 2003) with a B.A. in political science, and holds an M.A. in Biblical Studies from Asbury Theological Seminary (Class of 2009). He is a 2009 recipient of the Zondervan Biblical Languages Award for Greek. John holds memberships in the Evangelical Theological Society, the Evangelical Philosophical Society, and Christians for Biblical Equality.

John is an apologist for the Creator God and in helping people understand their faith heritage in Ancient Israel and Second Temple Judaism. Much of his ministry in the past has been campus based to the multitudes in evangelical Christianity who are associated with a wide variety of Protestant denominations and persuasions. John has introduced college students to things that are Messianic such as the original Hebrew name of our Savior, Yeshua HaMashiach (Jesus the Messiah), a name that he has known since 1983.

John's testimony before his Christian friends at college challenged much of their previous thinking about the whole of the Holy Scriptures and the need to follow the commandments of the Most High. His college peers asked him many questions: Why do you not believe in the pre-trib rapture? What do you think of the *Left Behind* books? Why do you observe the seventh-day Sabbath? Why do you eat kosher? Why do you wear a beard? Why do you celebrate the feasts of Israel? Why will you use a *tallit* and wrap *tefillin*/phylacteries during private prayer? Why do you consult original Hebrew and Greek language texts of the Bible? Why don't you come to church with us on Sunday? This led John into Messianic apologetics and the defense of our faith. John strives to be one who is committed to a life of holiness and methodical Bible study, as a person who has a testimony of being born again and who sincerely desires to obey the Lord.

As the editor of TNN Online, John's ministry has capitalized on the Internet's ability to reach people all over this planet. The Theology News Network speaks with challenging, provocative, and apologetic articles to a wide Messianic audience, and those Christians who are interested in Messianic beliefs. In the past decade (2005-2014), TNN Online has significantly emerged as a well-needed, moderate and Centrist voice, in a Messianic movement that is trying to determine its purpose, relevance, and mission to modern society—a voice which strives to sit above much of the posturing, maneuvering, and religious politics of the broad Messianic spectrum. Given his generational family background in evangelical

Christian ministry, as well as in academics and the military, John carries a strong burden to assist in the development and maturation of our emerging Messianic theology and spirituality, so that we might truly know the mission of God. John has had the profound opportunity since 1997 to engage many in dialogue, so that they will consider the questions he postulates, as his only agenda is to be as Scripturally sound as possible. John believes in demonstrating a great deal of honor and respect to both his evangelical Christian, Wesleyan and Reformed heritage, as well as to the Jewish Synagogue, and together allowing the strengths and virtues of both Judaism and Christianity to be employed for the Lord's plan for the Messianic movement in the long term future.

J.K. McKee is author of numerous books, dealing with a wide range of topics that are important for today's Messianic Believers. He has also written many articles on theological issues, and is presently focusing his attention on Messianic commentaries of various books of the Bible.

J.K. McKee is the son of the late K. Kimball McKee (1951-1992) and Margaret Jeffries McKee Huey (1953-), and stepson of William Mark Huey (1951-), who married his mother in 1994, and is the executive director of Outreach Israel Ministries.

John has a very strong appreciation for those who have preceded him. His father, Kimball McKee, was a licensed lay minister in the Kentucky Conference of the United Methodist Church, and was a very strong evangelical Christian, most appreciative of the Hebraic and Jewish Roots of the faith. Among his many ministry pursuits, Kim brought the Passover *sedar* to Christ United Methodist Church in Florence, KY, was a Sunday school teacher, and was extremely active in the Walk to Emmaus, leading the first men's walk in Madras, India in 1991. John is the grandson of the late William W. Jeffries (1914-1989), who served as a professor at the United States Naval Academy in Annapolis, MD from 1942-1989, notably as the museum director and founder of what is now the William W. Jeffries Memorial Archives in the Nimitz Library. John is the great-grandson of Bishop Marvin A. Franklin (1894-1972), who served as a minister and bishop of the Methodist Church, throughout his ministry serving churches in Georgia, Florida, Alabama, and Mississippi. Bishop Franklin was President of the Council of Bishops from 1959-1960. John is also the third cousin of the late Charles L. Allen (1913-2005), formerly the senior pastor of Grace Methodist Church of Atlanta, GA and First Methodist Church of Houston, TX, and author of numerous books, notably including *God's Psychiatry*. Among all of his forbearers, though, he considers his personality to be most derived from his late paternal grandfather, George Kenneth McKee (1903-1978), and his maternal grandmother, Mary Ruth Franklin Jeffries (1919-).

J.K. McKee is a native of the Northern Kentucky/Greater Cincinnati, OH area. He has also lived in Dallas, TX, Norman, OK, Kissimmee-St. Cloud, FL, and Roatán, Honduras, Central America. He presently resides in Dallas, TX, and is a member in good standing at Eitz Chaim Messianic Jewish Synagogue.

Bibliography

Articles

(2008). *Two-House Doctrine Debate. The Messianic Center.* Retrieved 14 August, 2011 from <http://www.themessianiccenter.com>.

Barabas, Steven. "Baal," in *NIDB*.

Bernis, Jonathan (2005). *The Scattering of the Tribes of Israel*, March/April 2005. *Jewish Voice Today.* Retrieved 17 April, 2011 from <http://www.jewishvoice.org>.

Bradshaw, Lonnie (2011). *The Origins of the Ephraimite Movement.* Retrieved 29 September, 2012 from <http://www.seedofabraham.org>.*

Charlesworth, James H. "Lost Tribes, The," in *ABD*.

Christensen, Duane L. "Nations," in *ABD*.

Delling, G. "*plēróō*," in *TDNT*.

Dralle, Seth. "The Emergence of Messianic Judaism" <u>Messiah Journal</u> Issue 102, Fall 2009/5770.*

Eby, Aaron, Toby Janicki, Daniel Lancaster, and Boaz Michael. (2009). *Divine Invitation: An Apostolic Call to Torah. First Fruits of Zion.* Retrieved 13 October, 2009, from <http://ffoz.org>.*

Editorial Staff. "Gentile," in *EJ*.

"Israel, Land of," in *Dictionary of Judaism in the Biblical Period.*

Gasque, W.W. "Jew," in *ISBE*.

"Gentiles," in *Dictionary of Judaism in the Biblical Period.*

Gilchrist, Paul R. "יָצָא," in *TWOT*.

Hegg, Tim. (2002). *The Two House Theory: Three Fatal Flaws. Torah Resource.* Retrieved 30 March, 2009, from <http://torahresource.com>.*

_____. (2009). *An Assessment of the "Divine Invitation" Teaching. Torah Resource.* Retrieved 06 October, 2009, from <http://torahresource.com>.*

Hicks, L. "Jacob (Israel)," in *IDB*.

Higginson, Richard E. "Gentiles," in *Baker's Dictionary of Theology.*

Hirschberg, Peter (1999). *Decoding the Priesthood*, 10 May, 1999. *The Jerusalem Report.* Retrieved 11 April, 2011 from <http://jpost.com/JerusalemReport>.

"Israel, Land of," in *Dictionary of Judaism in the Biblical Period.*

Juster, Daniel, and Russ Resnik (n.d.). *One Law Movements: A Challenge to the Messianic Jewish Community, UMJC.* Retrieved 26 February, 2008, from <http://www.umjc.org>.*

Kalland, Earl S. "dābār," in *TWOT*.

_____. "דנה," in *TWOT*.

Janicki, Toby. "What is a Gentile?" <u>Messiah Journal</u> Issue 101, Summer 2009/5770.

Johnson, D.H. "Shepherd, Sheep," in *Dictionary of Jesus and the Gospels.*

Kelle, B.E., and B.A. Strawn. "History of Israel 5: Assyrian Period," in *Dictionary of the Old Testament Historical Books.*

Krausz, Tibor (1999). *Report Card*, 10 May, 1999. *The Jerusalem Report.* Retrieved 11 April, 2011 from <http://jpost.com/JerusalemReport>.

Lewis, Jack P. "qāhāl," in *TWOT*.

Liber, David L. "Strangers and Gentiles," in *EJ*.

Lieske, Bruce J. (1999). *Something Old, Something New--The Messianic Congregational Movement. Christian Research Journal.* Retrieved 31 May, 2011 from <http://journal.equip.org/>.*

Michael, Boaz (2004). *Encounters with an Ephraimite: Identity through a Lost Heritage. First Fruits of Zion.* Retrieved 16 November, 2010, from <http://ffoz.org>.*

_____, and D. Thomas Lancaster. "'One Law' and the Messianic Gentile" <u>Messiah Journal</u> Issue 101, Summer 2009/5769.*

_____. "Messianic Judaism: Reconsidering the One Law, Two-House Trajectories" <u>Messiah Journal</u> Issue 111, Fall 2012/5773.*

---

* This is to acknowledge that this article has been read, not that it has necessarily been quoted in this publication.

North, R. "Smyrna," in *ISBE*.

Payne, J. Barton. "'āb," in *TWOT*.

_____. "שָׂרָה ;יִשְׂרָאֵל," in *TWOT*.

Pfeiffer, C.F. "Israel, History of the People of: Divided Kingdom," in *ISBE*.

Rabinowitz, Louis Isaac. "Ten Lost Tribes," in *EJ*.

Robinson, Rich (2001). *The Two-House (Messianic Israel) Theory that Ephraim is the Church. Jews for Jesus.* Retrieved 24 June, 2003, from <http://www.jfjonline.org>.*

Rudolph, David. "Mashiach" <u>Verge</u> Vol. 2, Iss. 2, February 2010.

Sanders, J.A. "Exile," in *IDB*.

_____. "Jew," in *IDB*.

Schmidt, K.L. "*ekklēsía*," in *TDNT*.

_____. "*éthnos*," in *TDNT*.

Scott, Jack B. "'ēl," in *TWOT*.

Silberling, Kay. (1999). *The Ephraimite Error: A Position Paper Submitted to the International Messianic Jewish Alliance.* Retrieved 14 April, 2011, from <http://umjc.org>.

_____. (1999). *A Short Summary of "The Ephraimite Error."* Retrieved 14 April, 2011, from <http://umjc.org>.

"tribes, ten," in *Dictionary of Judaism in the Biblical Period*.

Trotter, Perry (2003). *A Brief Assessment of Two House Theology,* 07 January, 2003. *Christian Witness Ministries.* Retrieved 24 June, 2003, from <http://www.christian-witness.org>.*

van Selms, A. "Gentile," in *ISBE*.

Vickers, Steve (2010). *Lost Jewish tribe 'found in Zimbabwe,'* 08 March, 2010. *BBC News.* Retrieved 08 April, 2012 from <http://news.bbc.co.uk>.

Bible Versions and Study Bibles

Abegg, Jr., Martin, Peter Flint, and Eugene Ulrich, trans. *The Dead Sea Scrolls Bible* (New York: HarperCollins, 1999).

American Standard Version (New York: Thomas Nelson & Sons, 1901).

Barker, Kenneth L., ed., et. al. *NIV Study Bible* (Grand Rapids: Zondervan, 2002).

Berlin, Adele, and Marc Zvi Brettler, eds. *The Jewish Study Bible* (Oxford: Oxford University Press, 2004).

Bratcher, Robert G., ed. *Good News Bible: The Bible in Today's English Version* (New York: American Bible Society, 1976).

Esposito, Paul W. *The Apostles' Bible, An English Septuagint Version* (http://www.apostlesbible.com/).

Garrett, Duane A., ed., et. al. *NIV Archaeological Study Bible* (Grand Rapids: Zondervan, 2005).

Green, Jay P., trans. *The Interlinear Bible* (Lafayette, IN: Sovereign Grace Publishers, 1986).

Green, Joel B., ed. *The Wesley Study Bible* (Nashville: Abingdon, 2009).

God's Game Plan: The Athlete's Bible 2007, HCSB (Nashville: Serendipity House Publishers, 2007).

Harrelson, Walter J., ed., et. al. *New Interpreter's Study Bible*, NRSV (Nashville: Abingdon, 2003).

Harris, W. Hall, ed. *The Holy Bible: The Net Bible*, New English Translation (Dallas: Biblical Studies Press, 2001).

Holman Christian Standard Bible (Nashville: Broadman & Holman, 2004).

Holy Bible, King James Version (edited 1789).

Holy Bible, New International Version (Grand Rapids: Zondervan, 1978).

LaHaye, Tim, ed. *Tim LaHaye Prophecy Study Bible*, KJV (Chattanooga: AMG Publishers, 2000).

Lattimore, Richmond, trans. *The New Testament* (New York: North Point Press, 1996).

May, Herbert G., and Bruce M. Metzger, eds. *The New Oxford Annotated Bible With the Apocrypha*, RSV (New York: Oxford University Press, 1977).

Meeks, Wayne A., ed., et. al. *The HarperCollins Study Bible*, NRSV (New York: HarperCollins, 1993).

Newman, Barclay M., ed. *Holy Bible: Contemporary English Version* (New York: American Bible Society, 1995).

New American Standard Bible (La Habra, CA: Foundation Press Publications, 1971).

New American Standard, Updated Edition (Anaheim, CA: Foundation Publications, 1995).

New English Bible (Oxford and Cambridge: Oxford and Cambridge University Presses, 1970).

New King James Version (Nashville: Thomas Nelson, 1982).

New Revised Standard Version (National Council of Churches of Christ, 1989).

Packer, J.I., ed. *The Holy Bible, English Standard Version* (Wheaton, IL: Crossway Bibles, 2001).

Peterson, Eugene H. *The Message: The Bible in Contemporary Language* (Colorado Springs: NavPress, 2002).

Phillips, J.B., trans. *The New Testament in Modern English* (New York: Touchstone, 1972).

Pietersma, Albert, and Benjamin G. Wright, eds. *A New English Translation of the Septuagint* (Oxford and New York: Oxford University Press, 2007).

Ryrie, Charles C., ed. *The Ryrie Study Bible*, NASB (Chicago: Moody Press, 1978).

Scherman, Nosson, and Meir Zlotowitz, eds. *ArtScroll Tanach* (Brooklyn: Mesorah Publications, 1996).

Siewert, Frances E., ed. *The Amplified Bible* (Grand Rapids: Zondervan, 1965).

Suggs, M. Jack, and Katharine Doob Sakenfeld, and James R. Mueller, et. al. *The Oxford Study Bible*, REB (New York: Oxford University Press, 1992).

Stern, David H., trans. *Jewish New Testament* (Clarksville, MD: Jewish New Testament Publications, 1995).

_____, trans. *Complete Jewish Bible* (Clarksville, MD: Jewish New Testament Publications, 1998).

Tanakh: The Holy Scriptures (Philadelphia: Jewish Publication Society, 1999).

The Holy Bible, Revised Standard Version (Nashville: Cokesbury, 1952).

The Jerusalem Bible (Jerusalem: Koren Publishers, 2000).

Today's New International Version (Grand Rapids: Zondervan, 2005).

Tree of Life Messianic Family Bible—New Covenant (Shippensburg, PA: Destiny Image, 2011).

Williams, Charles B., trans. *The New Testament: A Private Translation in the Language of the People* (Chicago: Moody Publishers, 1937).

Wright, N.T. *The Kingdom New Testament: A Contemporary Translation* (New York: HarperCollins, 2011).

Young, Robert, trans. *Young's Literal Translation.*

Zodhiates, Spiros, ed. *Hebrew-Greek Key Study Bible*, NASB (Chattanooga: AMG Publishers, 1994).

Books and Publications

Allen, Charles L. *God's Psychiatry* (Grand Rapids: Fleming H. Revell, 1953).

Allen, J.H. *Judah's Sceptre and Joseph's Birthright* (Merrimac, MA: Destiny Publishers, 1902).

Anderson, Sean Kendall, and Stephen Sloan. *Terrorism: Assassins to Zealots* (Lanham, MD and Oxford: The Scarecrow Press, 2003).

Archer, Jr., Gleason L., and Paul D. Feinberg, Douglas J. Moo, Richard R. Reiter. *Three Views on the Rapture* (Grand Rapids: Zondervan, 1996).

Baron, David. *The History of the Ten "Lost" Tribes: Anglo-Israelism Examined* reprint (London: Morgan & Scott Ld., 1915).

Beck, James R., ed. *Two Views on Women in Ministry* (Grand Rapids: Zondervan, 2005).

Ben-Dor Benite, Zvi. *The Ten Lost Tribes: A World History* (New York: Oxford University Press, 2009).

Berkowitz, Ariel and D'vorah. *Torah Rediscovered* (Lakewood, CO: First Fruits of Zion, 1996).

_____. *Take Hold* (Littleton, CO: First Fruits of Zion, 1999).

Bernis, Jonathan. *A Rabbi Looks at the Last Days: Surprising Insights on Israel, the End Times and Popular Misconceptions* (Bloomington, MN: Chosen Books, 2013).

Bloomfield, Sandy. *The Errors of "The Ephraimite Error": Disposing of the Lies and Hatred* (Lebanon, TN: Messianic Israel Alliance, 2008).

Bowman, Jr., Robert M., and J. Ed Komoszewski. *Putting Jesus in His Place: The Case for the Deity of Christ* (Grand Rapids: Kregel, 2007).

Boyd, Gregory A., and Paul R. Eddy. *Across the Spectrum: Understanding Issues in Evangelical Theology* (Grand Rapids: Baker Academic, 2002).

Brown, Michael. *Our Hands Are Stained With Blood* (Shippensburg, PA: Destiny Image Publishers, Inc, 1990).

_____. *Answering Jewish Objections to Jesus, Volume 3: Messianic Prophecy Objections* (Grand Rapids: Baker Books, 2003).

_____. *60 Questions Christians Ask About Jewish Beliefs and Practices* (Minneapolis: Chosen Books, 2011).

Bruce, Duncan A. *The Mark of the Scots: Their Astonishing Contributions to History, Science, Democracy, Literature and the Arts* (New York: Citadel Press, 1998).

Carson, D.A., and Douglas J. Moo. *An Introduction to the New Testament*, second edition (Grand Rapids: Zondervan, 2005).

Cassuto, Umberto. *The Documentary Hypothesis and the Composition of the Pentateuch* (Jerusalem: Shalem Press, 2006).

Chumney, Eddie. *Restoring the Two Houses of Israel* (Hagerstown, MD, Serenity Books, 1999).

Cohen, Michael. *Two into One will Go: Jews and Christians Destined to Become One* (San Giovanni Teatino, Italy: Destiny Image Europe, 2012). [eBook for Amazon Kindle]

Cohn-Sherbok, Dan, ed. *Messianic Judaism* (London and New York: Continuum, 2000).

_____, ed. *Voices of Messianic Judaism* (Baltimore: Lederer Books, 2001).

Collins, Kenneth J. *John Wesley: A Theological Journey* (Nashville: Abingdon, 2003).

Collins, Steven M. *The "Lost" Ten Tribes of Israel...Found!* (Boring, OR: CPA Books, 1995).

Cunningham, Loren, and David Joel Hamilton. *Why Not Women? A Fresh Look at Scripture on Women in Missions, Ministry, and Leadership* (Seattle: YWAM Publishing, 2000).

Davidy, Yair. *Lost Israelite Identity: The Hebrew Ancestry of Celtic Races* (Jerusalem: Brit-Am, 1996).

Dillard, Raymond B., and Tremper Longman III. *An Introduction to the Old Testament* (Grand Rapids: Zondervan, 1994).

Eby, Aaron. *Boundary Stones: Divine Parameters for Faith and Life* (Marshfield, MO: First Fruits of Zion, 2008).

_____, and Toby Janicki. *Hallowed Be Your Name: Sanctifying God's Sacred Name* (Marshfield, MO: First Fruits of Zion, 2008).

_____. *Biblically Kosher: A Messianic Jewish Perspective on Kashrut* (Marshfield, MO: First Fruits of Zion, 2012).

Edersheim, Alfred. *The Life and Times of Jesus the Messiah* (Peabody, MA: Hendrickson, 1993).

Egan, Hope. *Holy Cow! Does God Care About What We Eat?* (Littleton, CO: First Fruits of Zion, 2005).

Fee, Gordon D., and Douglas Stuart. *How to Read the Bible for All Its Worth* (Grand Rapids: Zondervan, 2003).

Fischer, John, ed. *The Enduring Paradox: Exploratory Essays in Messianic Judaism* (Baltimore: Lederer, 2000).

Franklin, Marvin A. *The Christ Who Makes Men Whole*, transcript (Atlanta: Joint Radio Committee of the Methodist Church, 1948).

Friedman, David. *They Loved the Torah* (Baltimore: Lederer Books, 2001).

Fructenbaum, Arnold G. *Israelology: The Missing Link in Systematic Theology*, revised edition (Tustin, CA: Ariel Ministries, 1996).

Gilbert, Martin. *Churchill and the Jews: A Lifelong Friendship* (New York: Henry Holt and Company, 2007).

Goldberg, Louis. *How Jewish is Christianity? 2 Views on the Messianic Movement* (Grand Rapids: Zondervan, 2003).

Gorenberg, Gershom. *The End of Days: Fundamentalism and the Struggle for the Temple Mount* (New York: Oxford University Press, 2000).

Gundry, Robert H. *The Church and the Tribulation* (Grand Rapids: Zondervan, 1973).

_____. *First the Antichrist* (Grand Rapids: Baker Books, 1997).

Guthrie, Donald. *New Testament Introduction* (Downers Grove, IL: InterVarsity, 1990).

Harris-Shapiro, Carol. *Messianic Judaism: A Rabbi's Journey through Religious Change in America* (Boston: Beacon Press, 1999).

Harrison, R.K. *Introduction to the Old Testament* (Grand Rapids: Eerdmans, 1969).

Harvey, Richard. *Mapping Messianic Jewish Theology: A Constructive Approach* (Milton Keynes: Paternoster, 2009).

Hegg, Tim. *Introduction to Torah Living* (Tacoma, WA: TorahResource, 2002).

_____. *The Letter Writer: Paul's Background and Torah Perspective* (Littleton, CO: First Fruits of Zion, 2002).

_____. *It is Often Said: Comments and Comparisons of Traditional Christian Theology and Hebraic Thought*, 2 vols. (Littleton, CO: First Fruits of Zion, 2003).

_____. *Fellow Heirs: Jews & Gentiles Together in the Family of God* (Littleton, CO: First Fruits of Zion, 2003).

Herman, Arthur. *How the Scots Invented the Modern World: The True Story of How Western Europe's Poorest Nation Created Our World & Everything in It* (New York: Three Rivers Press, 2001).

_____. *I Will Build My Ekklesia: An Introduction to Ecclesiology* (Tacoma, WA: TorahResource, 2009).

Hertzl, Theodor. *The Jewish State* (Mineola, NY: Dover Publications, 1989).

Hoffman, Bruce. *Inside Terrorism* (New York: Columbia University Press, 1998).

House of David. *Is The Church Ephraim? A Requested Response to the Union of Messianic Jewish Congregations* (White Stone, VA: House of David, 1994).

Huey, William Mark, and J.K. McKee. *Hebraic Roots: An Introductory Study* (Kissimmee, FL: TNN Press, 2003).

Hunt, Dave. *How Close Are We?* (Eugene, OR: Harvest House Publishers, 1993).

Janicki, Toby. *Tefillin: A Study on the Commandment of Tefillin* (Marshfield, MO: First Fruits of Zion, 2010).

_____. *God-Fearers: Gentiles and the God of Israel* (Marshfield, MO: First Fruits of Zion, 2012).

Juster, Daniel C. *Growing to Maturity* (Denver: The Union of Messianic Jewish Congregations Press, 1987).

_____. *Jewish Roots* (Shippensburg, PA: Destiny Image, 1995).

_____. *The Irrevocable Calling: Israel's Role as a Light to the Nations* (Clarksville, MD: Lederer, 2007).

_____. *Jewish Roots: Understanding Your Jewish Faith*, revised edition (Shippensburg, PA: Destiny Image, 2013).

Kaiser, Walter C. *The Messiah in the Old Testament* (Grand Rapids: Zondervan, 1995).

_____. *Mission in the Old Testament: Israel as a Light to the Nations* (Grand Rapids: Baker Books, 2000).

_____. *The Old Testament Documents: Are They Reliable and Relevant?* (Downers Grove, IL: InterVarsity, 2001).

_____. *The Promise-Plan of God: A Biblical Theology of the Old and New Testaments* (Grand Rapids: Zondervan, 2008).

_____. *Preaching and Teaching the Last Things: Old Testament Eschatology for the Life of the Church* (Grand Rapids: Baker Academic, 2011).

Keener, Craig S. *Paul, Women & Wives: Marriage and Women's Ministry in the Letters of Paul* (Peabody, MA: Hendrickson, 1992).

Kinzer, Mark S. *Post-Missionary Messianic Judaism: Redefining Christian Engagement with the Jewish People* (Grand Rapids: Brazos Press, 2005).

Kitchen, K.A. *The Bible In Its World: The Bible & Archaeology Today* (Exeter: Paternoster, 1977).

_____. *On the Reliability of the Old Testament* (Grand Rapids: Eerdmans, 2003).

Koniuchowsky, Moshe. *The Truth About All Israel: A Refutation of the I.M.J.A. Position Paper on the Two Houses of Israel* (Miami Beach: Your Arms to Israel, 2000).

_____. *Sex and the Believer: Shocking Freedom of Sexuality in Torah* (Margate, FL: Your Arms to Israel Publishing, 2008).

Koster, C.J. *Come Out of Her, My People* (Northriding, South Africa: Institute for Scripture Research, 1998).

Ladd, George Eldon. *The Blessed Hope* (Grand Rapids: Eerdmans, 1956).

Lancaster, D. Thomas. *The Mystery of the Gospel: Jew and Gentile in the Eternal Purpose of God* (Littleton, CO: First Fruits of Zion, 2003).

_____. *Restoration: Returning the Torah of God to the Disciples of Jesus* (Littleton, CO: First Fruits of Zion, 2005).

_____. *King of the Jews* (Littleton, CO: First Fruits of Zion, 2006)

_____. *Grafted In: Israel, Gentiles, and the Mystery of the Gospel* (Marshfield, MO: First Fruits of Zion, 2009).

_____. *The Holy Epistle to the Galatians: Sermons on a Messianic Jewish Approach* (Marshfield, MO: First Fruits of Zion, 2011).

Liberman, Paul. *The Fig Tree Blossoms: The Emerging of Messianic Judaism* (Kudu Publishing, 2012). [eBook for Amazon Kindle]

Martin, Walter. *Kingdom of the Cults* (Minneapolis: Bethany House, 1985).

McDowell, Josh, and Don Stewart. *Handbook of Today's Religions* (San Bernadino, CA: Here's Life Publishers, 1983).

McKee, J.K. *When Will the Messiah Return?* (Kissimmee, FL: TNN Press, 2002/2012).

_____. *Torah In the Balance, Volume I* (Kissimmee, FL: TNN Press, 2003).

_____. *The Dangers of Pre-Tribulationism* (Kissimmee, FL: TNN Press, 2003).

_____. *The New Testament Validates Torah* (Kissimmee, FL: TNN Press, 2004).

_____. *Introduction to Things Messianic* (Kissimmee, FL: TNN Press, 2005).

_____. *James for the Practical Messianic* (Kissimmee, FL: TNN Press, 2005).

_____. *Hebrews for the Practical Messianic* (Kissimmee, FL: TNN Press, 2006).

_____. *A Survey of the Apostolic Scriptures for the Practical Messianic* (Kissimmee, FL: TNN Press, 2006).

_____. *Philippians for the Practical Messianic* (Kissimmee, FL: TNN Press, 2007).

_____. *Galatians for the Practical Messianic*, second edition (Kissimmee, FL: TNN Press, 2007).

_____. *A Survey of the Tanach for the Practical Messianic* (Kissimmee, FL: TNN Press, 2008).

_____. *Ephesians for the Practical Messianic* (Kissimmee, FL: TNN Press, 2008).

_____. *Colossians and Philemon for the Practical Messianic* (Kissimmee, FL: TNN Press, 2010).

_____. *Acts 15 for the Practical Messianic* (Kissimmee, FL: TNN Press, 2010).

_____. *The Pastoral Epistles for the Practical Messianic* (Kissimmee, FL: TNN Press, 2012).

_____. *One Law for All: From the Mosaic Texts to the Work of the Holy Spirit* (Kissimmee, FL: TNN Press, 2012).

_____. *1&2 Thessalonians for the Practical Messianic* (Kissimmee, FL: TNN Press, 2012).

_____. *Are Non-Jewish Believers Really a Part of Israel?* (Richardson, TX: TNN Press, 2013).

Michael, Boaz, with Jacob Fronczak. *Twelve Gates: Where Do the Nations Enter?* (Marshfield, MO: First Fruits of Zion, 2012).

_____. *Tent of David: Healing the Vision of the Messianic Gentile* (Marshfield, MO: First Fruits of Zion, 2013).

Milton, John. *The Major Works* (New York: Oxford University Press, 2003).

Moreland, J.P., and John Mark Reynolds, eds. *Three Views on Creation and Evolution* (Grand Rapids: Zondervan, 1999).

Moseley, Ron. *Yeshua: A Guide to the Real Jesus and the Original Church* (Baltimore: Lederer Books, 1996).

Mozeson, Isaac E. *The Word: The Dictionary That Reveals The Hebrew Source Of English* (New York: SPI Books, 2000).

Neusner, Jacob. *The Way of Torah: An Introduction to Judaism* (Belmont, CA: Wadsworth Publishing Company, 1993).

Parfitt, Tudor. *The Lost Tribes of Israel: The History of a Myth* (London: Phoenix, 2002).

Payne, Philip B. *Man and Woman, One in Christ: An Exegetical and Theological Study of Paul's Letters* (Grand Rapids: Zondervan, 2009).

Provan, Iain, V. Philips Long, and Tremper Longman III. *A Biblical History of Israel* (Louisville: Westminster John Knox, 2003).

Ross, Hugh. *The Genesis Question: Scientific Advances and the Accuracy of Genesis*, second expanded edition (Colorado Springs: NavPress, 2001).

_____. *A Matter of Days: Resolving a Creation Controversy* (Colorado Springs: NavPress, 2004).

Roth, Sid. *The Incomplete Church: Bridging the Gap Between God's Children* (Shippensburg, PA: Destiny Image, 2007).

Rudolph, David J., and Joel Willitts, eds. *Introduction to Messianic Judaism: Its Ecclesial Context and Biblical Foundations* (Grand Rapids: Zondervan, 2013).

Schlatter, Victor. *Genetically Modified Prophecies: Whatever Happened to all the Sand and Stars God Promised to Abraham?* (Mobile: Evergreen Press, 2012).

Snell, Daniel C. *Life in the Ancient Near East* (New Haven and London: Yale University Press, 1997).

Stam, C.R. *Things That Differ* (Germantown, WI: Berean Bible Society, 1985).

Stern, David H. *Restoring the Jewishness of the Gospel* (Clarksville, MD: Jewish New Testament Publications, 1990).

_____. *Messianic Jewish Manifesto* (Clarksville, MD: Jewish New Testament Publications, 1992).

_____. *Messianic Judaism: A Modern Movement With an Ancient Past* (Clarksville, MD: Messianic Jewish Publishers, 2007).

Strickland, Wayne G., ed. *Five Views on Law and Gospel* (Grand Rapids: Zondervan, 1996).

Tenney, Merrill C., ed. *The New International Dictionary of the Bible* (Grand Rapids: Zondervan, 1987).

Thompson, David L. *Bible Study That Works* (Nappanee, IN: Evangel Publishing House, 1994).

Varner, William. *Jacob's Dozen: A Prophetic Look at the Tribes of Israel* (Bellmawr, NJ: Friends of Israel Gospel Ministry, 1987).

Walvoord, John F. *Israel In Prophecy* (Grand Rapids: Zondervan, 1962).

_____. *The Church In Prophecy* (Grand Rapids: Zondervan, 1964).

_____. *Every Prophecy of the Bible* (Colorado Springs: Chariot Victor Publishing, 1999).

Weiss, Myles. *An Epic Love Story: Jews & Gentiles One in Messiah* (Dallas: Zola Levitt Ministries, 2011). [eBook for Amazon Kindle]

Westerholm, Stephen. *Perspectives Old and New on Paul: The "Lutheran" Paul and His Critics* (Grand Rapids: Eerdmans, 2004).

Wilson, Marvin R. *Our Father Abraham* (Grand Rapids: Eerdmans, 1989).

Wolff, Robert F., ed. *Awakening the One New Man* (Shippensburg, PA: Destiny Image, 2011).

Wootten, Angus. *Restoring Israel's Kingdom* (St. Cloud, FL: Key of David, 2000).

Wootten, Batya Ruth. *Who Is Israel? And Why You Need to Know* (St. Cloud, FL: Key of David, 1998).

_____. *Who Is Israel?*, enlarged edition (St. Cloud, FL: Key of David, 2000).

_____. *Redeemed Israel—Restored and Reunited* (St. Cloud, FL: Key of David, 2006).

_____. *Israel's Feasts and their Fullness*, expanded edition (St. Cloud, FL: Key of David Publishing, 2008).

_____. *Who Is Israel? Redeemed Israel—A Primer* (St. Cloud, FL: Key of David, 2011).

Wright, Christopher J.H. *The Mission of God: Unlocking the Bible's Grand Narrative* (Downers Grove, IL: IVP Academic, 2006).

Christian Reference Sources

Alexander, T. Desmond, and David W. Baker, eds. *Dictionary of the Old Testament Pentateuch* (Downers Grove, IL: InterVarsity, 2003).

Arnold, Bill T., and H.G.M. Williamson, eds. *Dictionary of the Old Testament Historical Books* (Downers Grove, IL: InterVarsity, 2005).

Bauer, David R. *An Annotated Guide to Biblical Resources for Ministry* (Peabody, MA: Hendrickson, 2003).

Bercot, David W., ed. *A Dictionary of Early Christian Beliefs* (Peabody, MA: Hendrickson Publishers, 1998).

Bromiley, Geoffrey, ed. *International Standard Bible Encyclopedia*, 4 vols. (Grand Rapids: Eerdmans, 1988).

Buttrick, George, ed. et. al. *The Interpreter's Dictionary of the Bible*, 4 vols. (Nashville: Abingdon, 1962).

Cairns, Alan. *Dictionary of Theological Terms* (Greenville, SC: Ambassador Emerald International, 2002).

Crim, Keith, ed. *Interpreter's Dictionary of the Bible: Supplementary Volume* (Nashville: Abingdon, 1976).

Evans, Craig A., and Stanley E. Porter, eds. *Dictionary of New Testament Background* (Downers Grove, IL: InterVarsity, 2000).

Freedman, David Noel, ed. *Anchor Bible Dictionary*, 6 vols. (New York: Doubleday, 1992).

Geisler, Norman L., ed. *Baker Encyclopedia of Christian Apologetics* (Grand Rapids: Baker, 1999).

Green, John B., Scot McKnight, and I. Howard Marshall, eds. *Dictionary of Jesus and the Gospels* (Downers Grove, IL: InterVarsity, 1992).

Grenz, Stanley J., David Guretzki, and Cherith Fee Nordling. *Pocket Dictionary of Theological Terms* (Downers Grove, IL: InterVarsity, 1999).

Harrison, Everett F., ed. *Baker's Dictionary of Theology* (Grand Rapids: Baker Book House, 1960).

Hawthorne, Gerald F., Ralph P. Martin, and Daniel G. Reid, eds. *Dictionary of Paul and His Letters* (Downers Grove, IL: InterVarsity, 1993).

Keil, C., and F. Delitzsch, eds. *Commentary on the Old Testament*, 10 vols.

Longman III, Tremper, and Peter Enns, eds. *Dictionary of the Old Testament Wisdom, Poetry & Writings* (Downers Grove, IL: InterVarsity, 2008).

Martin, Ralph P., and Peter H. Davids, eds. *Dictionary of the Later New Testament & its Developments* (Downers Grove, IL: InterVarsity, 1997).

McKim, Donald S. *Westminster Dictionary of Theological Terms* (Louisville: Westminster John Knox, 1996).

Roberts, Alexander, and James Donaldson, eds. *The Apostolic Fathers*, American Edition.

Schaff, Philip. *History of the Christian Church*, 8 vols. (Grand Rapids: Eerdmans, 1995).

Tenney, Merril C., ed. *The New International Dictionary of the Bible* (Grand Rapids: Zondervan, 1987).

Cited Commentaries

Alexander, Ralph H. "Ezekiel," in Frank E. Gaebelein, ed. et. al. *Expositor's Bible Commentary* (Grand Rapids: Zondervan, 1986), 6:737-996.

Allen, Leslie C. *Word Biblical Commentary: Ezekiel 20-48*, Vol 29 (Dallas: Word Books, 1990).

Baldwin, Joyce G. *The Message of Genesis 12-15* (Downers Grove, IL: InterVarsity, 1986).

Barker, Kenneth L. "Zechariah," in Frank E. Gaebelein, ed. et. al. *Expositor's Bible Commentary* (Grand Rapids: Zondervan, 1985), 7:595-697.

Beasley-Murray, George R. "Ezekiel," in D. Guthrie and J.A. Motyer, eds. *The New Bible Commentary Revised* (Grand Rapids: Eerdmans, 1970), pp 664-687.

_____. *Word Biblical Commentary: John*, Vol 36 (Waco, TX: Word Books, 1987).

Blenkinsopp, Joseph. *Interpretation, A Bible Commentary for Teaching and Preaching: Ezekiel* (Louisville, KY: John Knox Press, 1990).

Block, Daniel I. *New International Commentary on the Old Testament: The Book of Ezekiel, Chapters 25-48* (Grand Rapids: Eerdmans, 1998).

Brownlee, William Hugh. "The Book of Ezekiel," in Charles M. Laymon, ed. *The Interpreter's One-Volume Commentary on the Bible* (Nashville: Abingdon, 1971), pp 430-431.

Bruce, F.F. *The Gospel of John* (Grand Rapids: Eerdmans, 1983).

_____. *New International Commentary on the New Testament: The Book of the Acts* (Grand Rapids: Eerdmans, 1983).

Brueggemann, Walter. *A Commentary on Jeremiah: Exile & Homecoming* (Grand Rapids: Eerdmans, 1998).

Carson, D.A. *Pillar New Testament Commentary: The Gospel According to John* (Grand Rapids: Eerdmans, 1991).

Cohen, Abraham, ed. *Soncino Books of the Bible: The Twelve Prophets* (London: Soncino Press, 1969).

Collins, C. John. *Genesis 1-4: A Linguistic, Literary, and Theological Commentary* (Phillipsburg, NJ: P&R Publishing, 2006).

Cooper, Lamar Eugene. *New American Commentary: Ezekiel* (Nashville: Broadman & Holman, 1994).

Craigie, Peter C. *Daily Study Bible Series: Ezekiel* (Philadelphia: Westminster Press, 1983).

Darr, Katheryn Pfisterer. "The Book of Ezekiel," in Leander E. Keck, ed., et. al. *New Interpreter's Bible*, Vol. 6 (Nashville: Abingdon, 2001), pp 1075-1607.

DeVries, Simon J. *Word Biblical Commentary: 1 Kings,* Vol 12 (Waco, TX: Word Books, 1985).

Duguid, Iain M. *NIV Application Commentary: Ezekiel* (Grand Rapids: Zondervan, 1999).

Ellison, H.L. "1 and 2 Chronicles," in *NBCR*, pp 369-394.

Esler, Philip F. *Conflict and Identity in Romans: The Social Setting of Paul's Letter* (Minneapolis: Fortress Press, 2003).

Feinberg, Charles L. *The Prophecy of Ezekiel: The Glory of The Lord* (Chicago: Moody Press, 1969).

_____. *The Minor Prophets* (Chicago: Moody Press, 1978).

_____. "Jeremiah," in *EXP*, 6:357-691.

Fisch, S. *Soncino Books of the Bible: Ezekiel* (London: Soncino, 1950, 1994).

Fishbane, Michael. *JPS Bible Commentary: Haftarot* (Philadelphia: Jewish Publication Society, 2002).

Freedman, H. *Soncino Books of the Bible: Jeremiah* (London: Soncino, 1968).

Fretheim, Terrence E. *Westminster Bible Companion: First and Second Kings* (Louisville: Westminster John Knox, 1999).

Garrett, Duane A. *New American Commentary: Hosea, Joel* (Nashville, B&H Publishing Group, 1997).

Goldingay, John. "Ezekiel," in James D.G. Dunn and John W. Rogerson, eds. *Eerdmans Commentary on the Bible* (Grand Rapids: Eerdmans, 2003), pp 623-664.

Guelich, Robert A. *Word Biblical Commentary: Mark 1-8:26*, Vol. 34a (Dallas: Word Books, 1998).

Hamilton, Victor P. *New International Commentary on the Old Testament: The Book of Genesis, Chapters 18-50* (Grand Rapids: Eerdmans, 1995).

Harrison, R.K. *Tyndale Old Testament Commentaries: Jeremiah & Lamentations* (Downers Grove, IL: InterVarsity, 1973).

Hodge, Charles. *A Commentary on Romans* (Edinburgh: Banner of Truth Trust, 1972).

Jamieson, Fausset & Brown's Commentary on the Whole Bible (Grand Rapids: Zondervan, 1961).

Keener, Craig S. *The IVP Bible Background Commentary: New Testament* (Downers Grove, IL: InterVarsity, 1993).

_____. *IVP New Testament Commentary Series: Matthew* (Downers Grove, IL: InterVarsity, 1997).

_____. *NIV Application Commentary: Revelation* (Grand Rapids: Zondervan, 2000).

_____. *The Gospel of Matthew: A Socio-Rhetorical Commentary* (Grand Rapids: Eerdmans, 2009).

Klein, George L. *New American Commentary: Zechariah* (Nashville: B&H Publishing Group, 2008).

Kruse, Colin G. *Tyndale New Testament Commentaries: John* (Grand Rapids: Eerdmans, 2003).

Lincoln, Andrew T. *Word Biblical Commentary: Ephesians*, Vol. 42 (Nashville: Thomas Nelson, 1990).

Marshall, I. Howard. *Tyndale New Testament Commentaries: Acts* (Grand Rapids: Eerdmans, 1980).

Mathews, Kenneth A. *New American Commentary: Genesis 11:27-50:26* (Nashville: Broadman & Holman, 2005).

McCartney, Dan G. *Baker Exegetical Commentary on the New Testament: James* (Grand Rapids: Baker Academic, 2009).

McComiskey, Thomas E., ed. *The Minor Prophets* (Grand Rapids: Baker Academic, 2009).

Moo, Douglas J. *Pillar New Testament Commentary: The Letter of James* (Grand Rapids: Eerdmans, 2000).

Morris, Leon. *New International Commentary on the New Testament: The Gospel According to John* (Grand Rapids: Eerdmans, 1971).

Mounce, William D. *Word Biblical Commentary: Pastoral Epistles*, Vol. 46 (Nashville: Thomas Nelson, 2000).

Beasley-Murray, G.R. *New Century Bible Commentary: Revelation* (Grand Rapids: Eerdmans, 1974).

Peterson, David G. *Pillar New Testament Commentary: The Acts of the Apostles* (Grand Rapids: Eerdmans, 2009).

Sarna, Nahum M. *JPS Torah Commentary: Genesis* (Philadelphia: Jewish Publication Society, 1989).

Slotki, I.W. *Soncino Books of the Bible: Chronicles* (London: Soncino Press, 1965).

Slotki, Judah J. *Soncino Books of the Bible: Daniel, Ezra, Nehemiah* (London: Soncino Press, 1973).

Smith, Billy K., and Frank S. Page. *New American Commentary: Amos, Obadiah, Jonah* (Nashville: Broadman & Holman, 2001).

Stuart, Douglas. *Word Biblical Commentary: Hosea-Jonah*, Vol. 31 (Nashville: Thomas Nelson, 1987).

Thompson, J.A. *New American Commentary: 1,2 Chronicles* (Nashville: Broadman & Holman, 1994).

Toussaint, Stanley D. "Acts," in John F. Walvoord and Roy B. Zuck, eds. *The Bible Knowledge Commentary: New Testament* (Wheaton, IL: Victor Books, 1983), pp 349-432.

Towner, Philip H. *New International Commentary on the New Testament: The Letters to Timothy and Titus* (Grand Rapids: Eerdmans, 2006).

Tuell, Steven. *New International Biblical Commentary: Ezekiel* (Peabody, MA: Hendrickson, 2009).

Walton, John H., and Victor H. Matthews and Mark W. Chavalas. *The IVP Bible Background Commentary: Old Testament* (Downers Grove, IL: InterVarsity, 2000).

Waltke, Bruce K. *Genesis: A Commentary* (Grand Rapids: Zondervan, 2001).

Walvoord, John F., and Roy B. Zuck, eds. *The Bible Knowledge Commentary: Old Testament* (Wheaton, IL: Victor Books, 1985).

Wenham, Gordon J. *Word Biblical Commentary: Genesis 16-50*, Vol 1b (Dallas: Word Books, 1994).

Williamson, H.G.M. *New Century Bible Commentary: 1 and 2 Chronicles* (Grand Rapids: Eerdmans, 1982).

_____. *Word Biblical Commentary: Ezra, Nehemiah*, Vol 16 (Waco, TX: Word Books, 1985).

Wright, Christopher J.H. *The Message of Ezekiel* (Downers Grove, IL: InterVarsity, 2001).

Yamachui, Edwin. "Ezra, Nehemiah," in *EXP*, 4:565-771.

Greek Language Resources

Aland, Kurt, et. al. *The Greek New Testament, Fourth Revised Edition* (Stuttgart: Deutche Bibelgesellschaft/United Bible Societies, 1998).

Black, David Alan. *Learn to Read New Testament Greek* (Nashville: Broadman and Holman, 1994).

Brenton, Sir Lancelot C. L., ed & trans. *The Septuagint With Apocrypha* (Peabody, MA: Hendrickson, 1999).

Bromiley, Geoffrey W., ed. *Theological Dictionary of the New Testament*, abridged (Grand Rapids: Eerdmans, 1985).

Danker, Frederick William, ed., et. al. *A Greek-English Lexicon of the New Testament and Other Early Christian Literature*, third edition (Chicago: University of Chicago Press, 2000).

Liddell, H.G., and R. Scott. *An Intermediate Greek-English Lexicon* (Oxford: Clarendon Press, 1994).

Metzger, Bruce M. *A Textual Commentary on the Greek New Testament* (London and New York: United Bible Societies, 1975).

Nestle, Erwin, and Kurt Aland, eds. *Novum Testamentum Graece, Nestle-Aland 27th Edition* (New York: American Bible Society, 1993).

Nestle-Aland Greek-English New Testament, NE27-RSV (Stuttgart: United Bible Societies/Deutche Bibelgesellschaft, 2001).

Newman, Jr., Barclay M. *A Concise Greek-English Dictionary of the New Testament* (Stuttgart: United Bible Societies/Deutche Bibelgesellschaft, 1971).

Rahlfs, Alfred, ed. *Septuaginta* (Stuttgart: Deutsche Bibelgesellschaft, 1979).

Rogers, Cleon L., Jr., and Cleon L. Rogers III. *The New Linguistic and Exegetical Key to the Greek New Testament* (Grand Rapids: Zondervan, 1998).

Thayer, Joseph H. *Thayer's Greek-English Lexicon of the New Testament* (Peabody, MA: Hendrickson, 2003).

Vine, W.E. *Vine's Expository Dictionary of New Testament Words* (Nashville: Thomas Nelson, 1968).

Wallace, Daniel B. *Greek Grammar Beyond the Basics* (Grand Rapids: Zondervan, 1996).

Zodhiates, Spiros, ed. *Complete Word Study Dictionary: New Testament* (Chattanooga: AMG Publishers, 1993).

Hebrew Language Resources

Arnold, Bill T., and John H. Choi. *A Guide to Biblical Hebrew Syntax* (New York: Cambridge University Press, 2003).

Baker, Warren, and Eugene Carpenter, eds. *Complete Word Study Dictionary: Old Testament* (Chattanooga: AMG Publishers, 2003).

Baltsan, Hayim. *Webster's NewWorld Hebrew Dictionary* (Cleveland: Wiley Publishing, Inc., 1992).

Brown, Francis, S.R. Driver, and Charles A. Briggs. *Hebrew and English Lexicon of the Old Testament* (Oxford: Clarendon Press, 1979).

Davidson, Benjamin. *The Analytical Hebrew and Chaldee Lexicon* (Grand Rapids: Zondervan, 1970).

Dotan, Aron, ed. *Biblia Hebraica Leningradensia* (Peabody, MA: Hendrickson, 2001).

Elliger, Karl, and Wilhelm Rudolph, et. al., eds. *Biblica Hebraica Stuttgartensia* (Stuttgart: Deutche Bibelgesellschaft, 1977).

Gabe, Eric S., ed. *New Testament in Hebrew and English* (Hitchin, UK: Society for Distributing the Hebrew Scriptures, 2000).

Gesenius, H.F.W.: *Gesenius' Hebrew-Chaldee Lexicon to the Old Testament*, trans. Samuel Prideaux Tregelles (Grand Rapids: Baker, 1979).

Harris, R. Laird, Gleason L. Archer, Jr., and Bruce K. Waltke, eds. *Theological Wordbook of the Old Testament* (Chicago: Moody Press, 1980).

Holladay, William L., ed. *A Concise Hebrew and Aramaic Lexicon of the Old Testament* (Leiden, the Netherlands: E.J. Brill, 1988).

Jastrow, Marcus. *Dictionary of the Targumim, Talmud Bavli, Talmud Yerushalmi, and Midrashic Literature* (New York: Judaica Treasury, 2004).

Kelley, Page H., Daniel S. Mynatt, and Timothy G. Crawford, eds. *The Masorah of Biblia Hebraica Stuttgartensia* (Grand Rapids: Eerdmans, 1998).

Koehler, Ludwig, and Walter Baumgartner, eds. *The Hebrew & Aramaic Lexicon of the Old Testament*, 2 vols. (Leiden, the Netherlands: Brill, 2001).

Seow, C.L. *A Grammar for Biblical Hebrew*, revised edition (Nashville: Abingdon, 1995).

Tov, Emanuel. *Textual Criticism of the Hebrew Bible* (Minneapolis: Fortress Press, 1992).

תורה נביאים כתובים והברית החדשה (Jerusalem: Bible Society in Israel, 1991).

Unger, Merrill F., and William White. *Nelson's Expository Dictionary of the Old Testament* (Nashville: Thomas Nelson, 1980).

Historical Sources

Aristotle: *Politics*, trans. Ernest Barker (New York: Oxford University Press, 1995).

Bettenson, Henry, and Chris Maunder, eds. *Documents of the Christian Church* (Oxford: Oxford University Press, 1999).

Dawood, N.J., trans. *The Koran With a Parallel Arabic Text* (London: Penguin Books, 2006).

Eusebius: *Ecclesiastical History*, trans. C.F. Cruse (Peabody, MA: Hendrickson, 1998).

González, Justo L. *The Story of Christianity*, Vol. 1 (San Francisco: Harper Collins, 1984).

Irvin, Dale T., and Scott W. Sunquist. *History of the World Christian Movement*, Vol. 1 (Maryknoll, NY: Orbis Books, 2001).

Josephus, Flavius: *The Works of Josephus: Complete and Unabridged*, trans. William Whiston (Peabody, MA: Hendrickson, 1987).

Judaeus, Philo: *The Works of Philo: Complete and Unabridged*, trans. C.D. Yonge (Peabody, MA: Hendrickson, 1993).

Plato: *The Republic*, trans. Desmond Lee (London: Penguin Books, 2007).

Pritchard, James B., ed. *The Ancient Near East Volume I: An Anthology of Texts and Pictures* (Princeton, NJ: Princeton University Press, 1958).

Shanks, Hershel, ed. *Ancient Israel: From Abraham to the Roman Destruction of the Temple* (Washington, D.C.: Biblical Archaeology Society, 1999).

Jewish Reference Sources

Cohen, A. *Soncino Chumash* (Brooklyn: Soncino Press, 1983).

_____. *Everyman's Talmud: The Major Teachings of the Rabbinic Sages* (New York: Schoken, 1995).

Eisenberg, Ronald L. *The JPS Guide to Jewish Traditions* (Philadelphia: Jewish Publication Society, 2004).

Enyclopaedia Judaica. MS Windows 9x. Brooklyn: Judaica Multimedia (Israel) Ltd, 1997.

Harlow, Jules, ed. *Siddur Sim Shalom for Shabbat and Festivals* (New York: Rabbinical Assembly, 2007).

Hertz, J.H., ed. *Pentateuch & Haftorahs* (London: Soncino, 1960).

_____, ed. *The Authorised Daily Prayer Book*, revised (New York: Bloch Publishing Company, 1960).

JPS Guide: The Jewish Bible (Philadelphia: Jewish Publication Society, 2008).

Kolatch, Alfred J. *The Jewish Book of Why* (Middle Village, NY: Jonathan David Publishers, 1981).

_____. *The Second Jewish Book of Why* (Middle Village, NY: Jonathan David Publishers, 1985).

Kravitz, Leonard, and Kerry M. Olitzky, eds. and trans. *Pirke Avot: A Modern Commentary on Jewish Ethics* (New York: UAHC Press, 1993)

Levine, Amy-Jill, and Marc Zvi Brettler, eds. *The Jewish Annotated New Testament*, NRSV (Oxford: Oxford University Press, 2011).

Lieber, David L. *Etz Hayim: Torah and Commentary* (New York: Rabbinical Assembly, 2001).

Neusner, Jacob, trans. *The Mishnah: A New Translation* (New Haven and London: Yale University Press, 1988).

_____, ed. *The Tosefta: Translated from the Hebrew With a New Introduction*, 2 vols. (Peabody, MA: Hendrickson, 2002).

_____, and William Scott Green, eds. *Dictionary of Judaism in the Biblical Period* (Peabody, MA: Hendrickson, 2002).

Robinson, George. *Essential Judaism: A Complete Guide to Beliefs, Customs, and Rituals* (New York: Pocket Books, 2000).

Scherman, Nosson, ed., et al. *The ArtScroll Chumash, Stone Edition*, 5th ed. (Brooklyn: Mesorah Publications, 2000).

_____, and Meir Zlotowitz, eds. *Complete ArtScroll Siddur, Nusach Ashkenaz* (Brooklyn: Mesorah Publications, 1984).

Wigoder, Geoffrey, ed. et. al. *The New Encyclopedia of Judaism* (Jerusalem: Jerusalem Publishing House, 2002).

Messianic Reference Sources

Cohn-Sherbok, Dan, ed. *Voices of Messianic Judaism: Confronting Critical Issues Facing a Maturing Movement* (Baltimore: Lederer, 2001).

Feinberg, Jeffrey Enoch. *Walk Genesis: A Messianic Jewish Devotional Commentary* (Clarksville, MD: Lederer, 1998).

Hegg, Tim. *Paul's Epistle to the Romans Volume 2: Chapters 9-16* (Tacoma, WA: TorahResource, 2007).

Stern, David H. *Jewish New Testament Commentary* (Clarksville, MD: Jewish New Testament Publications, 1995).

Miscellaneous Texts and Lexicons

Charlesworth, James H., ed. *The Old Testament Pseudepigrapha*, Vol 1 (New York: Doubleday, 1983).

_____. *The Old Testament Pseudepigrapha*, Vol 2 (New York: Doubleday, 1985).

Gruber, Daniel, trans. *The Messianic Writings* (Hanover, NH: Elijah Publishing, 2011).

HarperCollins Latin Concise Dictionary (Glasgow: HarperCollins, 1997).

Morwood, James ed. *The Pocket Oxford Latin Dictionary* (Oxford: Oxford University Press, 1994).

Langenscheidts New College German Dictionary, German-English (Berlin and Munich: Langenscheidt KG, 1995).

Vermes, Geza, trans. *The Complete Dead Sea Scrolls in English* (London: Penguin Books, 1997).

Young, Robert. *Young's Analytical Concordance to the Bible* (Grand Rapids: Eerdmans, 1977).

Webster's Intermediate Dictionary (Springfield, MA: Merriam-Webster, Inc., 1977).

Webster's New World Dictionary and Thesaurus (Cleveland: Wiley Publishing, Inc, 2002).

Miscellaneous

Mozeson, Isaac E. *The Word: The Dictionary That Reveals The Hebrew Source Of* English (New York: SPI Books, 2000).

Software Programs

BibleWorks 7.0. MS Windows XP. Norfolk: BibleWorks, LLC, 2006. CD-ROM.

BibleWorks 8.0. MS Windows Vista/7 Release. Norfolk: BibleWorks, LLC, 2009-2010. DVD-ROM.

E-Sword 8.0.8. MS Windows 9x. Franklin, TN: Equipping Ministries Foundation, 2008.

Judaic Classics Library II. MS Windows 3.1. Brooklyn: Institute for Computers in Jewish Life, 1996. CD-ROM.

Libronix Digital Library System 1.0d: Church History Collection. MS Windows XP. Garland, TX: Galaxie Software. 2002.

QuickVerse 6.0. MS Windows 95. Hiawatha, IA: Parsons Technology, 1999. CD-ROM.

The Babylonian Talmud: A Translation and Commentary. MS Windows XP. Peabody, MA: Hendrickson, 2005. CD-ROM.

The Essential Christian Library. MS-Windows 95. Coeur d'Alene, ID: Packard Technologies, 1998. CD-ROM.

World Book 2003. CD-ROM, Chicago: World Book, Inc., 2003.

Visual Media

The Gnome-Mobile Walt Disney Pictures, 1967, DVD 2004.

Quest for the Lost Tribes A&E, 1998, DVD 2006.

TNN Press is the official publishing arm of TNN Online, and its parent organization, Outreach Israel Ministries. TNN Press is dedicated to producing high quality, doctrinally sound, challenging, and fair-minded Messianic materials and resources for the Twenty-First Century. TNN Press offers a wide array of new and exciting books and resources for the truth seeker.

TNN Press titles are available for purchase at **amazon**.com.
www.outreachisrael.net or at

Hebraic Roots: An Introductory Study
is TNN Press' main, best-selling publication, that offers a good overview of the Messianic movement and Messianic lifestyle that can be used for individual or group study in twelve easy lessons

Introduction to Things Messianic
is an excellent companion to *Hebraic Roots*, which goes into substantially more detail into the emerging theology of the Messianic movement, specific areas of Torah observance, and aspects of faith such as salvation and eschatology

The Messianic Helper series, edited by Margaret McKee Huey, includes a series of books with instructional information on how to have a Messianic home, including holiday celebration guides. After reading both *Hebraic Roots* and *Introduction to Things Messianic*, these are the publications you need to read!

Messianic Spring Holiday Helper
is a guide to assist you during the Spring holiday season, analyzing the importance of *Purim*, Passover and Unleavened Bread, *Shavuot*, and the non-Biblical holiday of Easter

Messianic Fall Holiday Helper
is a guide for the Fall holiday season of *Yom Teruah/Rosh HaShanah*, *Yom Kippur*, and *Sukkot*, along with reflective teachings and exhortations

Messianic Winter Holiday Helper
is a guide to help you during the Winter holiday season, addressing the significance of *Chanukah*, the period of the Maccabees, and the non-Biblical holiday of Christmas

Messianic Kosher Helper
is a guide discussing various aspects of the kosher dietary laws, clean and unclean meats, common Jewish traditions associated with kashrut, common claims made that these are no longer important for Believers, and an extensive analysis of Biblical passages from the Tanach (OT) and Apostolic Scriptures (NT) about the Torah's dietary laws and their relevance

Messianic Sabbath Helper (paperback planned 2015)
is a guide that will help you make the seventh-day Sabbath a delight, discussing both how to keep the Sabbath and the history of the transition to Sunday that occurred in early Christianity

Messianic Torah Helper
is a guide that weighs the different perspectives of the Pentateuch present in Jewish and Christian theology, considers the role of the Law for God's people, and how today's Messianics can fairly approach issues of *halachah* and tradition in their Torah observance

Outreach Israel Ministries director **Mark Huey** has written Torah commentaries and reflections that are thought provoking and very enlightening for Messianic Believers today.

TorahScope Volume I
is a compilation workbook of insightful commentaries on the weekly Torah and Haftarah portions

TorahScope Volume II
is a second compilation workbook of expanded commentaries on the weekly Torah and Haftarah portions

TorahScope Volume III
is a third compilation workbook of expanded commentaries on the weekly Torah and Haftarah portions, specifically concentrating on the theme of faith

TorahScope Haftarah Exhortations
is a compilation workbook of insightful commentaries on the specific, weekly Haftarah portions, designed to be used to compliment the weekly Torah reading

TorahScope Apostolic Scripture Reflections
is a compilation workbook of insightful reflections on suggested readings from the Apostolic Scriptures or New Testament, designed to be used to compliment the weekly Torah and Haftarah readings

Counting the Omer: A Daily Devotional Toward Shavuot
is a daily devotional with fifty succinct reflections from Psalms, guiding you during the season between the festivals of Passover and Pentecost

Sayings of the Fathers: A Messianic Perspective on Pirkei Avot
is a daily devotional for two years of reflection on the Mishnah tractate *Pirkei Avot*, introducing you to some of the key views present in the Apostolic period as witnessed by the Jewish Sages (intended to be read during the counting of the *omer*)

TNN Online editor and Messianic apologist **J.K. McKee** has written on Messianic theology and practice, including studies on Torah observance, the end-times, and commentaries that are helpful to those who have difficult questions to answer.

The New Testament Validates Torah
Does the New Testament Really Do Away With the Law?
is a resource examining a wide variety of Biblical passages, discussing whether or not the Torah of Moses is really abolished in the New Testament

Torah In the Balance, Volume I
The Validity of the Torah and Its Practical Life Applications
examines the principal areas of a Torah observant walk of faith for the newcomer, including one's spiritual motives

Torah In the Balance, Volume II (planned 2015)
The Set-Apart Life in Action—The Outward Expressions of Faith
examines many of the finer areas of Torah observance, which has a diversity of interpretations and applications as witnessed in both mainstream Judaism and the wide Messianic community

Confronting Critical Issues
An Analysis of Subjects that Affects the Growth and Stability
of the Emerging Messianic Movement
compiles a variety of articles and analyses that directly confront negative teachings and trends that have been witnessed in the broad Messianic community in the past decade

TNN Press has produced a variety of **Messianic commentaries** on various books of the Bible under the "for the Practical Messianic" byline. These can be used in an individual, small group, or congregational study.

general commentaries:
A Survey of the Tanach for the Practical Messianic
A Survey of the Apostolic Scriptures for the Practical Messianic
The Apostolic Scriptures Practical Messianic Edition (a specialty NT version)

specific book commentaries:
Acts 15 for the Practical Messianic
Romans for the Practical Messianic
1 Corinthians for the Practical Messianic (coming 2015)
Galatians for the Practical Messianic
Ephesians for the Practical Messianic
Philippians for the Practical Messianic
Colossians and Philemon for the Practical Messianic
The Pastoral Epistles for the Practical Messianic
1&2 Thessalonians for the Practical Messianic
James for the Practical Messianic
Hebrews for the Practical Messianic

TNN Press has produced a selection of **confronting issues** mini-books, specifically designed to address controversial theological topics facing a widely divided Messianic movement

One Law for All
From the Mosaic Texts to the Work of the Holy Spirit
by J.K. McKee

addresses the different passages that are significant to the whole discussion of "one Law" or "one Torah" to be followed by the people of God, and the widespread polarization of the Torah being a Divine Invitation or Covenant Obligation for non-Jewish Believers

Are Non-Jewish Believers Really a Part of Israel?
by J.K. McKee

addresses the basic choices of ecclesiology for today's Messianic Believers: either God (1) has two groups of elect, or sub-peoples: Israel and "the Church"; or God (2) recognizes us all as a part of an enlarged Kingdom realm of Israel. How are we to approach non-Jewish Believers in the Messianic movement, and things like the Commonwealth of Israel (Ephesians 2:11-13), the Israel of God (Galatians 6:16), or being grafted-in (Romans 11:16-18)?

Confronting Yeshua's Divinity and Messiahship
by J.K. McKee

examines some of the top reasons given by Messianic people who deny Yeshua as being God, why the Godhead can indeed be plural, and some of the top reasons given by Jewish anti-missionaries against Yeshua being the Messiah of Israel

To Be Absent From the Body
by J.K. McKee

confronts the debate over the intermediate state, what occurs to a person between death and the resurrection, and how the Scriptures do indeed affirm that people will be in a disembodied condition in another dimension for a limited time

Why Hell Must Be Eternal
by J.K. McKee

addresses the rather uncomfortable and unpopular topic of eternal punishment, considering some of the common proof texts given in support of annihilationism, and also weighs in the perspective of the metaphorical view of eternal punishment present in theological studies since the Protestant Reformation

One of the goals of TNN Press is to always be in the mode of producing more cutting edge materials, addressing head on some of the theological and spiritual issues facing our emerging Messianic movement. In addition to our current array of available and soon-to-be available publications, the following are a selection of **Future Projects**, in various stages of planning and pre-production, most of which involve research at the present time (2014). Look for their release sometime over the next two to five years and beyond.

Salvation on the Line/in View
by J.K. McKee

is a planned/anticipated multi-volume series which will directly tackle the subject of apostasy in today's Messianic movement, first considering the Divinity of Yeshua, the doctrine of salvation, and later the Messiahship of Yeshua, the reliability of the Scriptures, and human origins

34980724R00157

Made in the USA
Lexington, KY
26 August 2014